DISCARD

In the Eye of the Animal

Published by
University of Pennsylvania Press
Philadelphia, Pennsylvania 19104-4112
www.upenn.edu/pennpress

Printed in the United States of America on acid-free paper
1 3 5 7 9 10 8 6 4 2

A catalogue record for this book is available
from the Library of Congress .
ISBN 978-0-8122-5035-0

To Wissen, Jessie, Sophie, and Ben

When God went forth to create the world, he took his dog along.
—Kato Indian creation myth

CONTENTS

Introduction

Reading ancient Christian texts for their imaginative engagement with images of animals is what occupies me in this book. I would, however, like to open not with a text but rather with an object of art. Around the year 400 or perhaps shortly thereafter, a Christian artist of unknown provenance carved an ivory diptych, now known as the Carrand diptych, whose left leaf features a nude Adam seated in a languid position (Figure 1).[1] Located in the upper central-right register of the diptych leaf, Adam looks out with a dreamy expression, not quite making eye contact with the viewer. Remarkably, he is accompanied by a cascade of animals who tumble down the leaf: to Adam's right there is an eagle, followed by a smaller bird, and then a leopard, a lioness, a roaring lion, a bear, a boar, a fox, a cartwheeling elephant, a horse, a goat, a lizard, a serpent, an ox, a grasshopper, a sheep, and finally a stag and doe, who are placed just above a representation of the four rivers of paradise.[2]

Adam floats in space in a topsy-turvy frolic with the beasts of paradise, a veritable "carpet of animality," as Glenn Peers has remarked.[3] In his approach, Peers argues for a positioning of this object as "a complexity that is constantly incubating," noting that it has been held captive by certain kinds of art-historical and patristic perspectives that limit the ivory's ability to assert itself "against our certainties and explanations."[4] One of those certainties has been a reading of the plaque as indebted to the Greco-Roman myth and art of Orpheus charming the animals with the magic of his song.[5] As one analyst remarked, "The gentle imagery of Orpheus and the beasts represents a world of animals in ancient art in which humans are very much in control, and the animals are idyllically at peace with one another."[6] This Orphic perspective, with its emphasis on taming the beasts, curiously deflects attention away from the very beasts that the ivory so prominently features: even though the animals are not attacking or otherwise harming each other, the depiction is hardly an idyll. As Peers sees it, the animals are "restless and roiled," appearing to be "in raucous relation, mouths open with expressive faces, running, falling, prancing."[7] This art object is alive with animal

FIGURE 1. Half of ivory diptych, depicting Adam among animals. From Magonza. Byzantine, fourth–fifth century CE. Museo Nazionale del Bargello. Photo: Scala/Art Resource, NY.

élan. In line with the ivory's celebration of animal being in the world, one goal of this book is to be attentive precisely to what the animals are saying and doing, so as to engage ancient Christianity's kinships with them that have often gone unnoticed.

A second art-historical certainty is based upon the presumed scriptural referent of this scene on the Carrand diptych's left leaf, Adam naming the animals in Genesis 2:19: "Out of the ground the Lord God formed every beast of the field and every bird of the air, and brought them to the man to see what he would call them; and whatever the man called every living creature, that was its name" (RSV). This verse has been understood, by an intertextual sleight of hand, in tandem with Genesis 1:26, the passage in which God gives humankind dominion over the fish, the birds, and the domestic and wild animals. In art-historical interpretation, the scene on the ivory plaque thus positions Adam, on top and larger even than the elephant, as one who controls the animals rather than harmonizing with them.[8] The supposed oratorical gesture of Adam's right hand, in this perspective, does not point to the roaring lion in wonder but instead establishes Adam's dominance and superiority as namer, even though the biblical passage on naming has no hint of this stance of domination. Such a view of the dominical Adam separates the human from the animal rather than placing the human in a continuum with the flesh-and-bones materiality of the natural world. To Peers's question "Can we say Adam (and animals) and ivory share relation to the world through their skins (which are the same, literally)?," this perspective would answer a resounding "no."[9] Adam is not open *to* the world but dominant *over* it.

The intertextual reading that understands naming as a being over rather than a being with is indebted to a particular strain of patristic commentary on Adam and the beasts. Especially, but not only, in the hexaemeral tradition as exemplified by such fourth-century theologians as Basil of Caesarea, Ambrose, and John Chrysostom, Adam's dominion over the animals as the one who names is attributed to his creation in the image of God; only humans have reason and hence are superior to the irrational beasts.[10] As Basil of Caesarea put the case for animals, "There is only one soul of brute beasts, for there is one thing that characterizes it, namely, lack of reason" (Μια δὲ ψυχὴ τῶν ἀλόγων. Ε γὰρ αὐτὴν τὸ χαρακτηρίζον ἐστὶν, ἡ ἀλογία).[11] As for Adam, John Chrysostom was especially enthusiastic about the exalted status of the human being: "Do you see the unrivalled authority? Do you see [Adam's] lordly dominance?"[12] Noting that Genesis specifies that Adam gave names to *all* the cattle, *all* the birds of

The humanities, too, have taken the animal turn—in the arts,[22] literature,[23] philosophy,[24] and religion.[25] It is a turn with important implications for disciplinary practice. As British historian of animal studies Erica Fudge has remarked about her field, scholarly work done under the aegis of animal studies moves "away from an earlier form of history which focused on human ideas about and attitudes towards animals in which animals were mere blank pages onto which humans wrote meaning" and instead "traces the many ways in which humans construct *and are constructed* by animals in the past."[26] In light of this remark, Wolfe has raised the broader issue for the humanities disciplines as a whole, and not just the discipline of history:

> But the larger question—and it is perhaps marked by the use of the cultural studies template, associated with ethically and politically attuned scholarship, to assimilate animal studies—is how the internal disciplinarity of history or literary studies or philosophy is unsettled when the animal is taken seriously not just as another topic or object of study among many but as one with unique demands. Rather than treat the animal as primarily a theme, trope, metaphor, analogy, representation, or sociological datum . . . scholars in animal studies, whatever their home disciplines, now appear to be challenged not only by the discourses and conceptual schemata that have shaped our understanding of and relations to animals but also by the specificity of nonhuman animals, their nongeneric nature (which is why, as Derrida puts it, it is "asinine" to talk about "*the* Animal" in the singular).[27]

Obviously, attending to and being the object of the gaze of the animal—or perhaps better, the gazes of animals—entails a shift in perspective and approach.

Scholars who participate in the turn to the animal disagree about what to call their collective endeavor. Some prefer the phrase "animal studies," defined as "work that explores representations of animality and related discourses with an emphasis on advocacy for nonhuman animals"; others prefer the phrase "animality studies," understood as "work that emphasizes the history of animality in relation to human cultural studies, without an explicit call for nonhuman advocacy," as well as work that questions the animal/human divide.[28] Both, however, embrace the critical challenges that Wolfe specifies in the quotation above. My book fits best under the rubric of animality studies; it has a historical focus, of course, but it also participates in the contemporary interrogation of the human/animal binary. In presenting positively those moments in ancient

Christian texts that sidestep or otherwise confound this binary, this book is in line with contemporary animal and animality studies in their quest to complicate and deepen views of animal-human relations.

My book has also been affected by the unsettling of disciplinarity (as noted by Wolfe) that occurs when the animal is taken seriously. Before addressing this issue of the unsettling of disciplinarity, however, I would like to engage what Wolfe calls "the single most important event in the brief history of animal studies," the work of Jacques Derrida, published posthumously, entitled *The Animal That Therefore I Am*.[29] At the heart of the argument Derrida offers, writes Kari Weil, is his realization that the question of "the animal"—a falsely homogenizing concept—is "a blind spot in philosophy, an unquestioned foundation upon which the notion of the human has been constructed."[30] As Mark Payne explains, "Real thought about animals is for Derrida 'what philosophy has, essentially, had to deprive itself of' in its efforts to secure the human subject."[31]

Derrida founds his realization both of the blind spot in the Western philosophical tradition and of the need to rethink animal-human relations in a now-famous encounter with his little cat, "the moment when, caught naked, in silence, by the gaze of an animal, for example, the eyes of a cat, I have trouble, yes, a bad time overcoming my embarrassment."[32] In terms of my study of the ancient Christian zoological imagination, Derrida's insistence on the particularity of this gazing cat is important: "I must immediately make it clear, the cat I am talking about is a real cat, truly, believe me, *a little cat*. It isn't the *figure* of a cat. It doesn't silently enter the bedroom as an allegory for all the cats on the earth, the felines that traverse our myths and religions, literature and fables. . . . An animal looks at me. What should I think of this sentence?"[33] Although many of the animals in this book are indeed figures and allegories, what is significant about this body of material, and what makes of it a genuine countercurrent to the exclusivist argument about human dominion, is that the animals are *particular* animals, not a simplified category of being. As Derrida characterizes his own perspective that developed out of being caught in his cat's gaze, "it is rather a matter of taking into account a multiplicity of heterogeneous structures and limits: among nonhumans and separate from nonhumans, there is an immense multiplicity of other living things that cannot in any way be homogenized, except by means of violence and willful ignorance."[34]

This embrace of multiplicity is crucial for the kind of rethinking that Derrida proposes. If, as he writes, "thinking begins" when we are naked before the gaze of an animal, what "ends" is an ontological hierarchy of value based upon a binary opposition of human to animal that refuses kinship and compassion.[35]

Derrida's shame in the face-to-face encounter with his cat leads him to argue for the decentering of the human and to shoulder the weight of animal suffering.[36] As Matthew Calarco remarks, "Derrida sees the embodied vulnerability of animals as the site where one's egoism is called into question and where compassion is called for."[37] Likewise, in their various subversions of anthropocentric arrogance, many of the animal images and stories in this book are expressive of a profoundly ethical outlook, one in which the foibles of humans, if not precisely their egos, are held up for scrutiny and critique in the light of their animal others.

Further in concert with Derrida's concerns, the shared suffering and vulnerability of the animal condition *tout court* is on display, especially in stories about desert ascetics who reach out with healing comfort to other animals. It is as though their own bodily vulnerabilities, discovered in the course of ascetic practice, have inculcated in them a deep sense of compassion toward the suffering of their animal kin. Linking mortality with the ability to suffer, Derrida writes: "Mortality resides there, as the most radical means of thinking the finitude that we share with animals, the mortality that belongs to the very finitude of life, to the experience of compassion, ... the anguish of this vulnerability, and the vulnerability of this anguish."[38] The countercurrent explored in this book is witness to the fact that, in ancient Christian thought as well as in contemporary philosophy such as that of Derrida, the concept of human exceptionalism falters in the face of the compassion born of anguish and finitude.

Much of the ancient Christian material presented here recognizes and even celebrates a shared creatureliness. Caught in the uncanny gaze of their animal images and stories, these Christian texts, when considered as a whole, anticipate the (re)thinking that Derrida calls for, especially in terms of dismantling the animal-human binary that disallows mutuality. As many of the ancient Christian images, exegeses, and stories included in this book attest, that binary simply does not hold when humans and animals can reflect each other in ways both emotional and ethical. Derrida, in fact, imagining himself reflected full-length in a mirror, wonders whether his cat "can find itself caught in the same mirror." And then he asks, "But cannot this cat also be, deep within her eyes, my primary mirror?"[39] One might think that Derrida had been reading Rilke's poem about a black cat:

> as if awakened, she turns her face to yours;
> and with a shock, you see yourself, tiny,
> inside the golden amber of her eyeballs
> suspended, like a prehistoric fly.[40]

One interpreter understands the mirroring in this poem as a form of self-reflection that "comes to block our access to the animal's gaze."[41] If one only saw the fly-self and not the cat's own gaze, one would surely be correct. Derrida, however, seems to have a more generous sense of mutuality in mind. Although he does not specify what he means by the mirroring depth of the cat's eyes, he does embrace the idea of *zoo*tobiography, as contrasted with autobiography, as an appropriate genre for his work.[42]

This striking neologism suggests to me that his sense of mirroring embeds animal and human in a shared subjectivity that sidesteps human exceptionalism. Indeed, as Calarco points out, "The question 'Who am I?' seems, for Derrida, to necessitate a rather paradoxical answer."[43] That answer comes as a play on the French title of Derrida's book, *L'animal que donc je suis*, where the verb *suis* can mean either "I am" or "I am following." Derrida writes: "And by wondering whether one can answer for what 'I am (following)' means when that seems to necessitate an 'I am inasmuch as I am *after* [*après*] the animal' or 'I am inasmuch as I am *alongside* [*auprès*] the animal. Being *after*, being *alongside*, being *near* [*près*] would appear as different modes of being, indeed of *being-with*. With the animal."[44] Calarco offers the following conclusion about this passage: "According to Derrida's account I come to myself and arrive at self-consciousness only in and through other animals, that is, other living beings, whether human, animal, or otherwise."[45] The mirroring is a question of self-knowledge that does not negate the animal but rather develops in conjunction with it. In the chapters that follow, we shall encounter the animal-mirror again, most prominently in the exegetical work of Origen of Alexandria and Augustine of Hippo, where the ethical depths of the animal gaze anticipate (again!) Derrida's philosophical reflections.

As I suggested earlier in this Introduction, these transforming possibilities *of* and *for* reading animals—that is, of finding oneself "in the eye of the animal"—entail a shift in perspective and approach as well as an unsettling of disciplinarity. In my own case, the first step toward "seeing otherwise" beyond ancient Christian exceptionalism was to begin to look past the rhetoric of human dominance over, and hence separation from, animals. Doing so—that is, reading ancient Christian texts for the animals rather than for the rhetoric—disclosed another kind of awareness at work. Instead of reinforcing alienation between humans and animals, this awareness finds a shared ground of bodily, emotional, and ethical life. My work of imagining ancient Christian texts imagining animals has led me to see that such texts need not be read as depriving Christianity of genuine thought about animals in order to secure the human subject; instead, in their engagement with animals and in their willingness not

only to construct but also to be constructed by animals, there is an intersubjective gaze in play. Crucial to arriving at these conclusions was stepping outside
the comforts of my discipline. During the months I spent immersed in contemporary animal and animality studies, above all in cognitive ethology, I came to
appreciate and was in fact surprised by the ways in which the study of actual
animals and the study of animal imagery in texts intersect and can be mutually
illuminating. The phenomenon of the intersubjective gaze just mentioned is
one such result of that immersion. The textual/actual wolf of Chapter 4, as well
as the reflections on zoomorphism and anthropomorphism in Chapters 2 and 3,
are other examples of what I experienced as a fruitful unsettling of both discipline and perspective.

Reading ancient Christian texts for animals also discloses the remarkable
diversity of animal life that teems in such texts. Following Derrida in his desire
to particularize talk about animals, the philosopher Bailly takes a step further
in celebrating the "prodigious diversity" of animals' names. He imagines sustaining "a language scarcely spoken and almost never written, a language that
would still have in itself something of the Adamic denomination, minus the
will to mastery."[46] By Adamic denomination, Bailly seems to mean the fresh-
ness, surprise, and delight that the initial summoning of animals into language
entailed, and he gives as an example this list of northern European freshwater
birds: "*red-throated loon, Arctic loon, little grebe, horned grebe, little egret, night
heron, Eurasian spoonbill, shelduck, widgeon, mallard, gadwell, garganey, red-
crested pochard, common pochard, eider, common goldeneye, smew, merganser,
great bittern. . . .*"[47] It is difficult to tell which is more prodigious, the animals or
the names that language has endowed them with. My own list, though not quite
as colorful, happily coincides, at least partially, with the animals that roil the
surface of the Carrand diptych: eagle, leopard, lion and lioness, elephant, serpent, sheep, deer (and many more). As is the case on the ivory, so in this book
speech belongs to the animals, whether it is literal or metaphorical.

As the following chapters make clear, the images, exegeses, and stories of
the ancient Christian tradition are very diverse. Thus I have coined the collective phrase "zoological imagination" in order to suggest that this disparate
material in fact belongs together because it exposes an animal richness that
ancient Christian exceptionalism obscures. As I remarked earlier, I have positioned this concrete, often earthy and sensuous, material as a countercurrent to
the abstract rhetoric of domination and superiority that runs like a leitmotif
through ancient Christian literature. In the purview of the zoological imagination, animals are not primarily passive beings that carry the burden of irratio-

nality. Instead, they actively signify. In other words, these images and stories of animals are performative: that is, they both conjure up and participate in a human-animal "contact zone" of engagement, intimacy, pathos, intercorporeal sensibility, fantasy, and sheer wonder.

A brief rehearsal of the concerns of each of the book's chapters will suggest just how complex and diverse are the active significations of animal images in ancient Christian thought. Chapter 1, "Animals and Figuration: The Case of Birds," begins the discussion of ways in which ancient Christian texts establish relations between animals and humans that do not reinforce or buy into human exceptionalism. In this regard, this chapter introduces the concept of animal interiority, a centuries-long phenomenon in which animal imagery is used to imagine the contours of human identity and self-knowledge. Figuration in many of its senses—metaphor, symbol, allegory—is explored for ways in which it is used to shape human self-understanding, using avian imagery as a test case. How is human subjectivity inflected by birds? From the development of an aerial sensibility all the way to the very material use of dove-shaped lamps in churches, birds are this book's first instance of ancient Christian views of human-animal intertwining. Finally, attention to birds introduces a feature of ancient Christian interest in animals that appears in several chapters of the book, namely, the role of biblical exegesis in bringing animals forward for analysis and contemplation.

Chapter 2, "The Pensivity of Animals, I: Zoomorphism," and Chapter 3, "The Pensivity of Animals, II: Anthropomorphism," are linked by a phrase from Bailly's meditative work. Bailly introduces this phrase while contemplating a line from Rilke's *Duino Elegies*: "And yet, sometimes a silent animal looks up at us and silently looks through us."[48] Animals, says Bailly, are participant in a world of gazes, which is a world of "significance," of the making and conveying of meaning.[49] The presence of the animal gaze establishes a "pensive path."[50] About the pensivity of animals, Bailly remarks: "My concern is not that we should credit animals with access to thought; it is that we should move beyond human exclusivity, that we should let go of the eternally renewed credo according to which our species is the pinnacle of creation and has a unique future. The pensivity of animals . . . is neither a diversion nor a curiosity; what it establishes is that the world in which we live is gazed upon by other beings, that the visible is shared among creatures."[51] Bailly's point about the pensivity of animals is not that animals think in the same way as humans but rather that they are worthy of thought and of thoughtful regard as fellow creatures. Further, animals are not only passively contemplated; they are provocateurs *of* thought.

In these two chapters, then, the pensivity of animals rests on two kinds of gazing: seeing humans as animal (zoomorphism) and seeing animals as human (anthropomorphism).

Chapter 2, "The Pensivity of Animals, I: Zoomorphism," introduces terms that will be central to the arguments of the rest of the book: anthropocentrism, anthropodenial, anthropomorphism, and zoomorphism itself. These terms are discussed in the context of the anxieties that arise when the intelligence of animals is at issue, with a spotlight on bees, particularly in the thought of Origen of Alexandria. The bulk of the chapter focuses on ancient Christian biblical exegeses that interpret animal images in biblical texts in such a way that human beings are imagined as animals or as having characteristics of animals. The exegeses explored in this chapter—from Augustine's asses and deer through Gregory of Nyssa's fawns and the lion of the *Physiologus*—support an understanding of ancient Christian exegesis of biblical imagery as animal friendly insofar as figural appropriations of animals provoke anthropological and theological thought.

Chapter 3, "The Pensivity of Animals, II: Anthropomorphism," examines texts that present animals as human or as humanlike. Drawing from such novelistic literature as the *Acts of Philip* and the *Acts of Paul* as well as from Basil of Caesarea's *Hexaemeron*, this chapter explores two qualities—the possession of reason or speech and the ability to act ethically—that have typically been reserved for humans and hence denied to animals. Here the focus is on talking animals and on animals that "speak" with their gestures as well as on stories about ethical animals whose virtues are frequently said to surpass those of human beings. This chapter introduces the theme of the *fabula*, storytelling that conveys truth, and continues the discussion begun in Chapter 2 of ancient Christian views of animal-human relations, connections, and kinship. Like zoomorphism, anthropomorphism unsettles ontological certainties of an abyssal divide separating humans from animals. Hence in this chapter, ancient Christian anthropomorphism is presented as an interpretive strategy for imagining how humans and animals are mutually entangled.

The literature of desert asceticism is the focus of Chapter 4, "Wild Animals: Desert Ascetics and Their Companions." Most of the stories in this literature feature compassion as the signal character trait linking animals and humans. In this chapter, as in others, the negative stereotype of ancient Christian views of animals as merely irrational and as supportive of a reductive binary opposition between humans and animals is shown to be incorrect. Instead, these stories of intimate animal-human encounters can better be described as developing relationships that are based on intersubjectivity and intercorporeal sensibilities. Drawing on contemporary affect theory, the chapter argues that representations of monks' relationships with animals were fraught with emotional, affective, and ethical complexity. The circuit of intensities that such stories cultivate is sustained in many of the narratives by a sharing of the body language of touch, which emphasizes animal-human engagement, not alienation.

In Chapter 5, "Small Things: The Vibrant Materiality of Tiny Creatures," concepts drawn from new materialist theory are used to give expression to the distinctive vibrancy of tiny animals in many ancient Christian texts. The rhetoric and assumptions of human dominion are countered by this vibrancy, such that the dominical perspective that places human beings at the apex of a hierarchy of value can be seen to be at odds with the zoological imagination. Senses of wonder, whether theological or cosmological, often accompany the intensity with which the being of such creatures as worms, frogs, flies, and mosquitos is evoked and explored. But whether these small things incite theological wonder and theophanic glimmerings or an outpouring of moral disgust, the fact is that small things are a locus of surplus value. The vital materiality of tiny bodies shows matter at its most vibrant.

Given the complexly disparate nature and function of all this material, the chapters that explore it are not arranged in linear or chronological fashion. Instead, as the chapter summaries have indicated, each chapter explores a distinct theme (like figurations of birds or the vibrancy of tiny creatures) or body of material (like stories from desert asceticism) or conceptual category (like anthropomorphism and zoomorphism). Perhaps one might imagine that the chapters tumble through the book like the animals cavorting about on the Carrand diptych. They are an attempt to imagine what the animals are saying and doing in ancient Christianity.

CHAPTER I

Animals and Figuration

The Case of Birds

The poet Ted Hughes once remarked that he thought of poems "as a sort of animal" because they have "a life of their own," separate from the author, and "they have a certain wisdom."[1] Of the many poems by Hughes that feature animals, none is perhaps more "animal" than the poem entitled "The Thought Fox." Sitting late in the evening before "this blank page where my fingers move," the poet, looking through the window, imagines "the midnight moment's forest" where "something else is alive." The poet first sees the fox's nose, and then its two eyes that "serve a movement, that now / . . . / sets neat prints into the snow." The fox appears and just as suddenly disappears: "The clock ticks, / the page is printed."[2] The fox's footprints and the "prints" on the poet's page merge. It would seem that not only is the poem an animal but also the animal is a poem. In this chapter I would like to turn Hughes's poem-as-animal simile around, so that animals can be seen as "a sort of poem."

As we shall see, birds have been particularly prominent animals as poems because of their metaphoric possibilities. The idea of the bird as poem is strikingly present in the following tableau from the writer Annie Proulx. In one of her stories that evoke scenes from Wyoming, she envisions an evening, "just before darkness," when one can see "the herons flying upstream, their color matching the sky so closely they might have been eyes of wind."[3] Proulx's herons lend their color to the sky, their onrushing flight giving poetic expression to a force of nature, the wind.

As "eyes of wind," these herons are beautifully illustrative of a long-standing use of birds in flight, by poets and theologians alike, to evoke what poet Billy Collins calls "imaginative freedom" as well as various forms of elation.[4] Birds' movement—especially when experienced as beautiful—has also been used to evoke human thought and language in a poetic mode, as when for the nineteenth-century English poet John Clare "the wild duck startles like a sudden thought," or when the contemporary American poet Henry Carlile writes about watching a cardinal in winter: "He shocks us when he flies / like a red verb over the snow."[5] This "shock" and "startle" of the poetic bird as a metaphor of human thought was well conveyed by Thoreau: "Nothing was ever so unfamiliar and startling to a man" as his "winged thoughts" that "are like birds, and will not be handled."[6] Like their flight, the singing of birds, too, has been connected with a poetry of expression. Ambrose of Milan, for example, likened birds' singing, which "charms the sky with song," to Christians' ritual singing of the psalms.[7] Much later, Wallace Stevens mused: "I do not know which to prefer, / The beauty of inflections / Or the beauty of innuendoes, / The blackbird whistling / Or just after."[8] Whether flying or singing, the bird as poem is an enchantment, both charming and disturbing.

The connection between humans and birds is very old. Among the Paleolithic paintings in the caves of Lascaux, there is only one portrayal of a human being: "a stick figure," as Alphonso Lingis points out, "with the head of a bird."[9] It is of course impossible to know whether the artist who painted that bird-headed image intended to convey the flight of thought, shamanic vision, or even the flight of artistic inspiration as enacted in the paintings on the walls of the cave. Yet Lingis's comment, that there is "an animal vigor of the mind that seduces us," seems particularly apt in the case of birds.[10] This vigor was not lost on ancient Christian writers, for whom such interior vigor was sheathed not only with feathers but also with shaggy coats. Origen of Alexandria, for example, attempting to find psychological meaning in the discussion of sacrificial animals in Leviticus, wrote, "Understand that you have within yourself herds of cattle, flocks of sheep and flocks of goats, and that the birds of the air are also within you. You see that you have all those things that the world has."[11] The phenomenon of animal interiority, not least regarding the connection of birds and thought, has had a lasting attraction since Origen assured his parishioners, "[You can] find [the animals] within your soul."[12] Wallace Stevens wrote in one poem, "The blackbird is involved in what I know," and Carl Sandburg found, among the "menagerie, inside my ribs, under my bony head," an eagle flying "among the Rocky Mountains of my dreams" and a mockingbird gushing "over the blue Ozark foothills of my wishes."[13] Winged thoughts, indeed.

On the topic of animals and interpretation, whether exegetical or poetic, Origen, Stevens, and Sandburg seem to be in agreement with Rainer Maria

Rilke: "Before one can write a single verse, one must get to know the animals."[14] In this chapter, the animals in question are birds. But before dealing more specifically with the patristic treatment of birds, it is important to note the broader context within which the association of birds and thought was articulated. Gregory of Nyssa attempted a quasi-biological explanation for the interrelationships among what he considered to be the three types of soul, the nutritive vegetable, sensing animal, and rational human souls. In his view, the human being contains or replicates all previous stages of living things. In *On the Making of the Human Being*, he writes: "For this rational animal, the human being, is mixed from every idea of soul. He is nourished in accordance with the vegetative species of soul; but, in addition to the [vegetative] faculty of growth, there arose that of sense perception [characteristic of animals], which stands in the middle between the proper natures of the intellectual and the more material nature.... Then there takes place a certain appropriation as well as a blending of the intellectual essence to the fine and luminous part of the sensible nature, so that the human being is constituted by all three [souls]."[15] Given this ascensional view of nature, it is not surprising that knowledge of animal life would be important for human self-knowledge, a fact that Gregory explores primarily through his consideration of "brutish" passions.[16]

Ambrose of Milan voiced a different perspective in terms of the necessity of knowing the animals: "We cannot fully know ourselves," he wrote in his *Hexaemeron*, "without first knowing the nature of all living creatures."[17] Although Ambrose does go on to offer descriptions of the behaviors of various birds, fish, reptiles, and mammals, his real goal is not science but exegesis, as his rather humorous depiction of his congregation's mindset suggests. Signaling that he is about to open his discussion of "the origin of beasts," he anticipates objections (and the crowd's boredom!): "I already hear some who murmur and say: how much time are we to spend discussing matters alien [*aliena*] to us, while knowing nothing of what really concerns us? How long are we to learn of other living creatures while we do not know ourselves? Let him tell me what is to be for my benefit, that I may know myself. That is a just complaint. The order which scripture laid down must, however, be retained. We cannot fully know ourselves without first knowing the nature of all living creatures."[18] Ambrose's point is not only that animal nature is not alien to human nature but also that, in preaching on the days of creation in the opening chapters of Genesis, scriptural order is paramount and must be respected. Animals in Genesis, while crucial for human self-knowledge, are nonetheless only one part of the much larger project of biblical interpretation.

Origen and Aerial Sensibility

With this situating of animals in the context of exegesis that is aimed at self-knowledge, we can turn once again to Origen, now with a focus on humans and birds. When Origen wrote in his *Homilies on Leviticus*, "The birds of the air are within you," what exactly did he mean? That is, in what way was he using these animals to shape the landscape of the interior human being?[19] The contours of the avian inner self become evident in Origen's *Homilies on Genesis*, in the section in which he comments on Genesis 1:20: "And God said: 'Let the waters bring forth both creeping creatures having life and birds flying over the earth in the firmament of heaven.' And it was so done" (quoting from the biblical text as given by Origen).[20] As Origen proceeds to give the spiritual sense of this passage, he specifies that both "the waters" and "the firmament of heaven" signify the human mind or heart, which are interchangeable in this section of his commentary.[21] Out of the depths of the human being, then, the "creeping creatures" and the "birds that fly" proceed: they signify, respectively, "the evil and good thoughts, that there might be a distinction of the good thoughts from the evil, which certainly both proceed from the heart."[22] Origen continues: the flying birds embody our explorations within ourselves of the "meaning and plan of heavenly things," and knowledge of such "birds" then enables the human mind to recognize and "fly away" from the evil thoughts that it harbors.[23] In very short compass, Origen has sketched a dynamic vision of human subjectivity brought into view through birds. In this passage, flight is fundamentally ethical, as the "birds," which activate the human ability to discriminate between good and evil impulses and thoughts, open up a vertical pathway for and in the self.

As the French philosopher Gaston Bachelard remarked in his book *Air and Dreams*, "What is primordially beautiful about birds is their flight," and this certainly seems true of the aerial avian sensibility articulated by Origen.[24] Of course these birds as thoughts are part of his allegorical exegetical program in which Origen finds a spiritual metanarrative encoded in biblical texts.[25] Accordingly, the birds (and the creeping reptiles, for that matter) are supremely poetic because they are figural. As Origen explained, when read allegorically, the birds and other animals of the creation story in Genesis are figures, interior embellishments of the "little world" that is the human being.[26] Figurative readings like these were part of Origen's allegorical program, which he called "plumbing the depths of God's wisdom,"[27] by which spiritual reading would induce spiritual transformation in the interpreter.[28]

It is important to note at this point that, in contemporary animal studies, there is real concern that using animals like birds as figures or metaphors for human characteristics risks losing the animal altogether. As Tim Ingold has remarked, "Metaphor should be apprehended as a way of drawing attention to real relational unities [between animals and humans] rather than of figuratively papering over dualities."[29] Aaron Gross has put the case even more strongly: "One danger of scholarly work on animals is that it can function to render 'actual animals' absent." When animals are used to interpret aspects of human nature, the animals themselves "seem beside the point" as they are transformed into "absent referents (beings made absent as they are being referenced)."[30] A similar critique has been lodged against allegorical interpretation per se, which would of course include animal allegories: when a literal text is said to have a "higher" spiritual meaning, that spiritual meaning can supersede and so occlude or even erase the literal sense of the text. This erasure is especially egregious when allegory—as in the hands of Origen when he interprets the history of Israel in the Hebrew Bible—results in the dualism of the "dead" letter and the "living" signification.[31] As David Dawson notes, summarizing one of the major objections to allegory as articulated by Daniel Boyarin: "Supersession occurs when meanings are preferred over texts, history, and embodied persons."[32]

I would argue, however, that allegorical interpretation—at least in the case of scripture's animals—can be read as relational rather than destructively hierarchical. Once Origen invites birds into the human psyche, how can one think about thinking and ethical judgment without imagining wings, feathers, and flight? Rather than dismissing birds from the biblical text, Origen's interpretation apprehends and actualizes them as figures. Birds become part of interpretive plurisignification. Thus the effect of allegorical interpretation need not be read as "dissolving concreteness into abstract meaning."[33] Rather, Origen's allegory is based on a "conception of reality consisting of two deeply interpenetrating realms: a non-sensible realm of spiritual realities (τὰ νοητά) and a sensible realm of material realities (τὰ αἰσθητά)."[34] The task of allegorical reading is to find the "deep coherence" or interrelationships between these realms.[35] Origen's reading of the aerial sensibility of human beings does not occlude real birds but actually brings them forward for examination.

Thus rather than transforming birds into absent referents, Origen releases them into their skyward element, and draws a relational unity between their flight and human thought. In a more modern idiom—reflecting the long pedigree that this way of thinking about birds has—philosopher Jean-Christophe Bailly notes about actual birds the joy that human beings feel when watching them fly, the joy being a response to "the miracle of that escape from gravity that birds epitomize in their upward soaring." And then he brings the flight of the birds inward, as they "open space up, as though from within, so that our contemplation is impregnated by it and our thinking flooded by the radiant and dilated sense of what opens up and is nothing but opening up."[36] For modern and ancient thinker alike, birds embody a liberating sense of openness.

The Winged Soul

Origen was not, of course, alone in his appropriation of the mobility of birds for evoking human thought and emotion in an ascensional mode. Many centuries earlier, Sappho had written about the sight of her beloved, "Oh it puts the heart in my chest on wings."[37] Such avian fluttering caught the attention of patristic authors, too. Basil of Caesarea, for example, thought of birds as "wonders in the air" (τὰ ἐναέρια θαύματα), and his astonishment was shared by his contemporary Ambrose, who exclaimed that "the speedy flight [of birds] often dazzles human eyes."[38] One is reminded of the line from Carlile, quoted earlier, that expresses the shock of a cardinal's flight over the snow. As Bailly, echoing Basil and Clement's sense of aerial dazzle, has it, the flight of birds inscribes "a rapid and ephemeral line that is erased no sooner than it appears, erased indeed in its appearing."[39] For ancient Christian writers, however, birds were more than "acrobats of speed and sheen," to quote a modern poet.[40] Most of all, birds gave image to the human soul as, released from earthbound concerns, it makes its vertical flight toward the heavens. Augustine was blunt: "Birds represent spiritual souls. Winged creatures symbolize the hearts of spiritual persons which enjoy the freedom of the air."[41]

Many other Christians, too, placed the soul as bird in the cluster constituted by air, freedom, and liberation that Bachelard argued was characteristic of the dynamic imagination of the aerial psyche.[42] In the course of his typological interpretation of the animals that God created, Theophilus of Antioch, for example, contrasted the negatively charged land animals—"a type of human beings who are ignorant of God and sin against him and do not repent"—with the positively valued birds: these represent those people who "repent of their iniquities and live righteously" and "take flight in soul like birds, minding things above and taking pleasure in the will of God."[43] The idea that souls might "run the upward course to the divine nature" because they are winged like birds was a popular one.[44] Clement of Alexandria highlighted the aesthetic aspect of the aerial soul: "It is not without singular grace," he wrote, "that the soul is winged and rises on high, laying aside all weight and giving itself over to what is akin to it."[45] Envisioning psychic flight as a form of spiritual agility that sheds the "serpentine" complications of earthbound attachments, Clement wrote, "Cease to act like serpents. Lift up your head from earth to sky, look up to heaven and marvel. . . . Become wise and yet harmless; soon, perhaps, the Lord will give you wings of simplicity (for it is his purpose to give wings to earth-born creatures) in order that you may leave behind the holes of earth and have heaven for your dwelling."[46] Clement's wings of simplicity offer a vision of a lightness of being that characterizes the true home of human beings.

Other interpreters followed Origen in connecting wings with thoughts. At one point in his *Second Theological Oration*, Gregory of Nazianzus was attempting to thrill his audience with proofs of "the majestic working of God" by envisaging God's creative cosmological genius.[47] He asks his audience to indulge his lofty rhetoric, allowing him to "luxuriate a little in my language when speaking of the luxuriant gifts of God": "And now, leaving the earth and the things of earth, soar into the air on the wings of thought, that our argument may advance in due path; and then I will take you up to heavenly things, and to heaven itself, and things which are above heaven; for to that which is beyond, my discourse hesitates to ascend, but still it shall ascend as far as may be."[48] Here our overarching motif of the bird as poem seems especially marked, as Gregory's (somewhat overwrought) rhetoric takes flight to the empyrean on the wings of "luxuriant" language. Didymus of Alexandria, too, connected winged flight, words, and thoughts. In an aside in his *Commentary on Genesis*, Didymus remarks that those who devote themselves to interpreting the Old and New Testaments in terms of each other, especially comparing prophecies in the Old Testament with their fulfillment in the New Testament, are given wings that are thoughts that have "elevation and celestial loftiness."[49] Apparently, there really is "no wing like meaning."[50]

These images of the winged soul flying upward had in their background Plato's image of the winged soul in his dialogue *Phaedrus*, an image that was part of the cultural encyclopedia embedded in the textual communities available to ancient Christian (and other) authors.[51] In Plato's telling, wings are natural to the soul, but it can lose them and fall to earth from the heavens when it is "burdened with forgetfulness and evil."[52] The soul grows back its lost wings in an erotic context of seeing beauty in the person of a beloved; the resulting "flood of passion" nurtures the feathers, and so the soul regains its winged, ascensional nature once more.[53] As is obvious from the foregoing examples, Christian writers adopted this centuries-old image of the birdlike soul, including its emphasis on the verticality of the soul's movement as well as the necessity of ethical behavior for retaining the soul's winged nature. What they did not retain, however, was the erotic context in which the soul's wings are nourished and grow again after their loss. If pleasure is mentioned at all, it is the pleasure of obedience to God and the promise of a heavenly dwelling place.

Peacocks and Other Divine Birds

The winged soul was not, however, the only role that birds played in the ancient Christian imagination. The male peacock, for example, condensed in its tail a poetry of the glory of the cosmos, "glittering like gold and studded with stars," in Gregory of Nazianzus's telling.[54] With this description, Gregory placed himself in good company. As Henry Maguire has pointed out, "Poets from Ovid to George of Pisidia compared the eyelike markings of [the peacock's] tail to stars."[55] The peacock's tail was not notable only for its sidereal beauty, however; it also figured the theological doctrine of resurrection, due to its annual shedding and regrowing of its feathers.[56] As Maguire, again, has observed, the peacock's association with rebirth, immortality, and eternal life accounts for its frequent appearance "in Christian funerary art, in tomb paintings, on carved sarcophagi, and in the mosaics that covered graves in North Africa."[57] Figure 2 shows one such funerary peacock, which is on the sarcophagus of Bishop Theodore in S. Apollinare in Classe. This peacock is decorative, but not merely so. It is an emblem of a religious belief structure that gave meaning to the life and death of the person whose remains the sarcophagus held.

Perhaps it was its association with resurrection that led to the view that the peacock's flesh was incorruptible. In a "scientific" experimental mode (as we shall see again in Chapter 5 with regard to worms), Augustine put the lore about the incorruptibility of the flesh of the peacock to the test. He relates his experiment in the *City of God* in the context of a discussion about bodies that are not destroyed by fire (thus proving the reality of eternal torment by hellfire). But, in the middle of this discussion, there is a digression that introduces a new angle on the topic: now the focus is not the body's failure to disintegrate under fiery punishment but rather on its integrity in the afterlife (hellish or otherwise, presumably). Here is Augustine on the peacock:

> Who but the Creator of all things gave to the peacock the power of
> resisting putrefaction after death? I had heard of this property and

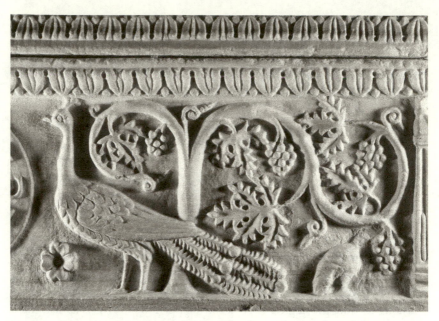

FIGURE 2. Sarcophagus of Bishop Theodore with peacocks and olive
branches, close-up. Early Christian, fifth century CE. S. Apollinare in Classe.
Photo: Alfredo Dagli Orti/Art Resource, NY.

had thought it incredible, until one day at Carthage I was served with
a roast peacock, and I gave orders that what seemed a sufficient quantity of meat should be cut from the breast and kept. After an interval
of some days, long enough to have ensured the putrefaction of any
other kind of cooked meat, this was brought out and presented to me;
and I found it had no offensive smell. It was then put back in store,
and after more than thirty days it was found to be in the same condition; and there was no change in a year's time except that the flesh
was somewhat dry and shriveled.[58]

Despite the difficulty of imagining eating peacocks for those of us accustomed
to seeing them in the zoo and to thinking of them as ornamental rather than
culinary, Romans did indeed eat peacocks, and, according to the late Roman
cookbook attributed to Apicius, croquettes of peacock were very highly prized
"if they [were] fried so as to make the hard skin tender."[59] Augustine's interest,
however, was not in cuisine but in the eternal life of the body after death, a state
of being that he (amusingly) "proves" on the basis of a cutlet of peacock. In this

case the peacock adds to the motif of the bird as an image of the aerial, ascensional aspects of human existence in a Christian context.

Other birds in the ancient Christian imagination functioned as vehicles of the expression of divine presence in the human world. One noteworthy example involves the child Jesus at play. The *Infancy Gospel of Thomas*, probably dating to the second century, opens with a scene of the five-year-old Jesus playing in a stream: "He made pools of the rushing water and made it immediately pure; he ordered this by word alone." Next, "he made soft clay and modeled twelve sparrows from it. It was the Sabbath when he did this." A passerby who sees the child thus "working" goes to complain to Jesus's father about this violation of the holy day: "Joseph came to the place, and seeing what Jesus did he cried out, 'Why do you do on the Sabbath what it is not lawful to do?' Jesus clapped his hands and cried to the sparrows, 'Be gone.' And the sparrows flew off chirping."[60] This picture of the child Jesus intervening in the course of nature—gathering and purifying water and vivifying the inanimate matter of the clay sparrows—has been read as "a recapitulation of the creation story in Genesis 1–2."[61] Jesus' act of animating the sparrows by his words may well be this gospel's attempt to associate the child Jesus with the creative power of his heavenly father.

This interpretation, however, seems to me to be somewhat grandly cosmic if it stands alone, because it misses the playful aspect of the story, envisioning as it does a child playing in the mud and making shapes out of it. Stephen Davis's recent study *Christ Child* has taken the play seriously. As Davis shows, Roman children played with toys in the shape of birds, and they kept birds as pets—no less a personage than St. Augustine, for one, had pet sparrows when he was a child; perhaps he held his sparrow like the boy holding his parrot in Figure 3.[62] Given the association of children and birds in antiquity, Davis thus argues "that for many ancient readers and hearers Jesus' childlike play and wonder-working in the story of the sparrows would have simultaneously signaled two things: his experience of a typical human childhood, and his embodiment of divine potency."[63] The *Infancy Gospel of Thomas*, I would add, has used the chirping sparrows to think with in terms of the miracle-working biography of its hero. The sparrows are metaphors that embody the thought of the text.

As I noted at the outset of this chapter, birds have been prominent animals as poems because of their metaphoric possibilities. This has been no less true in modernity than in antiquity, as the poet and literary critic Howard Nemerov has demonstrated. Here is his story about purple finches, a homage in fact to the lasting appeal of sparrows as birds to think with.

FIGURE 3. Boy with bird and stick (*Mosaics of Jordan*, fig. 79 on p. 97). From
Madaba, Church of the Apostles, 578 CE. Courtesy of the Franciscan
Custody of the Holy Land, Mount Nebo, and the American Center of
Oriental Research, Amman.

While I am thinking about metaphor, a flock of purple finches
arrives on the lawn. Since I haven't seen these birds for some years, I
am only fairly sure of their being in fact purple finches, so I get down
Peterson's *Field Guide* and read his description: "Male: About size of
House Sparrow, rosy-red, brightest on head and rump." That checks
quite well, but his next remark—"a sparrow dipped in raspberry
juice"—is decisive: it fits. I look out the window again, and now I
know that I am seeing purple finches.

   That's very simple. So simple, indeed, that I hesitate to look any
further into the matter, for as soon as I do I shall see that its simplic-

ity is not altogether canny. Why should I be made certain of what a purple finch is by being led to contemplate a sparrow dipped in raspberry juice? Have I ever dipped a sparrow in raspberry juice? Has anyone? And yet there it is, quite certain and right. Peterson and I and the finches are in agreement.[64]

Nemerov's experience of recognizing purple finches by way of the metaphor of sparrows dipped in raspberry juice is not so different from the experience of a reader of the *Infancy Gospel of Thomas*, who is led to recognize the true nature of the child Jesus by way of the animated clay sparrows. Nemerov concludes, "It is like being told: If you really want to see something, look at something else."[65] In the ancient text, looking at the flying, chirping sparrows conveys an insight about divine power that no merely discursive statement could do.

The final notable example of the use of a bird to express the presence of divine power in the world involves not Jesus but rather a saint, who uses a bird in order to effect a miraculous cure. In one of the miracle stories in the fifth-century *Life and Miracles of St. Thecla*, the sanctuary grounds of the saint are described as containing a number of different kinds of birds—swans, cranes, geese, doves, and so on—to whom visitors throw grains of wheat and barley. Among those present in St. Thecla's sanctuary is a child with a diseased eye. The text imagines a charming scene in which the child, giggling, chases after a bird and is in turn pursued, a scene that provokes delighted laughter from the onlookers. The delight quickly turns to horror when the child snatches grain away from one of the cranes and thus prevents it from eating. Seemingly in angry retaliation, the crane pecks at the child's diseased eye, and the child cries out in anguish at the blow. As it turns out, the crane has used its beak as a "lancet"—and the eye is healed. The crane has in fact acted as a surgeon at the behest of the saint herself; this bird was the vehicle through which the saint's healing power expressed itself.[66]

Long-Billed Birds and Ethics

This story of the violent but healing crane brings to mind a similar tale by a contemporary author, whose long-beaked bird is a great blue heron. Written by Annie Proulx, this story is also fictional, but it is more chill in its realism. One of Proulx's "Wyoming stories" includes the brief tale of Ned, who comes from a family that collects wild bird eggs, the more exotic the better, just for show.

Carrying on the family tradition, Ned sets out to steal the egg of a great blue heron: "Ned had climbed a hollow tree stub in a black-water swamp to get the egg of a great blue heron while Sen [his friend] waited in the boat below, and as Ned came even with the nest, the violent bird, defending her egg, had pierced his eye and brain with her beak," killing him.[67] In contrast to the healing violence of the ancient crane's beak, here the beak's thrust is defensive, as the heron protects her future progeny from theft and destruction. The modern tale is a cautionary story aimed at curbing—or curing?—human cupidity. As one of the people attending the egg thief's funeral says, "If they piled up all the birds' eggs in the world in front a [*sic*] me I would turn the other way."[68]

In antiquity, too, both the defensive posture of long-billed birds, as well as their function as models of behaviors that expose character foibles of human beings, were a topic for discussion. In the hexaemeral literature, cranes and storks, while not directly manifesting divine power, nonetheless exhibit traits that demonstrate their place in God's providential design of nature. As noted by Aristotle and then by the Greco-Roman naturalists Pliny and Aelian, cranes were notable for their use of sentries to protect the community of birds sleeping at night.[69] This defensive behavior was recorded by Basil of Caesarea without comment, but Ambrose made the crane into a didactic poem as he laid out the appeal of the actions of this bird.[70] In his *Hexaemeron*, after running through some generalities about birds, Ambrose turns to particular species, the first of which is cranes: "Let us begin," he writes, "with those birds that have become examples for our own way of life. These birds [cranes] have a natural social and military organization, whereas with us this service is compulsory and servile."[71] Immediately one sees what the stakes are in Ambrose's presentation of cranes: their forms of community provide the standard against which human behavior is shown in a negative light in terms of compulsion and servility. He goes into some detail about the nighttime "watchers" over the sleeping flock, who accept sentry duty gladly, whereas "we are loath to give up our sleep."[72] Unlike soporific human beings, the crane "rises eagerly from its resting place, performs its duty, and repays with equal care and courtesy the favors that it has received. Hence there are no deserters, because their loyalty is a natural one. Hence their guard duty furnishes real protection, because their wills are free."[73]

Ambrose's congregants might well already have begun to entertain the idea that they should think about emulating the virtuous behavior of this bird, and they were right, but there is much more to Ambrose's crane lore. Not only are cranes the paradigm of freedom, they are also exemplary of a communal lifestyle based on "equal participation in both labor and office," sharing responsibilities in "an ideal state where no one became accustomed to unbroken power," because the dignity of shared work was affirmed.[74] By woeful contrast, human beings are afflicted with "lust for domination" that led to power-hungry behavior and a hierarchical social organization: arrogance, lack of good will, and injurious social striving are the lot of the human community because they lack the equanimity and humility of cranes.[75] At first, the cranes as Ambrose presents them seem as though they might be an image of the ideal social and ethical conditions of paradise, but in fact the principal paradisal virtues as Ambrose lists them in his treatise *On Paradise*—prudence, chastity, fortitude, and justice—do not map precisely onto the virtues that he associates with cranes.[76]

The cranes are not, then, a feathered dream of paradisal bliss. They are, rather, a utopian model of what communal social cooperation and generosity could be like for human beings now. Thus the cranes fall more appropriately into the tradition of moral exhortation as modeled by Basil of Caesarea in his *Hexaemeron*, where the emphasis on the ethics of animal behavior is aimed at shaming and so reforming human misbehavior.[77] Even so, the fact is that Ambrose holds up cranes as a mirror into which his congregants are forced to gaze. One wonders whether they could look at their preacher's figuration of the cranes and imagine themselves living such lives of orderly freedom, or whether they thought to themselves, "The bird's after-image is more than I can take."[78]

For Basil (as indeed, for Ambrose as well), sometimes a bird is just a bird.[79] Birds' feet were apparently of considerable interest to Basil, who opens his discussion of birds with the following comments:

> None of the winged creatures is without feet [unlike fish, which he
> has just discussed], because food for all of them comes from the earth
> and all necessarily require the assistance of feet. To the birds of prey
> sharp pointed claws have been given for catching their prey; but for
> the rest the service of feet has been granted as an indispensable means
> for procuring their food as well as for the other needs of life. A few of
> the birds have poor feet, not suitable for walking nor for seizing the
> prey, like the swallows, which are able neither to walk nor to seize
> prey, and the so-called swifts, for whom food is provided from insects
> borne about in the air. However, the flight of the swallow, which is
> close to the ground, serves them as a substitute for feet.[80]

And this is about all that Basil has to say about the physiology of birds; presumably their feet were one more aspect of all that the "Master Craftsman" accomplished "wisely and skillfully."[81] When, however, he turns to the stork—one more long-billed bird—we find providential design bending back in feathered figures upon human comportment once more. Basil is most impressed with the hospitality and solicitude that storks exhibit, leading him to describe their conduct as "not far from reasoning intelligence" (οὐδὲ πόρρω ἐστὶ συνέσεως λογικῆς). The image picture that he paints of the behavior of storks is worth quoting in full.

> The conduct of the storks is not far from reasoning intelligence; thus
> they all reside in these regions at the same time, and likewise all
> depart at one signal. Our crows attend them as bodyguards and escort
> them, as it seems to me, providing a certain auxiliary force against
> hostile birds. And a proof is, first, that the crows do not appear at all
> during that time; then, that, returning with wounds, they carry clear
> proofs of their protective and defensive alliance. Who prescribed the
> laws of hospitality among them? Who threatened them with an
> indictment for military desertion, so that no one deserts the escort?
> Let the inhospitable listen, who close their doors and do not share
> shelter in winter and at night with travelers. The solicitude of the
> storks for their old would suffice to make our children devoted to
> their fathers, if they were willing to heed it. For, surely, no one at all is
> so lacking in intelligence as not to judge it deserving of shame to be
> inferior in virtue to irrational birds. They, surrounding their father
> when from old age he has shed his feathers, warm him through with
> their own feathers; they also procure food in abundance for him and
> furnish powerful aid on the flight, gently lifting him on each side
> upon their wings. This fact has been so commonly proclaimed among
> all that already some call the repayment of benefactions "antipelargo-
> sis" (ἀντιπελάργωσις).[82]

As Euripides' play *Alcestis* demonstrates, hospitality in antiquity involved entertaining and sharing one's goods with strangers, a practice that continued in ancient Christianity.[83] In this passage, storks are hospitable in that they take in, as it were, the crows as fellow travelers, hence Basil's exhortation to inhospitable human beings, who turn their backs on travelers in need. More notable, perhaps, is the familial solicitude shown by young storks for their elders. Indeed, it is the thought of this loving behavior that prompts Basil to exclaim that these "irrational birds" surpass human beings in their virtuous comportment.

Once again, as with Ambrose's cranes, members of a congregation are compelled to look in an animal mirror, and what they see is, in this case, shaming indeed. Surely Basil's point is that his congregation should develop an avian sensibility in regard to strangers and elders. But—as we shall see in subsequent chapters—he expresses that wish in terms that are contradictory, declaring that the storks are models of virtue "not far from reasoning intelligence," and yet at the same time "irrational." This simultaneous embrace and distancing of animals in terms of their continuity, even their shared moral being (even their superiority) with humans is part of the paradox that lies at the center of this book. The rhetoric of human dominance due to reason clashes with the narrative of the virtuous behavior of actual storks, and there is no resolution.

Christological Birds

Some birds in the ancient Christian imagination escaped the binarism just noted, however, perhaps because the bird as animal has almost disappeared into its role as symbol, so much so that there is no reason to question its actual intelligence, or lack thereof. This was particularly true of birds that served as Christological images. There was, for example, the pelican. This bird was embedded in fantasy rather than biological fact even by ancient naturalists. These writers were interested in the pelican because of its supposed habit of eating large mussels whole and then vomiting up the shells following digestion.[84] Although pelicans in fact eat fish rather than shellfish, ancient "observers" were fascinated by the pelican's supposed ability to regurgitate food somewhat like a ruminant.[85] So much for ancient naturalists' knowledge of the "real" bird. Adding to such lore were Christian authors. Both the *Physiologus* and Augustine approached the pelican exegetically, starting from a verse in Psalm 101:7 (Vulgate): "I have become like a pelican in a lonely place [or, in loneliness]" (*Similis factus sum pellicano solitudinis*). Christians too thus began with lore, since pelicans are sociable birds that live in colonies, not in isolation, and in any case the solitude of the pelican played a very minor role in both their exegeses. Thus actual pelicans—"those lovely ungainly / pelicans [that] fished there, dropping / like rocks, with grace, from the air"—have from the beginning receded into a symbolic world where reason, or lack thereof, is not really the point.[86]

The point, rather, was seizing upon the verse mentioning the pelican as an opportunity to anchor Christological doctrine in the Old Testament and in this way to link it to the New Testament and so to Christian truth. The section on the pelican in the *Physiologus* is exemplary in this regard.

> David says in Psalm 101, "I am like the pelican in loneliness" [Ps. 102:7]. Physiologus says of the pelican that it is an exceeding lover of its young. If the pelican brings forth young and the little ones grow, they take to striking their parents in the face. The parents, however, hitting back kill their young ones and then, moved by compassion, they weep over them for three days, lamenting over those whom they killed. On the third day, their mother strikes her side and spills her own blood over their dead bodies (that is, of the chicks) and the blood itself awakens them from death. Thus did our Lord speaking through Isaiah say, "I have brought forth sons and have lifted them up, but they have scorned me" [Is. 1:2]. The Maker of every creature brought us forth and we struck him. How did we strike him? Because we served the creature rather than the creator [cf. Rom. 1:25]. The Lord ascended the height of the cross and the impious ones struck his side and opened it and blood and water came forth for eternal life [cf. Jn. 19:34 and 6:55], blood because it is said, "Taking the chalice he gave thanks" [Mt. 26:27 and Lk. 22:17], and water because of the baptism of repentance [Mk. 1:4 and Lk. 3:3]. The Lord said, "They have forsaken me, the fountain of living water," and so on [Jer. 2:13]. Physiologus, therefore, spoke well of the pelican.[87]

Aside from the fact that the hapless pelican suffers from near-death by referential overkill, in this passage the supposed behavior of the bird toward its young provides a touching symbolic picture of divine love in the face of various kinds of impious behavior. An entire Christian credo of persecution, death, resurrection, and Eucharistic ritual is emblazoned on the body of the pelican.

Notably missing from this image of the pelican is the avian complex of air, freedom, and liberation. Far from being aerial, this bird stays on the ground—unless one counts the "flight" of elevated doctrine that the lore about its behavior accords it. Augustine's petitioning of the pelican followed suit. In his exegesis of Psalm 101 (Vulgate), Augustine attempts first to account for the pelican living "in solitary places" (rather than "in loneliness" as the *Physiologus* has it). Very briefly, he finds that the pelicans in solitary places represent the Christian preacher who "must visit non-Christian peoples," and thus is the single believer in a crowd of unbelievers. Or perhaps, he thinks later on in his exegesis, the pelican in a solitary place represents Christ's unique virginal birth.[88] Augustine is quick, however, to move to the Christological import of the pelican that emphasizes the redemptive shedding of blood: "Pelicans are alleged to kill their chicks by pecking them, then for three days to mourn the dead chicks in the nest. Finally the mother is said to wound herself gravely and pour her blood over her babies, which come back to life as her blood flows over them. This report may be true or false; but if it is true, observe how apt a symbol it is of him who gave his life by his own blood."[89] While Augustine wonders whether the lore about the pelican is accurate, he decides to accept it because of its symbolic richness.[90] Unlike the *Physiologus*, he notices that the mother pelican is both persecutor (she pecks her chicks to death) and persecuted (she sheds her blood to bring the chicks back to life). This is an odd Christological image in that it requires the symbol of the pelican to carry both a positive valence, referring theologically to Christ's redemptive shedding of his blood, and a negative valence, referring historically to the persecution of Christ and his death on the cross. Augustine, of course, has an exegetical solution for this seeming oddity: "If the story about the pelican is true, then, this bird is a very apt image of the flesh of Christ—Christ, by whose blood we have been given life. But does her killing of her chicks fit into that picture? Yes, it does fit, for he declares, 'I will kill, and I will give life; I will strike, and I will heal' (Dt. 32:39). Would the persecutor Saul have died, if he had not been struck from heaven? And would he have been raised to a new life as a preacher, if he had not been given life by Christ's blood?"[91] Here Augustine solves a problematic symbol by introducing an oddity of his own, an intertext from the Old Testament about a vengeful God that seems wildly inappropriate as it veers off into yet another story concerning Saul/Paul in the New Testament. The "real" pelican has been long lost in this swirl of signification.

There is another oddity about the symbolic pelican, unremarked by the *Physiologus* but capitalized upon by Augustine. Following his observation, as above, that the symbol of the pelican is apt, he wrote, "It fits him very well, even though it is the mother bird who with her blood gives life to her squabs, for Christ called himself a mother hen, caring for her young: 'Jerusalem, Jerusalem, how often I wanted to gather your children to myself, as a hen gathers her chicks under her wings, but you would have none of it!'" (Mt. 23:37). He has both a father's authority and a mother's tenderness."[92] In this passage Augustine neatly glosses over a gender problem by introducing another intertext that presents Christ under the symbol of yet another bird, the domestic hen. And, lest this new bird feminize Christ further, Augustine is quick to note Christ's fatherly authority, although on what basis it is difficult to discern in the context as it stands.

Nonetheless, Augustine was very attracted to the hen's maternal, nurturing qualities, to which he returned in his exposition of Psalm 58 (Vulgate). As we shall see more fully in Chapter 4, Augustine viewed the narrative voice of the psalms as that of Christ, both "head" and "body," divine and human, as he put it. In this psalm, according to Augustine, the reader hears the persecuted Christ speaking.[93] In a digression on Christ's dignity and weakness—or perhaps better, the dignity of his weakness—Augustine remarks,

> He became weak even to the point of dying; he assumed our weak flesh in order to gather the chicks of Jerusalem under his wings, like a hen that is weakened with her babies. We have never seen this phenomenon in any other bird. . . . We are unaware of any other bird that becomes so weak with its young. . . . How does the hen reduce herself to weakness? What I am talking about is a familiar sight, something that takes place daily as we watch. We know how her voice becomes hoarse, how she makes her whole body a fluffy muddle. Her wings droop, the feathers are relaxed, and she looks almost ill over her chicks. This is maternal love, expressing itself as weakness. For what other reason did our Lord liken himself to a hen in scripture? "Jerusalem, Jerusalem, how often I wanted to gather your children to myself, as a hen gathers her chicks under her wings, but you would have none of it!" (Mt. 23:37). But the Gentiles he did gather, as a hen her chicks, he who became weak for our sake by taking flesh from our race, and being crucified, despised, slapped, scourged, hung on the tree and wounded with a lance. All this is the mark of a mother's weakness, not of lost majesty. This was the state to which Christ was reduced, and this is why he was despised, why he became a stone to trip people and a rock to stumble over, and why many did trip over him. Because he was so weakened, and yet had assumed flesh without sin, we confess that he participated in our weakness, but not in our iniquity, to the end that by sharing weakness with us he might destroy our iniquity.[94]

From the perspective of the animal as poem, this passage begins quite promisingly, as Augustine appeals to the image of a broody hen to give expression to the love of Christ for humanity. Like the pelican, this bird is (literally) grounded, but its sphere of meaning is not folklore but rather animal husbandry. One can imagine the farmers in Augustine's congregation thinking that their chickens would never look the same again (and indeed, in another sermon, Augustine assures his listeners, "You must not think it irreverent to use the hen as a symbol of God").[95] Yet this figure of the mother hen weakened by loving care of her chicks is ultimately overwhelmed by Augustine's staccato-like recitation of Christ's passion. The Christological point toward which the passage drives leaves any connection between the "fluffy muddle" of the hen's body and Christ's sinless flesh unexplored.[96]

Doves

Thus far this chapter has dealt with birds whose poetizing function has conveyed Christian meaning of one sort or another. The chapter concludes with a coda that explores the phenomenon of birds that don't *mean* anything. Prior to that coda, however, is one final meaningful bird, one that brings together the two most prominent attributes of the bird as poem, flight and song, and adds a new dimension, color. This bird is the dove, which has been an enduring Christian emblem of the avian complex of air, freedom, and liberation ever since the Gospels pictured the Holy Spirit descending upon Jesus at his baptism in the form of a dove.[97] Although, biblically speaking, the dove was an early image of human salvation and the reestablishment of peace with God after the Flood (Gen. 8:8–12) as well as a figure of innocence (Mt. 10:16), the attributes of the dove that appealed to patristic authors were its association with spiritual heights and with love.[98]

First, love. In the section of his *Hexaemeron* that deals with the parts of the human body, Ambrose devoted one (not very well organized) section to the lips. After exclaiming about the ways in which humans' "corporeal lips" utter "oracular words" of divine wisdom, Ambrose abruptly asks, "What shall I say of the kiss which is a symbol of affection and love? (*Quid autem loquar de osculo oris, quod pietatis et caritatis est signum?*) Doves exchange kisses, but what is this compared to the charm of a kiss of a human being in which the note of friendliness and kindliness is conspicuous, and where is expressed the indubitable sense of our sincerest affection?"[99] In positioning doves as kissers, Ambrose may have been referring to the bonding rituals of pairs of male and female doves, in which the two "preen each other with gentle nibbles around the neck" and then progress to "grasping beaks and bobbing their heads up and down."[100] An earlier author, Cyprian, adds an important ingredient to this picture of doves kissing: their "kiss of the mouth" is a recognition of "the concord of peace" and thus shows how appropriate is the dove as a figure and channel for the Holy Spirit.[101] Ethology has shaded into theology. It is interesting to note here how doves' kisses have been co-opted for expressing themes of peace, unity, and pious interpersonal relations, in light of the fact that in non-Christian ancient literature the kiss is erotic, an exchange between lovers.[102] Furthermore, Cyprian and Ambrose ignore a widespread association of the dove with lascivious sexuality in Greco-Roman culture.[103] In the Christian passages, this positively Venusian bird and its "lingering" kisses, as Martial describes them, have been de-eroticized as a way of "defending the widespread use of the dove as icon of the Holy Spirit."[104]

It is intriguing to imagine that Ambrose passed along the triangulation of dove, love, and kisses to his one-time pupil Augustine, who in a sermon states that the person who "has the Holy Spirit ought to be simple as the dove, to have true peace with his brethren, that peace which the kisses of the dove signify."[105] Thus Augustine too places the dove in a de-eroticized context of Christian unity and the ritual kiss of peace—de-eroticized, that is, until he states in another sermon that doves conceive by kissing rather than by sexual intercourse, a view that brings the kiss back into the ambit of *amor* proper.[106] In the early seventh century, Isidore of Seville made the connection between the dove's kiss and sexual passion explicit: in his *Etymologiae*, he observed that "the ancients called [the dove] 'of Venus' because they frequently visit their nests and make love with a kiss."[107]

And then there was Augustine's own addition to the mix of the dove's qualities: the sound of its song. There are two substantial passages in which Augustine addresses the sound made by doves. The first is in his sermon on Psalm 55 (RSV), a psalm in which the narrator, overcome with anguish due to attacks by adversaries, cries, "Oh that I had wings like a dove! I would fly away and be at rest" (Ps. 55:6). Augustine explains that the wings of a dove are appropriate to long for because the dove "does not let go of love." He continues, "A dove is considered to be the symbol of love, and its moaning is a loveable sound [*columba enim pro signo dilectionis ponitur, et in ea gemitus amatur*]. No creature is as much given to moaning as a dove; it moans all day long and at night, evidently thinking the place where it lives to be one appropriate to moaning."[108] Given the amatory context in which he places the dove's moaning, one might think that Augustine agreed with Basil of Caesarea, who comments on the dove in his *Hexaemeron* in a section in which he is discussing the sounds that distinguish the various birds from each other; the sound of the dove, for Basil, is "lust-ful" or "lecherous" (λάνιοι αἰπεριστεραὶ).[109] However, the word that Augustine uses for moaning, *gemitus*, denotes a sighing or groaning that shades off into lamentation or complaint,[110] and indeed, Augustine follows the passage above with the following statement attributed to the persecuted "I" of the psalm: "So, then, this is the voice of a lover, and what has he to say? 'I cannot bear all this abuse. People hiss at me, they are beside themselves with savagery, they are incandescent with rage, their anger is a dark cloud over me. I can do noth-ing to help them, so I want to get some rest elsewhere, distant from them in body, but not in love, simply so that the love that is in me may not be agitated anymore.'"[111] This passage makes clear that the dove and the narrative voice of the psalm have merged. The moaning, however "loveable," pertains more to plaintive lament than to lust. Perhaps Augustine would have agreed with what a modern poet wrote about mourning doves. When she read in a guide-book that the name of the bird was not "morning dove" but rather "mourning dove," this poet wrote: "I noticed their ash-gray feathers, / like shadows / on the underside / of love."[112]

This was not Augustine's only perspective on the dove, however. In yet another sermon, the amatory moaning of the dove is spiritualized, taking on the character not of complaint or lament but of deep-seated longing. In one of his homilies on the Gospel of John, Augustine has set himself the task of explaining why the Holy Ghost appeared in the form of a dove. He begins by noting that he and his congregation love each other in Christ, and then he writes: "Let our love mutually sigh towards God, for the song of the dove is a sighing or moaning."[113] Augustine continues: "Now if the dove's song is a moaning, as we all know it to be, and doves moan in love [*gemunt autem columbae in amore*], hear what the apostle says, and wonder not that the Holy Ghost willed to be manifested in the form of a dove. 'For what we should pray for as we ought,' he says, 'we know not; but the Spirit himself intercedes for us with groaning which cannot be uttered' [*gemitibus inenarrabilibus*]" (Rom. 8:26).[114] On the authority of the apostle Paul, Augustine is able to link the "groaning" of the dove with that of the Holy Spirit. He explains that the Holy Spirit does not "groan" as a member of the Trinity; rather, "in us he groans because he makes us to groan," and this is an important inner song, because

he gives us to know that we are sojourners in a foreign land, and he teaches us to sigh after our native country, and through that very longing do we groan. . . .

The person who knows that he is . . . a pilgrim "absent from the Lord" [2 Cor. 5:6], that he does not yet possess that perpetual blessedness which is promised to us, but that he has it in hope, and will have it in reality when the Lord shall come openly in glory who came in humility concealed; he, I say, who knows this doth groan. And so long as it is for this he groans, he does well to groan; it was the Spirit that taught him to groan, he learned it from the dove.[115]

For Augustine, groaning is a deep longing for eternal bliss as taught by the Holy Spirit, our interior dove.

In the foregoing sermon, Augustine has turned the song of the dove into an eschatological hope for "flight" to our "native country," the heavenly realm. This positioning of the dove in terms of spiritual flight brings this chapter back to its beginning, where the bird as poem was linked with lofty thoughts and winged souls. So too with the dove of Augustine's imagination. The sighing of the amatory dove gives figure and tone to a very lofty thought, the theological concept of eternal life, better than any discursive explanation could do. Many centuries later, Augustine's linking of the dove, longing, and homecoming achieved another kind of poetic expression in the following poem by Rilke:

Ah, not to be cut off
not through the slightest partition
shut out from the law of the stars.
The inner—what is it?
If not intensified sky,
Hurled through with birds and deep
With the winds of homecoming.[116]

Rilke had probably not read Augustine's sermon on the groaning dove, but the figures of his poem capture beautifully the celestial heights and avian inner depths of Augustine's own intense longing for "home."

For other patristic interpreters, it was the dove of the Song of Songs that struck them as spiritually significant. Gregory of Nyssa, for example, was arrested by Song of Songs 1:15: "Behold, you are beautiful: your eyes are doves." In his *Homilies on the Song of Songs*, the identification of the dove with the Holy Spirit is implicit in Gregory's Platonizing view that "people receive in themselves the likeness of whatever they gaze upon intently." It is fitting then, he continues, that the person "who no longer gazes upon flesh and blood" and "looks toward the spiritual life . . . is attested as having in its eyes the shape of the dove—that is, the imprint of the spiritual life is beheld in the clear vision of the soul."[117] In his view of the dove as the "stamp" (χαρακτῆρα) that enables the soul to see the beauty of Christ the bridegroom, Gregory is following in the footsteps of Origen, who in his *Commentary on the Song of Songs* says straightforwardly, "Nobody can perceive and know how great is the splendor of the Word, until he receives dove's eyes—that is, a spiritual understanding."[118] As was so typical of Origen's perspective, spiritual understanding pertains to a type of scriptural reading; thus "to understand the Law and the Prophets in a spiritual sense is, therefore, to have the eyes of a dove" because "the dove is the emblem of the Holy Spirit."[119]

Gregory's preoccupation with the dove and beauty and Origen's focus on spiritual insight into a book seem rather distant and disconnected from the desirously moaning dove of Augustine's imagination. In the same passage in which he equates spiritual understanding with possession of eyes of a dove, however, Origen changes the metaphor of the dove by switching scriptural passages: "But in the Psalms [68:14] a soul of this sort longs to be given 'the wings of a dove,' that she may be able to fly in the understanding of spiritual mysteries, and to rest in the courts of wisdom."[120] Now there are wings rather than eyes. Here again, as in a passage quoted earlier in this chapter, Origen's aerial avian sensibility is at work, as the soul hopes to fly—perhaps "in a spasm of wing-beats"—in the medium of heavenly wisdom.[121]

In a final reference to the winged dove, Origen's evocation of it takes on the gleam of "the color of felicity afire," as the "burnished plumage" of one particular biblical dove glitters in his commentary.[122] In one of his homilies on the Gospel of Luke, Origen is remarking on the swiftness of the dovelike Holy Spirit, which rises "up to the heights."[123] He continues,

> For this reason, we say in prayer, Who will give me wings like those of a dove? I shall fly and take rest [Ps. 55:6–7, RSV]. In another place the prophetic word promises: if you sleep between the plots of the land, the wings of a dove are of silver, and the pinions of its tail are made of gleaming gold [Ps. 67:14, LXX and Vulgate]. For, if we rest "between the plots" of the Old and New Testaments, "silver wings of a dove" will be given to us, that is, the words of God, and the pinions of its tail, radiant with the gleam of gold, so that our senses might be filled with perceptions of the Holy Spirit.[124]

There is an oddity in this passage, since in the Hebrew of Psalm 67 the silver and gold doves are spoil divided among women who "stay among the sheepfolds" (Ps. 68:12–13, RSV). As the translator of Origen's passage notes, the wording of the psalm that he was using doesn't make very much sense literally, but his allegorical appropriation of it, the resting "between the plots"—the sacred words—of the two testaments, enables Origen to highlight an aesthetic reading of both the dove and the scriptural words and perceptions that it represents. Gleaming with the sheen of precious metals, this embellished dove shows just how much value and meaning Origen placed in the dove poem of winged thoughts. It is impossible to know whether Origen had seen the silver and gold lamps in the shape of doves that hung in some ancient Christian churches, since surviving examples of these most popular of the zoomorphic lamps of antiquity date between the fourth and sixth centuries (Figure 4).[125] But the brilliance of their shining surely matched the silver and gold intensity that Origen hoped might fill our senses.

Coda

Such an impossibly bright bird also captured the imagination of a modern poet.[126] Wallace Stevens's last poem is entitled "Of Mere Being," in which the word "mere" may have a variety of referents, from simple to slight to pure, but "being" is evoked by a bird something like Origen's dove.[127] In this poem, Stevens imagines a "palm at the end of the mind/beyond the last thought." A "gold-feathered bird" sits in this palm, singing; but its song is "without human meaning . . . a foreign song." The bird simply is: "its fire-fangled feathers dangle down." The radiant golden pinions of Origen's dove and the fire-fangled feathers of Stevens's golden bird seem uncannily like doubles of each other. Across the centuries, the feathers gleam. But there is a remarkable difference: Stevens's bird sings a song that is foreign, without human meaning, whereas Origen's dove is full of meaning. Interestingly, in a nonscriptural context, Origen himself could imagine birds that didn't mean anything, and it is those meaningless birds whose "song" ends this chapter.

In Book 4 of his *Contra Celsum*, Origen engages in a sharp critique of the philosopher Celsus's view that animals are rational.[128] Adopting what was basically the Stoic position on animal minds (or better, the lack thereof), Origen explains that Celsus "has not seen the difference between actions done as a result of reason and thought and those which are the product of irrational nature and are merely natural characteristics."[129] In this particular passage, Origen

FIGURE 4. Dove-shaped lamp, bronze, fourth–fifth century CE. Courtesy of the Virginia Museum of Fine Arts, Richmond. Gift of Dr. Richard H. Howland. Photo: Travis Fullerton. © Virginia Museum of Fine Arts.

exemplifies his point by reference to ants and bees: they are not intelligent city planners, he says; rather, their social organizations are simply the result of innate impulse—"of mere being," as it were. What Origen finds especially shocking in Celsus's position is the conviction that not only are animals rational, some of them have ideas of God. Here is where the topic of birds enters the discussion. Origen attributes the following passage to Celsus:

> If because man has laid hold of notions of God he is thought to be superior to the other animals, let those who maintain this realize that many of the other animals would lay claim to this. And quite reasonably. For what would anyone say to be more divine than to foreknow and declare the future? Well then, men learn this from other animals, and especially from birds; and those who understand the indications which they give are diviners. If then the birds and all other prophetic animals which are given foreknowledge by God teach us by means of signs, they seem to be naturally so much nearer in communication with God and to be wiser and dearer to God.[130]

Augury, then, as a specific form of divinatory practice, will provide the context for Origen's declaration of the meaninglessness of birds.

Origen argues that divination by birds is neither prophetic nor genuine. If birds really had prophetic souls, he reasons, they would not get trapped in nets set for them by human beings and they would know ahead of time where archers

trying to shoot them were located and so avoid those spots.[131] And as for perceptions and ideas of God, Origen tosses out this notion on the basis of lack of
reason: birds have no idea of God at all and thus cannot act even as intermedi-
aries between divine intention and human life. The very idea, says Origen, is
repellent, and besides, the chances are good that demons, not God, are responsible for any "signs" that birds and other animals might give.[132]

In his blunt dismissal of birds as giving meaningful signs, Origen was in
fact sweeping away an entire cultural system of meaning. As Mary Beard has
pointed out, Roman augury "was deeply embedded at the centre of Roman
political and religious life, defined and regulated in the written tradition of the
priestly books; it made sense according to the logic of the symbolic inheritance
of Rome and Roman views of the operation of the gods in the world. . . . Roman
augury involved no predictive element, but was concerned rather simply to
ascertain divine approval for the undertaking contemplated."[133] In fact, Origen
not only dismissed this tradition, he replaced it with another, biblical one: "For
knowledge of the future, the true God uses neither irrational animals nor ordinary men, but the most sacred and holy human souls whom He inspires and
makes prophets"—a position guaranteed, as far as Origen was concerned, by
several passages from the Hebrew Bible that forbid augury.[134] Thus the question
of the meaning of birds has become a battle of religious traditions.

For Origen, birds were the losers in terms of being bearers of meaning. He
refuted the idea "that there exists a positive interaction between gods and birds,
whereby beneficent gods send reliable signs to expert mortals by means of certain birds, which act as the gods' messengers."[135] If these birds were to sing, the
song would truly be "without human meaning, a foreign song." Centuries later,
Bailly apparently agreed with Origen that a poetics of augural birds is really not
possible. In his meditative work *The Animal Side*, he wrote about the "Roman
custom of Etruscan provenance—that of observing the flight of birds in a pre-
determined portion of the sky called the *templum*." He continued: "The augurs
avidly sought signs of destiny in the flight of birds crossing the *templum*. As for
the birds themselves, they were passing by. It is almost caricatural: on one side,
men, subject to anxiety and seeking to recognize, in the free play of the forms of
the universe, signs personally addressed to them; on the other side, birds, who
could not care less about signs and who fly freely in the open."[136] Here is a rejection of augury as a meaningful sign system similar to Origen's, only this rejection takes the part of the birds' eye view: the birds were just passing by! And in
this form of rejection lies an important shift in worldview. Origen's dismissal of
augural birds was based on the thoroughly anthropocentric position of human

superiority to animals, while Bailly's position, by taking the side of the birds in flight, resolutely rejects anthropocentrism as an anxious ploy to harness cosmic meaning for solely human purposes. Writing about grackles in a maple tree, the poet Bob Hicok echoes Bailly's point: "I do ask them something / by looking at them, as they ask me nothing / by not looking at me."[137]

Ultimately Bailly positions birds in what Rilke called "the open," a space, for Bailly, of "pure unfolding . . . the one in which wonders occur—for example, one evening on the Loire and over a period of hours, the perpetual movement of a flock of starlings endlessly forming liquid figures, a triangulation of black dots departing, then suddenly turning back like iron filings attracted by an invisible magnet moving in the sky. Nothing more, perhaps: only flight, the idea of flight, embodied in flight as we see it and as it comes and goes before our eyes."[138] With this idea of birds in flight as "the signature of pure intoxication with living," we return full circle to the beginning of this chapter, where birds' flight connotes imaginative freedom for ancient and modern authors alike.[139] Bailly's birds simply *are*, in the sense of mere being, and their song, if they sang, would be "beyond the last thought"; but the bird in flight as poetic figure continues on.

CHAPTER 2

The Pensivity of Animals, I

Zoomorphism

In November 386 CE, Augustine produced the first of the dialogues that he wrote while on philosophical retreat at Cassiciacum, the *Contra Academicos*.[1] At one point in the first book of this treatise, the discussants are worrying the issue of what constitutes true knowledge. The astonishing prescience of a diviner named Albicerius is raised as a possible instance of real knowledge, only to be dismissed as flamboyant cleverness, liable to falsehood. His knowledge is a pretention to wisdom, not the real thing. As the clincher to this dismissal of the diviner's kind of knowledge as true wisdom, one of Augustine's pupils remarks: "For even if we express wonder that a little bee, after putting away its honey, flies to it again and again with a sagacity that surpasses that of a human being, we ought not for that reason to prefer it to or even to compare it with ourselves."[2] Presumably, the bee in this remark is like the diviner: it excites wonder (*miror*) because of its acute perception (*sagacitas*), but ultimately it fails in comparison with human beings. But: fails at what, exactly? And isn't the diviner a human being too, even if possessed of flawed knowledge?

The implied comparison of the bee with the diviner and his false pretentions to knowledge is odd at the very least because, unlike the diviner's "knowledge," the bee's sagacity *surpasses* that of human beings. In December of the same year, Augustine in effect clarified his position regarding bees in the dialogue entitled *De ordine*. There, in a comment on homebuilding, Augustine remarks: "I am no better, in this respect, than the swallow or the bee: for the one builds its nest artistically, and the other its honeycomb. But I am better than these, because I am a rational animal [*Sed his melior, quia rationale animal sum*]."[3] Bees, then, might have a flair for domestic architecture and an unerring sense of memory for the location of their hives, both of which talents seem to elicit a certain sense of lack in human abilities, but they don't possess reason, hence Augustine's repeated assertion that humans are better. Yet this uncomfortable jostling of admiration *and* contempt for the bee betrays a certain anxiety about animal-human relationships, and it is this (over)insistence on human superiority vis-à-vis animals, as well as alternatives to it, that this chapter explores.

My argument is that the anxiety that arose at the thought of comparing human beings and bees (as well as other animals) and the concomitant possibility of finding humans wanting, together with trumpeted assertions of human superiority, constitute an early Christian version of "anthropocentrism and its discontents."[4] The position that "human beings are primary and central in the order of things" seems to rest on shaky psychological and ontological ground when the question of animals is posed.[5] As Aaron Gross has pointed out, the history of Western thought, including Christian theology, has been characterized by an insistence on an animal/human binary that has been naturalized as fact. And yet, as Gross continues, "Far from being a datum given in the natural order, the human/animal binary has always been and remains unstable, disputed, and negotiated."[6] Augustine's defensive assertion of his superiority to bees is a case in point of the uneasiness of this presumption of a chasm between human and animal being. Indeed, as I show throughout this book, the conceptual stability of an animal/human binary is challenged again and again, and in several ways, by ancient Christian texts.

To return to Augustine's defensiveness: imagine the rise in his level of anxiety were Augustine to have read the view of the bee expressed by Philo's nephew Alexander: "Its intelligence [*ingenio*] is hardly distinguishable from the contemplative ability of the human mind."[7] Some years later, the views of Greco-Roman naturalists only underscored this high estimation of apian ability. Pliny, for example, expostulating on the creative power of nature, wrote, "Nature is so mighty a power that out of what is almost a tiny ghost of an animal she has created something incomparable! . . . What men, I protest, can we rank in rationality [*ratione*] with these insects [bees], which unquestionably excel humankind in this, that they recognize only the common interest?"[8] Aelian agreed: "There was never any creature more gracious than the bee, just as there is none wiser [σοφώτερον]."[9] Such statements about the relative mental capacities of animals vis-à-vis human beings have led one contemporary observer, the ecocritic Timothy Morton, to ask, "What if [human] consciousness were not 'higher' but 'lower' than we have supposed?"[10] That is, what if there is not a chasm separating human and animal but rather a continuum of animal intelligence, including human animals?

Anchoring his viewpoint in Darwin's *Descent of Man* (rather than in the thought of the more ancient Pliny and Aelian), Morton expounds upon animal intelligence without a shred of Augustinian anxiety: "Nonhumans can reason and imagine; they have a sense of beauty and wonder."[11] He continues:

> Do nonhumans possess language? Yes. How about imagination?
> Check. Reason? Copy that. A sense of mind? No doubt. Can they
> use tools? Indeed. Do they display improved skills and learning over
> time? Absolutely. Can nonhumans feel compassion? Of course.
> Do they have a sense of humor? Why not? How about wonder? Yes.
> Choice? Also yes. Humans are fairly uniquely good at throwing and
> sweating: not much of a portfolio. Read Darwin on female insects:
> "when we see many males pursuing the same female, we can hardly
> believe that the pairing is left to blind chance—that the female exerts
> no choice, and is not influenced by the gorgeous odours or other
> ornaments with which the male is decorated." If butterflies have the
> capacity to make a choice, then surely it's game over for rigid distinc-
> tions between humans and nonhumans?[12]

Morton ends his catalogue of nonhuman consciousness with an amusing—but serious—question aimed at those who bend over backward to deny cognition in nonhumans: "If it walks like a mind and quacks like a mind, why not call it one?"[13]

Origen, Bees, and Anthropocentrism

The foregoing question is one that Origen of Alexandria, like Augustine after him, answered in the negative, and he did so while discussing not ducks but bees. However, Origen's firm espousal of human superiority when compared with bees belies the way in which early Christian thought was haunted by what Jean-Christophe Bailly has called "the pensivity of animals."[14] For Bailly, anthropocentrism of the sort espoused by Origen is an anxious play to harness cosmic meaning for solely human purposes and validation, whereas in Bailly's view each animal is a "thought" of Being dispersed in and traversing the world in an "infinite dissemination."[15] In order to delve more deeply into the very different thought world of ancient anthropocentrism and its discontents, then, it will be instructive to spend time with Origen's arguments.

In his work *Contra Celsum*, Origen went to great lengths to refute a second-century Platonist, Celsus, who had written a treatise, *The True Doctrine*, criticizing and even lampooning various aspects of Christian belief as credulous and unphilosophical.[16] Origen's comments on bees follow a section of the *Contra Celsum* in which Origen upholds the view that everything in nature was made for human beings against Celsus's position that everything was made as much for nonhuman creatures as for human beings.[17] Origen seems especially piqued at Celsus's critique of his claim that such cosmic elements as the sun and night were made for the sake of humankind. "Why do they exist for us any more than for ants and flies?" Celsus asks, a comment that undermines Origen's anthropocentric outlook and anticipates a remark by the Scottish philosopher David Hume: "But the life of a man is of no greater importance to the universe than that of an oyster."[18] Origen, however, seems undaunted by Celsus's critique of human beings' centrality in the cosmos. He presses on to the issue of humankind's superiority to those whom he consistently calls "irrational animals," a position that is strangely at odds with his willingness to treat birds as thoughts, as we saw in the previous chapter. Many animals, Origen observes, are physically stronger than human beings, but "we overcome wild beasts by intelligence."[19] Following such generalized opening salvos, Origen then latches onto Celsus's remarks about bees and ants in order to give focus to the debate about animal intelligence (or lack thereof).

Bees and ants were widely admired in antiquity and often spoken about in the same breath and for the same reasons, namely, their social organization and industry.[20] Here I shall focus on the bee. Origen begins by charging Celsus with a failure to perceive "the extent of the harm done and the hindrance to piety which results from believing that in God's sight man is no better than ants and bees."[21] He then quotes from Celsus's treatise as follows: "He says that 'if the reason why men appear to be better than the irrational animals is that they live in cities and have a state and positions of authority and leadership, this proves nothing at all. For ants and bees do this too. At any rate, the bees have a leader, they have attendants and servants, wars and conquests, they slay the vanquished, they have cities and even suburbs, they pass work on from one to another, they condemn the idle and wicked—at least they drive out and punish the drones.'"[22] To this Origen replies that Celsus has been unable to see "the difference between actions done as a result of reason and thought [τὰ ἀπὸ λόγου καὶ λογισμοῦ ἐπιτελούμενα] and those which are the product of irrational nature and are merely natural characteristics [τῶν ἀπ᾽ ἀλόγου φύσεως καὶ κατασκευῆς ψιλῆς γινομένων]."²³ Origen concludes this line of reasoning by seeming to cede to Celsus the fact that bees do indeed have cities, only not by virtue of reason: "But the supreme Son of God, king of all that exists, has made an unreasoning instinct [φύσιν ἄλογον] which, as such, helps those beings not worthy of reason."²⁴ Although he goes on to insist that "cities with many arts and with legislation"— note the qualifications—"have come to exist only among men," he concludes as follows, with a statement that deserves to be quoted in full.

> We ought not to praise ants and bees for these [i.e., the "rational soci-
> ety, city, states, and positions of authority and leadership" that he has
> just listed] since they do not act from reason. But we ought to admire
> the divine nature which has gone so far as to give irrational beings the
> ability to copy [μίμημα] as it were, the rational beings, perhaps in
> order to put the latter to shame, that by considering ants they may
> become more industrious and thrifty with things which are useful to
> them, and that by understanding the ways of bees they may obey their
> rulers and divide among themselves the work beneficial to the state
> which will preserve their cities.²⁵

Herein lies the chink in the armor of the anthropocentric onslaught that Origen unleashed when he first brought up the topic of Celsus's bees. The absolute binary between rational human beings and irrational animals has been compromised in two ways. First, implicit in Origen's statement is a recognition that bees do indeed have cities, even if they are copies, and furthermore, it is "the divine nature" that has endowed the bees with the ability to mimic—or shadow or haunt?—these human institutions. Second, not only does the binarism not hold, the tables are actually turned: bees are such *good* mimics, that is, they have such superior political and social order in their "cities" that they become the ideal against which humans are evaluated and shamed into more a harmonious life in the state. Could this aspect of "bee culture" lie behind Origen's initial worry that Celsus's (and, ironically, his own) elevation of bees might harm a piety focused on divine reason (*logos*) and humans' exclusive claim to participation in it?

In any case, anthropocentrism has a way of undermining itself from within, and the note of anxiety that runs through Origen's discussion is hard to deny. Yes, bees are irrational animals, but they threaten human uniqueness, which is what anthropocentrism wants to proclaim and protect, by copying human society so well that they surpass it; the copy becomes the model, and a shaming one at that. I doubt, however, that Origen intended his discussion to soften his anthropocentric stance, since he spends the rest of Book 4 of the *Contra Celsum* ridiculing Celsus's views—isn't it the "height of absurdity," he chortles, to "speak of ants as though they had discussions with one another"—and pointing out again and again how degrading it is to humans to liken them to irrational animals.[26] Origen was very firm on one point: only humans have reason. Celsus, meanwhile, had no ability to talk back, since he exists only as textual fragments embedded in Origen's text. Nonetheless, it is clear from Origen's quotations of *The True Doctrine* that Celsus was one of the few thinkers in Greco-Roman antiquity who made the case for animal reason, citing such capacities as social and political organization and language, as we have just seen, as well as virtuous behavior, practical skills, and even knowledge of God.[27] Thus the disagreement over the cognitive capacities of bees is just one instance of a much larger debate, one that in fact continues to the present.

Thinking Animals: Bees as a Test Case

In order to understand how early Christian anthropocentrism participates in an ongoing and lively debate about animal-human relationships, it will be instructive to view that debate in its contemporary form, focusing again on bees as a flashpoint for disagreement. As Gary Steiner has pointed out, there is a "controversy over the mental lives of bees" that concerns whether they can think and grasp problems consciously.[28] This controversy is neatly encapsulated by one question: "How do flowers look to a bee?"[29] That is, do bees have cognitive capabilities and experience, and how do these manifest themselves?

The phenomena around which much of contemporary scientific discussion revolves are the so-called round and waggle dances that foraging bees perform to alert their hive mates to new sources of pollen or nectar. First decoded in 1947 by the Austrian zoologist Karl von Frisch, the dance language of bees has been called "the most significant example of versatile communication known in any animals other than our own species."[30] Foraging bees that have discovered a new source of food close to the hive perform the round dance, which consists of a circling movement that has alternating clockwise and counterclockwise directions; this dance alerts nest mates to the presence and odor of the new food source and "stimulates them to fly out and search in all directions" for the food.[31] The waggle dance is much more complex: it consists of figure-eight movements over the vertical surface of the honeycomb inside the hive that alert the forager bee's hive mates to the location of a more distant source of food. As two prominent entomologists describe it,

> The essential element in the performance [of the waggle dance] is the waggle run, or straight run [during which the dancing bee waggles her body from side to side at a rate of about fifteen times a second]; it is the middle piece of the figure-eight pattern, and it conveys the direction of the target during the outbound flight. Straight up on the vertical surface represents the direction of the sun the follower will see as she leaves the nest. If the target is on a line 40° to the right of the sun, say, the straight run is made 40° to the right of vertical on the comb. The remainder of the figure eight consists of a circling back at the end of the run, during which the bee first goes left, then right to reach the departure point of the waggle run.[32]

Scientists do not disagree that the honeybee's communicative dances are impressively complex. The disagreement is in regard to the dance and its relation to the honeybee's mental capacities. Positive evaluations of bees' cognitive abilities come from Donald Griffin, who views the dancing as symbolic communication, and from E. O. Wilson, who calls the waggle dance "a ritualized reenactment of the outward flight to food."[33] A more negative assessment, one akin, perhaps, to Origen's view of bee behavior as instinctual rather than rational, comes from Tim Ingold, who argues that the waggle dance "is not a symbol that connotes an idea but a sign that commands action."[34] According to this perspective, bees do not possess the kind of cognitive ability that acting on the basis of symbol and ritual would entail: their dance language is not conscious problem-solving but rather innate behavior.[35]

The dance language is thus at the heart of the question about the mental lives of bees and whether they share some form of ideation with human beings. Steiner offers a succinct summary: "A central issue in apian ethology is whether the ability of bees to convey complex information about objects remote in space and time (for some time has elapsed since the dancing bee located the desired object, and the bee is now at some distance from the object) is to be construed as a sign of inner mental states such as belief or of programmed information-processing more along the lines of a computer than a human being."[36] Although there is scholarly disagreement over whether observers as ancient as Aristotle had observed the waggle dance of honeybees, there is no indication that either

Origen or Celsus knew about the phenomenon, yet it is clear which side each would take in the modern controversy about the mental capacity of bees.[37]

This controversy about bees and cognition is actually part of a much larger debate about whether there are shared characteristics between humans and other animals—characteristics such as intelligence, emotion, empathy, morality, and so on. Contemporary cognitive ethologists oppose the implied anthropocentrism of behaviorists, who claim that "behavior can and should be studied without appeal to motives, intentions, or internal states—that is, to thought or feelings."[38] The eminent primatologist Frans de Waal, a leader in the field of cognitive ethology, has coined the term "anthropodenial" to describe "the a priori rejection of shared characteristics between humans and animals."[39] De Waal offers the following anecdote, which gives a concrete example of the positions of the two sides in the contemporary debate about animal/human relationships:

> As a student of chimpanzee behavior, I myself have encountered resistance to the label "reconciliation" for friendly reunions between former adversaries. Actually, I should not have used the word "friendly" either, "affiliative" being the accepted euphemism. More than once I was asked whether the term "reconciliation" was not overly anthropomorphic. Whereas terms related to aggression, violence, and competition never posed the slightest problem, I was supposed to switch to dehumanized language as soon as the affectionate aftermath of a fight was the issue. A reconciliation sealed with a kiss became a "post-conflict interaction involving mouth-to-mouth contact."[40]

From the perspective of the animal behaviorists, the principle of "nature red in tooth and claw" applies when the shared violence of humans and other animals is at issue, but where positive behaviors and values come into play, animals and humans cannot share the same descriptors due to the implied superiority of human beings.

One of the key terms in this debate is the term "anthropomorphism," and a discussion of its new positive meaning among contemporary ethologists will take us back to early Christianity's anthropocentrism and especially to its discontents. Two rhetorical questions asked by biologist Stephen Jay Gould lead into the heart of contemporary ethologists' embrace of anthropomorphism as an analytical tool or methodology: "Why should our nastiness be the baggage of an apish past and our kindness uniquely human? Why should we not seek continuity with other animals for our 'noble' traits as well?"[41] Seeking continuity is key. In his book *The Animal Part: Human and Other Animals in the Poetic Imagination*, classicist Mark Payne aptly sums up the ethological perspective: "Since we share the ground of our being with all the other animals, thinking our way into the life of any one of them only requires us to extend to them the same imaginative sympathy that we use to think about the lives of other human beings."[42] Making what de Waal calls a "clean break with the Cartesian view of animals as automatons," cognitive ethologists study "how animals think and what they feel, and this includes their emotions, beliefs, reasoning, information processing, consciousness, and self-awareness."[43]

Anthropomorphism provides a crucial entrée into this kind of study. Noting that anthropomorphism has often been used to "bash" his field, cognitive ethologist Marc Bekoff counters with the following observation: "As humans who study other animals, we can only describe and explain their behavior using words with which we're familiar from a human-centered point of view. So when I try to figure out what's happening in a dog's head, I have to be anthropomorphic, but I try to do it from a dog-centered point of view. Just because I say that a dog is happy or jealous, this doesn't mean that he's happy or jealous as humans are, or for that matter as other dogs. Being anthropomorphic is a linguistic tool to make the thoughts and feelings of other animals accessible to humans."[44] Bekoff's fellow ethologist Jonathan Balcombe agrees: "We inescapably anthropomorphize because we can't help it—we are anthropoid apes, and we cannot know absolutely what other animals are feeling. But we can make reasonable conjectures backed by good science."[45]

What underlies anthropomorphism, then, is a "recognition of shared creatureliness."[46] Anthropomorphism uses human qualities to portray animals, and one of its goals is to discern a genuine connectedness between humans and animals. As Wendy Doniger has pointed out, anthropomorphism as an interpretive strategy has a counterpart, zoomorphism, in which humans are imagined as animals or with characteristics of animals. Zoomorphism, too, relies on likeness and it, too, is a challenge to the anthropodenial of anthropocentrism. As Doniger argues, "Anthropomorphism and zoomorphism are two different attempts to reduce the otherness between human and animals, to see the sameness beneath the difference"—but not, she continues, to erase the difference.[47]

It is important for my purposes to come to terms with anthropomorphism and zoomorphism—seeing animals as human and seeing humans as animal—because they are interpretive strategies used, in complicated ways, by early Christian authors, and in my view they function as "end runs" around the tradition's undeniable anthropocentric rhetoric. Focusing on early Christian anthropomorphism and zoomorphism also provides a crucial corrective to the so-called Lynn White thesis. In an article entitled "The Historical Roots of Our Ecologic Crisis," White argued that Christianity is, of all the world's religions, the most anthropocentric and, due to its privileging of humanity over nature, responsible for reducing nature to a utilitarian use value and causing the concomitant ecological destruction that has ensued.[48] By focusing on zoomorphism in this chapter, and on anthropomorphism in the next chapter, I show that it is absurdly reductive virtually to equate Christianity and anthropocentrism, and that certain early Christian texts offer ways of imagining human/animal relationships that, perhaps surprisingly, blur the supposed boundary between human and animal just as effectively as contemporary ethology. That blurring is a central interest of this book, as is a focus on the conundrum that accompanies it, namely, that the blurring often occurs in the very texts that also subscribe to a version of the rhetoric of human superiority.

Augustine's Asini

Origen's wish that humans would act more like bees is essentially a zoomorphic gesture that, as we have seen, undermines his overall anthropocentric stance. More thorough in his zoomorphic stance was Augustine in two sermons in which he addressed the topic of the ass that Christ rode into Jerusalem on Palm Sunday. In the first of these expositions, Augustine broached the topic of the Lord's donkey by way of his commentary on Psalm 31:9 (RSV 32): "Do not be like a horse or a mule, devoid of understanding. Rein in their jaws with bit and bridle, those who will not approach you." Reading animals as figures for certain kinds of human beings, as he often did in his expositions on the Psalms, Augustine imagines that the horse/mule in this verse is a sinner afflicted with the worst of the sins, pride.[49] Speaking directly to his congregation, Augustine asks: "Do you aspire to be a horse or a mule; do you want to throw your rider? Your mouth and your jaws will be reined in with bit and bridle; yes, that mouth of yours with which you vaunt your merits but keep quiet about your sins will be reined in."[50] As the sermon continues, one can feel Augustine beginning to relish this bit of "therotheology":[51]

The sinner wanted to be an unbroken animal, and so must be subdued with bit and whip; and let us hope that he or she can be broken

in. The fear is that such persons may resist so obstinately that they
deserve to be left in their unbroken state and allowed to go their own
sweet way, until of them it can be said, "Their iniquity will leak out as
though from folds of fat" [Ps. 72 (73):7], as it is of those whose sins go
unpunished for the present. May such people, when the whip catches
them, be corrected and subdued, as the psalmist tells us he too was
tamed. He admits that he was a horse or a mule, because he was obstinately silent; and how was he subdued? By the whip.[52]

By the end of this passage, Augustine's metaphor has really taken hold as he
teaches his listeners how this text of the psalm mirrors the behavior of the
"horses" and "mules" among them. By blurring the boundary between the horse/
mule and the prideful sinner, and by showing the consequences of mulish behavior, Augustine is asking his audience to reformulate their understanding of their
subjectivity and agency, all through the medium of the animal.[53]

In this sermon, animals do not shape the contours of the human only negatively. Augustine's zoomorphic interpretation of the horse/mule of Psalm 31
takes on a Christological edge when he asserts, rather abruptly, "God tames the
beast of burden [iumentum] he rides, because it is to the beast's own advantage
to be ridden."[54] Now the horse/mule has become a beast of burden with a
divine rider and, in the midst of a flurry of intertextual quotations, rider and
beast become Christ mounted on the colt of an ass. Following his statement
that it is to the beast's advantage to be ridden, Augustine inserts the Palm Sunday story into what is becoming a very extended metaphor:

It is not because God is weary of walking on his own feet that he
mounts. Isn't it a very mysterious episode, when a donkey [asellus] is
led to the Lord [Mk. 11:1–7 and parallels]? This donkey is the humble and docile people who provide a good mount for the Lord, and
it is making for Jerusalem. "He will guide the meek in judgment,"
as another psalm predicts; "he will teach his ways to the gentle"
[Ps. 24 (25):9]. Who are these gentle ones? Those who do not toss
their heads in defiance of their trainer, who patiently accept the
whip and the rein, so that later, when they have been broken in,
they may walk without the whip. . . . If you refuse your rider, it is
you who will fall, not he. "There is many a scourge for the sinner;
but everyone who hopes in the Lord is encompassed with mercy"
[Ps. 31 (32):10].[55]

In this passage, the beast of burden is now imagined positively: the ass that has given up its pride and learned humility is a fitting mount for Christ. The figures that really matter in this zoomorphic rendering of the psalm and the Palm Sunday story are the god and the beast, because they provide the crucial context for transforming human beings from sinners to Christians with commendable ethics. Augustine's interpretive maneuvers in this sermon are strikingly reflected in a trenchant remark by Jacques Derrida in *The Beast and the Sovereign*: "There are gods and there are beasts, there is, there is only, the theo-zoological, and in the theo-anthropo-zoological, man is caught, evanescent, disappearing, at the very most a simple mediation, a hyphen between the sovereign and the beast, between God and cattle"—or asses, as in Augustine's case.[56]

In his study of the "surprising prominence" of the ass in early Christian liturgy and art, Thomas Mathews remarks, "The image of a God riding on an ass is an image of extraordinary power," as the mounted Christ in Figure 5 stunningly visualizes.[57] Augustine, too, apparently thought it was an extraordinary image, because he returns to the topic of "the Lord's beast" (*iumentum domini*) in another sermon. Psalm 33 (34) begins, "I will bless the Lord at all times." In his exposition of this psalm, Augustine asks, "What prompts a person to bless the Lord at all times? Being humble."[58] He then goes on to develop the contrasting themes of humility and its sinful opposite, pride, just as he does in his exposition of Psalm 31 (32). Moving on to the next verse, Augustine asks his audience,

> So you don't want to be proud? All right: in order to be humble,
> make the words of the psalm your own: "In the Lord shall my soul
> be praised; let the gentle hear it and rejoice." Those who do not want
> to be praised in the Lord are not gentle; they are savage, rough, arro-
> gant and proud. The Lord wants gentle, compliant animals for his
> use; so you be the Lord's beast; be gentle. I mean, he sits on you, he
> himself controls you. Do not fear that you may stumble or fall head-
> long. Weakness is characteristic of you, certainly, but think who
> your rider is. Donkey's colt [*pullus asini*] you may be, but you are
> carrying Christ.[59]

Here again is the now familiar picture of the humble Christian as the ass that carried Christ on Palm Sunday, but now Augustine's point about embracing—even performing—an asinine identity is clear: those who embrace humility have Christ as their permanent "rider." Palm Sunday has been extended from the past

FIGURE 5. Christ on a donkey and two angels. From Egypt, allegedly Deir Amba Schenute (so-called White Monastery). Limestone, 42 × 62 cm. Inv. 4131. Photo: Jürgen Liepe. Bpk Bildagentur/Staatliche Museen Berlin/Art Resource, NY.

into the present; that is, it has ceased to be only an historical event and assumes the role of a stunning, if brief, meditation on Christian anthropology, one that is thoroughly zoomorphic.

In writing this way, Augustine was enacting a view of scripture perfectly suited to the kind of therotheological interpretation he offers in his sermon on Psalm 33 (34). At several points in his expositions on the psalms, Augustine exhorts his listeners to view the scriptures as a mirror. Sometimes the reflection is positive: "Listen to it [Psalm 123 (124)] as though you were looking at your own reflection in the mirror of scriptures. When you gaze into the scriptural mirror your own cheerful face looks back at you."[60] And sometimes the reflection is negative: In his exposition of Psalm 103 (104), Augustine says, "Your first duty is to see clearly what you are. . . . 'But where shall I look, to see myself,' you ask." Augustine answers: "He has provided his scriptures as a mirror for you, and there you are told, 'Blessed are the pure of heart, for they shall see God' [Mt. 5:8]. In that text a mirror is held out to you. See whether you are one of the pure-hearted it mentions, and grieve if you are not yet like that; grieve in order to become so. The mirror will reflect your face to you. You will not find the mirror flattering you, and neither must you beguile yourself. The reality that is yourself, that is what the mirror shows forth. Look at what you are."[61] As Michael Cameron has remarked, for Augustine "all understanding of Scripture is at the same time understanding of oneself."[62] Thus taking his own perspective seriously, the normally anthropocentric Augustine departed from the rhetoric of human superiority when the mirroring function of scripture was at work—even when the mirror reflected the face and body of an ass.

Gerald Bruns has argued that Augustine saw scripture as "a work of figural eloquence with designs upon its audience."[63] The way in which scripture's mirroring worked was often figural, and those figurations "had designs" on their readers and hearers in terms of provoking changes in consciousness, as we have seen above.[64] Being in the clutches of figures like the Palm Sunday ass, however, was apparently objectionable to some in Augustine's congregation, because they seem to have made the very mistake that Augustine had cautioned against in his *De doctrina christiana*, namely, they had taken a figurative expression literally (or perhaps they found it distasteful to contemplate their own subjectivity from the perspective of a beast of burden, however metaphorical).[65] As he continued his exploration of the anthropological import of the Palm Sunday ass, Augustine anticipated retorts from his audience: "Perhaps some people are angry with me for comparing them to the donkey's colt [*asello*] on which the Lord sat? Proud and arrogant folk will say, 'Listen to that! He thinks we're asses [*ecce asinos nos fecit*]!' But anyone who feels like objecting should try to be the Lord's ass, and try not to be like a horse or a mule that cannot understand; for you are familiar with another psalm that says, 'Do not be like a horse or a mule, devoid of understanding'" (Ps. 31[31]:9).[66] Did Augustine think they were asses? Yes and no. He certainly knew that "metaphor necessarily involves simultaneous similarity and difference," as his oscillation back and forth between simile and metaphor in the passage above shows.[67] There is likeness, though not identity, since his parishioners were not literally *asini*. Yet there *is* identity too as Augustine exhorts his congregants to "become this meek animal" about whom they are hearing. Zoomorphic interpretations such as this one depend on a willingness to become entangled with an animal, and to explore the possibilities of meaning that such a venture opens up. By asking the arrogant people among his parishioners to embrace—even to perform—the humble identity of the Palm Sunday ass, Augustine compromised the absolute binary between humans and animals upon which his anthropocentric rhetoric depended, and thereby undermined it. In his sympathetic engagement with the Palm Sunday ass, he let go of "the credo of human superiority," at least for a moment.[68]

Exegesis, Zoomorphism, and Deer: Augustine

Part of the shortsightedness of anthropocentrism is that it misses this "pensivity of animals," to recall the phrase of Jean-Christophe Bailly. Zoomorphism abandons the human exclusivity fostered by anthropocentrism, and in the interesting case of Augustine in his treatment of animals in the Psalter, the figural dimension of the text seems to be what enables the attribution of value to the animal images in his exegeses. In his engagement with the animals of the psalms, Augustine rarely indulges in the rhetoric of human superiority and domination of the rest of creation as he does in other works.[69] Instead there is in the *Enarrationes in Psalmos* a marked reduction of animal/human otherness that produces an "animalized" version of the human self that is quite striking. The *Enarrationes* are, of course, commentaries, and, as Marco Formisano has argued, late antiquity was a culture of the commentary in terms of its literary productivity. He not only notes "the innovative power of the commentary within a literary system" but also observes that "normally the phenomenon of commenting can be seen among strongly traditional cultures, although it can often include a certain subversive potential."[70] Taking this comment in my own direction, I am interested in entertaining the idea that the "traditional" position of anthropocentrism as often espoused by Augustine (and others) was subverted by the exegetical mode. Engaging in commentary on a plurisignificant text of a Bible itself bursting with meaning, Augustine approached the Psalter's images— including its animals—as images steeped in religious value and not as part of a monolithic rhetorical hierarchy that rests on a human being/animal binary opposition.

In ancient Christianity, zoomorphism occurs most often in exegeses of scriptural animals. Augustine, like other exegetes, relished what he variously called the symbolic, figural, and allegorical meanings of the Bible's images.[71] Given this perspective, scriptural animals were freed from animals' debased position on the biological scale of being and took on a contemplative value that the ontological positioning of animals did not support. Exegesis freed animals to signify zoomorphically. A second example of Augustine's engagement with an animal from the psalms will demonstrate just how complex his zoomorphic exegeses could be.

In the introduction to his sermon on Psalm 41 (42), Augustine notes that the psalm "begins with holy longing [*sancto desiderio*], for the singer says, 'As a deer longs for springs of water, so does my soul long for you, O God' [v. 1]."[72] He continues with a pointed question: "Who is saying that?" And he answers, "If we will, it is we ourselves. Why bother to inquire any further who it is, when it is within your power to be yourself the answer to the question?"[73] Having specified the intimate relationship between person and biblical text, Augustine then cautions, "Remember, though, that the speaker is not a lone individual, but a single body: the Church, which is the body of Christ. A longing like this is not found in everyone who comes into church, yet those who have tasted the sweetness of the Lord, and recognize the savor in this song, should not think they are alone in this experience. They must believe that similar seeds have been sown widely in the Lord's field all over the world, and that it is a single, united Christian voice that sings, 'As a deer longs for springs of water, so does my soul long for you, O God.'"[74] Augustine thus positions what he characterizes as intense longing to be both individual and corporate. Not every Christian has been seized by the intensity he evokes, but those who do experience it are bound up in the community of the church. Since Augustine will eventually compare and then identify the desirous Christians with the longing deer, we see him inviting the animal not only into the individual believer's psyche but also into the collective Christian body and its signifying system as a whole.

The *desiderium*, longing, that Augustine petitions in this passage is "kindled" to a great intensity in those "who know where their pilgrimage is tending."[75] As John Burnaby pointed out long ago, "There can be no question of what is dominant in [Augustine's] conception of Christian love. It is *desiderium*—the unsatisfied longing of the homesick heart."[76] In another sermon, Augustine seems to have had the panting and thirsty deer/soul in mind when he wrote, "The man in whom is the faith that works through love must hope for that which God promises. Hope therefore is faith's companion . . . and with them is the love with which we long [*desideramus*], with which we strive to attain, with which we are inflamed, with which we hunger and thirst."[77] As Augustine famously wrote in his *Tractates on the Gospel of John*, *desiderium sinus cordis est*: "It is longing that makes the heart deep." He continued: "We shall receive, if we extend our longing as wide as we can."[78]

The longing deer makes only one appearance in Psalm 41 (42), at the very beginning. Yet given the fiery intensity of Augustine's sense of desiderium, it is perhaps not surprising that he chose to emphasize the yearning animal in his exposition of Psalm 41 (42), for as Bekoff has observed, "Animals' emotions are

raw, unfiltered, and uncontrolled. Their joy is the purest and most contagious of
joys and their grief the deepest and most devastating. Their passions bring us to
our knees in delight and sorrow. If animals didn't show their feelings, it's
unlikely that people would bond with them."[79] It is not, however, just any animal that traverses and inflects the human being with this intense longing for
God. As Augustine will insist, it is the deer. Here is how he introduces the deer's
special standing. "Into what kind of comprehension will the singing of this
psalm lead us?" Augustine asks, and then he answers as follows:

> I will tell you, boldly I will tell you: since the world was first created
> men and women have seen the invisible realities of God, understood
> through things that are made. Well then, brothers and sisters, catch
> my eagerness, share my longing. . . . Let us burn together with this
> thirst; let us run together to the fountain of understanding. Let us
> long for it as a hart yearns for a spring. I do not mean that spring
> which the baptismal candidates long for, that their sins may be for-
> given; let us who are baptized long rather for the wellspring of which
> scripture says, "With you is the fountain of life"; for God is both a
> spring and a light, as that other psalm goes on to say: "In your light
> we will see light" [Ps. 35 (36):9].[80]

Augustine goes on to develop the theme of the "inward radiance" and the "interior light" that characterize those Christians who understand that their spiritual
goal is to see that light, which is also a fountain, which is also God.[81]

While he doesn't say so explicitly, Augustine's opening statement about
seeing the invisible realities of God through the created world positions the
longing deer as a medium through which such seeing takes place. As he continues to address the theme of inner seeing, it becomes clear that Augustine is using
this animal to visualize the contours of a deeply spiritual human self. Here is the
next passage of the sermon: "Your inner eye is being prepared to see that light,
and your inner thirst is burning ever more fiercely for that fountain. Run to the
fountain, long for the fountain; but do not run to it in any random fashion, do
not run like any animal you may chance to think of: run only like a deer. Why
like a deer? Because there must be no tardiness about your running. Run ener-
getically, long untiringly for the fountain. I say this because a distinguishing
characteristic of the deer is speed."[82] Augustine's bit of biological data at the end
of this passage is something of an emotional letdown given what comes before
it, although it does not detract from the sense of identity between human seeker

and deer that Augustine is building. Those preceding passionate exhortations leave no doubt, however, about the intensity of the "animal" emotion and the almost physical urgency of the spiritual quest that Augustine is pressing upon his fellow seekers after divine illumination.

As I noted at the outset of this discussion of Augustine's exposition on Psalm 41 (42), his engagement with the deer is a particularly complex zoomorphic interpretation. Having established the deer as the very figure of the Christian impelled ever forward by the longing quest for spiritual satiation, Augustine then muses, "Perhaps this is not the only characteristic of deer that scripture wished us to consider. There may be something else."[83] Of course, in the kind of figurative mind-set in which Augustine finds himself in this sermon, there is always "something else." "Listen now," he says, "to another peculiarity" of deer:

> A hart kills snakes, and after killing them he burns with a more intense thirst than before; so after dealing with the snakes he runs to the wellsprings even more urgently. These snakes are your vices; put the snakes of your iniquity to death, and you will long all the more keenly for the font of truth. Perhaps a miserly spirit is hissing dark suggestions in you, hissing something opposed to God's word and forbidden by his commandments? You know what you are told: "Give that thing up, and stay clear of sin." But if you would rather commit the sin than turn your back on some temporal gain, you are choosing to be bitten by the snake instead of killing it. If you prefer your vice, your lust, your greed, your snake, when am I going to find in you the kind of longing that will send you running to the wellspring? How are you going to yearn for the font of wisdom, if you are still floundering in the venom of ill-will? Kill off whatever in you is opposed to the truth.[84]

In this passage, a "snake self" is added to the already complex "deer self" as Augustine moves from the spiritual dimensions of the deer to its ethics. Snakes encompass a dark interior, where hissing thoughts provoke a sinful lifestyle of lust, greed, and ill will. They are the very opposite of the wellspring of truth toward which the deer runs in its longing. That the deer self has a pronounced ethical agency becomes clear as Augustine notes how it "slaughters" its own serpentine tendencies.[85] Here is "a leap of identification across the species gulf" that works zoomorphically to shape conscience—that is, moral identity—and to undergird an entire ethics of behavior.[86]

In a manner reminiscent of his exhortation to his congregation to become the Palm Sunday ass and to perform its character, Augustine next says, "I know that if you are a good deer you are going to say to me, 'God knows . . . I no longer have these [various] sins,' and so you look for something you can enjoy, don't you? Long for what will truly give you delight, long for the fountains of water."[87] As though in answer to Stephen Jay Gould's question, quoted earlier in this chapter, "Why should we not seek continuity with other animals for our 'noble' traits?," Augustine goes on to give the "good deer" of his address a striking example of what is at stake in performing one's deer nature.

> There is another point to notice about deer. People have seen them doing what I am about to describe; it would not have been recorded about them in writing unless previously observed. It is said, then, that when deer are walking in single file, or want to swim to a different place to find fresh grazing, they rest their heavy heads on each other. One goes in front, another rests its head on him, and others on them, and so on until the whole line is supported. When the hart who has been bearing the weight in the foremost position is exhausted, he moves to the rear, and another takes his place to carry what the first one was carrying, while this previous leader rests himself by supporting his head on another, as all the others have been doing. They go on like this, carrying the heavy weight for each other; so they make good progress, and do not let each other down. Was it not deer like these that the apostle had in mind? "Bear one another's burdens," he says, "and so you will fulfill the law of Christ" [Gal. 6:2].[88]

Although Augustine is following traditional lore in picturing this mutually supportive behavior of deer, his intertextual quotation from the New Testament shows that his deer are otherwise quite different from deer as imagined, for example, by Pliny: "The deer is a simple animal and stupefied by surprise at everything."[89] Far from being an *animal simplex*, Augustine's good deer fulfills the law of Christ. As an aside, it would be difficult, after Augustine's insertion of deer into the apostle's imagination, to read Paul's statement in Galatians about bearing one's fellows burdens without thinking of a procession of head-on-rump deer, which Paul most certainly did not have in mind. Immediately preceding the command to "bear one another's burdens," Paul wrote: "Brethren, if a man is overtaken in any trespass, you who are spiritual should restore him in a spirit of gentleness. Look to yourself, lest you too be tempted. Bear one another's burdens, and so fulfill the law of Christ" [Gal. 6:1–2, RSV]. What Paul *did* have in mind was empathy, a trait of those who are "spiritual," like Augustine's deer. Thus the quotation from Paul gives the biblical foundation for the vivid picture that Augustine offers of the behavior of his spiritual deer in terms of their ability to care for others. Augustine's intertextual gesture gives a Christian gloss to the deer's empathic camaraderie.

There is one final step in Augustine's zoomorphic interpretation of the deer in Psalm 41 (42). Returning to the opening topic of his exegesis, the desiderium of the deer, Augustine quashes any possible flatfooted appropriation of the psalm's first verse, "as a deer longs for springs of water, so does my soul long for you, O God." He says, "Did I hear someone ask, 'Perhaps the deer is longing for springs of water because he needs a wash?' We can't tell whether it was for drinking or for washing, but listen to the next line, and don't ask questions: 'My soul has been athirst for the living God' [Ps. 41(42):2]. The line, 'as a deer longs for springs of water, so does my soul long for you, O God,' means the same as 'my soul has been athirst for the living God.' What was this soul thirsting for? 'When shall I reach him and appear before the face of God?'" [Ps. 41 (42):2].[90] As with the mistaken literalizing of the ass in the earlier psalm discussed above, here Augustine shows that missing the spiritual dimension of the psalm's image of the deer misconstrues the way in which scripture mirrors the depths of the human self, especially, in this psalm, the self that longs to be in the presence of God, contemplating him with delight. Had any among Augustine's listeners happened to walk across the floor of the church in Carthage pictured in Figure 6, their appreciation of its mosaic was no doubt considerably enhanced by Augustine's insistence on the spiritual sense of the deer.

At the end of the portion of the sermon that discusses the deer, Augustine goes back and forth between "deer," "soul," and "people" as though they were interchangeable. Although it would be false to say that Augustine had taken "a turn to the animal" as many contemporary theologians, ethologists, philosophers, and others have done in their interrogation of the human/animal binary, still his blurring—even erasing—the boundary between human and animal in this exposition is quite marked.[91] Even in the thought of one for whom the rhetoric of anthropocentrism was ingrained, the binary between the animal and the human was unstable, as indeed it is in Augustine's final point about the deer: "Once a deer of this kind is established in faith, but does not yet see the object of that faith and yearns to understand what he or she loves, this deer has to endure other people who are not deer at all, people whose understanding is darkened, who are sunk in their inner murk and blinded by vicious desires. Nor

FIGURE 6. Mosaic pavement, late Roman, Carthage.
© Trustees of the British Museum.

is this all, for they jeer at the believer who cannot yet point to the reality in which he or she believes. . . . Let us listen to how our hart handled these attacks, so that we may meet them in the same way if we can."[92] In this concluding zoomorphic passage, being a deer is fraught with difficulty! Augustine advises that the deer's best defense is to quote the first two verses of Psalm 41 (42), emphasizing desire and its future satisfaction.

Exegesis, Therotheology, and Deer: Gregory of Nyssa

Augustine was not the only ancient Christian interpreter whose biblical exegesis was more animal friendly than his anthropocentric rhetoric, nor was he alone in using the deer of Psalm 41 (42) to think theologically about human comportment and subjectivity. Gregory of Nyssa, too, subscribed to the rhetoric of anthropocentrism, distinguishing sharply between irrational animals and rational human beings.[93] According to his view, the creation of the world proceeded in an ascending order, culminating in the creation of the human being who, as John Behr observed, "is not simply another part of the world but is called to be its lord and sovereign."[94] When he was thinking cosmically about an ascendant order of being crowned by the kingly human, there was no room for therotheology in Gregory's thought. Gregory was no ancient version of Descartes, however. In his view, although animals are undoubtedly irrational they possess both vegetative and sensitive powers of soul and in that regard are related to human beings, in whom the powers of soul, including those related to nutrition and sensation, were brought to perfection.[95] Thus the Cartesian *bête-machine*, a term coined to describe Descartes's view of animal behavior as utterly mechanistic and completely unlike human behavior, finds no place in Gregory's thought.[96] Still, from the perspective of his ontology, animals were definitely inferior to humans.

From the perspective of Gregory's exegesis, however, the animal-human relation is much more complicated. Animal images help Gregory think about human nature and give him a vocabulary, indeed, a storyline, to use for relating the human and the animal. Here, for example, is Gregory's zoomorphic appropriation of the desirous and thirsty deer of Psalm 41 (42):1:

> The person who has once tasted virtue and has come to understand
> its nature by his own experience of the good . . . has an excessive thirst
> for what is superior. For the Word compares unrestrained and exces-
> sive desire to thirst. The most thirsty nature among the beasts was
> sought out so that the intensity of desire might be shown. . . . It calls
> this beast a "hart," whose nature it is to be fattened by the eating of
> venomous creatures. Now the juices of these creatures are warm, even
> extremely hot, and when the hart has eaten them it necessarily
> becomes dryer, having been purged by the juice of the creatures. This
> is why it has an excessive desire for water, to quench the dryness it
> experiences from such food.[97]

Here is the thirsty deer self, familiar from Augustine, whose thirst stems from eating snakes, but Gregory added an explanatory bit of "biology," namely, that snakes have hot bodily juices that induce extreme thirst when consumed. With the deer established as the appropriate animal to figure human intense desire, Gregory brought his interpretation to its conclusion as follows: "The person, therefore, who has been initiated into the life of virtue in the first part of the Psalter, and has discovered how sweet that which is desired tastes, and has consumed every creeping form of desire in himself, and with the teeth of self-control has devoured the passions in place of creatures, 'thirsts' for participation in God *more than* 'the hart longs for the fountains of water.' And it follows that the person who finds the fountain after this excessive thirst draws in as much water as the abundance of his desire draws off."[98] In this passage, zoomorphism serves Gregory's anthropology of the exemplary self that frees itself from the passions so as to ascend from the perceptible to the intelligible cosmos, with participation in spiritual abundance as the goal.[99] Interestingly, the deer self here breaks out of its own animal metaphor as the person who thirsts does so "more than" the hart. This fact may reflect one of Gregory's hermeneutical principles: as articulated by Alden Mosshammer, for Gregory "interpretation deconstructs all understandings of self and world. Interpretation reveals difference and teaches that difference can be the basis of a more authentic existence through an unending search for new meanings. . . . Thus the only criterion of a valid interpretation is that it should reveal its inadequacy"—as demonstrated in the passage above.[100] The deer image cannot contain the desiring self, although it *can* inflect that self with a particular set of meanings.[101]

Gregory's interaction with biblical animal figures could be just as intricate as Augustine's. Staying with the figure of the deer—actually, fawns, in this case—we see Gregory the therotheologian at work as he exploits the "enigmas" and "below-the-surface meanings" of the Song of Songs.[102] The fawn first appears at Song of Songs 2:8–9: "Behold, he comes leaping over the mountains, bounding over the hills. My kinsman is like a gazelle, or a young hart on the mountains of Bethel." Like Origen before him, Gregory understood the female character of the Song, the bride who speaks this line, to be the human soul, while the male character, the bridegroom, is Christ. These verses, then, constitute part of what "the purified and discerning eye of the soul" must investigate.[103] Here is Gregory's interpretation:

> He who marks out the mountains and hills with his leaps is likened to a fawn—that is, one who treads down and destroys the wicked heights of demonic evil. For "mountains" means the things that are shaken "by his might," even as David says [Ps. 45:4]: the things "that are moved in the heart of the sea and sunk in the place of the abyss" [Ps. 45:3]. Concerning these, the Lord said to his disciples, "If you have faith as a grain of mustard seed, you will say to this mountain [Mt. 17:20]"—signifying by this word the evil demon that brings on lunacy—"Rise up and be cast into the sea" [Mk. 5:1–20].

This passage contains Gregory's somewhat unusual gloss on the serpent-destroying nature of the fawn, which he refers to in his next statement.[104] The fawn becomes part of an allegory that is shored up in part by naturalists' lore about deer and in part by intertextual quotations from scripture. Gregory first uses a passage from the psalms to make mountains signify demonic evil. Next he turns to the New Testament, quoting Jesus's saying about faith moving a mountain. Finally that saying is subtly merged with the Gospels' story about the Gerasene demoniac, so that the demonic evil of the mountain is the source of a lunacy that is cast into the sea like the swine that contained the Gerasene demoniac's demons. As we shall see in later chapters' discussions of animals in the *Physiologus*, here too the animal mediates and so connects the two scriptures.[105]

Following a subsequent paragraph full of observations about hills, mountains, and rebellious powers that are trampled and trodden down, and including yet more scriptural references to prophets, a psalm, and the serpents and scorpions of Luke 10:19, Gregory seems to have sighed perplexedly about how to pull all this into coherence. He remarked:

> What I mean is something like this: in the crowds that followed Jesus, in the synagogues, in the territory of the Gerasenes, in many other places, there were demonic heights, exalted against humankind and towering. Among these there were both hills and mountains, the preeminent and the inferior. But the young hart—who destroys serpents and who likewise forms his disciples so that they may be deer when he says in their presence, "I have given you authority to tread on snakes and scorpions" [Lk. 10:19]—sets his foot upon all of them equally, both putting them to flight and leaping from the one set to the other, so as through them to make it perfectly plain that the stature of those whom virtue lifts up is no longer overshadowed by the hillocks of evil.[106]

As was often the case, ancient Christian biblical exegesis linked animals and human beings in the context of ethics. In this passage, the fawn is crucial to Gregory's determination to find virtue as the central meaning of Song of Songs 2:8–9. Note also that Gregory showed no hesitation in attributing an animal persona to the incarnate Christ, as indeed did the *Physiologus* before him, memorably writing about a lion-Christ and a panther-Christ, among others.[107] The fawn is no hindrance to theologizing but rather is a spur to creating webs of relations among texts, animals, human beings, and divinity.

Just as Augustine spun out the storyline of the deer, so Gregory continued to amplify the image of the fawn in his *Homilies on the Song of Songs*. In Song of Songs 4:1–2, the bridegroom extols the bride's beauty by appealing to features of several animals (doves' eyes, goats' hair, ewes' teeth), and then in v. 5 he says: "Your breasts are like two twin fawns that feed among the lilies." Here is the first part of Gregory's interpretation of this verse:

> This will surely be the right time to introduce the mystery of the two fawns into our scrutiny of the passage, the fawns whose birth is that of twins, whose food is the lily, whose pasture is the good and plenteous earth. According to the word of the Lord's parable, this earth is the heart [see Lk. 8:15], and they are fattened as they graze on it and from it gather the flowers of pure thoughts. Now the blossom of the lily naturally has a double beauty: it mingles an appealing scent with lovely coloration, so that in both respects it is an object of desire for those who pluck it; either it will draw people by its scent, or it will delight the eyes with the splendor of its beauty. For the smell is full of the sweet scent of Christ, while its appearance signifies what is pure and spotless.[108]

In this passage, both the bride and the fawns seem to be eclipsed by the lily, whose olfactory and visual beauty Gregory celebrates because the lily is Christological, as the final sentence declares.[109] Yet it is important to remember that the image being developed here is also anthropological, since earlier in the passage Gregory notes that the lilies are "pure thoughts" that the "fawns" eat.

The fact that Gregory is using a turn to animals—the fawns—in order to develop a model of enlightened human consciousness and behavior becomes evident in the second part of his exegesis of the verse in question. The verse makes clear, Gregory argues, that

> there are two human beings to be discerned in each individual. The one is corporeal and visible, while the other is intelligible and invisible; yet the birth of the two is twin, since they come jointly into life at the same time. For the soul does not exist before the body, nor is the body constituted before the soul, but they come into life simultaneously. Now the food that naturally suits these is purity and fragrance and the like, which are born of the virtues, but there comes a time when certain folk set a higher value on what harms them than on what nourishes them. These do not feed on the flowers of the virtues but take delight in "thorns and thistles" [Mt. 7:16]—for this is the

name that the parable in the Gospel assigns to sins—whose evil shoot was introduced by the curse laid on the serpent.[110]

The two fawns, then, give figure to our inner and outer selves, both of which originally delighted in the virtues but lost that purity of vision when their delight was sinfully misdirected. It is significant that the two fawns carry a condensed anthropology of the emergence of the human self as well as an entire cosmology regarding the paradisal and earthly placement of human beings as narrated in Genesis. One might think that the animal imagination has no bounds—or else one might agree with Susan Ashbrook Harvey's observation that "Gregory's work to interpret the Song of Songs surely tests the limits of allegory as a reading strategy."[111] At the very least, Gregory's exegesis has come a long way from the Song's image of a bride with beautiful breasts.

As the second part of his interpretation of Song of Songs 4:5 concludes, Gregory finds even more layers of meaning in the original image with the help of intertextual quotation. He concludes:

> Since, then, the business of discerning eyes that can distinguish exactly between lily and thorn is to choose what is saving but dismiss what is destructive, for this reason our text refers to the person who, after the fashion of the great Paul, becomes a breast for the little ones and feeds the church's newborn with milk as a pair of breasts that are born together and likened to the fawns of a deer. In this way it bears witness to the esteem that belongs to such a member of the church: both because in each case, seeing sharply and distinguishing the thorn from nourishing food, he shows the way toward the pasture of pure lilies.[112]

In this concluding passage the image of the fawns that are breasts swerves away from cosmology and anthropology and toward the sociology of the early Christian community. Gregory gets interpretive help from the apostle Paul's self-characterization in 1 Corinthians 3:2: "I fed you with milk, not solid food," and also from an etymological pun, since the word translated as "seeing" (δεδορκώς) recalls the word for "deer" (δορκάς).[113] The result is that the deer (or fawn) with discerning vision becomes a pastoral image of one able to give ethical guidance to fellow Christians, "feeding" them, as it were, with lilies rather than thorns. Once again, the animal enters human consciousness as an upholder of virtue.

As I remarked earlier, Gregory, like Augustine, was an interpreter whose biblical exegeses were more animal friendly than his anthropocentric rhetoric. As his treatment of harts and fawns shows, he was perfectly willing to find in an animal figure the depths of the human psyche as well as the sweep of cosmological history and anthropological development. It was not unusual, of course, that Gregory allowed himself as interpreter to be addressed by the multisignification of an animal image in a biblical text, since being attuned to multiple meaning was typical of his approach to all of scripture's figures. What does seem unusual is that, in his treatment of the animals, there is not a trace of the "anthropodenial" so characteristic of early Christian ontological rhetoric of human dominance and superiority, including Gregory's own. The exegetical perspective that values the depth of every scriptural word folds animals into the Christian consciousness along with everything else. Far from producing "a landscape of inert presences," Gregory's zoomorphic interpretations, like Augustine's, blur the supposed binary between human and animal and activate an animal subjectivity that is deeply therotheological.[114]

Zoomorphism in the *Physiologus*

As we have already seen in Gregory's use of the hart to figure Christ, zoomorphism in ancient Christianity could attribute animal characteristics to the incarnate Christ as well as to human beings. The most extravagant examples of this form of zoomorphic interpretation are on offer in the *Physiologus*, where one might say that the pensivity of animals has run amok.[115] One might also say, however, that this text is proof of Wallace Stevens's view of imagination, namely, that "it does not create except as it transforms," because the *Physiologus* is an unusually transformative text both in its structure and in its contents.[116] Probably written in the late third century in Egypt, the *Physiologus* is a collection of fifty-some chapters, most of which feature animals—mammals, birds, fish, and reptiles.[117] These animals figure realities both theological and psychological, and they often give rise to allegories of a most bestial sort, embodying as the stories unfold such activities as mockery, reversal, deadly pretense, trickery, disguise, deception, metamorphosis, and a good deal of killing and devouring.

Although the text has parallels to some of the animal lore in Origen's work and may well have used Origen as a source, its interpretive procedure is different from Origen's allegorical exegesis.[118] As Alan Scott has observed, by contrast with Origen's meticulous engagement with the minutiae of the text of scripture, for the author of the *Physiologus* scriptural images "serve as little more than a cipher. In fact, in the *Physiologus* it is clear that biblical passages have been chosen with paradoxographical interests in mind: finding the beasts comes first, aligning them with a passage of scripture is second."[119] Although I agree with Scott that the interest of the author of the *Physiologus* is more paradoxigraphical than exegetical, I think that the text's imaginative structure deserves emphasis because of the way in which it serves the author's therotheological perspective.

As for structure, the narratives in the *Physiologus* follow a fairly standard format: each chapter is introduced by a quotation from the Hebrew Bible in which the featured animal is mentioned. Then the animal's characteristic behavior is noted, and that is followed by an allegorical interpretation in a Christian context; the chapter closes with a quotation from the New Testament that sometimes also mentions the animal in question but more often appeals to the spiritual significance of the whole narrative. Thus in each narrative there are three and sometimes four groups of images placed in juxtaposition: a quotation from the Hebrew Bible, an animal's character plus its allegorical significance, and a quotation from the New Testament. Not surprisingly, the relation among all these is often asymmetrical, and it is difficult to plot a smooth flow of meaning from one image or group of images to the next. What is significant about this structure, however, is that the animal is the focal point, the imaginative ground that gives rise to connections between two scriptural texts and also to an engaging, if often fantastical, form of zoomorphism. There is no anthropodenial in *this* text!

A few examples will suffice to demonstrate how the *Physiologus* used an animal to portray the incarnate Christ. What follows is the first chapter of the *Physiologus*, "On the Lion," which deserves to be quoted in full.

> We shall begin by speaking about the lion, the king of wild beasts, indeed of all animals. For Jacob, praising Judah, said: "Judah is a lion's cub; out of this shoot, my son, you have sprung up. He reclined calmly like a lion and like a cub; who will awaken him" [Gen. 49:9]?
>
> The Physiologus has said about the lion that it has three characteristic behaviors. The first is this: when the lion walks and travels about in the desert, and the scent of the hunter comes to it, the lion covers its tracks with its tail, lest the hunter, following its tracks, discover its lair and capture it. Thus also my savior, the victorious spiritual lion out of the tribe of Judah, the root of David, who was sent by the eternal Father, covered his spiritual tracks, that

from the Gospel of John? And what is one to make of the passage in which the
"king of glory" is declared to be Lord of the very hosts whom he has just erased?[125]
Like a canny lion erasing its tracks, the text plays with the expectations that its
seemingly simple one-to-one correspondence between animal and Christ (and
God and the Virgin Mary) sets up.

Unlike the monovision upon which anthropocentrism rests, the vision of
zoomorphic interpretation tends to be more generous in its extension of variega-
tion and complexity to animals, be they fantastical or "real." A second example
from the *Physiologus* demonstrates just how complex this text can be in its presentation of an animalized Christ. Here is *Physiologus* 16, "On the Panther."

> The prophet prophesied and said, "I have become like a panther
> to Ephraim" [Hos. 5:14, LXX]. The Physiologus has said that the
> panther has the following trait. It is the friendliest of all animals,
> although it hates the serpent. It is many-colored like Joseph's coat
> [Gen. 37:3]. It is gentle and very tame. After it eats and is satisfied, it
> falls asleep in its lair. On the third day, it wakes from its slumber and
> roars, howling with a mighty voice. Animals both near and far hear
> this sound. From the panther's throat comes forth every sweet smell
> of spices, and the animals are guided by the sweet fragrance of the
> smell of the panther, and they run quickly close to it.
>
> Just so, Christ, awakening on the third day and rising from the
> dead, was every sweet fragrance for us peaceful ones both far and
> near [Eph. 2:17]. Many-colored is the spiritual wisdom of God
> [Eph. 3:10]. As the Psalmist said [Ps. 44:10], "The queen stands at
> your right hand, clothed in a many-colored robe interwoven with
> gold," which is the church. Many-colored is Christ, since he is virgin-
> ity, self-control, mercy, faith, virtue, patience, oneness of mind, and
> peace [Gal. 5:22].[126]

Christ as panther is a strikingly beautiful image recalling Paul's "aroma of Christ"
as well as Origen's "Christ who comes breathing sweet odors."[127] The panther
pictures a gentle, tame, peaceful Christ whose roar is reassuring.

However, for a reader familiar with the prophetic passage that evokes these
lovely images, there is a startling omission. Hosea goes on to say that the God
who will be like a panther to Ephraim will prey upon Ephraim, rending, carrying off, with no hope of rescue.[128] Furthermore, for a reader familiar with natu-

ralists' lore about the panther, this tale would be more astonishing still. Such a reader would recognize that the text's message lies as much in what is not reported as in what is narrated and would see immediately that antipathy lurks insidiously in the shadows of this sympathetic portrayal.[129] Hidden complexities inhere in the animal guise of Christ as panther.

The *Physiologus*'s zoomorphism with regard to the panther leads Christology in some unusual directions. Prominent religiously and mythologically as the animal companion of the god Dionysus, the panther was a much-discussed animal in Greco-Roman naturalist literature.[130] One of its most remarkable features was its appearance. Set in what Pliny described as its "savage" head are shining eyes, "gray-green at once and red within, flaming as if on fire," and in the mouth "the teeth are pale and venomous." Marked on the shoulder by a crescent moon, the panther's coat is described as ποικίλος, "many-colored."[131]

This adjective, *poikilos,* is a fitting description of the panther, which was thought to be one of the supreme embodiments of cunning intelligence in the animal world. As Marcel Detienne and Jean-Pierre Vernant have shown, *mētis,* the term for cunning intelligence, was for the Greeks a way of being in the world: "Its field of application was the world of movement, of multiplicity, and of ambiguity." Mētis, they continue, denoted a means of conniving with shifting reality, with "fluid situations which are constantly changing and which at every moment combine contrary features and forces that are opposed to each other." To be poikilos, many-colored, was one of the marks of a figure possessing mētis: poikilos refers to "the sheen of a material or the glittering of a weapon, the dappled hide of a fawn, or the shining back of a snake mottled with darker patches. This many-colored sheen or complex of appearances produces an effect of iridescence, shimmering, an interplay of reflections." Indeed, Detienne and Vernant conclude that "shimmering sheen and shifting movement are so much a part of the nature of *mētis* that when the epithet *poikilos* is applied to an individual it is enough to indicate that he is a wily one, a man of cunning, full of inventive ploys and tricks of every kind."[132]

The *Physiologus* says that the panther is *pampoikilos*—an intensification of an already intense word—and goes on to describe the seductive sweetness of its breath, which attracts other animals to it. What it does *not* describe, however, was reported by Pliny: animals are indeed attracted by the panther's fragrance, but they are frightened by the savage appearance of its head, "for which reason panthers catch them by hiding their head and enticing by other attractions."[133]

Aelian gave the specifics of the panther's mode of enticement. He said that the panther catches other animals by concealing itself in a dense thicket, and having thus made itself invisible, "it just breathes."[134] Unsuspecting animals are drawn by its marvelous fragrance and close in on the thicket, at which point the panther springs out and devours them.

The panther's smell, seemingly so sweet, is a deadly trap that gives the hidden animal more presence than the visible one. Further, in keeping with the complexity of the *Physiologus*'s zoomorphic Christology, I would suggest that the story is itself a panther, a trap that hides its savage message with a sweet perfume. Its prophetic introduction, which conceals within it a flesh-rending God; its repetition of the adjective "pampoikilos," which suggests the shimmering, shifting qualities of spiritual wisdom; its cunning reversal of the received tradition about the animal—all these suggest that the text itself is a panther, an interpretation that is completely bestial, as the word itself says: *pan-ther*, all beast. Thus at least in this case, the zoomorphism of the *Physiologus* is truly a bestial poetry, one that reflects the divine realm in images and likenesses that flame like the panther's inner eye.

Although it offers an unusually transformative version of the attribution of animal characteristics to a nonanimal figure, the *Physiologus* differs only in degree, not kind, from the other zoomorphic interpretations treated in this chapter. As a mode of thought that is fundamentally different from the anthropocentric perspective expressed in so much early Christian rhetoric on the ontological scale of being, zoomorphism regularly underscores relation rather than separation where animals and humans are concerned. In fact, as we have seen again and again, from Augustine's asses and harts to Gregory of Nyssa's deer and fawns, zoomorphic exegesis so blurs the boundary between human and animal that humans are said *to be* animal in terms of the characteristics being accorded to them. That is, zoomorphism connects human and animal to the point of identity, a fact that is surely a surprise in the face of the contempt shown toward animals by the rhetoric of superiority and domination. In my view, there is much in ancient Christian zoomorphism that anticipates contemporary ethologists' call for finding continuity in behavior with other animals. Finally, given the ethical contexts to which animals lead humans in many of the exegeses explored in this chapter, it is certain that the statement by the sociobiologist William Hamilton that "the animal in our nature cannot be regarded as a fit custodian for the values of civilized man" would find no sympathy among the likes of Augustine and Gregory of Nyssa.[135]

Coda

It seems appropriate to end this chapter where it began, with Origen of Alexandria. As we saw, when he was in an anthropocentric frame of mind, as he was when discussing bees, Origen was little inclined to find continuity between humans and animals. When he was engaging in biblical exegesis, however, he found continuity indeed, both in the sense of an interior bestial soul and a wearing of bestial masks.[136] In fact, it was Origen who gave the most forceful and extended defense of zoomorphism that I know of among ancient Christian authors. Discussing the laws pertaining to clean and unclean foods and animals in Leviticus, Origen, in one of the few autobiographical remarks in his entire corpus, wrote:

> Let us ascend from the foods which were spoken through the shadow to those which are true foods through the spirit. But in this investigation, we are in need of the witness of divine Scripture lest anyone think—for people love "to sharpen their tongues with a sword" [see Ps. 63:4]—lest anyone, I say, think that I do violence to divine Scriptures, and ascribe to human beings what is related in the Law about clean or unclean animals, quadrupeds, or even birds, or fish, and depict these words to be said about persons. Perhaps one of the hearers may say, "Why do you do violence to Scripture? They are called animals; they are understood as animals." Therefore, lest anyone believe these things to be perverted by human thinking, we must call forth the apostolic authority in these matters.[137]

Origen goes on to defend his attribution of animal characteristics to human beings by appealing to "two luminaries of the apostles, Paul and Peter, as witnesses."[138] From Paul, Origen draws support for a spiritual interpretation of scripture, including its references to animals, by quoting (among other passages) I Corinthians 10:14, where Paul refers to the followers of Moses eating "spiritual food" and "spiritual drink."[139] Peter's vision of animals in Acts 10:9–16 provides Origen with his second apostolic witness. In the vision, a heavenly voice declares that all animals are clean. Peter is perplexed by the vision until he joins people gathered at the house of Cornelius, a Gentile, whereupon he suddenly realizes that the intent of the vision was to abolish barriers between Jews and Gentiles: "God has shown me," declares Peter, "that I should not call any human being

the glory of the Lord, are being changed into his likeness" [2 Cor. 3:18]. . . . If you were impure, and the Word touched your soul, and if you offered yourself to be shaped by the Word, you were changed from a swine into a human being.[153]

Here, Origen suggests that it is just when we are thoroughly molded by the μορφή, the shape, of the beast that the resolve to be transformed is awakened. The quotation from Paul about unveiled faces is suggestive in this context of bestial masks: we must not only wear the animal mask but see through it as well, and then take it off, thereby exposing the inner reflective self—achieved, it is important to emphasize, not apart from the beast but with and deeply within it.[154]

As with Origen's bees, so also here: zoomorphism capitalizes on anthropo-centrism's discontents, and so undermines it. While Origen's position might not be called theriophily, it definitely qualifies as therotheology, and of a most profound sort.

CHAPTER 3

The Pensivity of Animals, II

Anthropomorphism

In the *Acts of Xanthippe and Polyxena*, a Christian apocryphal text dated between the fourth and sixth centuries, one of the heroines, Polyxena, escapes from her kidnapper into a dense forest and hides in the hollow of a tree, not knowing that it is the den of a lioness.[1] When the lioness returns from hunting, Polyxena addresses her thus: "By the God of Paul, have mercy on me, wild beast [τὸ θηρίον], and do not tear me apart until I receive baptism." The text continues: "The beast was frightened by this oath and immediately went away. Standing far away it looked at [Polyxena] intently. She said, 'Look, the beast has obeyed me; I will give up this place for her house,'" at which point the lioness guides Polyxena out of the forest, so that she ultimately encounters the apostle Andrew, who baptizes her.[2] This is the first of two encounters with this lioness in which the human being in question is caught in the gaze of the animal. In the second encounter, Andrew is preparing to baptize Polyxena when another captive woman, Rebecca, joins them and asks for mercy. Here is the narrative: "Then the apostle stood and prayed, and behold the lioness came running and stood and looked intently at him. The apostle of the Lord, Andrew, said: 'What does this wild beast want?' And the lioness opened her mouth and said in a human voice, 'Apostle of Christ, Andrew, the prayer of the one standing on your right side overwhelmed me. Therefore, establish them, hold them fast, and admonish them in the right and true faith in Christ, because they greatly desire the name of the Lord.'"[3] At this point the author of the text exclaims how wonderful it is that God so extends himself "that even on the irrational and untamed beasts he has poured out his mercy." Andrew then baptizes the women, and the lioness runs off to the mountain.[4]

What is the significance of the lioness's commanding gaze, which is clearly so full of understanding and compassion? The lioness appears to be the very embodiment of the pensivity of animals, which is premised upon a world of shared gazes among all animal beings.[5] On the other hand, given that she speaks as well as gazes, one might be tempted to place her in the context of Alice Kuzniar's discussion of contemporary authors who supply thoughts (and speech) to dogs, and by extension to other animals as well: "Clearly," she writes," the imaginative leap into the dog's thoughts arises from the desire to supply what is missing; it is compensatory for both the animal's silence and human incomprehension."[6] Kuzniar is herself wary of such anthropomorphic gestures. She asks, "How, in thinking through our similarities with animals, can we resist anthropomorphization," especially of the "mawkish, sentimental" kind?[7] Moreover, she refers to "the ridiculous anthropomorphizing of this talking animal" in a modern novel.[8] And yet, more sympathetically, she can ask, "Is the accusation of anthropomorphism itself a quick means of denying animals emotional sensibilities?" Such a question, she concludes, probes "the ontological certainty of the divisions between mankind and the so-called brute."[9]

The intelligent gaze of the ancient text's lioness is undoubtedly an "imaginative leap," but not, I think, in the compensatory and mawkish fashion disliked by Kuzniar. Cartoonish Disneyfication seems beside the point in the *Acts of Xanthippe and Polyxena*'s presentation of an animal that understands human speech as well as the importance of religious ritual (baptism); that serves as a guide out of a fearful situation (the forest) and into one of salvation (the meeting with the apostle Andrew); and that, when she speaks with a human voice, shows greater empathic understanding of the prayerful wishes of the story's young women than the apostle himself, who appears to be just standing by, praying. Indeed, referring to the fact that a number of apostles show up in this text, Richard Pervo remarks that this group of apostles "is about as thin in assistance as thick on the ground."[10] In any case, on the basis of her authority in this situation, the lioness spurs—in fact, commands—the apostle to "do the right thing" by initiating the women into Christianity. To be held in *this* lioness's gaze is to have one's fears and deepest desires understood, and to be called to account in terms of performing one's sacramental duty.

The talking lioness with the captivating gaze of the *Acts of Xanthippe and Polyxena* is a striking example of ancient Christian anthropomorphism, which entails the attribution of human characteristics to animals. As I explained in Chapter 2, anthropomorphism, like zoomorphism, is premised on connection between animals and humans and so constitutes a countertradition to anthropocentrism, which is premised on separation. That separation has typically had language as a focal point: Kuzniar refers in general to a centuries-long Western "predisposition against animals, namely, the onto-theological tradition of denying them access to ethics and *logos*."[11] One sign of the denial of logos (understood as language) is the very word "animal"; as Derrida has exclaimed, "The animal, what a word!"[12] He continues with the following elaboration.

> *Animal* is a word that men have given themselves the right to give. These humans are found giving it to themselves, this word, but as if they had received it as an inheritance. They have given themselves the word in order to corral a large number of living beings within a single concept: "The Animal," they say. And they have given it to themselves, this word, at the same time according themselves, reserving for them, for humans, the right to the word, the naming noun [*nom*], the verb, the attribute, to a language of words, in short to the very thing that the others in question would be deprived of, those that are corralled within the grand territory of the beasts: The Animal.[13]

The problem with "the animal" as a "catch-all concept" is that it confines the vast array of animals to what Derrida calls "this general singular," thus blinking the particularities of all (other) living creatures, and, as the passage above implies, it denies language to animals.[14]

Derrida asks: "The animal that I am (following), does it speak?"[15] To this question ancient Christian writers had basically two responses. The negative response has been indicated in other chapters but bears repeating in this one. Here is Gillian Clark's succinct summary:

> When a Greek philosopher [and an ancient Christian theologian] says that humans have *logos*, this means both that we can make sense of the world and that we can express our understanding in words; and our understanding includes awareness of God and of the choices we should make in our own best interests. Animals do not use words, and it was assumed that they lack *logos* in other ways and have a soul ... only in that they are alive and sentient; they do not have a rational or spiritual soul as human do. They were often referred to as *aloga zôa*, "living creatures without *logos*" or, in the common translation, "irrational animals."[16]

This negative position is what I have variously named a "rhetoric of domination" or a "rhetoric of superiority." In ancient Christian articulations of this "blithe assumption of [human] ascendancy,"[17] the plural phrase "irrational animals" is indeed often used, as Clark states and as we have seen in the writings of Origen, Gregory of Nyssa, and Augustine; but the gist of that plural phrase actually coheres with Derrida's "general singular" rather than petitioning the genuine plurality of the animal world.

There was, however, another option in ancient Christian literature that did not simply relegate all animals (other than human beings) to one mute category. To Derrida's question, "The animal that I am (following), does it speak?" several ancient Christian texts answered "Yes." The talking lioness of the *Acts of Xanthippe and Polyxena* is one such response. Here it is important to underscore the fact that, in the context of the ancient Christian anthropocentric mind-set signaled by its rhetoric of human exceptionalism, a talking animal comes as a shock because it is such a surprising and unexpected reversal of the positioning of animals as irrational. While we are not privy to the authorial intentions of the anonymous writer of the *Acts of Xanthippe and Polyxena* and so cannot say whether he or she set out deliberately to unseat that human exceptionalism by supporting a pensivity of animals, still one can say that the *function* of the talking animal is to destabilize the human/animal binary that anthropocentrism exists to inscribe and uphold.[18] I say "destabilize" rather than "demolish" because there is a curious paradox in the narrative of the talking lioness, one that we have seen in other ancient Christian texts. In the scene in which the lioness speaks to the apostle Andrew "with a human voice," the text expresses its wonderment that God has favored such "irrational and untamed beasts" (τὰ ἄλογα καὶ ἀτίπασα θηρία) as the talking lioness. Here in short compass there is the anthropocentric bias against animals along with the very animal whose presence in the text subverts that bias, rendering it in effect untenable in the face of what the lioness is, an intelligent animal. Anthropocentrism is stubborn in its persistence, but at least in this text it is not powerful enough as a perspective to silence the expression of human/animal kinship that the *Acts of Xanthippe and Polyxena* envisions and enacts.

There is one other feature of this text that deserves discussion at this point. It is that the lioness is able to "see" both holiness (she knows that Andrew is an apostle of Christ) and piety (she knows that the two young women are yearning for baptism). And yet the text presents her as completely bestial by using the Greek term "τὸ θηρίον," which connotes a wild and even savage animal. What is the point of embedding this kind of theological awareness and insight in a creature belonging to the untamed natural world? The text itself suggests an answer. The first heroine who appears in the *Acts of Xanthippe and Polyxena*, Xanthippe, has been converted to Christianity based on what she has heard about the preaching of the apostle Paul. At one point, she goes out into her garden and sees it with new eyes, exclaiming,

> "O beauty of the world, for up to now we thought that it had come
> about on its own, but we now know that all things were created beau-
> tifully by the beautiful one. O power and invention of Wisdom,
> because not only did it put into men countless languages, but it also
> distinguished in birds many sounds, as if from their calls and
> responses it receives sweet-voiced and heart-pricking hymns from its
> own works. O pleasantness of the air, which points to the incompara-
> ble creator. Who will change my sorrow into gladness?" And again
> she said, "O God who is celebrated in song by all, give me rest and
> encouragement."[19]

What Xanthippe sees is the "beauty of the world" (εὐπρέπεια κόσμου), which she now experiences as a divine gift. As Pervo has noted, in this moment Xanthippe discerns, "for the first time, the creator behind the beauty of the world. This is an effective piece of natural theology within a narrative context."[20] François Bovon agrees that apocryphal acts like the *Acts of Xanthippe and Polyxena* "are not satis-fied with a salvation limited to humans; they open cosmic windows and do not hesitate to connect redemption to the animal world."[21] To these comments I would add that Xanthippe emphasizes nature's speech; she draws a parallel between human languages and bird songs (ἀτιφώνων καὶ ὑπηκόων) that she hears as "hymns." Even the birds are not denied logos here. This, I think, is the kind of "cosmic window" that opens onto the phenomenon of the lioness who speaks. She is part of the beauty of a world that is rich in relational possibilities. In the case of the *Acts of Xanthippe and Polyxena* and, as we shall see, in other texts as well, the wild animal who talks is a gesture of ancient Christian anthro-pomorphism toward establishing what the French phenomenologist Maurice Merleau-Ponty called the "strange kinship" between humans and animals.[22]

(Re)Imagining Ancient Christian Anthropomorphism

In the discussions that follow, my position is that ancient Christian anthropo-morphism questions and unsettles—in one case to the point of overthrowing—what Kuzniar called "the ontological certainty of the divisions between mankind

and the so-called brute."[23] Anthropomorphism will be viewed not as an accusation that modern readers lodge against a text but rather as an ancient interpretive strategy for imagining how humans and animals are mutually entangled.
Curiously—or perhaps fittingly—the ancient Christian material to be treated in
this chapter falls into the very categories—logos and ethics—that, as Kuzniar
noted, the ontotheological tradition has denied to animals. The question is,
aside from its implied critique of anthropocentrism, what does anthropomorphism disclose to human consciousness and understanding that the concept
"The Animal" does not?

In this chapter, the concept of the pensivity of animals is expanded to refer
to the ways in which animals assume significance, as well as the ability to
signify, when they are seen, presented, and interpreted through the lens of
anthropomorphism, with reference particularly to language and to ethical
comportment. At this point, however, I hasten to note that, in the hands of
ancient Christian writers, anthropomorphic interpretation is not used as it is in
contemporary cognitive ethology to help explain the behaviors, emotions, and
thought processes of actual animals in their native habitats. Instead, as a species
of the sympathetic imagination, its function is relational; ancient Christian
anthropomorphism exposes "how we use animals to shape the landscape of our
humanity."[24] In addition, like the zoomorphism discussed in the previous chapter, anthropomorphism provides an alternative to anthropodenial, which as we
have seen is the word that primatologist Frans de Waal coined to denote "the a
priori rejection of shared characteristics between humans and animals" as well
as a "willful blindness to the human-like characteristics of animals or the
animal-like characteristics of ourselves."[25] Finally, anthropomorphism embeds
certain central tenets of Christianity deeply in the corporeal matrix of the created world.

As we saw in Chapter 2, at least one ancient Christian author, Origen of
Alexandria, mounted an articulate defense of zoomorphic interpretation,
although of course the term "zoomorphism" was not available to him. Similarly,
the term "anthropomorphism" as it is used positively today was not available to
ancient Christian authors, and I know of no ancient Christian thinker who
articulated the conceptual territory upon which anthropomorphic interpretation was grounded.[26] Thus prior to addressing first the narratives of intelligent
and sometimes talking animals, which entail a relationship between animals
and logos, and then narratives that posit a relation between animals and ethics,
I would like to draw on ideas from a contemporary theorist in order to try to

imagine the fundament in which anthropomorphic tales in ancient Christian texts are rooted and which supports the power of their pensivity.

Martin Heidegger famously declared animals to be "poor in world," in contrast to stones, which are "worldless," and human beings, who are "world-forming."[27] In declaring that "the animal is separated from man by an abyss," Heidegger meant that animals are in effect trapped in their instinctual behavior and do not have the capability of conscious self-reflection and intellection.[28] Stepping aside from this kind of "metaphysical anthropocentrism," Merleau-Ponty, whose phrase "strange kinship" has already been invoked, argued instead for continuity and against the notion of a separating abyss.[29] The continuity that founds human-animal kinship is not, however, evolutionary or hierarchical but is instead a lateral connectedness by virtue of embodiment.[30] "Animality and human being are given only together," he argued.[31] Thus the notion of strange kinship "allows for an intimate relation based on shared embodiment without denying differences between lifestyles or styles of being," as Kelly Oliver has explained.[32]

There are two ideas in Merleau-Ponty's work that undergird the phenomenon of shared embodiment. One is what he called "wild" or "brute" being (*l'Être sauvage*), and the other is "the flesh of the world."[33] Both refer to the fundament that supports the emergence and intertwining of all animal life, human included. Of l'Être sauvage he wrote, "This environment of brute existence and essence is not something mysterious: we never quit it, we have no other environment."[34] Similarly, of the flesh of the world he explained, "The flesh is not matter, is not mind, is not substance. To designate it, we should need the old term 'element,' in the sense it was used to speak of water, air, earth, and fire, that is, in the sense of a *general thing*, midway between the spatio-temporal individual and the idea, a sort of incarnate principle that brings a style of being wherever there is a fragment of being."[35] Louise Westling has summed up the relation of these two concepts succinctly: "All organisms exist intertwined and in constant interaction with the flesh of the world around them, which is the wild or brute being in which we are immersed."[36] Flesh opens the possibility of strange kinship. But because neither flesh nor brute being entails sheer oneness or sheer multiplicity, "we can neither draw a sharp ontological boundary between human and nonhuman animals nor arrange their relations hierarchically."[37]

For Merleau-Ponty, all life is rich, and when he expressed his ontology in a musical metaphor, he described the differences in style among the various "fragments of being" as different ways of "singing the world," itself viewed as a sustaining melody.[38] With his emphasis on being, Merleau-Ponty thus positioned the relations between human and animals ontologically. By contrast, in Greco-Roman antiquity a positive view of animal-human relations was articulated not in terms of Being but rather in terms of reason and speech. As Richard Sorabji has pointed out, "The questions whether animals have speech and whether they have reason were closely connected in Greek thought. This was partly because the same word *logos* could be used equally for speech or reason."[39] Two thinkers were responsible for the positive estimation of animals based on logos: Plutarch, writing in the first century CE, and Porphyry, writing in the late third.[40]

Both Plutarch and Porphyry were opposed to the Stoic position on animals, which "imparted a moral dimension to Aristotle's zoology by focusing on his denial of reason to nonhuman species and by concluding therefrom that because only humans are rational, other species are so alien to them that they can have nothing in common with humans."[41] In his treatise "On the Cleverness of Animals" (*De sollertia animalium*), Plutarch states his basic position bluntly: "Every living creature has the faculty of reasoning" (τοῦ λογικοῦ πᾶσι τοῖς ἐμψύχοις μέτεστιν).[42] Since, as he says elsewhere (and often) in this treatise, "animals have their share of reason" (τὸ μετέχειν λόγου τὰ ζῷα), he has in effect, as Stephen Newmyer explains, challenged "the Stoic denial of kinship (*oikeiōsis*) between humans and nonhuman species if this kinship rests, as the Stoics demanded, on the possession of reason."[43] Plutarch explicitly links the reasoning ability of animals to their ability to speak when he discusses various birds that, he says, "are endowed both with rational utterance [προφορικοῦ λόγου] and with articulate voice [φωνῆς ἐνάρθρου]."[44] Indeed, he exclaims—with a sentiment directly relevant to Xanthippe's praise of the "hymns" of birds—"What music, what grace do we not find in the natural, untaught warbling of birds! To this the most eloquent and musical of our poets bear witness when they compare their sweetest songs and poems to the singing of swans and nightingales."[45] For Plutarch, animals and humans are akin by virtue of sharing in reason and speech.

Porphyry, whose ideas on the topic of animals were influenced by the earlier Plutarch, was just as forthright in his declarations of animals' possession of rationality. In an extended passage of his treatise *On Abstinence* (*De abstinentia*) that deserves to be quoted in full, Porphyry argues, against the Stoics, that animals possess both internal (ἐδιάθετος) and external (προφορικός) logos, which transforms internal discourse into spoken language:

> Now since there are two kinds of *logos*, one in expression and one in
> disposition, let us begin with expressive *logos*, *logos* organized by voice.
> If expressive *logos* is voice signifying with the tongue that which is

experienced internally and in the soul ... what in this is absent from those animals that speak? And why should a creature not first have thought what it experiences, even before it says what it is going to say? I mean by "thought" that which is silently voiced in the soul. Now since that which is voiced by the tongue is *logos* however it is voiced, whether in barbarian or Greek, dog or cattle fashion, animals which have a voice share in *logos*, human speaking in accordance with human customs and animals in accordance with the customs each has acquired from the gods and nature.[46]

Porphyry goes on to describe cases in which animals understand human language, and in which humans understand animal language. Indeed, in those cases in which animals speak "clearly and meaningfully" to each other and, moreover, even learn to speak Greek, "who would be so brazen," Porphyry asks, "as to deny that they have *logos* just because he cannot himself understand what they say?"[47]

Not only was Porphyry clearly opposed to anthropocentrism, he also strongly supported the idea of animal-human kinship. That kinship was based not only on the use of language but also on animals' and humans' mutual possession of an internal logos, which varied in degree but not in kind. In a passage that sounds uncannily like Merleau-Ponty's idea of embodiment as the ground of the "strange kinship" between humans and animals, Porphyry writes:

> Almost everyone agrees that animals are like us in perception and in organization generally with regard both to sense-perception and to the flesh. They share like us not only in natural experiences and the movements they cause, but even in unnatural and unhealthy experiences which are observed in them. No sensible person would say that animals are incapable of a rational disposition because they are quite different in their bodily constitution, seeing that in human beings too there is great variation of constitution according to race and people, yet also agreeing that all are rational.[48]

Perception, Porphyry emphasized, is "the origin of kinship [οἰκείωσις]."[49] Although Porphyry's argument for animal-human kinship relies first and foremost on the possession of logos, still his discussion of flesh and bodily constitution hints at an ontology as well. In any case, he mounted the most powerful argument in antiquity for animal-human kinship, an οἰκείωσις that constituted a deep acknowledgment of relationship.[50]

though they tend to deflect interpretative attention laterally away from the role of the lion rather than deeply into his function in the *Acts of Paul*. The perspective regarding OIKONOMIA is one that I agree with insofar as it highlights the redemption of the natural world. The problem is that placing the baptized lion in such an abstract domain as God's administration or ordering of the cosmos neglects the element of real kinship—like Porphyry's warmer, familial sense of οἰκείωσις—that I have argued for above.[54]

Symbolic interpretations of the lion have also been offered. Han Drijvers, for example, saw in the lion's appearance "out of the valley of the burying-ground" a reference to the valley of the dry bones in Ezekiel 37:1 and thus posited that the lion symbolizes death. Arguing that the worldview of the *Acts of Paul* is encratite, in which death and sexuality were linked, Drijvers noted that, following his baptism, the lion spurns intercourse with the lioness. Once he is thus "dead" (in a second, positive, sense) to sexuality, the lion can then symbolize new life in an encratic form of Christianity.[55] Similarly emphasizing the text's encratic character as well as the lion's link with sexuality, Willy Rordorf argued that the lion's baptism symbolizes Paul's own embrace of sexual continence rather than the lion's initiation into Christianity.[56] The problem with these symbolic linkings of the lion with sexuality, death, and ultimately continence is that only the lion's baptism is in focus; the fact that he is a *talking* lion is shunted to the side. Ignoring the fact that the animal possesses logos seems to me to constitute a tacit uneasiness with the text's anthropomorphism, which of course pervades *both* the baptism *and* the ability to speak.

In antiquity, at least one ancient Christian author decided not to interpret the text at all. In his treatise *De viris illustribus*, completed between 392 and 393 CE, Jerome wrote: "Igitur περιόδους Pauli et Theclae et totam baptizati leonis fabulam inter apocrypha computemus."[57] Giving his own opinion using the imperial "we," Jerome thus says in his typically blunt manner: "Therefore we count the *Journeys of Paul and Thecla* and the whole tale of the baptized lion among the apocrypha." Jerome refused to consider the *Acts of Paul* as a sacred (canonical) text both because Tertullian before him had already exposed the text as a pious fraud and because he regarded the story of the baptized lion as a *fabula*, a "fictional narrative, story, or tale."[58] It is impossible, of course, to know whether Jerome was one of those little boys whose rhetorical education began with the recitation, copying out, and narratizing (from verse into prose) of the fables of Aesop, a practice advocated by the influential first-century CE rhetorician Quintilian.[59] Had he been, he might well have considered the genre of fabula to be fitting only for children and not for consumption by serious-minded Christian adults. *Pace* Jerome, however, fables were a popular form of literature in Greco-Roman society, and at least one rhetorician thought that they contained a kernel of truth. As Ben Edwin Perry has noted, one of Quintillian's contemporaries, the Alexandrian rhetorician Theon of Alexandria, wrote in his own influential work, the *Progymnasmata*, a definition of fable "in the Aesopic sense of the term in just four words: λόγος ψευδὴς εἰκονίζων ἀλήθειαν, that is, a fictitious story picturing a truth."[60]

I think that the story of the talking, baptized lion in the *Acts of Paul*, as well as the talking lioness in the *Acts of Xanthippe and Polyxena*, might well be included in the genre of fabula, only not in terms of Jerome's dismissive understanding but rather in terms of Theon's definition, which allows for such storytelling to convey truth. Indeed, Kalman Bland has argued of the literature of fables that they "presuppose cultures that deny speech and moral agency to animals."[61] Given this presupposition, fables constitute "a deceptively profound genre" because, "by pretending that animals speak . . . fables playfully radiate subversion."[62] Bland elaborates as follows:

> The fantastic component of animals conversing in human language signals a refusal to dilute the doctrine that space, drama, and emotion shape the life of all creatures. Fables therefore mock human pretentions of uniqueness and grandeur. By insisting that animals are moral agents who speak, fables destabilize conventional rationality; they disrupt so-called common sense. A form of "spiritual exercise" described by Hadot, fables assert themselves as transformative "efforts to practice objectivity in judgment," as liberating "efforts to become aware of our situation in the universe. Such an exercise of wisdom [is] thus an attempt to render oneself open to the universal."[63]

What Bland has attributed to the fable as a genre, I have attributed to ancient Christian anthropomorphism as a storytelling perspective that flaunts the anthropodenial of ancient Christian anthropocentrism. It is, indeed, a storytelling perspective that embraces the pensivity of animals as fellow creatures in a shared world.

Ancient Christian Animals and Logos: The *Acts of Philip*

The next "fictitious story picturing a truth" to be considered in this chapter is indeed a transformative spiritual exercise that offers to the reader a view of the cosmos that is not rent by an animal/human binary—or does it offer such a view? The text in question is the *Acts of Philip*, which originated in a rigorist, most probably encratite-oriented Christian community in Asia Minor at the end of the fourth century.[64] In the imagination of this text's author, as presented by Ingvild Gilhus, "a strange party was thought to have once been travelling through the mountainous areas of Asia Minor. The company included the apostles Philip and Bartholomew (cf. Matthew 10:3), Mariamne dressed as a man, along with a leopard and a [goat] kid."[65] The leopard literally explodes into the text: while the group (of human beings) were walking in a wilderness, "suddenly a great leopard came out from the mountain woods."[66] Like the talking, baptized lion of the *Acts of Paul*, this cat is μέγας, huge. Fearsomely confrontational it may be, but like the lion this leopard recognizes human holiness, that is, it has both a sense for the presence of the divine and a religiously informed consciousness, and it can talk. The text continues: "When he [the leopard] saw the apostles of the Lord, he ran over to them, threw himself at their feet, and spoke to them with a human voice: 'I prostrate myself before you, servants of the divine greatness [τοῦ θείου μεγέθους] and apostles of the only-begotten Son of God. Command me so that I might speak perfectly.' Philip said: 'In the name of Jesus Christ, speak!'"[67] As with the talking lioness of the *Acts of Xanthippe and Polyxena*, so here the animal gives the apostle a command, and the apostle obeys with alacrity. Even more impressive is the leopard's theological correctness with regard to the proper Trinitarian title of Christ and—more astonishingly still—the fact that the leopard is intimately related not to the apostles but to Christ by virtue of the text's (perhaps inadvertent?) adjectival pun that relates the leopard's status as μέγας to Christ's status as μεγέθος, a word derived from μέγας. This chapter of the *Acts of Philip* is off to a promising start as a therotheological tale that envisions what I have been calling, with Merleau-Ponty, a strange kinship among humans and animals, and now the divine as well.

As the text continues, the leopard says, "Listen to me, Philip, you who conduct us to the divine word as one who leads the bride to the bridegroom" (νυμφαγωγέ τοῦ θείου λόγου).[68] This is a passage that creates an even stronger link between the leopard and Philip, the animal and the human being. As Frédéric Amsler has pointed out, the title νυμφαγωγός and "the image that it carries of a man leading the fiancée to her future husband was applied, by various fathers of the church from the fourth century onward, to apostles who lead believers to Christ."[69] Hence Philip affiances the animals to the divine word, but they are structurally analogous to human believers. At this point the leopard, having received "a perfect human voice," begins to tell the following story.[70] During the previous evening, he had come upon a flock of goats and had seized and carried away a kid with the intention of eating it. The kid, taking on a human voice and crying like a small child, said,

> "Leopard, put off your fierce heart [τὴν ἀγρίαν καρδίαν] and savage intent [τὸ θηριῶδες τῆς γνώμης] and put on tameness [ἡμερότητα]. For the apostles of the divine greatness are about to pass through this wilderness to fulfill perfectly the promise of the glory of the only-begotten Son of God." While the kid was admonishing me with these words, I was at a loss with myself, and little by little my heart was changed [ἠλλάγη μου ἡ καρδία], and my fierceness was turned into tameness [ἡ ἀγριότης μου ἐστράφη εἰς ἡμερότητα] and I refrained from eating it.[71]

As modern commentators have noted, the pairing of a goat kid with a leopard was not an arbitrary choice on the part of the author of the *Acts of Philip*. It is an allusion to Isaiah 11:6: "The wolf shall dwell with the lamb, and the leopard shall lie down with the kid, and the calf and the lion and the fatling together, and a little child shall lead them" (RSV). The taming of the savage leopard and his reconciliation with the kid, normally his prey, picture eschatological peace in paradise in Isaiah's messianic oracle. In the *Acts of Philip* the oracle is given a Christological interpretation.[72] Thus the leopard's change of heart is what "fulfills the promise of the glory of the only-begotten Son of God," as the text declares. Indeed, as François Bovon has argued, the tale of the leopard and the kid is a defense of "the utopian conviction that God (through Christ) was reconciling not only the human heart but also the whole of creation, casting out the rule of violence and overcoming the law of the jungle."[73]

It seems that the cosmic window of this text opens upon a paradisiacal scene. In this regard, as Bovon has observed, "when the Gospel is preached, when the apostolic presence is visible, when the heart is transformed, an anticipation of the Kingdom, a limited but real one, can be observed. The leopard and the kid have their place as animals, reconciled and redeemed, in the Christian community."[74] While I agree that the *Acts of Philip* does adopt a perspective of reconciliation, I think that the text's embrace of animals may go too far in the direction of humanizing them rather than establishing a strange kinship that values difference between animals and human beings as well as connectedness or a sharing of "the flesh of the world," as Merleau-Ponty would have it.[75]

One indication of this kind of humanization occurs in Philip and Bartholomew's address to Jesus following the scene in which the leopard declares his tameness and then leads the apostles to the kid, which has been physically healed of its wounds just as the leopard has been "healed" of its savage nature. The apostles deliver this petition: "Let a human heart [καρδία δὲ ἀνθρωπίνη] be born in them and they will follow us wherever we go, eating the same things we eat for your glory, and that they might speak like human beings, glorifying your name."[76] With this interior transformation, the animals become in effect mini-apostles. They react to this change as follows: "And at that moment the animals rose up, both the leopard and the kid, lifted up their forefeet and glorified God, and said with human voices: 'We glorify and bless you [δοξάζομεν καὶ εὐλογοῦμέν σε], you who have visited us and remembered us in this wilderness, you who have transformed our savage and wild nature into tameness, and freely given us the divine word [τὸν θεῖον λόγον] and placed in us a tongue and a mind [νόημα] so that we might speak and confess your name, because your glory is great.'"[77] At this the apostles reaffirm their decision to include the leopard and the kid in their missionary wanderings, and the section ends with a striking visual image: "So they went along together, praising and glorifying God."[78]

As in the *Acts of Paul*, whose talking lion was doxologically literate, so in the passage above the leopard and the kid offer glory and bestow blessings; they are both doxologically and ritually informed. Significantly, not only have they been given human voices, they are possessed of logos and even mind. At least in this respect, this text challenges the anthropocentric rhetoric of human superiority and exceptionalism by endowing animals with reason and of course speech. The ontological and epistemological certainty of the divisions between humankind and animals has most surely been unsettled. However, unlike the baptized lion, who runs off joyfully back to the countryside, the leopard and the kid stand upright and assume the posture of human orants, lifting up furry paws and cloven hooves during their prayer. And they not only mimic human behavior, they have undergone a dramatic transformation in their very core, their hearts having become human. The category of human being seems to be on the way to becoming a "general singular," to adapt Derrida's phrase, as it takes the animals into itself.

The text's totalizing of the human gathers steam when the leopard and the kid make their next appearance in the narrative. This episode pictures Philip administering the Eucharist to Bartholomew and Mariamne. The two animals look on, "crying exceedingly and grieving in their own tongue. And their tears were flowing upon their jaws because they had not been considered worthy of the holy communion."[79] Adding to their earlier display of theological knowledge, the animals now demonstrate, by virtue of their distress at being excluded, their recognition of the significance of this particular Christian ritual. They seem to know that the apostles' failure to include them in the Communion means that they have been judged unworthy to participate in the charmed religious circle formed by the human apostles; perhaps this explains why the animals revert to speaking their own language as they suffer the deep slight that has been inflicted on them by their companions. The leopard then makes the following plea on behalf of himself and the kid:

> Therefore have mercy on us, as you have been commanded, without envy, since he himself [Christ] is in everyone, because he has given us the word [τὸν λόγον] without envy. And this is a great wonder, that we, a wild beast and a goat's kid, have forsaken our own nature and become like human beings, and truly God lives in us. Now we beseech you, apostles of the good Savior, in order that you might freely grant to us without hesitation this part that we still lack, and that our beast-like bodies might be transformed by you and we might forsake the animal form [τὴν ζωοτύπον μορφήν].⁸⁰

Asking thus that their bestial bodies be transformed into human bodies just as their hearts had been so transformed, the leopard seems to be complicit with the text's attempt to erase the animals by turning them into human beings. Ironically, anthropomorphism here edges uncomfortably close to anthropocentrism. Kinship is about to give way to ontological sameness: it seems that animals can be "rich in world," theologically speaking, only if they are no longer animals. The leopard and the kid are on the brink of losing their pensivity.

As the text continues, however, ambiguities surface. The leopard himself, having just asked for physical humanization to match his psychic one, declares that God "watches over every nature, even that of wild animals, on account of his great compassion" (τοῦ θεοῦ ἐπισκοποῦντος πᾶσαν φύσιν ἕως καὶ τῶν ἀγρίων διὰ τῇ πολλὴν αὐτοῦ εὐσπλαγχνίαν).⁸¹ The leopard's invocation of God's compassionate oversight that encompasses "every nature" is then echoed and even strengthened by Philip. "Listen to me, you animals who have become worthy so that the word of God has reached you. For this is clear, that God has visited all creation [ὁ θεὸς ἐπεσκέψατο τὸ πᾶν] through his Christ, providing [οἰκονομῶν] not only for human beings but also for the domestic animals and all the varieties of animals. Who can tell of his good providence [τὴν καλὴν πρόνοιαν] which works incessantly in us?"⁸² In this passage, Philip describes God's cosmic

oversight and beneficent providential care without a shred of human exceptionalism. Animals and human beings alike are gathered into the divine embrace.

However, in what is perhaps the oddest moment in the *Acts of Philip* vis-à-
vis animal-human relationships, the narrative veers back into anthropocentrism—but with a decidedly ambiguous twist. Following his speech affirming
that divine providence is rooted in the entire corporeal world, Philip raises his
hands in prayer and makes the following request.

> "Come, our Lord Jesus Christ, if it is your will, and just as you
> changed the form of the soul of these animals, so make them appear to
> themselves in the bodily appearance of human beings [οὕτως ποίησον
> φαίνεσθαι αὐτὰ ἑαυτοῖς πρὸς τὸ σχῆμα τοῦ σώματος τῶν ἀνθρώπων] for
> the glory and honor of your name. . . ."
>
> Philip then took the cup and filled it with water, and he sprin-
> kled it upon them.[83] And at that moment, little by little, the forms of
> their faces and bodies were transformed into the likenesses of human
> beings [κατὰ τὴν ὁμοιότητα τῶν ἀνθρώπων]. And they stood upon
> their feet and stretched out their forefeet in the place of hands [ἥπλω-
> σαν τοὺς ἐμπροσθίους πόδας ἀντὶ τῶν χειρῶν] and glorified God,
> speaking in this way: "We glorify you, Lord, the only begotten Son,
> on account of the undying life into which we have been born, having
> received in place of an animal body a human one. Truly you are the
> genuine judge of those who approach you, you who have granted us
> today the glorious word in order to make us associates [μετόχους] of
> your evangelists. For you have stripped off our beastly uncleanness
> and clothed us with the gentleness of the saints. . . . We believe that
> there is no life among either creature or human being unless God
> should visit for our salvation."[84]

As Christopher Matthews has pointed out, fundamental to the *Acts of Philip* is
the conviction that "animals possess an innate sense for the divine and a desire to
serve God and the servants of God"—though I would point out that the animals
do much more than *serve* the servants; they become their partners, μέτοχοι. Matthews adds that "the apostles for their part either recognize the appropriateness
of the animals' inclusion in Christian salvation as a matter of course . . . or they
are persuaded by the rhetorical arguments of the animals and the testimony of
heaven on their behalf."[85]

At the very least, animals and human beings share a providential world in this text, in which, as Amsler notes succinctly, "salvation is understood as transformation."[86] Surely this is true, but what kind of transformation has "really" happened to the leopard and the kid? While it certainly seems that they have been made human in the exterior as well as the interior sense, there is some odd diction in the description of their transformation. For example, Philip asks that they be made to appear *to themselves* in the *appearance* of human beings. Is this mere appearance, given the range of meanings of the term "σχῆμα" from form or shape to show and pretense? Furthermore, when the transformation actually occurs, it is into the *likeness* (ὁμοιότητα) of human beings rather than into their substance (οὐσία). And compounding this ontological uncertainty is the fact that, once the transformation has occurred, the animals stretch out their forefeet *in the place of* hands; they still have paws and hooves. Finally, despite the leopard's conviction that he and the kid have received human bodies that replace their bestial ones, further mention of the animals in the text unsettles the status of their transformation. Somewhat later in the narrative, in response to a prayer of Philip in praise of Christ, the text says, "And the apostles and the animals cried out, 'Amen.'"[87] In addition, the following chapter indicates that, while Philip and Mariamne were baptizing men and women converts, respectively, "All the crowds were exceedingly amazed because the leopard and the kid of the goat were pronouncing the amen."[88] The animals who supposedly have human bodies participate in the ritual—as animals, however marvelous is their articulate role in it.

This text subverts its own subversive gestures, and then subverts them again. The animals are certainly akin to human beings by virtue of their possession of logos as well as by their religious astuteness, but are they embraced by the Christian providential vision as animals, or not? Must they literally become human before they can enter the salvific order, thus rendering this text very thoroughgoing in its anthropodenial? In my view, this text's presentation of the leopard and the kid flirts with anthropocentrism, but it doesn't finally succeed in succumbing to it. There is too much ambiguity about the precise nature of the animals' transformation.

Perhaps it would be more useful to ask whether there are indications in the *Acts of Philip* that, as in the *Acts of Paul*, animals and human beings share an Être sauvage. There is no doubt that this text views human and animal life as intertwined. We have just seen, as with Merleau-Ponty's concept of strange kinship, that it is impossible finally to draw a sharp ontological boundary between human and nonhuman animals in the *Acts of Philip*, nor is it possible to rank humans and animals on a hierarchical scale; they are partners in their performance of Christian mission and ritual. Despite its ambiguity, the text also preserves difference in styles of being in its vision of kinship based on shared embodiment in a cosmos inhabited, ordered, and blessed by God through Christ, as the text repeatedly argues. Those paws and hooves create "a certain alienation effect" that underscores the "strange" component of the strange kinship of animal and human in this text. "Alienation effect" is the phrase used by Jean-Christophe Bailly to describe his view of how animal fables work to detach the human "from its canker of pride" and to "inflect things towards a modesty born of astonishment."[89]

Considered as fabula, the animal storytelling of the *Acts of Philip* indeed does rely on a modesty born of astonishment as the human characters accept the soteriological requests and tearful rebukes of the animals without hesitation; as Philip says at one point, "O benevolent Jesus, you precede us and correct and instruct us through these animals, so that we might believe still more and complete with zeal that which was entrusted to us."[90] As in Bland's view of the function of fable, here too the animals are moral agents, and conventional rationality is destabilized by their actions as pedagogues to the apostles and by their strange kinship with them. The intimacy of that kinship permeates the text, from the apostles' and animals' crying out of the "Amen" together to the desire of the human Philip to have his body transformed into angelic glory, a desire that is structurally and even linguistically parallel to the bestial characters' desire for transformation.[91] Thus despite this text's occasional nod in the direction of anthropocentrism, its anthropomorphic aspects shore up rather than destroy animal-human connectedness. Although the perspective of this text challenges anthropomorphism, it does not defeat the text's crisscrossing of the boundary between human and animal. Even in the *Acts of Philip*, then, the rhetoric of human exceptionalism is challenged by the zoological imagination.

Ancient Christian Animals as Masters of Silence

Talking animals, that is, animals endowed with expressive logos, were the most radical form of intelligent animals in ancient Christianity, but they didn't exhaust Christians' deployment of anthropomorphism to imagine human-animal connectedness.[92] There were many stories of animals—perhaps we could dub them "masters of silence," following Bailly—whose embodiment of interspecies communication continued one of the themes explored above, namely, the embeddedness of Christian values in the created world. These "masters of silence" were the many mute but intelligent animals in ancient Christian literature who recognize human saintliness—that is, they know a holy man or a holy woman when they see one. One particularly moving story involves Macarius, one of the most famous of the miracle-working monks of the Egyptian desert in the fourth century. The anonymous author of the *History of the Monks in Egypt* relates the following tale:

> Another time, they say, Macarius was praying in his cave in the desert. There happened to be another cave nearby which was the den of a hyena. While he was at prayer the hyena suddenly appeared and began to lick his feet. And taking him gently by the hem of his tunic, she drew him towards her own cave. He followed her, saying, "I wonder what this animal wants to do?" When she had led him to her own cave, she went in and brought out to him her own cubs, which had been born blind. He prayed over them and returned them to the hyena with their sight healed. She in turn, by way of a thank-offering, brought the man the huge skin of a large ram and laid it at his feet. He smiled at her as if at a kind and sensitive person, and taking the skin, spread it under him. This skin is still in the possession of one of the brothers.[93]

Here is a touch that expects a response. The hyena is Macarius's neighbor, and she appears to know that he is a healer, indeed, a healer in the tradition of Jesus, healing the blind. Her knowledge of Macarius as a miracle worker gives her agency, impelling her to seek his help for her cubs.

The intimacy of the animal-human exchanges in this passage is striking. The hyena licks Macarius's feet—a sign, perhaps, that her wildness is not a threat. Then she takes Macarius gently by the hem of his tunic to guide him to her cave. Her logos is expressed bodily; her powers of reasoning, we might say, are embodied rather than abstract. Meanwhile Macarius, his curiosity piqued, allows himself to be led to the cubs, and he prays for them to be healed without regard for their bestial rather than human status. Like Derrida, he "follows the animal," as it were, and in so doing he ignores the hierarchical structure of value separating human and animal that the doctrine of human exceptionalism posited.[94] As the text continues, this intelligent hyena positions her compassionate monk in a relationship of gift exchange. Culturally savvy, she presents him with a thank offering, to which he responds, not with licks, but with a smile that acknowledges the animal's status as one who is equally embedded in a creation suffused with the power of the holy. In a final act of intimate touch, Macarius takes the gift of the ram skin and settles into it. The picture of animal-human relationships offered by this story envisions a reciprocity of call and response. It could not be more different from the situation today, as described by Bailly, who writes that "contact between humans and wild animals is above all this complex system of avoidance and tension in space, an immense entanglement of uneasy, self-concealing networks."[95] The monk and the hyena are decidedly entangled (and at the animal's initiative, it should be noted), but their "network" is one of intimate touch that is neither uneasy nor self-concealing. This text's anthropomorphism captures the intimacy that would otherwise be lost by the rhetoric of domination imposed by ancient Christianity's anthropocentric impulse.

Sometimes, mute but intelligent animals turn the tables and perform the "saving" act themselves by recognizing human holiness and acting to protect it. A well-known example comes from the second-century *Acts of Paul and Thecla*.[96] In this text, the young woman Thecla, a follower of the apostle Paul, is accosted on the streets of Antioch by one of its leading citizens, a certain Alexander. When she defends what she perceives as a threat to her virginity by ripping his cloak and knocking the crown off his head, thereby humiliating him, he brings her before the governor, who condemns her to the beasts.[97] Prior to the *damnatio ad bestiam* proper, there is a procession, part of which features Thecla "bound to a fierce lioness [λεαίνῃ πικρᾷ]."[98] In the very next sentence, we hear that Thecla is actually riding the lioness: "And as Thecla sat upon her back, the lioness licked her feet, and all the crowd was amazed." Here once again is a very compelling image of intimate touch in a human-animal relationship, as Thecla rides the lioness who licks her feet. Does contact with the holy woman soften the fierceness of the animal? Or does the lioness lick Thecla's feet because she perceives the woman's holiness? The latter would appear to be the case, since when Thecla is flung into the stadium the next day, "lions and bears were set upon her, and a fierce lioness [λεαίνῃ πικρᾷ] ran to her and lay down at her feet. And the crowd of women raised a great shout. And a bear ran upon her, but the lioness ran and met it, and tore the bear asunder. And again a lion trained against men . . . ran upon her; and the lioness grappled with the lion, and perished with it. And the women mourned the more, since the lioness who was her helper was dead [ἐπειδὴ καὶ ἡ βοηθὸς αὐτῇ λέαινα ἀπέθανεν]."[99] This "fierce lioness" is presumably the same "fierce lioness" who had licked Thecla's feet the day before and now functions as her "helper."[100]

The term for "helper," βοηθός, is used later in the *Acts of Paul and Thecla* as a Christological title, as Thecla prays, "Christ Jesus the Son of God, my helper in prison, my helper before governors, my helper in the fire, my helper among the beasts, thou art God, and to thee be the glory forever. Amen."[101] The application of this term both to the lioness and to Christ elevates the animal's status considerably; she is not only Thecla's literal "helper among the beasts," she is also the vehicle through which Christ's power was manifested soteriologically in Thecla's moment of peril.[102] This intelligent animal not only recognizes human holiness but also enables divine intercession to protect it. Finally, the lioness also has a human dimension as Thecla's supporter. As Stephen Davis has noted, in this strongly feminized text, "by punctuating the battle between the lioness and the male beasts with the supportive responses of the anonymous 'crowd of women,' the story incorporates the lioness into that community of female supporters, and portrays the animal herself as a martyr for Thecla's cause."[103] In the *Acts of Paul and Thecla*, anthropomorphism has produced a bestial heroine who is polysignificative and thoroughly embedded in the religious matrix inhabited by the human heroine.

There are other ancient Christian texts in which the motif of "lion (or lioness) to the rescue" plays a part in the plot and provides snapshots of animals who are "masters of silence" but are nonetheless possessed of conscious awareness and an ability to evaluate a situation accurately.[104] The appearance of helpful lions in a hagiography will provide further brief but compelling testimony to the striking paradox of the intelligent animal. In Jerome's *Life of Paul*, an aged St. Antony has set out from his monastery at the behest of a dream to find a monk who is better than he is. After a journey through the desert, Antony finds Paul, who informs Antony that God has sent him to perform Paul's eventual burial. First, though, Antony must return to his monastery and bring back a cloak intended for Paul's shroud. Upon his return, Antony discovers that Paul has died. Having no shovel, Antony finds himself in a predicament; how to dig a grave for the holy man? To his surprise, two lions, "their manes streaming back from their shoulders," come running up out of the deep desert.[105] Here is what happens next:

> The lions came directly up to the corpse of the blessed Paul and
> stopped still. Then, with their tails thrashing, they reclined at the
> feet of the corpse and let out a mighty roar, so that you would think
> that they were offering lamentation in the only way they could.
> Next, the lions began to paw the ground nearby, competing with one

another to excavate the sand, until they had dug out a space big
enough for a man. Then, with waggling ears and downcast heads,
they approached Antony and, as if requesting wages for their labor,
began to lick his hands and feet. Antony realized that they sought his
benediction and so straightaway he poured out his praise to Christ,
rejoicing that even dumb animals recognize that God exists [*quod
muta quoque animalia Deum esse sentirent*].[106]

In this thoroughly anthropomorphized scene, the perceptive lions intuit Antony's grave-digging predicament and help him out of it. Further, like Macarius's hyena, they "speak" with their bodies, roaring their lamentations and seeking the saint's blessing with licks (again!) to the hands and feet. Finally, the text makes it clear that these lions are informed theologically as well as ritually; they know that God exists, even though they are *muta*, a word meaning "speechless" that, when applied to animals, carries a brutish connotation.[107] Here is yet another of those ironic moments when anthropomorphism can't quite silence the anthropocentric view of animals, and yet the anthropomorphic rendering of the lions is so compelling that the text's resort to the term "muta" seems quite out of place.[108]

A final set of stories concerning ancient Christian animals and logos addresses the phenomenon of the obedient animal. One tale features, once again, St. Antony. As his hagiographer Athanasius narrates Antony's move to the inner mountain, he notes Antony's desire to be self-sufficient by planting grain and so supplying himself with bread rather than relying on others to bring it, and he notes his desire to be hospitable to visitors by maintaining a vegetable garden.[109] Trouble arises: "At first, however, when the beasts in the wilderness came for water [there was a stream at the foot of Antony's mountain], they often would damage his crop and his planting. But gently capturing one of the beasts, he said to all of them, 'Why do you hurt me, when I do you no injury? Leave, and in the name of the Lord do not come near here any longer.' From then on, as if being afraid of the command, they did not come near the place."[110] Obviously possessed of the ability to understand human speech, the wild animals follow Antony's reasoning regarding reciprocal relationships and obey the saint's command.[111]

In another part of the same desert, the monk Abba Helle also had a problem: he needed to cross a river that was inhabited by a crocodile "which had devoured many people."[112] Upon hearing this, "the father did not hesitate. At once he jumped up and rushed into the ford. And immediately the beast took him onto its back and set him down on the other side. . . . [When Helle wanted to return] he let out a cry calling the crocodile to him. The animal obeyed him instantly and offered its back as a raft. . . . He crossed the ford with the beast, came ashore, and hauling the beast out of the water, said to it, 'It is better for you to die and make restitution for all the lives you have taken.' Whereupon the animal at once sank onto its belly and died."[113] This animal is obedient even unto death, although one might wonder at the monk's ingratitude. Presumably eating people is worse than wreaking havoc in a vegetable garden, but the sentient crocodile who obeys the monk's call is every bit as impressive as the wild animals who obey Antony.

A final story of obedient animals is the most comically anthropomorphic of the tales related here. The *Acts of John* pictures the apostle and his traveling companions arriving at an inn. There was only one bed, which his companions beg John to lie on, while they sleep on the floor.

> But when he lay down he was troubled by the numerous bugs; and as they became more and more troublesome to him, and it was already midnight, he said to them in the hearing of us all, "I tell you, you bugs, to behave yourselves, one and all; you must leave your home for tonight and be quiet in one place and keep your distance from the servants of God." And while we laughed and went on talking, John went to sleep. . . . As the day was breaking . . . we saw by the door of the room a mass of bugs collected. . . . When [John] woke up we explained to him what we had seen. And he sat up in the bed and looked at them and said to the bugs, "Since you have behaved yourselves and avoided my punishment go (back) to your own place." And when he had said this and had got up from the bed, the bugs came running from the door towards the bed and climbed up its legs and disappeared into the joints. Then John said again, "This creature listened to a man's voice and kept to itself and was quiet and obedient; but we who hear the voice of God disobey his commandments and are irresponsible; how long will this go on?"[114]

Given the serious signifying nature of the stories of intelligent animals that opened this chapter, the tale of the obedient bedbugs might seem like a shift from the sublime to the ridiculous. The text itself refers to the incident as a παίγνιον, a "plaything" or "toy" or perhaps "comic performance" or "trifle," and the companions laugh, presumably at the spectacle of an apostle addressing insects as though they could understand what he was saying.[115] And yet of course the bugs can and do comprehend John's command—twice! While on its surface this tale might seem like anthropomorphic slapstick, it is used in the true style of ancient fabulae to point to a moral; the contrast between the obedient bedbugs and the disobedient Christians is a shaming device of a sort that we encounter frequently in the second part of this chapter.

One might think that the relationships between humans, on the one side, and garden-wrecking wild beasts, a man-eating crocodile, and swarming bedbugs, on the other, constitute strange kinship indeed, yet these relationships also show the generous range of the pensivity of animals in ancient Christian thought. The intelligent animals of these stories are intelligent because they understand human speech and are responsive to the commands delivered to them. They are solidly rooted in logos, even if they don't speak. Like the tales of intelligent animals discussed earlier, these stories also "playfully radiate subversion" by endowing the animals with a logos that anthropocentrism denies to them.[116] And finally, again like the preceding stories, these tales, however amusing, depict how deeply in touch Christian holy men are with the created order. They are positive models of human/animal entanglement.

Ethical Economies

As indicated earlier in this chapter, anthropomorphic interpretation questions the ontological certainty of the existence of an abyss between human beings and other animals, and at the same time it in effect exposes what Alice Kuzniar termed "the onto-theological tradition of denying them access to ethics and *logos*."[117] In the foregoing stories of talking and intelligent but mute animals, we have seen how ancient Christian anthropomorphism gives animals access to logos. The second part of the chapter explores how ancient Christian anthropomorphism imagines the connection between humans, animals, and ethics. Subtending this connection is a perspective well expressed by Basil of Caesarea, who remarked in his *Hexaemeron* that "all things bear traces of the wisdom of the Creator."[118] Animals in particular bear such traces, and in doing so they function for Basil and others as natural pedagogues who provoke (or should provoke) certain kinds of self-awareness in human beings.[119] In this reliance on animals as pedagogues we moderns are not so different from our ancient predecessors, as the *New Yorker* cartoon in Figure 7 demonstrates.[120]

The ancient Christian texts to be explored in this section of the chapter are notable for their ethically therapeutic use of animal lore designed to entice

FIGURE 7. "Everything I Know About Being Human I Learned from Animals."
Cartoon by William Haefeli, *New Yorker*, November 26, 2013.
Courtesy of William Haefeli, New Yorker Collection/The Cartoon Bank.

human beings into a shared moral economy. These texts emphasize what Bailly
has called "the immediacy of living things to themselves." Their world is "a
world of actions"—"actions whereby animals, according to their abilities as species and as individuals, seem to wrap themselves in the world and create it before
our eyes, certainly just as we ourselves do, but also in another way, with quite
different styles and, it must be said, a gift for envelopment that surpasses ours."[121]
What seemed remarkable to ancient Christian interpreters was the animals'
"gift for envelopment" in an ascetic lifestyle as well as in a moral universe marked
by social harmony.

When ancient Christian anthropomorphism focuses on ethics, animal
images function at the intersection of self and world. The self in question here
is the self of ascetic striving, in which body and soul were inseparable and in

which control of physical and emotional passions was paramount. It is important to note that using animals as models for goading human beings toward a more perfect ascetic self produces a very different angle on human nature than using that other measure of the ascetic self, angels.[122] While angel images show a self that is transparent to its own spiritual radiance, anthropomorphic animal images often disclose a darker, even unpleasant, self. Again, whereas images of light-filled angels petition a sense of human transcendence, images of ethical animals reveal an implicit shared embodiment—that is, human cohabitation with animals in "the flesh of the world"—that might otherwise remain unrecognized.[123] In other words, anthropomorphic images that highlight ethical behavior keep the flesh—whether literal or figurative—in the forefront of the ascetic endeavor.

Ancient Christian Animals and Ethics: The *Physiologus*

In the previous chapter, the zoomorphism of the *Physiologus* was analyzed; now one of its anthropomorphic tales will be considered. Among the many stories about animals that constitute this text, which is marked by the increasing ascetic fervor of the period in which it was written, there is a curious tale about elephants.[124]

> There is an animal called the elephant whose copulating is free from wicked desire. If the elephant wishes to produce young, he goes off to the east near paradise where there is a tree called the mandrake. And he goes there with his mate, who first takes part of the tree and gives it to her husband and cajoles him until he eats it. After the male has eaten, [they join together] and the female immediately conceives in her womb. . . . The male guards her while she gives birth because of the serpent who is an enemy to the elephant. . . . The great elephant and his wife represent the persons of Adam and Eve. While in a state of virtue (that is, while they pleased the Lord), before their transgression, they had no knowledge of copulation, nor any awareness of the mingling of their flesh. When, however, the woman ate of the tree (that is, the intelligible mandrake) and gave to her husband, she became big with evil; because of this act they were expelled from paradise.[125]

The story continues at some length to detail the plight of an elephant that falls due to a hunter's trick and recounts all the elephants that try but fail to raise up the elephant who had fallen: one, very large elephant, the Law, is followed by twelve more elephants, the prophets; all try but do not succeed in coming to the aid of the fallen one. Finally a tiny elephant, "the holy intelligible elephant (that is, the Lord Jesus Christ)," succeeds where the others have failed.[126]

These elephants have been thoroughly anthropomorphized so as to conform to the sexually ascetic ideals of the text's author. In fact this picture of a monogamous twosome could hardly be farther from the nature of real elephants, which are polygynous and live in matrilineal family groups. Further, the text's picture of elephants' sexual chastity is far off the mark. Sexually mature bull elephants do not need the aphrodisiacal mandrake to excite them. As ethologist Marc Bekoff explains, these males go through musth—a state of rut—every year for a period of one to two months:

> They don't exactly hide it, excreting a cocktail of chemicals from a bulbous gland on their cheeks that can swell to the size of a basketball, passing more than 300 litres of urine a day (equivalent to 24 buckets), and—not surprisingly—smelling like a herd of goats. What's more, during this dramatic advertisement of his sexuality the male appears to undergo something of a personality change; indeed, the word musth is derived from a Persian word meaning drunk. They become very aggressive and obsessed with sex, probably as a result of their high testosterone levels, which can increase by up to 60 times.[127]

So much for elephantine continence in paradise!

It seems clear that one goal of the *Physiologus* was to embed ascetics' view of ideal human sexual relationships in animal behavior and thus to naturalize it as proper to the created order. In crafting this anthropomorphic fantasia on the elephant, the author was indebted to Roman zoological lore. Pliny the Elder, for example, thought that elephants were close to humans in intelligence and that they possessed virtues—honesty, wisdom, and justice—rare even in human beings.[128] According to Aelian, not only do the gods love elephants, elephants themselves are religious, waving their trunks as well as branches from trees in obeisance to the sun and moon.[129] Indeed, in an aside that appears to be critical of humankind in light of elephant behavior, Aelian remarked that "elephants for their part worship the gods, whereas human beings are in doubt whether

in fact there are gods, and, if there are, whether they take thought for us."[130]
Although attributing worship of pagan cosmic gods (sun and moon) to elephants
is obviously anthropomorphic, the naturalist tradition was correct concerning
the complex morality of these animals.[131] In any case, in the view of the ancient
zoological literature, elephants embody high ethical ideals and are fitting vehicles for religious reflection, and the testimony of the story of Adam, Eve, and
the elephants in the *Physiologus* bears this out.

The most obvious aspect of elephant lore adopted by the *Physiologus* was
the ancient naturalists' discussion of elephants' sexual propriety. According to
both Pliny and Aelian, elephants are chaste and modest; living in continence
with their mates, they do not commit adultery and in fact engage in intercourse
only once in their lives, doing so in private, away from the gaze of other animals.[132] The Christian appropriation of elephant lore in the *Physiologus* is ultimately a Christological allegory, but a central focus of this tale, even though the
analogy is inexact, is precisely the chaste mating behavior of the elephants. In a
break from the overall allegorizing aspect of the story, the sexual chastity of the
elephants is *not* mirrored in the sexual behavior of Adam and Eve, whose min-
gling of the flesh is so tinged with "wicked desire" that Eve becomes "big with
evil." Instead of serving as psychological figures for base human desires and
emotions, as we saw in some zoomorphic texts in the previous chapter, here the
animals turn the tables: in the mirror of these ascetically correct elephants, it is
human behavior that is shown to be in need of proper embodiment.

Ancient Christian Animals and Ethics:
The Menagerie of Basil of Caesarea

As we have seen, ancient Christian anthropocentrism denied reason to animals,
but it granted that they possessed a sagacity that is natural and connected to
instinct.[133] In this perspective, animals' basic nature was summed up in the terms
phūsis and *aisthēsis*; the success of their envelopment in the world was said to rest
on their "possession of the faculty of sensation."[134] Augustine can speak for many
of his fellow Christians on this point: "Many beasts surpass us in sense perception" because "the brute soul is more closely bound to the body."[135] One might
argue that it was precisely because animals were seen as so closely connected to
the sensuous and the material that they were perfect vehicles for ascetic reflection. Their sheer physicality was aligned with the "animal" human bodies on
which so much of ascetic practice was focused. As Blake Leyerle has remarked

about desert ascetics, "Animals were a powerful way in which monks thought and spoke about the encounter with the body."[136] This is surely the case, but there is one ingredient missing in the face of the phenomenon of the ethical animal: ethical comportment is not only a matter of the body, it is also a matter of the mind. Hence there is a real irony in the kind of anthropomorphism engaged in by Basil of Caesarea, who is considered next. He constantly plays on the opposition between bestiality ("irrational animals") and reason (human beings); and yet he holds up animal after animal as models of behavior (whether positive or negative) that humans would do well either to emulate or to avoid. What was at stake in positioning the actions of "dumb beasts" as a mirror into which "smart humans" are invited to gaze? We shall soon see.

In his *Hexaemeron*, Basil tended to craft images of animals for use in his program for human beings' recovery of what he called "natural virtues" (αἱ ἀρεταὶ κατὰ φύσιν); as Philip Rousseau has pointed out, Basil "did not think that the Fall had destroyed nature in any fundamental way."[137] As Rousseau explains further, nature (φύσις) was for Basil "the hidden presence of God's creative word" in animal as well as human bodies.[138] Hence while "the soul of animals is something earthy" (γῆ ἐστι τῶν κτηνῶν ἡ ψυχή), at the same time "the word of God [ῥῆμα θεοῦ] flows through all creation."[139] Animal souls might be lowly, but they are energized by God's creative word. Perhaps it is this complexity of the animal soul that makes animals such fitting vehicles for both positive and negative reflections on the ethical character of human beings.

Although Basil's *Hexaemeron* is not usually considered to be a member of the canon of ascetic texts from Christian antiquity, I shall consider it to be so here, for the following reasons. Basil purported to be writing about what he saw as the beauty and wondrousness of the created world.[140] Eschewing allegory for the plain sense of scripture, he wrote: "When I hear 'grass,' I think of grass, and I do the same with plant, fish, wild animal, and ox. I take everything just as it is said."[141] And yet as he detailed the natural characteristics and behaviors of the various birds, beasts, and creatures of the sea, Basil frequently introduced interjections in which he used animals to measure humans, and he often did so anthropomorphically by attributing human ethical ideals to animal comportment. These punctuations in the text have largely to do with Basil's shaping—or perhaps better, *reshaping*—of human ethical subjectivity not only with a view toward personal responsibility and social harmony but also along ascetic lines of the control of the passions: "Let the passions of the incontinent," he wrote in the seventh homily, "be restrained and trained by these examples from land and sea."[142] Thus Basil often (though not always) engaged in anthropomorphic interpretation when dealing with animals in the *Hexaemeron* (*pace* his assertion to the contrary, grass is *not* always grass in this text). In such presentations of animals, one sees what I would call a therapeutic use of animal pictures in order to craft an ascetic self devoted to an ethic of poverty, self-control, and charity.[143]

Basil was especially impressed by the self-discipline of birds. One of his descriptions of avian behavior provides a brief but nonetheless apposite example of his use of animals to promote an ascetic human self: "They say that the turtle-dove, when once separated from her mate, no longer accepts union with another, but, in memory of her former spouse, remains widowed, refusing marriage with another. Let the women hear how the chastity of widowhood, even among irrational creatures, is preferred to the unseemly multiplicity of marriages."[144] Here Basil anthropomorphizes the turtledove in order to promote the ascetic ideal of sexual self-control among women who have been widowed. Although it is true, behaviorally speaking, that turtledoves are monogamous and so seem to be a fitting "natural" choice for Basil's moral point about Christian marriage, the fact is that they are *serially* monogamous; if one dies, the other finds a new mate. But this biological fact is missing in Basil's anthropomorphic portrait of the ethical turtledove: the bird is presented in human terms as a "widow" who spurns "marriage" with another "spouse." The turtledove is a model of ascetic discipline (even though it is, in an irony we have seen before, "irrational"). In this and other passages, Basil hopes that Christians might enter the ethical economy established by a bird (!) and share its style of being. For an author committed to the rhetoric of human superiority, this positive ethical positioning of the turtledove is a stunning instance of the conundrum that pervades ancient Christian thought on animals.

Along with such overt appeals to ascetic values, there is the broader perspective on Basil's later works, including the *Hexaemeron*, provided by Philip Rousseau, who has noted that "the importance of self-knowledge, the need for inner purification, the ideal of a freedom that rises above the enslavement of property and fame—all occur again and again in the teaching of the mature Basil." Such achievements, he continues, were "not limited to an ascetic life but considered the only worthy goal of any human."[145] On Basil's extension of an ascetic mode of life to all Christians, Rousseau remarks further: "Genuine authority, he said, sprang from the self-possession and the inner control achieved by the holy ones. But the Church itself was involved in that victory: by siding with the traditions of the fathers, by adopting an ascetic mode of life, by remaining 'sons of the bride of Christ,' Christians could share with the Church a dominion over the whole world."[146]

Concerns for self-knowledge and ethical behavior, especially in the context of promoting social harmony among his fellow Christians, are strikingly evident in Basil's presentation of the crab. This is an unusual story in that, as Basil proceeds in his anthropomorphic description, the crab takes on *both* positive *and* negative aspects of human comportment. As a mirror into which humans are invited to gaze, this animal reflects a complicated anthropology. Referring to the crab as an "evildoer" (κακοῦργος) not to be imitated, Basil continues:

> The crab craves the flesh of the oyster, but its prey is hard to get because it is enveloped by a shell. For nature has protected the softness of the oyster's flesh with this unbreakable enclosure—hence the name testacean or hard-shelled. Thus when the two shells, which fit each other exactly, enclose the oyster completely, the crab's claws are necessarily powerless. What is the crab to do? When it sees an oyster in a sheltered spot warming itself voluptuously [μεθ' ἡδονῆς] and opening its shells to the sun's rays, then the crab furtively flicks a pebble into it, making it impossible for the oyster to close its shells. With this trick the crab is able to obtain what it could not by force. Such is the immorality of animals who partake neither of reason nor of speech. I myself wish that, while emulating the resourcefulness and inventiveness of crabs, you refrain from harming those near you. That person is [like a crab] who approaches his brother with cunning, is attached to the mishaps of those near him, and delights in the misfortunes of others. Flee any resemblance to these wretches! Be satisfied with what you have! For poverty that is truly self-sufficient is for the wise more honorable than any other pleasure.[147]

So much for the plain sense of scripture! In this anthropomorphized world of voluptuous oysters and maliciously furtive yet imaginatively resourceful crabs, Basil has offered an object lesson in the ascetic value of poverty as well as in proper social relationships based on care for the other.

Although it is amusing to imagine that anyone would entertain the idea of imitating a crab, whether for good or for ill, the effect of such a fancy is to highlight the kinship between crabs and human beings. In Basil's telling, they are mutually implicated in a social world of actions and their consequences. In this regard, one might say that Basil's description of the crab and the oyster, when considered as an extended image, has succumbed to the lure of the storytelling potential of the image's own craving. That is, this narrative image as a whole is itself a "crab," working its own furtive trick on the unsuspecting reader, for what Basil has done here is to insert an anthropology into his catalogue of nature and nature's appetites. When one "reads" animals along with Basil, one is also reading the human self. Like zoomorphism, anthropomorphism can be psychologically revealing: moving from the crablike to the human realm, Basil positions the carnal appetite of the crab as a double mirror of human ethical striving and failure. Emulate the crab's resourcefulness, he counsels, but not so as to inflict harm on "oysters," those defenseless others who are prey to the furtive flicks of the cunning selves whom Basil condemns. The text's abrupt switch from descriptive narrative to direct address is surely a jolt to the reader, a moment in which perception is altered by forcing one to inhabit this testacean story that Basil converts into a tale of strange kinship indeed.

This is of course no ordinary crab. It is not, as the literary critic J. Hillis Miller would say, an innocent image.[148] Not only does it generate an "unexpected fusion of images," as the human and the natural worlds envelop each other; and not only does it "lead to make believe," asking the reader to imagine himself or herself as a crab; but it also masks—or better, unmasks—an erotic exuberance that the stern ethical stance of the text cannot quite suppress.[149] Basil's text presents the crab's quest for the soft flesh of the voluptuous oyster in unmistakably sexual terms. What the reader sees is in this anthropomorphic tale is a humanized scene of seduction: the canny crab, unable to use force, tricks the oyster into satisfying its desire. Paradoxically, the image of the crab and the oyster petitions the erotic while at the same time condemning it as bestially immoral. It is truly a fabula, wily in its subversiveness.

On the face of it, Basil's fall into the sensuous allure of this image may seem surprising, since he was a leader in the ascetic movement in late fourth-century Christianity. Founder of monastic brotherhoods and devoted to relief of the poor, Basil spoke the stern language of sexual renunciation and the embrace of celibacy and virginity that swept through late ancient Christianity. Given his renunciatory stance toward the body and its pleasures, Basil's image of the crab is what the poet Ezra Pound might have called a "luminous detail," that is, one of those moments when a text confounds itself in "aporiae, those tears where energies, desires, and repressions flow out into the world."[150] Seduced, perhaps, by his own suppressed eros, the ascetic Basil displaced his sense of the seductive and the voluptuous onto the animal world while giving expression to that sense at the same time. Furthermore, his attempt to convert the story into a moral lesson confounds the very story it petitions; by recommending, at the end of his narrative, the embrace of poverty as the ultimate wisdom of the story, Basil

denies the satisfaction of the crab's carnal desire even as he narrates its fulfillment. At the very least, one can say that his crab-and-oyster story shows that
anthropomorphic interpretation can be sublimely erotic; it is a striking instance
of what Virginia Burrus has called the "eruption of a powerful crosscurrent of
asceticized eroticism" in late ancient Christianity.[151] As we saw in the previous
section concerning the convoluted tales of some of the talking animals, there is
more than meets the eye, as it were, in the eye of the animal.

The "force field of desire" into which Basil's *Hexaemeron* places its ethically oriented animals is concerned not only with the inculcating of an ascetic
self but also with the picturing and promoting of social harmony, as noted
earlier in this chapter.[152] In this context, what one interpreter has called "theriophily"—the notion that animals are in some ways superior to humans
because, ironically, they embody human ideals—comes strongly and surprisingly to the fore, surprisingly, given Basil's repeated adherence to the rhetoric
of human superiority.[153] Some animal tales, in other words, function as a
technē of the social self. What I wish to explore, however, is not simply the fact
that animal behavior can be pedagogical but that it can be pedagogical as a
shame-inducing exemplum. Like the *Physiologus*'s story of the ascetically correct elephants who function as a reproach to Adam and Eve's lust, Basil's
therapy of the human by means of the earth's creatures was frequently based
on shame. For example, when describing the migratory patterns of fish, Basil
wrote:

> I have seen these wonders myself and I have admired the wisdom of
> God [τοῦ θεοῦ σοφίαν] in all things. If the irrational animals [τὰ
> ἄλογα] are able to contrive [ἐπινοητικὰ] and look out for their own
> preservation, and if a fish knows what it should choose and what
> avoid, what shall we say who have been honored with reason, taught
> by the law, encouraged by the promises, made wise by the Spirit, and
> who have then handled our own affairs more unreasonably than the
> fish? Even though they know how to have some foresight for the
> future, yet we, through hopelessness for the future, waste our lives in
> brutish pleasure. A fish traverses so many seas to find some advantage;
> what do you say who pass your life in idleness?[154]

In this passage, anthropocentrism and anthropomorphism clash head-on: how
can fish be both irrational and conceptually mindful? Basil admires the "gift for
envelopment" in their world that fish have, to recall Bailly's phrase; if only

humans would exercise the foresight that is rightfully theirs (but more successfully exercised by fish), he laments.[155]

More striking still in terms of the thematic of shame is Basil's story about
the symbiotic relationships among storks and crows.

> The conduct of the storks is not far from reasoning intelligence
> [συνέσεως λογικῆς]; thus they all reside in these regions at the same
> time, and likewise all depart at one signal. Our crows attend them as
> bodyguards and escort them, as it seems to me, providing a certain
> auxiliary force against hostile birds. And a proof is, first, that the
> crows do not appear at all during that time; then, that, returning
> with wounds, they carry clear proofs of their protective and defensive
> alliance. Who prescribed the laws of hospitality among them? Who
> threatened them with an indictment for military desertion, so that
> no one deserts the escort? Let the inhospitable listen, who close their
> doors and do not share shelter in winter and at night with travelers.
> The solicitude of storks for their old would suffice to make our chil-
> dren devoted to their fathers, if they were willing to heed it. For,
> surely, no one at all is so lacking in intelligence as not to judge it
> deserving of shame to be inferior in virtue to irrational birds.[156]

Here once again the anthropocentric and anthropomorphic characterizations of
the animals clash, although Basil's attribution of defensive and protective maneuvers, military alliances, and hospitality to crows, and parental devotion to storks,
seems to elevate the virtue of these birds to such a degree that the resort to the
debasing language of irrationality seems out of place and beside the point. These
birds are highly ethical social creatures, and they put human beings to shame.

Like Derrida caught standing naked before his cat and feeling ashamed of
his destitution, Basil showed human beings denuded, as it were, or stripped
down to their shameful anti-ethical selves in the face of animal behavior.[157] Derrida's rhetorical question "But cannot this cat also be, deep within her eyes, my
primary mirror?" would surely have been answered positively by Basil.[158] The
function of the shame intended by such mirroring in the *Hexaemeron* is a call to
action to embody the sorts of virtuous behavior that lead to salvation. If we can't
even imitate the brute (but smart) beasts who take care of their lives, Basil
wrote, "we'll be condemned."[159] As Philip Rousseau commented, Basil intended
"to touch his audience at the level of motive, self-image, guilt, and confidence; to
awaken in them a desire for spiritual and moral growth."[160] Such shame-inducing

awakenings as we have just seen in his animal tales had, Basil hoped, the positive effect of refunctioning the imagination, "bringing new criteria and new desires into the world" of Christian life.[161]

In *Saving Shame*, Virginia Burrus notes that shame need not be "a sheerly destructive or paralyzingly inhibiting force."[162] "There is no escape from shame," she continues, "but there may be many possibilities for a productive transformation of shame and through shame."[163] "In shame, desire, whatever its object, is not so much decisively blocked as tantalizingly arrested, caught like a deer in the headlights of (self-) scrutiny."[164] Indeed, shame is "the place where the question of identity arises most originarily and most relationally."[165] Shame, desire, self-scrutiny, and the question of identity form a set of interrelated concerns that well describe the function of the shaming animal stories in Basil's *Hexaemeron* as well as in the *Physiologus*.

Whether the subject of discussion in this chapter has been animals possessed of logos or animals that either enact or provoke a certain ethical being in the world, one concept that has repeatedly surfaced has been "strange kinship," a concept that posits an entanglement, a connectedness, indeed an intimacy between animals and human beings that is, I argue, promoted by anthropomorphic interpretation. Perhaps the most fitting way to end this chapter is with a final story of deep intimacy between a human being and animals. The *Historia monachorum in Aegypto* tells the story of the desert monk Theon, who had practiced silence for thirty years: "One could see him with the face of an angel giving joy to his visitors by his gaze and abounding with much grace." The text continues: "They say he used to go out of his cell at night and keep company with wild animals, giving them to drink from the water that he had. Certainly one could see the track of antelope and wild asses and gazelles and other animals near his hermitage. These creatures delighted him always."[166] This was possibly a Christomimetic scenario, for it was when Christ was in the wilderness with wild beasts that angels ministered to him (Mk. 1:13). But perhaps the story has more to do with the strange kinship fostered by brute being: Theon existed with animals in the world "like water in water," in an intimacy so profound that the animal and the angel were one.[167] The pensivity of animals is enhanced by a special warmth in this story.

Coda

Actually, human-animal intimacy has been the theme that unites the discussions of both zoomorphism and anthropomorphism. Hence what better image with which to close these two chapters than Jerome's centaur, a hybrid figure made up of a human head and torso attached to a horse's body that throws the distinction between zoomorphism and anthropomorphism into confusion: is the centaur an anthropoid horse, or an equine human? And what does such a hybrid creature signify?

The centaur appears in Jerome's *Life of Saint Paul*. In this hagiography, St. Antony, the other main (human) character, sets off into the desert to find Paul, whom a dream has declared to be "a better monk" than the spiritually self-preening Antony, whom the dream jolts out of his presumption of monkish superiority. Along the way, Antony encounters two hybrid creatures, a centaur and a satyr, who helpfully point the way to Paul's cave. Because the satyr—half human, half goat—is essentially a double of the centaur in terms of hybridity, I shall engage only the centaur, who appears first in the narrative. As Jerome tells the tale, Antony boldly sets out to find Paul, but he has no idea where to go.

> By midday, the sun blazed overhead, but [Antony] did not falter and stayed his course, saying, "I trust in my God that he will show me that servant of his whom he promised." No sooner had he said this than Antony spied a man-horse [*hominem equo mixtum*]. (The fancy of poets names this creature a "hippocentaur.") At the sight of this creature, Antony protected himself by making upon his forehead the sign of the cross. "Hey, you!," said Antony, "where does this servant of God dwell?" The beast gnashed its teeth and tried to speak clearly, but only ground out from a mouth shaking with bristles some kind of barbarous sounds rather than lucid speech; the creature indicated the sought-for route by extending its right hand and then, as Antony watched in amazement, it fled swiftly over the open ground and vanished.[168]

Oddly, Jerome concludes this episode by indicating how terrifyingly monstrous the centaur is. And yet Antony, though he protects himself with the sign of the cross, doesn't seem to be particularly afraid; in fact, he assumes that the creature understands human language and arrests it with a question, a question that assumes further that it knows where the holy man Paul dwells. The centaur does in fact possess that knowledge, and indicates it not in human speech but with a gesture of its arm, replacing logos with a language of the body.

One might well wonder what this bolt out of the mythological blue is doing in a Christianized desert. The centaur is a discordant figure that calls attention to itself and is crucial to the movement of the plot. Why? My argument will be that the centaur, as a figure in a text about ascetic identity, plays a central role in picturing the "mobile subjectivity" of desert ascetics.[169] It is significant that Jerome's hagiography drives toward the revelation of Paul, the very founder of asceticism according to this text, and that this holiest of monks is presented as a wild and hairy anchorite.[170] As we shall see, as "wild men" the monk and the centaur are related. "Paul" is the answer to the text's question about ascetic identity, "Who is the better monk?" and the centaur is the sign of that knowledge, knowing as he does how to find Paul. Furthermore, Jerome makes it clear that the hybrid centaur is indigenous to the desert (it gave him birth, he speculates), and by the time we meet the 113-year-old Paul in the text, he has been "native" to the desert, as it were, for almost a hundred years.[171]

Like the crab discussed earlier in this chapter, the centaur is not an innocent image. In Greek myth, the cross-species centaurs were notable for two main traits: their hypermasculine and violent sexuality, and their hostility to what ancient Greeks saw as foundational norms of culture, especially relations of guest-friendship and hospitality and the institution of marriage.[172] As Page duBois has argued, in Greek myth the figure of the centaur "permitted speculation about boundaries and kinds. The centaurs formed an asymmetrical, overly masculine, violently bestial alternative to the norm of what was seen by the Greeks as human culture."[173] As figurations of wildness and animal appetite, centaurs were opposed to culture—and yet it is important to emphasize that it was only through them that civilized society recognized itself as civilized. Centaurs were a strange mixture of the animal and the human, of bestiality and civilization; negatively, they figured not only a literal "other" but also an intimate other, the wildness within the human.

But there was another dimension to the centaur, one that accented a positive aspect of this union of animal and human. The myth of the centaur had two poles, "one as a wild man who was humanoid and the other as a wise and just man who was bestial."[174] As Roger Bartra has observed, it was possible for "a human with wild characteristics to represent wisdom and culture" due to "the superhuman qualities of nature itself. . . . Not only did nature savagely assault civilized man, but nature also communicated the signs and symbols of a profound knowledge."[175] DuBois adds the following to this complex portrait: "They [centaurs] lived in nature both as violent, uncivilized beasts, and as characters from a long past, before the necessity for a separation between gods and men, before work, cooking, death, all the evils that culture brings. . . . The world before culture was viewed with nostalgia as well as loathing."[176]

As Hayden White has shown, this doubleness is itself doubled in the tradition of the wild man in which the centaur figured prominently. The wild man held in a tensive balance two contrary views of the relation of the human to nature and the animal: on the one hand, identifying with the wild man signified a regressive return to bestiality, while on the other, sympathizing with him signaled a radical rejection of the values, norms, and institutions of a civilization now viewed as cramping and corrupt.[177] Thus the wild man could be an idealized metaphor used to rebel *against* culture as well as a corrupt image of all that civilization had rejected in constituting itself *as* culture. Most significant in terms of what I have called the hybrid's "mobile subjectivity" is that the animal and the human aspects of the wild man were not neatly aligned respectively with the degraded and the idealized dimensions of life. The animal could carry either, as could the human. In the case of the centaur, the "animal" aspect could connect the "human" aspect with a lost Arcadian world still present in a latent way in corrupt human culture, or it could connect the human with its own barbarous longings, particularly regarding sexual desire. Likewise, the "human" aspect could either tame the beast or corrupt its profound natural knowledge with the trappings of civilization's social controls. In this uncanny hybrid, both the animal and the human can carry both negative and positive metaphorical charges.

As a sign of the ascetic self, then, the centaur pictures a wildness that the ascetic ideal of the human unleashed at the same time as it tried to control it. Ascetics, after all, willingly courted a "wildness" that was both literal—the desert—and psychological—the unleashing of the passions. The centaur encapsulates both the hopes and the fears that centered on the person of the monk as he confronted the inner wildness that was the source of the ascetic's strength (courting temptation in order to resist it), and also his weakness (succumbing to out-of-control thoughts and feelings).[178] In this "circuit of intensities," the centaur was a paradoxical image of the monk in which animal and human forms were conjoined *and* in which contrary or different readings coexisted in a single figure.[179]

The centaur both advertises and collapses the animal-human divide. This is why it is so difficult to decide whether such a hybrid image is anthropomorphic or zoomorphic. It doesn't simply attribute human characteristics to animals, nor does it simply attribute bestial characteristics to human beings. It does both. Its dividedness is also its connectedness. In this image, human-animal intimacy is so profound that each provides the depth of the other. Finally, the centaur subverts any attempt to keep anthropomorphism and zoomorphism apart. They both have strange kinship as their fundament.

CHAPTER 4

Wild Animals

Desert Ascetics and Their Companions

In the *Historia monachorum in Aegypto* there is a curious story about Macarius the Egyptian: "After much fasting and prayer he asked God to show him the paradise which Jannes and Jambres had planted in the desert in the desire to make a copy of the true paradise."[1] Why Macarius so desired to see a simulacrum of paradise—merely a copy of the real paradise and worse, concocted by the magicians of Pharaoh—is not clear.[2] Nonetheless, off he goes, apparently with divine approval, and after much wandering in the desert, "an angel set him near the place." Although the entrances of this paradise are guarded by demons, Macarius succeeds in entering and finds two holy men. The fact that two holy men dwell in this garden gives the space a more positive aspect, which is reinforced by its large and colorful fruit, its huge trees, the springs that well up to water all of this luxurious vegetation, and Macarius's request, after spending a week there, that he might go back to his community and bring his fellow monks to this marvelous place. "Taking some of the fruit as proof" of the paradise, Macarius returns, trying—in vain, as it turns out—to persuade the monks to leave for paradise. The monks object that the garden might be a destructive hoax that, by posing as the real paradise, threatens to nullify the striving for virtue that was a mainstay of the monastic endeavor. If paradise is already at hand in this life, why continue the ascetic discipline, and what reward would there be in heaven?[3]

What goes unremarked in this story is what makes it relevant to the focus of this chapter on desert monastics and their bestial companions: in a fake paradise, there are no animals. If it is fair to say, with Peter Brown, that the monks of texts like the *Historia monachorum* "were men believed to have touched, and to have released for others, the huge, frankly physical exuberance of Adam's

Paradise," it is also fair to say that along with Adam came the animals who were made to be his companions.[4] Indeed, many interpreters of desert Christianity view stories of monks' friendly and even intimate relationships with wild animals as conceptualizations, in narrative form, of monastic life as offering the hope of the recovery of a peaceable kingdom. As Tim Vivian has noted, "The restoration of paradise is a recurrent theme in early monastic literature," and his quotation of Isaac of Nineveh, a seventh-century Syrian monk, is apposite: "The humble person approaches ravening beasts, and when their gaze rests upon him, their wildness is tamed. They come up to him as to their Master, wag their heads and tails and lick his hands and feet, for they smell coming from him that same scent that Adam exhaled before the fall, when they were gathered together before him and he gave them names in Paradise."[5] Catherine Osborne agrees. She writes, "The true holy man, unlike the city-dweller, will be in a position to recognize that the beasts are not vicious, but that they serve for us as models of justice. . . . The desert, unlike the human city, is a society in which justice is respected and nature's proper order is restored, as before the Fall. Thus the desert becomes a model of heaven."[6]

All was not entirely well between monks and animals in the desert, however. The author of the *Historia monachorum*, for example, gave as proof of the faith Egyptian monks had in Christ that "they have slain wild beasts."[7] There is a chilling example of such slaying in the *Life of Macarius of Alexandria*:

> Another time he [Macarius] dug a well in the middle of some reeds.
> There was an asp sleeping there that no one knew about. That asp
> was a killer and it was hiding in the rushes on account of the cold.
> When the sun rose, the earth warmed up. The old man came and
> stood on the earth without knowing about the asp. The asp was
> injured and bit the old man on the leg. He caught the asp alive in his
> hands and said to it, "What harm have I done to you that you attempt
> to eat me? God has not given you authority to do this; therefore it's
> your evil nature to do so. I will do to you according to your own evil
> nature." And the old man seized the two lips of the asp in his two
> hands, pulled them apart, and tore it in half down to its tail. He left it
> in two pieces and in this way the old man did not suffer at all but was
> like someone who has been struck by the point of a reed.[8]

Even if the "evil" asp is an allusion to the "cursed" serpent of Genesis 3:14, and even if Macarius's escape from suffering is an allusion to the apostle Paul's escape from harm following a bite from a viper in Acts 28:3–6—that is, even if this anecdote is a piece of hagiographical exegesis tying Macarius's life to biblical events—still I agree with Vivian that "the violent reaction of Saint Macarius is disquieting, even repulsive: it reminds us of our inherently violent natures."[9] Indeed, the repulsiveness of the violence rests in part on the fact that it is gratuitous: presumably the asp would not have bitten Macarius had he not stepped on and so injured it.

Monastic benevolence toward animals was not marred only by killing, however. Relationships with animals could also be occasions for lapses in the exercise of monastic virtues. In his *Spiritual Meadow*, John Moschos tells the story of Abba Paul in conversation with Abba Alexander.[10] Once when Alexander was visiting Paul in his cave, there was a knock on the door; Paul "went out and opened to him," and then "he took out and set before him bread and soaked peas, which he wolfed down." Alexander, thinking that the visitor was a (human) stranger, "looked through the window and saw that it was a lion." The text continues:

> I [Alexander] said to the elder, "Good elder, why do you feed that animal? Explain to me." He said: "I have required of it that it harm neither man nor beast; and I have told it to come here each day and I will give it its food. It has come twice a day now for seven months— and I feed it." Some days later I met him again . . . and I said to him, "How are things, good elder? How is the lion?" He answered, "Badly," and I asked, "How so?" He told me: "It came here to be fed yesterday and I noticed that its muzzle was all stained with blood. I said to it: 'What is this? You have disobeyed me and eaten flesh. Blessed Lord! Never again will I feed you the food of the fathers, carnivore! Get away from here.' He would not go away, so I took a rope, folded it up into three and struck it three blows with it. Then it went away."[11]

In this tale, the lion is of course guilty of disobedience, but the monk's fall from grace is worse: he has failed to embody and to enact two of the cardinal virtues of the desert, forgiveness and compassion.[12] Further, Abba Paul's beating of the animal whom he had befriended suggests that the monk had not come to terms with his own ability to inflict harm—the very trait that he was trying to reform in the lion.[13]

Despite these stories' violence and moral transgression, however, tales of monks killing or mistreating animals are rare in the literature of desert monasticism. Tim Vivian is right: "Within a larger monastic context, what is most striking about Macarius's encounter with the asp [and, I would add, Paul's with the lion] is how unrepresentative it is. . . . Although monks lived in close proximity with spiders, snakes, scorpions, jackals, wolves, and lions, most of them appeared to have lived quite peaceably with their animal companions in the desert."[14] This view of monk-and-wild-animal companionship as constituting a prelapsarian peaceable kingdom takes us partway but, I would argue, not all the way into the import of stories about desert ascetics and their encounters with wild animals, which are fraught with emotional, affective, exegetical, and ethical complexity. In fact, the various kinds of mutual entanglement between human and animal that have been analyzed in preceding chapters come stunningly to the fore in these stories of engagement. Such tales are not merely illustrative of a concept such as the realization of a lost paradise in the desert; instead, they constitute a storytelling knowledge that draws its power from an "intimacy that subtends the snare of calculative thought."[15] In this type of desert literature, understanding of human-animal relations is shaped by stories whose cognitive content cannot be separated from their storytelling form.[16] In this these tales are like the fabulae discussed in Chapter 3: they are fictitious stories picturing—and embodying—a truth.

One path that can lead into an exploration of the intercorporeal sensibility that obtains between monks and wild animals in the literature of desert asceticism is a focus on affect. As understood in contemporary affect theory, "affect arises in the midst of *in-between-ness*: in the capacities to act and be acted upon. Affect is an impingement or extrusion of a momentary or sometimes more sustained state of relation *as well as* the passage . . . of forces or intensities."[17] Denoting thus "those intensities that pass [from] body to body," affect can be defined as "those resonances that circulate about, between, and sometimes stick to bodies and worlds."[18] Overall, it seems clear that "affect is in many ways synonymous with forces of encounter"; "it marks a body's belonging to a world of encounters."[19] Thus encounter, intensity, and belonging characterize the relation that is signified by the term "affect."

Desert Ascetics, Animals, and Affect

According to Jean-Christophe Bailly, affect encompasses the entire human relation with animal worlds.[20] One of the benefits of focusing on affect is that it allows the interpreter to sidestep, even to counter, the perspective that hardens rather than loosens the supposed boundary between humans and animals. In terms of the stance that separates rather than intermingles, Maurizio Bettini has noted the centuries-old use of animals to reinforce, explain, and critique human culture. At the root of this process of representation, he argues, lies the paradox that Ludwig Wittgenstein so clearly articulated: "If lions could speak we could not understand them."[21] Animals, that is, are insuperably other, good for constructing systems of thought, but not much else. It seems to me that affect theory is one of the contemporary methods that is attempting to step away from this perspective, a perspective that has been embraced, of course, by much of the Western philosophical tradition that has defined human beings in dualistic terms as "essentially outside of nature, functioning as disembodied minds with access to timeless spiritual realms" and standing over against animals as rational subjects to irrational objects.[22] As previous chapters have noted, this perspective was articulated in religion as well as philosophy, as the ancient Christian rhetoric of domination amply demonstrates.

To exemplify the possibilities opened up by focusing on affect, I offer two stories from the modern world before turning to Christian antiquity. The first story comes from Mark Rowlands's book *The Philosopher and the Wolf.* It is an anecdote about philosopher Rowlands and his companion for ten years, a timber wolf named Brenin. Here is Rowlands's story of an encounter that affect theory would, I think, present as an instance of the inseparability of affect and cognition.[23]

> One evening, when Brenin was around a year old, I found myself in front of the TV eating the staple diet of all self-respecting U.S. bachelors—a microwaveable plate of monosodium glutamate known as a Hungry Man meal. Brenin lay next to me, watching like a hawk just in case something should tumble off the plate. The phone rang and I went to answer it, leaving the plate on the coffee table. You know when [the cartoon character] Wile E. Coyote is chasing Road Runner and he runs off the cliff? Think of the moment just after he has run off the edge, the moment when he realizes that something horrible has happened but he's not quite sure what—the moment just before he begins his mad but futile scramble back. He stands there in mid-air, frozen in place, with a look on his face that gradually transforms from enthusiasm to confusion to impending doom. It was that sort of scene that awaited me on my return to the room. Brenin, having quickly devoured my Hungry Man meal, was making his way rapidly

over to his bed on the other side of the room. My return, unwelcome but not entirely unexpected, caused him to freeze in mid-stride; one leg in front of the other, his face turned towards me and gradually coalesced into a look of Wile E. Coyote apprehension. Sometimes, just before he began his plunge into the chasm, Wile E. Coyote would hold up a sign that read "Yikes!" I'm pretty sure that if Brenin had had this sign available, he would have done the same thing. Wittgenstein once said that if a lion could talk, we would not be able to understand him. Wittgenstein was undoubtedly a genius. But, let's face it, he didn't really know much about lions. A wolf talks with his body; and it was clear what Brenin's body was saying: busted! They can talk. And what's more, we can understand them.[24]

Bodily intensity indeed! In this anecdote, an intimacy of companionship trumps calculative thought as the basis of understanding; here subjectivity does not float free of the body but is deeply embodied. In other words, this story of the encounter between philosopher and wolf embodies a forcefield of relationship, an affective relationship that is the fundament of animal-human understanding. Intimacy is key: as Georges Bataille, in a mind frame very different from that of Wittgenstein, observed, "Not being simply a thing, the animal is not closed and inscrutable to us. The animal opens before me a depth that attracts me and is familiar to me. In a sense I know this depth: it is my own."[25]

For a narrative about another kind of affective opening, here is an anecdote from zoologist David George Haskell, who in his book *The Forest Unseen* recounts his yearlong observations of a patch of forest in Tennessee.[26] He sets the scene of one day's observation as follows: a group of three raccoons, apparently unafraid, approach the spot where Haskell is sitting. Slightly anxious at the sound of continuous rustle, Haskell slowly turns his head toward the source of the noise.

My first reaction to the raccoons was that of surprise, a jolt of excitement as the strange sound resolved into the advancing trio. Then the raccoons' appealing faces came close: dark velvet masks set in crisp white borders, obsidian eyes, rounded ears perked jauntily, and slender noses. All this set in ruffs of silver fur. One thing was evident: these animals were adorable. My zoological self was immediately embarrassed by these thoughts. Naturalists are meant to have outgrown such judgments. "Cute" is for children and amateurs, especially when applied to a common animal like a raccoon. I try to see animals for what they are, independent beings, not as projections of desires leaping unbidden from my psyche. But, like it or not, the feelings were there. I wanted to pick up a raccoon and tickle it under the chin. Surely this was the ultimate humiliation of the zoologist's scientific hauteur.[27]

Here again, affect has given the lie to calculative thought as the basis of human-animal relationship. As a zoologist, Haskell has made "a clean break with the Cartesian view of animals as automatons."[28] In this story, unbidden desire—a good definition of affect, I think—trumps the kind of scientific objectivism that regards perceiving one's own animal fellow feeling as a defect.[29] Hauteur is replaced by connection and the fantasy of touch.

Both of these stories contain a certain "circuit of intensities" that founds engagement between animals and humans.[30] Such a circuit of intensities, plus a deployment of touch that goes beyond fantasy, characterizes the following set of tales from the ancient Christian desert. In a work entitled *Dialogues* written around the turn of the fifth century, the Gallic historian and hagiographer Sulpicius Severus staged a series of snapshot descriptions of monks as narratives spoken in the first person by his friend Postumianus, who had just returned from a visit to the Egyptian desert. In one of these stories, Postumianus and his guide are being entertained by a monk who had, in concert with his one ox, created a mini-paradise in the desert sand, using water from a well to produce a flourishing vegetable garden. After dinner, the monk invites his guests to accompany him to a date tree (to get dessert), and there they meet up with a lion. The visitors quake with fear; meanwhile, the monk picks some dates and holds them out to the lion, who runs up and takes the dates just "as readily as any domestic animal could have done," eats them, and then runs back off into the desert.[31] This is a striking portrayal of the kind of spirituality spawned by the desert from this text's point of view, which attributes the intercourse of the monk with the lion to the power of his faith. Especially notable is the juxtaposition of fear and familiarity. To the visitors, the lion is a terrifying monster; to the holy man, it is a fellow denizen of the desert as deserving of the gift of food as the human beings and clearly accustomed to receiving it. Bodily gesture and touch—the outstretched hand from which the lion eats—found and sustain their relationship, which resonates with unspoken but very real feeling. Monk and lion belong together in the charmed circle of their intimacy.

In another of Sulpicius's narratives, two monks from Nitria spend seven months seeking an especially virtuous anchorite who had once been a member of their monastery. They find him, and, after spending time together, the anchorite is seeing the monks off on their homeward journey when the group is approached by a lioness "of astonishing size" (*leaenam mirae magnitudinis*). She makes a beeline for the virtuous anchorite and, weeping, throws herself at his feet, expressing both sorrow and supplication. All of the monks were moved, "especially the one [the anchorite] who perceived that he was sought for" (*movet omnes et praecipue illum, qui se intellexerat expetitum*). The lioness makes it clear that the men should follow her: stopping and looking back from time to time, she "clearly made it understood that the anchorite should follow wherever she led" (*facile poterat intelligi id eam velle, ut quo illa ducebat*). At her den are her five cubs, all blind. The lioness deposits them one by one at the feet of the holy man who, finally understanding what she wants, touches their closed eyes with his hand, healing them. Some days later, the lioness brings the monk the gift of an exotic animal's skin, which he accepts and wears with gratitude.[32]

This story of the grateful lioness is akin to the story of the date-eating lion by virtue of their implicit rejection of the rhetoric of human domination of animals that seems to have been something of a default mode in ancient Christian theology. In these stories, there is no hint of hierarchical relationships that would position the animals as ontologically or mentally lower or inferior to the human beings with whom they interact. Interestingly in this regard, both stories link human holiness with friendly encounters with animals, whose fearsome mien does not deter the monks in their gestures of care. Here religion—in the form of Christian faith and holiness—is actually what enables human-animal relations, as the animals recognize and seek out the virtuous ascetics. These stories give expression to a different kind of subjectivity when compared with the rhetoric that positions humans as rational and animals as irrational. This is very clear in the story of the lioness, whom the text links with the anchorite by applying the verb "intellegere" (to perceive or understand) to them both. As subjects, they share a perceptual bond. The intensity of the resonance that circulates between them, to use the language of affect theory, is based not on calculative reason but rather on compassionate understanding on the part of the monk, who has been moved by the animal's emotion, and on the lioness's intelligent use of her body, especially her gaze, to achieve her goal of leading the monk to her cubs. They share a sensibility, and they also share touch: their belonging is deeply physical in terms both of the monk's healing touch of the cubs' eyes and the lioness's gift of an animal skin, which the monk dons. This gift exchange—of sight and skin—concludes with a very poignant image of animal-human entanglement, as the reader visualizes the anchorite clothed in an animal's pelt.

Intimacy as a chief characteristic of encounters between humans and wild animals in the desert is powerfully on display in the final two stories that I use to delineate the intercorporeal sensibility that comes into view when affect is the interpretive key. The first concerns Abba Macarius of Egypt:

> When Abba Macarius was speaking openly to the brothers, he said, "One time when I was in the wadi gathering palm branches, an antelope came up to me, tearing out her fur, weeping as though she were a he-goat, her tears flowing to the ground. She threw herself down on top of my feet and moistened them with her tears, and I sat down and stroked her face and anointed it with my hands, amazed at her tears, while she gazed back at me. After a while, she took hold of my tunic and pulled on me. I followed her through the power of our Lord Jesus Christ and when she took me to where she lived, I found her three young lying there. When I sat down, she took hold of them one by one and placed them in my lap and when I touched them I found that they were deformed: their chins were on their backs. I took pity on them as their mother wept; I groaned over them, saying, "You who care for all creation, our Lord Jesus Christ, who have numerous treasures of mercy, take pity on the creature you made." After I said these words accompanied by tears before my Lord Jesus Christ, I stretched out my hand and made the saving sign of the cross over the antelope's young, and they were healed. When I put them down, their mother immediately gave them her attention. They went underneath to her nipples and sucked her milk. She rejoiced over them, delighting in them, looking into my eyes with great joy. I marveled at the goodness of God and the love for humanity of our Lord Jesus Christ as shown by his tender mercies for me and for the other beasts he cares about.[33]

Here is a mute but profoundly communicative interspecies relationship, a "living flow of transactional energies between one animal and another," to quote Mark Payne's description of imaginative sympathy.[34] Locked together as subjects by their mutual gaze and their mutual tears, the monk Macarius and the antelope are enmeshed in what Virginia Burrus, in another context, has called "a radical relationality of bodies."[35] After all, Macarius places humans and animals on a par when he positions them all as creatures showered with divine mercy: Christ cares for Macarius *and for the other beasts.*

The intimacy of this relationship is expressed in gestures of touch: the antelope's weeping prostration upon the monk's feet, the monk's caress of the animal's face, and his holding of her young in his lap. Further, the human and the animal are each the object of the other's perception, and each exercises dynamic agency as the antelope tugs at the tunic of the monk and the monk, following, takes pity and makes the healing sign of the cross over the young animals. Here is a compassion born from fellow feeling; as Vivian remarks, a "universal language of suffering" marks human and animal belonging.[36]

This tale of animal-human encounter, which turns on the twin themes of shared creatureliness and compassionate contact, is shadowed by a biblical image.[37] As I remarked above, stories of desert monks and their animal companions are not just ciphers for ideas like paradise regained; they are complex tales, and exegesis—that is to say, biblical allusion of various kinds—is sometimes part of that complexity. The story of Macarius of Egypt and the antelope, like the story of Macarius of Alexandria and the asp at the beginning of this chapter, has such an exegetical dimension. The action of the weeping antelope who moistens the monk's feet with her tears recalls the scene in the Gospel of Luke in which a sinful woman wets the feet of Jesus with her tears. This allusion casts Macarius in the role of Jesus and so gives a scriptural anchor to his healing abilities. Oddly, though, when Macarius then anoints the face of the animal, *he* enacts the role of the sinful woman, who anointed Jesus' feet with the ointment she had brought with her.[38] Their intersubjectivity is such that monk and animal inhabit the same scriptural persona, a figure whose affect is expressed by touch. Thus in the Gospel of Luke as well as the *Virtues of Saint Macarius*, touch is the primary medium for the imparting of forgiveness and love in the biblical story and of compassion for all of creation in the monastic tale.

In the story of Macarius and the antelope, one aspect of the affective "circuit of intensity" that characterizes the relationship between the human and the animal is their mutual gazing into each other's eyes. Such gazing was, of course, a form of touch, since many in Greco-Roman antiquity thought that the eye and its gaze were active rather than passive, the eye sending out rays to touch the object of its vision. From this perspective, seeing was connective and embodied, in a word, participatory in effecting an intertwining of the two gazers.[39] Monk and antelope thus share a subjectivity constituted by their mutual exercise of the gaze that touches.

The deep sense of touch as the fundament for the relationship between animal and human in the foregoing story is, if anything, deepened in the following tale, this time a tale about Macarius of Alexandria.[40] Macarius relates that on one occasion, while traveling in the desert, he ran out of water and bread. In the midst of this life-threatening situation, he saw a herd of antelope and went up to it.

> [Macarius said], . . . "[One of the antelope] immediately turned over
> and [showed] me her breasts streaming with milk. Then I knew right
> away that God wished to keep me alive and I heard a voice, 'Macarius,
> arise, go to the antelope, drink the milk, and recover your strength
> and go to your cell.'" He went and drank her milk and slept a little.
> The antelope went away and one of them, either her or another one,
> gave him milk each day. "And [Macarius continues in the first person]
> when I drew near my cell and was a day's walk from it, all the antelope
> went away and left me. I returned to my cell on the eighth day."[41]

This tale presents a truly radical relationality of bodies. Here we see not just a monk clothed in an animal's skin, like the virtuous monk in Sulpicius's *Dialogues*; instead, Macarius takes the animal's very substance, her milk, into his body. In that sense, the two become one. Further, the tale has not just an affective but also an ethical dimension: the lactating antelope who offers her body to the monk in peril demonstrates what Kate Rigby, discussing the parable of the Good Samaritan (Lk. 10:25–37), has called a "corporeal capacity to be touched by the plight of another."[42] Animal-human intimacy has reached its apex in this story of compassionate contact. The magnanimous gesture of the antelope might well be described, in Jane Bennett's terms, as an instance in which affect has been disciplined into "a sensibility of generosity."[43]

Ethics and Emotion: The Lion

Although affect will continue as an important feature of tales of desert ascetics' relationships with animals, I turn now to two final stories, each of which will receive extended treatment, that feature ethics and exegesis along with affect and emotion. The animal featured in the first of these stories is a lion. As told by John Moschus in his late fifth- or early sixth-century work entitled *The Spiritual Meadow*, this lion, roaring with pain from a paw inflamed from a wound made by an embedded reed tip, met up with the saintly head of a monastery, Abba Gerasimos, on the banks of the Jordan River. The lion showed the monk his paw, "whimpering and begging some healing of him." Responding to the distress of the animal, Gerasimos sat down, cleansed and bandaged the wound, and told the lion to leave. "But the healed lion would not leave the elder. It followed him like a noble disciple [ὡς γνήσιος μαθητὴς] wherever he went. The elder was amazed at the gentle disposition of the beast [τὴν τοσαύτην εὐγνωμοσύνην τοῦ θηρίου] and, from then on, he began feeding it, throwing it bread and boiled vegetables." As the story continues, the monks of the lavra in effect adopted the lion and gave it the responsibility of pasturing the ass that fetched their water from the river. One day, when the ass had wandered off a bit, some Arabian camel drivers stole the ass.

> Having lost the ass, the lion came back to the lavra and approached Abba Gerasimos, very downcast and dismayed. The Abba thought that the lion had devoured the ass. He said to it: "Where is the ass?" The beast stood silent, hanging its head, very much like a man [ὥσπερ ἄνθρωπος]. The elder said to it: "Have you eaten it? Blessed be God! From henceforth you are going to perform whatever duties the ass performed!" From that time on, at the elder's command, the lion used to carry the saddlepack containing the four earthenware vessels and bring water.

Fortunately for the lion, the camel driver who had stolen the ass returned to the area with the ass in tow to sell grain and, crossing the Jordan, found himself face to face with the lion. He ran away in fear, and the lion, recognizing the ass, took it as well as three camels back to the monastery. "It brought them to the elder, rejoicing and roaring at having found the ass which it had lost. The elder had thought that the lion had eaten the ass, but now he realized that the lion had been falsely accused. He named the beast Jordanes and it lived with the elder in the lavra, never leaving his side, for five years." The story concludes with the death and burial of Abba Gerasimos, which occurred when the lion was not in the lavra. When it came back, it searched for its companion. The rest of the story deserves to be quoted in full.

> The elder's disciple, Abba Sabbatios [the Cilician], saw it and said to it: "Jordanes, our elder has left us orphans, for he has departed to the Lord; but come here, eat something." The lion, however, would not

eat, but continually turned his eyes this way and that, hoping to see its elder. It roared mightily, unable to tolerate this bereavement. When Abba Sabbatios and the rest of the fathers saw it, they stroked its mane and said to it: "The elder has gone away to the Lord and left us," yet even by saying this they did not succeed in silencing its cries and lamentations. The more they tried to mollify and comfort it by their words, the more it roared. The louder were its cries by which it expressed its grief; for it showed by its voice, its countenance and by its eyes the sorrow which it felt at not being able to see the elder. Then Abba Sabbatios said to it: "Since you do not believe us, come with me and I will show you where our elder lies." He took the lion and led it to where they had buried the elder. The spot was about half a mile from the church. Abba Sabbatios stood above the grave of Abba Gerasimos and said to the lion: "See, this is where our elder is," and he knelt down. When the lion saw how he prostrated himself, it began beating its head against the ground and roaring, then it promptly died; there, on top of the elder's grave.

This did not take place because the lion had a rational soul [ψυχὴ λογικὴ] but because it is the will of God to glorify those who glorify him—and to show how the beasts were in subjection to Adam before he disobeyed the commandment and fell from the comfort of paradise.[44]

The end of this story tries to explain away the lion's extraordinary persona and behavior by invoking the now-familiar anthropocentric position that denies rational subjectivity—or indeed any subjectivity at all apart from instinct—to animals. But the features of the story itself, which presents a picture of a "living flow of transactional energies" across species if there ever were such, refutes the anthropocentric conclusion.[45]

Prior to exploring the various dimensions of this complex tale, a few comments on its Greco-Roman context are in order. As Robert M. Grant observed, "Stories about lions and their humane relations with human beings were not uncommon in the first century."[46] Pliny, for example, tells a simplified version of the tale of Androcles and the lion in which a man pulled a thorn out of a lion's foot and so "set the creature free from torment."[47] An expanded version of this tale a century later in Aelian's *On the Nature of Animals*, which narrates the subsequent relations of friendship between the human and the lion, may well be the prototype upon which John Moschus modeled his Christianized version of

the story, especially given the fact that Aelian's story "portrays a lion who is
equal to, or better than, the man, in intelligence, in memory, and in the power
of communication," as Catherine Osborne has remarked.[48] Although Aelian
noted lions' carnivorous ferocity elsewhere in his work, he was taken with the
notion of a tame lion:

> If he [a lion] has been domesticated since the time when he was a cub,
> he is extremely gentle and agreeable to meet, and is fond of play, and
> will submit with good temper to any treatment to please his keeper.
> For instance, Hanno [a Carthaginian general] kept a lion to carry his
> baggage; a tame lion was the companion of Berenice [a Ptolemaic
> queen?] and was no different from her slaves: for example, it would
> softly wash her face with its tongue and smooth away her wrinkles; it
> would share her table and eat in a sober, orderly fashion just like a
> human being. And Onomarchus, the Tyrant of Catana, and the son
> of Cleomenes both had lions with them as table-companions.[49]

Christians, too, imagined lions that, if not exactly pets, were at least either submissive to humans or else protective of them.[50] Hippolytus of Rome, for example,
had heard doubts expressed about the story of Daniel escaping harm in the lions'
den. In response he declared that the lions "rejoiced by shaking their tails as if
submissive to a new Adam; they licked the holy feet of Daniel and rolled on
his footprints in their desire to be trodden by him."[51] In addition to Gerasimos
and his lion, John Moschus offered this brief vignette: "There was another elder
at that place [the Jordanian desert] whose virtue was so great that he would wel-
come the lions which came into his cave and feed them at his lap, so full of divine
grace was this man."[52] Finally, there was the famously protective lioness who kept
the martyr Thecla safe in the arena, as well as the helpful lions who showed up
unexpectedly to bury the desert saints Mary of Egypt and Paul of Thebes.[53]

Even in art one can find the motif of the tame or peaceable lion, as in the
image of the grinning lion with demurely crossed paws pictured in Figure 8.[54]
Oddly enough, given the prominent role of lions in the blood sport of the gladi-
atorial arena, there was clearly a cultural expectation that lions can be friendly,
so friendly in fact as to be pets. To return to the story of Gerasimos and *his* lion
with "the gentle disposition," as John Moschus describes him: asking about the
meaning of this tale, Blake Leyerle remarks, "It is certainly possible that a Palestinian monastery had a tame lion that was known to pasture the community's
donkey."[55] However, she goes on to argue, "this story, with its 'narrative luxury,'

FIGURE 8. Lion, detail of mosaic, Mount Nebo (*Mosaics of Jordan*, fig. 219
on p. 169). Chapel of the Priest John at Khirbat-al-Mukhayyat, Jordan, 565 CE.
Courtesy of the Franciscan Custody of the Holy Land, Mount Nebo,
and the American Center of Oriental Research, Amman.

appears to function semiotically every bit as much as Aesop's fables."[56] Leyerle
here uses the provocative phrase "narrative luxury," which is a nod in the direction of Roland Barthes's "reality-effect," a hyperrealistic or pictorially theatrical
narrative that creates an illusion of reality that masks its own complexity. In
doing so, her perspective, especially in its brief but telling reference to fable,
dovetails nicely with my own view of such early Christian animal stories as
fabulae, deceptively profound fictions, often with a subversive edge, that picture
a truth (or truths).[57]

The lion-as-pet motif certainly carries this story's narrative excess, since in fact lions like the full-grown Jordanes eat massive amounts of raw meat (not boiled vegetables and bread), and, "even when born in captivity and hand-raised, these wild animals [lions and tigers] retain their predatory instincts. They can (and do) injure and kill people."[58] We have seen above that friendly relations with lions had a cultural appeal in antiquity; what underlies the charming surface of the story of Gerasimos and his leonine companion? In her analysis, Leyerle uncovers two ways in which the tale signifies, one theological and one ethical. First, theology: as she remarks, the story's purpose "is undoubtedly theological— to provide a 'living example' of how monasticism is even now instantiating the peaceable kingdom."[59] Even more striking is the story's portrayal of what Leyerle calls "behavior modification": the lion becomes a monk, eating a vegetarian diet, doing menial work, and thus overcoming its reputation for pride, overall living "the exemplary life of a devoted disciple."[60] I would add that this anthropomorphization of the lion has two further theological effects. On the one hand, the conversion of lion to monk constitutes a virtual Christian takeover of animal wildness; monastic Christianity is positioned as the civilizing force par excellence, but it achieves this victory over supposed natural savagery at the expense of the animal. On the other hand, the presentation of the lion in this story as a creature who befriends and understands human beings and adopts a monastic lifestyle endows the animal with a subjectivity that undermines the story's denial of a rational soul to the lion, thus subverting the hierarchical ontology upon which Christian theological anthropocentrism was dependent.

As for ethics, Leyerle argues that the story's "protreptic" purpose is "to shame prideful monks with the example of an obedient lion."[61] This reading in effect places John Moschus's tale in the tradition of Basil of Caesarea's treatment of animals in his *Hexaemeron*. As discussed in earlier chapters, Basil often presented animals as exemplars of ethical comportment intended to expose and so to transform human misbehavior. Especially interesting is Leyerle's placement of this story in the context of Christian mosaics of the peaceable kingdom. Such mosaics dramatically revise mosaics of the hunt by showing animals coexisting companionably rather than killing each other. Both the Christian mosaics and stories such as that of Gerasimos and the lion "have as their subject ethical formation . . . . Instead of domination, the ideal is restraint."[62] Leyerle elaborates this point as follows:

> When elite males were encouraged to dominate over their passions,
> they were both trained and entitled to exercise dominion over subor-

dinate others such as women, slaves, barbarians, and, of course, animals. Early Christian monastics, to the contrary, were encouraged to restrain themselves. And it is this formation that explains the remarkably consistent hesitation of monastics to eat meat, to assume positions of leadership, or even to give advice. In Greco-Roman terms, such behavior was servile, appropriate only for the dominated factions, for, if you will, the donkeys. The tale of Jordanes asserts, to the contrary, that it is leonine. Thus the animal stories from the desert, like those of Aesop, can sustain a reading that challenges the status quo.[63]

The subversive aspect of the Gerasimos-Jordanes story, on this reading, concerns not the undermining of the rhetoric that denied subjectivity to animals but rather the championing of a monastic ideal of self-control with a lion as its model. Moving from nature to culture, the figure of a domesticated lion functions to revise the character of both.[64]

Yet another interpretive twist on the story of Gerasimos and the lion is offered by Catherine Osborne. Noting the lion's "lack of verbal resources," she focuses on the moment in the story in which the lion, having lost the ass, returns to the monastery "downcast and dismayed."[65] Confronted by Abba Gerasimos and accused of eating the ass, the lion can only hang his head. The accusation is, as the reader of the story knows, false: "The abbot unjustly accuses the lion of a crime it did not commit, because he cannot understand the innocent dumb beast. Gerasimos is too quick to assume that he knows, and too stupid to understand the animal."[66] Osborne goes on to observe that the lion "wouldn't dream of eating the monastery donkey, yet he accepts his undeserved disgrace with Christ-like fortitude."[67] Her overall point is that this episode in the story shows the animal to be ethically superior to the monks. Noting that the humans in this tale "underestimate the moral capacities of the beasts," she continues as follows:

> Gerasimos's lion was more self-controlled than the monks gave it credit for. They were wrong to jump to the conclusion that it had slipped back into its beastly ways, or that it had (all too predictably) fallen into temptation. They jumped instantly to that conclusion because they misjudged the capacities of beasts, and they assumed that beasts were basically beastly and were readily tempted to be beastly. In the hagiographic context, this is a telling criticism, for the

trials of the desert focus heavily on the difficulty that human beings
have in resisting temptation, and how hard it is to avoid falling into
beastly ways, even when they put themselves well beyond the reach of
the things that would tempt them to impurity. Humans—even
saintly ones—are quick to imagine that animals are beastly, but in
reality the natural beasts are the human beings.[68]

The dignity of the animal and the cruelty and ultimate remorse of the human
being are paramount in this reading of the story. Significantly, once Abba Gerasimos realizes his mistake, he gives the lion a name, Jordanes. The unjust accusation is undone, as it were, by an act that recognizes the subjectivity of the animal,
and thus the disturbed state of relation between human and animal is overcome.

This overcoming of the disturbed state of relation between human and
animal implicitly taps into what Richard Bauckham has called "the classic
scriptural expression of the hope of peace between humans and wild animals,"
Isaiah 11:6–9:

> The wolf shall dwell with the lamb,
> and the leopard shall lie down with the kid,
> and the calf and the lion and the fatling together,
> and a little child shall lead them.
> The cow and the bear shall feed;
> their young shall lie down together;
> and the lion shall eat straw like the ox.
> The suckling child shall play over the hole of the asp,
> and the weaned child shall put his hand on the adder's den.
> They shall not hurt or destroy
> in all my holy mountain;
> for the earth shall be full of the
> knowledge of the Lord
> as the waters cover the sea. (RSV)[69]

The obedient, devoted lion certainly fits into this expression of eschatological
harmony that is realized, in the final analysis, in the relationship of Gerasimos
and Jordanes. What the lion does not fit—except initially in the faulty judgment
of the monk—is the frequent scriptural figuring of lions as ravening and destructive beasts.[70] The echoes of paradise regained really do seem to reverberate
through ancient Christian lions.[71]

A more explicit scriptural dimension of this text concerns the bestowal of a name. This act of naming positions Gerasimos as Adam, who gave his companion animals names in Eden. Here once again is the peaceable kingdom motif, which, in this part of the story, seems centered precisely on companionship: once named, the lion did not leave the abba's side for five years. The conclusion of this tale is a remarkable portrait of cross-species intimacy. Once Abba Gerasimos dies, the affective and emotional depth of that intimacy becomes clear. The lion expresses his grief with his restless gazing, his sorrowful eyes, his cries and roaring. So deep is his feeling that it evokes the compassionate stroking of his mane by the other monks in an attempt to console him. This lion may "lack verbal resources," as Osborne noted, but just as surely as Brenin the wolf, Jordanes can talk. He talks with his body, and the humans around him understand his expressions of loss. As Marc Bekoff has remarked, "Animal emotions are not restricted to 'instinctual responses,' but entail what seems to be a good deal of conscious thought."[72] Darwin proved long before Bekoff's work that animals share with humans what he specified as six universal emotions: happiness, sadness, anger, fear, disgust, and surprise; newer research shows that they express a wide range of secondary emotions as well.[73]

The inconsolable grief of Jordanes the lion would not have been a surprise to Darwin. Indeed, the story of Gerasimos and Jordanes seems to me to anticipate what Bekoff calls "a paradigm shift in how we think about animals and how we study animal emotions and animal sentience."[74] The story pictures a social, emotional, and affective bond between humans and an animal that breaks the stereotypes of animal (and human) behavior fostered by ancient Christian anthropocentrism. Further, insofar as the end of this story—the lion's grief and its death—turns upon a "language of feelings," to borrow a phrase from Bekoff, it can be compared to other, earlier stories in Greco-Roman antiquity in which animals feel deeply and cognitively.[75] Pliny, for example, told stories of dolphins in love with young men. In one of them, "the boy became ill and died. The dolphin kept returning to their usual meeting-place—saddened, like one in mourning—and eventually died; no one doubted that it was out of longing [*desiderio*] for the boy."[76] The story of Jordanes the lion repeats this motif of intense longing and subsequent death. Is the tale of Gerasimos and Jordanes ultimately a love story? Although it lacks the technical vocabulary of love, its emotional evocation of deep affection between a human being and an animal highlights the cross-species relationships that the desert fostered in the ancient Christian imagination. Here indeed is "an intimacy that subtends the snare of calculative thought."[77]

In interpreting such stories of relationships between monks and wild animals, my approach is like that of Craig Williams in his study of tales about animal-human love. He writes of such material, "I suspend questions of historicity (did a dolphin *really* fall in love with a young man of Pozzuoli in the time of Augustus?)."[78] I likewise suspend questions of historicity. Thus I do not ask whether there was really a monk who had a lion as his constant companion in a Palestinian monastery in the late Roman Empire. Instead I join Williams in reading these narratives *as narratives*, looking for "recurrent patterns and considering what kinds of answers this body of material suggests" for the question of the shaping of the ancient Christian zoological imagination.[79] I add these comments here (which are really just another way of stating the point I made earlier in this chapter about narrative luxury) because the final story of this chapter's discussion of monks and their wild-animal companions is so seductive in its realism that one might forget its function in ancient Christian storytelling knowledge about human-animal relationships.

Ethics and Emotion: The She-Wolf

Here once again is a tale from the *Dialogues* of Sulpicius Severus. In this portrayal of a quiet intimacy that is disrupted and then touchingly reinstated, one can clearly see both how affect can be disciplined into a magnanimous sensibility and how ethics plays a role in the circuit of intensities between bodies. Set in the Upper Thebaid of Egypt, the story concerns the relationship between a monk and his companion, a she-wolf. Postumianus, Sulpicius's narrator, recounts the following:

> We saw another remarkable man living in an impoverished hut that could hold only one person at a time. Concerning him we were told that a she-wolf [*lupa*] was accustomed to stand near him at his meal, and that the beast [*bestia*] never failed to come at the appointed time or to wait by the door until the man offered her whatever bread had been left over from his meager meal. Then she would lick his hand and, as if her duty were done and the comfort of her presence given, she would go away. But it once so happened that this holy man, escorting on his way home a brother who had come to visit him, was gone a long time and did not get home until nightfall. Meanwhile the beast had come at the usual mealtime. Sensing that her friendly patron

[*familiarem patronum*] was absent, she entered the vacant cell, curious to find where its inhabitant might be. As it happened, a palm basket containing five loaves of bread was hanging close at hand. She
took one of these and devoured it and then, having committed the
wicked deed, she took off. When he returned, the hermit saw his little
basket damaged and missing a loaf. Realizing, then, the loss of his
household goods, he recognized near the threshold some crumbs
from the stolen loaf; he had little doubt as to the identity [*persona*] of
the thief. Then as the days went by and the beast did not come as she
used to do—[being] too conscious of her audacious act to come to the
one she had wronged and affect innocence—the hermit suffered
greatly at the loss of the comforting presence of his pet [*alumnae sola-
cio*]. Finally, called back through his prayers, there she was after seven
days, as he sat at his meal as of old. But it was easy to perceive the penitent's feeling of shame [*verecundiam paenitentis*]: she did not dare to
come near, her eyes fixed in profound shame [*profundo pudore*] upon
the ground and, as was obvious to see, begging for forgiveness. Pitying
her confusion, the hermit bade her come close and with a caressing
hand [*manu blanda*] he stroked the sad head [*caput triste permulcet*],
and he refreshed his penitent with two loaves for the one. And she,
forgiveness won and her grieving ended, resumed her usual practice.
Behold, I beg you, in this example of it the power of Christ, with
whom every brute beast [*brutum*] is wise, and every savage creature
gentle. A she-wolf discharges duty! A she-wolf acknowledges the
crime of theft! A she-wolf is confounded with a sense of shame!
When called for, she presents herself; she offers her head to be
stroked; and she has a perception [*sensum*] of the pardon granted to
her, just as if she had a feeling of shame on account of her misconduct.
This is your power, O Christ, these, O Christ, are your miracles.[80]

This text wavers intriguingly between denigration and elevation of the animal.
On the one hand, the she-wolf is described as *bestia* and *brutum*, terms that relegate animals to a savage, irrational realm. On the other hand, she is endowed
with a persona, which puts her on a par with human subjectivity, and she is
called the monk's *alumna*, which in the context of the story can properly be
translated as "pet," but the word itself designates the one so described as a "foster
daughter" or "disciple." In my reading, the text's elevation of the animal wins out
over its anthropocentric aspects in part due to the ending, in which a "beast"

being made "wise" is attributed to the power of Christ. It is the value of the animal as a vehicle of divine action that is affirmed, not human superiority.

In any case, Sulpicius has crafted a story full of verve, visual power, and raw affect. Indeed, it is precisely the story's drama, its appeal to the mind's eye, and its strong emotion that contribute to its realism. In terms of realism, here once again is an ancient presentation of an animal and its emotion that seems remarkably consonant with contemporary ethological findings. I have already referred several times to Bekoff's detailed study of the complex emotions of mammals and his view that, "lacking a shared language, emotions are perhaps our most effective means of cross-species communication."[81] Wolves, in particular, are notable for their amiability and friendliness. According to a leading expert on lupine behavior, "It appears that the personality of the wolf is related most directly to the animal's social nature. Probably the creature's strongest personality trait is its capacity for making emotional attachment to other individuals."[82]

When Sulpicius describes the wolf of his story with the term "sensum," a word that connotes a form of perception and feeling that is both corporeal and mental, and when he endows her with complex emotions, he would seem to align his wolf (several centuries early) with the best of ethological research—except that the ethologists' observations pertain to intraspecies, not cross-species, lupine emotions.[83] Here is one place where the story's narrative luxury shows itself, as it does not only with the lupa's friendliness toward the monk but also with her strong expressions of shame (*pudor* and *verecundia*), expressions that anthropomorphize her because they carry such heavy cultural and religious freight. As we shall see later in this chapter, this tale's cross-species exchanges are a significant feature, not of ethology, but rather of the ways in which early Christian storytelling subverts Christianity's anthropocentric bias by picturing the mutual entanglement of human and animal.

As we saw in Leyerle's argument concerning the story of Gerasimos and the lion, a story's narrative luxury suggests its semiotic, rather than realist, function. So also in Sulpicius's tale: a further indication of its narrative luxury is its positioning of the wolf as the monk's friendly pet. According to an eminent student of the ecology of wolves, David Mech, "the wolf is one of the wildest and shyest of all animals" and, although it *is* possible to tame wolves (as the story of philosopher Mark Rowlands and his wolf Brenin attests), socializing them is difficult and time consuming; Mech concludes that it is not a good idea.[84] In antiquity, Basil stated forthrightly: "The wolf is untameable."[85] In addition, wolves were thought to be loners "of a solitary habit, who walk alone and love solitude," as Augustine, for one, attests.[86] In light of both ancient views and modern observations, then, the wolf as pet is not a convincing scenario when read literally. A final blow to the supposed realism of this story pertains to diet. It was as well known in antiquity as it is today that wolves are meat-eating predators; indeed, "a wolf can consume almost twenty pounds of prey at a feeding"; thus it is highly unlikely, in fact impossible, that a wolf could subsist on even two loaves of bread, let alone the crumbs left over from an ascetic's humble meal.[87]

If, then, one suspends questions of historical veracity, what does this narratively rich tale connote? Recall that narrative luxury is one way to describe the phenomenon that Barthes named "the reality effect," in which narratives use alluring details in order to instantiate themselves in historical reality.[88] The "effect of the real" makes "the reader believe the truth of the illusion that is being constructed."[89] In this kind of narrative, representation rests on poetic or figural effects rather than on straightforward perception and description. The remainder of this chapter's discussion focuses precisely on the figural effects of the story of the monk and the wolf. In Sulpicius's zoological imagination, ethics as well as emotional bonding are paramount in the animal-human relationship that the story depicts, but the story is also interestingly contextualized by the wolf's figural significance in scripture and patristic thought as well as in Greco-Roman culture; to these I turn first.

Scripturally speaking, wolves did not fare any better than lions in terms of negative portrayals. Here are a few examples from the Hebrew Bible. Genesis 49:27 says, "Benjamin is a ravening wolf, in the morning devouring the prey, and at evening dividing the spoil."[90] Jeremiah 5:6 presents a similar picture: "Therefore a lion from the forest shall slay them, a wolf from the desert shall destroy them." Ezekiel 22:27 agrees: "Judah's princes are like wolves tearing prey, shedding blood, destroying lives to get dishonest gain." Even in the eschatological context of Isaiah 11:6 as quoted above, "the wolf shall dwell with the lamb," the vision of peace works only because opposites—the predatory wolf and the meek lamb—are paradoxically at one with each other. Moving to the New Testament, one finds the familiar image of the wolf in sheep's clothing, as in Matthew 7:15: "Beware of false prophets, who come to you in sheep's clothing but inwardly are ravenous wolves." The New Testament is consistent in imagining dangerous or violent people as wolves. In Acts 20:29, for example, Paul says: "I know that after my departure fierce wolves will come in among you, not sparing the flock."

This unrelentingly negative image of the wolf was carried on by patristic authors. Clement of Alexandria, for example, defined wolves clad in sheepskins as beasts of prey in the form of human beings.[91] Irenaeus was more specific, using the image of wolves in sheep's clothing to portray arch-heretics, the Valentinians.[92] For Athanasius, one of St. Antony's tormenting demons took the form of "an onrushing wolf [that] made straight for him."[93] John Moschus told the story of one Cyriacos the robber: "He became so cruel and inhuman that they called him 'the wolf.'"[94] Perhaps we should simply let Origen have the last word, patristically speaking: "A wolf is never referred to with a good connotation."[95]

Given this powerful and one-sided interpretive tradition, which lies in the background of our modern, cartoonish stereotype, "the Big Bad Wolf," it is very interesting that, aside from her one rash act as a starving animal devouring a loaf of bread, Sulpicius's lupa does not conform to the scriptural and patristic image of the fearsome wolf. Indeed, his representation of the lupa is one of the most positive anthropomorphic images in ancient Christian literature, so strikingly does it characterize the she-wolf's relationship with the monk in terms drawn from the Roman social order. Thus the she-wolf is situated socially in the late Roman system of patronage: the monk is described as her *familiarem patronum*, her friendly patron, and she then is his client. The patron-client relationship was a hierarchical one, with the patron occupying a higher social, economic, and political position and the client occupying a lower one. While hierarchical, this relationship was a mutual one that entailed reciprocity: the patron offered various kinds of protection, financial and otherwise, and the client offered loyalty and witness to the largesse of the patron.[96] The *patronus*-monk's largesse, in Sulpicius's story, is presumably the crumbs that he offers to the she-wolf each day, and her thanks and support take the form of licks and her "comforting presence." Intriguingly, though couched in the language of patronage, the monk-wolf relationship actually works to undo its terms. Crumbs of bread are hardly comparable to a real patron's wealth, and the wolf's bestowal of her comforting presence bespeaks a warmth of relationship not characteristic of the patronage system. In this story, reciprocity trumps hierarchy—and the devoted she-wolf, described as the monk's alumna—disciple or foster daughter—trumps the negative figure of scripture's ravening beast.

How can one account for Sulpicius's positive figuring of his lupa, especially given the harsh portrayal of wolves in scripture and patristic literature? In light of his use of biblical imagery in his *Life of Saint Martin* and other writings, one can certainly not accuse Sulpicius of ignorance of the Bible.[97] In fact, the ending of his story of the monk and the wolf itself betrays his knowledge of the traditional characterization of wolves as the text breaks into exclamations that show how surprisingly different this she-wolf really is: "A wolf discharges its duty! A wolf acknowledges the crime of theft! A wolf is confounded with a sense of shame!" One can almost hear Sulpicius's exclamations of delight at the transgressive image that he has crafted. Sulpicius has, I suggest, engaged in what Burrus has called "allusive citation," which in this case is a form of citation that turns its host image upside down.[98] Also helpful for understanding the transgressive aspect of Sulpicius's image of the she-wolf is Derrida's notion of the supplement, "a word that suggests both 'addition to' and 'replacement for' an original text or practice."[99] While claiming to add on to an original, the supplement actually displaces it. As a supplement in Derrida's sense, the she-wolf alludes to the biblical wolf but reconstitutes its reality, effectively replacing the image of a head that has a ravening mouth with a head that can be gently stroked. This wolf, then, is a source and lure of meaning that focuses attention on issues beyond the predatory physicality of the biblical image that is one of its allusive precursors. In its impossible reality, that is, Sulpicius's lupa recontextualizes the scriptural and patristic image of the wolf for work in a far different context.

The broadest context is one that I have repeatedly drawn attention to in previous chapters, namely, the scholarly position that ancient Christianity was based entirely in metaphysical anthropocentrism and thus denigrated both animals and animality per se. Although, as we have seen, there *was* a theological rhetoric, as presented by such notables as Basil of Caesarea, John Chrysostom, and Augustine, that did in fact disparage animal life as brutish and possessed only of an irrational soul, we have also seen that it is incorrect to suppose that all Christian literature embraced what philosopher Giorgio Agamben termed the "anthropological machine," a perspective in Western thought that supports reductive binary oppositions between humans and animals.[100] Stories like that of Sulpicius's monk and wolf offer instead a vision of shared sensibility and profound animal-human relationship, and in so doing they put the lie to this stereotype of ancient Christian views of animals. The history is more complex when the zoological imagination is given its due as a phenomenon that was alive and well in the early centuries of Christian thinking "in the eye of the animal."

The more immediate context for the work of the wolf is the material in the present chapter, which examines the late ancient ascetic imagination that makes friendship with wild animals seem possible, attractive, even normal. As we have seen in a number of texts analyzed above, picturing close relations with wild animals seems to have been a function of the monastic imaginary that has appropriated certain animal images from the Bible and from the ancient cultural encyclopedia for its own purposes. The close relationships that the monks establish with these animals—hyena, antelope, lion, wolf—suggest that, in the perspective of the tales about them, their desert habitat is not a fallen world but rather a world of embracing warmth. These are fabulae in the true sense of the subversion of dominant, perhaps even unthinking, assumptions that relegate animals to the lump-sum category "the animal" and in the sense of according value to the plural singularity of individual animals.[101] Disrupting metaphysical discourses about animals surely entails disrupting such discourses about human beings as well. Mutually entangled with the animals, the monks open their hearts to an embodied sensibility that embraces touch and emotion (and not only reason) as signal characteristics of being human in the world.[102]

The story of the monk and the she-wolf is a good example of what one contemporary author has called "the tangled and circular ways that human communities imagine themselves—their subjectivity, their ethics, their ancestry—with and through animals."[103] Indeed, this story is a testament to the human penchant for "finding in the being of other animals powerful expressions of many of our most important experiences—suffering, love, friendship, hunger."[104] As novelist Jonathan Safran Foer has observed, "When thinking back to my most extreme experiences—extremes of terror, joy, pleasure, and pain—I think of them in the language of animality: 'I howled like an animal'; 'I hungered for it like an animal'; [I was like] 'a wounded animal' . . . 'like a bloodthirsty animal.'"[105] Our self-conception seems to depend upon how we imagine other animals, especially in terms of extreme experiences and emotions.[106] There is a corporeal continuum here, a shared "flesh of the world," to recall the phrase of Merleau-Ponty discussed in Chapter 3. "We have met the animal's body," declares one contemporary commentator, "and he is us. There are no animal Others."[107] In what follows I consider the ways in which Sulpicius's she-wolf is "us" by looking at the text's presentation of the extremes of intimacy and shame.

The primary affective bond in the monk-lupa story is conveyed by touch: the wolf's licks, the monk's caress. Encounter, intensity, and belonging are all on display in these contacts. Anyone who has a pet knows that the experience of caressing its head (and being licked in return) is an intimate one. But being intimate in this way with a domestic animal is one thing; being intimate with a wild animal is something else. I want to focus on the monk's caress. As Sulpicius tells the story, the monk suffered deeply when the she-wolf stayed away out of shame at her rash act of theft; about the loss of a pet, Bailly notes "the inexpressible aspect of the kind of pain we feel" upon such a loss—"a sort of enormous woe, specific, distinct, and oppressive."[108] The she-wolf stayed away, but the monk wanted her back, and he prayed until she reappeared. Upon her return, she did not dare to look him in the eye, but he was looking at her. I think it is fair to say that "his heart shone right out of his eyes" as he entreated her to come up to him.[109] Then, "with a caressing hand he stroked the sad head." Forgiveness lay in his touch, as did a fondness so intense I can only call it love. Indeed, the verb used to describe the monk's stroking touch, *permulceo*, goes in the directions of both fondness and forgiveness. One group of meanings pertains to touching with tender intimacy: to rub gently, stroke, touch gently, fondle; another group refers to the kind of touch that mitigates strong emotion (here, the wolf's shame): to soothe, appease, allay. What the suffering animal evokes is a powerful expression of deep compassion and tender care. Such virtues rest in an animal touch.

Thus the rupture in the relationship of monk and wolf serves ultimately to reaffirm the mutuality of animal and human. Indeed, the wolf is as necessary to the monk's emotional equilibrium—his happiness—as he is to hers. All this is embodied in the caressing touch. Here is a poem by Galway Kinnell that addresses just how important touch is.

Saint Francis and the Sow

The bud
stands for all things.
even for those things that don't flower.
for everything flowers, from within, of self-blessing;
though sometimes it is necessary
to reteach a thing its loveliness,
to put a hand on its brow
of the flower
and retell it in words and in touch
it is lovely
until it flowers again from within, of self-blessing;
as Saint Francis
put his hand on the creased forehead
of the sow, and told her in words and touch
blessings of earth on the sow, and the sow
began remembering all down her thick length,
from the earthen snout all the way
through the fodder and slops to the spiritual curl of the tail,
from the hard spininess spiked out from the spine
down through the great broken heart

to the sheer blue milken dreaminess spurting and shuddering
from the fourteen teats into the fourteen mouths sucking and
　　blowing beneath them:
the long, perfect loveliness of sow.[110]

Just as the touch of St. Francis conveys to the sow her own loveliness, so the touch of the monk reenvelops the she-wolf into the fond embrace of his friendship. In the desert, the animal provides the occasion for the monk's exercise of the signal ascetic virtues of forgiveness and compassion. Animal fellow feeling is not a defect but, one might say, a blessing that is a flowering.

Touch subtends the intimacy not only between monk and she-wolf but also, as we saw earlier in the chapter, between monks and a lioness, lions, and antelopes. What is all this intimate hands-on experience with wild animals in the desert about? In the coda to Chapter 3, I wrote about the centaur and satyr who appear in Jerome's *Life of Saint Paul* in terms of their hybridity: they are double creatures who combine the human and the animal to produce a wildness that is both positive (a state of being untouched by corrupt civilization) and negative (a state of being marked by unbridled physicality). As indigenous to the desert (in Jerome's view) and so emblematic of its monastic inhabitants, these creatures show both the ascetic's accomplishment and failure in coming to terms with his wildness. In other words, as hybrid figures, the centaur and the satyr carry both idyllic and barbaric connotations; they function as markers of a wildness that was fundamental to ascetic identity.

Although the essential wildness of wolves, lions, and even antelopes cannot be denied, I think that the stories about the animal caress—and I intend the ambiguity of this phrase—are different in tone and intent from Jerome's tale. Sulpicius's wolf, for example, is not a mythological hybrid. Far from it: as the client of the patron-monk, the lupa makes the desert a city, or at least a mini-society in which wild animal and human befriend each other. Furthermore, they are as one in their affective being: licking, caressing, slumping in grief, hanging the head in dejection. In the desert, body language matters. Furthermore, the wild animal, especially when it is suffering, petitions a caress, not a rejection, a taming, or a sublimation. Even more, it is specifically *wild* animals in these stories that carry extremes of woundedness, grief, and abjection. These are features of life with which ascetics cultivated intimacy, and in so doing they discovered deep wells of kindness and healing power in themselves. They had met the animal body, and it was them.

Yet another approach to Sulpicius's story of the monk and the she-wolf has been suggested by Catherine Osborne. Pairing the she-wolf with Jordanes the lion, she argues that both animals are associated with the "motif of the resistance to temptation so beloved of the Desert Fathers."[111] The lion, as we have seen, succeeds at resisting temptation, while the she-wolf does not. According to Osborne, the she-wolf's reaction to her failure—"genuine remorse"—is more important than her thieving lapse when she snatched a loaf of bread.[112] Ultimately, I think that this observation is correct. I would, however, like to take the wolf's "wicked deed," as the text calls it, seriously as constituting a moment of doubt regarding the tameness of this animal. Such a flicker of untamed desire, which coexists with the tale's portrayal of the lupa as calling forth, and so embodying, the caring dimension of human nature, suggests another historical and cultural context in which to consider this wolf.

Could there really have been anyone in late antiquity who when hearing the word "lupa" did not think of the tutelary animal of Rome and her role in its founding? This lupa was everywhere—on "coins, engraved gems, sculpted cuirasses, altars [like the Ara Pacis], tombstones, and urns."[113] Her story as the savior and nurturer of Romulus and Remus, told here by Ovid, was well known:

> A whelped she-wolf (marvel!) came to the abandoned twins.
> Who'd believe the boys weren't hurt by the beast?
> Far from harming, she even helps them: a she-wolf suckles
> Those whom kindred hands were braced to kill.
> She stopped; her tail caresses the delicate babes,
> And she shapes the two bodies with her tongue.[114]

There are striking congruences between this lupa and the lupa in Sulpicius's story. The Roman she-wolf literally gives "the comfort of her presence," to recall Sulpicius's characterization of *his* she-wolf's behavior, by suckling abandoned babies. The stories are linked by the motifs of the giving and taking of food, of caressing—the Roman lupa's tail being paralled by the monk's caressing hand—and of licking. Further, in both stories a fearsome, predatory animal turns out to be a gentle nurturer, whether figuratively, as in Sulpicius's tale, or literally, as in the case of the Roman lupa.

Yet if Sulpicius's she-wolf wittingly or unwittingly carries these positive connotations of this most famous animal integral to Rome's origins, she must also carry that animal's negative aspects. Apparently an alternative understanding of the Roman lupa was well known, for in his *City of God*, Augustine, after briefly narrating the suckling of the twins by the she-wolf, wrote: "There is no lack of people who say that, when the exposed babies lay wailing, they were first taken in by some unknown prostitute, and that hers were the first breasts they suckled—for 'she-wolves' [*lupae*] was the name given to prostitutes, which is why houses of ill repute are even now called 'wolf-houses' [*lupanaria*]."[115] Augustine clearly knew that, in Latin slang, "lupa" was the term for "the lowest of prostitutes in ancient Rome (i.e., those who beckoned to men in the streets and cemeteries)."[116] The lupa was a streetwalker, then, and in the minds of both pagans and Christians "prostitutes and she-wolves smelled alike, prowled in similar ways, and shared a common indecency."[117]

As Cristina Mazzoni argues, the lupa was an image of "unbridled female sexuality."[118] Thus the licking wolf who draws a monk's caress might after all embody the danger of temptation, a danger marked specifically as female eroticism. As noted above, the resistance to temptation (as well as courting it in order to resist it) is a well-known structure of ascetic practice in Christian antiquity. Flirtation with the very eros that one went to the desert to resist might well be a dimension of the striking intimacy between Sulpicius's she-wolf and her monastic patron. As Virginia Burrus has argued, there was in late ancient Christian hagiographical tales an "eruption of a powerful crosscurrent of asceticized eroticism"; thus the touching relationship between lupa and monk can be contextualized in terms of "the inherent excessiveness of asceticism, as well as its paradoxical carnality."[119] "A polymorphous creature," as Charles Goldberg has observed, the she-wolf implies both "sustenance and civilization" but also "bestial rapacity and erotic sensuality."[120]

I am reluctant, however, to privilege whatever erotic charge Sulpicius's she-wolf might carry, because the situation that draws the loving caress is actually—or also—a moral one. Recall that, in answer to the monk's prayers, the she-wolf returns to the monk after an absence of seven days, "her eyes fixed in profound shame [*profundo pudore*] upon the ground." What the monk sees are thus not her eyes but rather her eyelids, the very dwelling place of shame.[121] The lupa, "crushed by her own awareness of disgrace," sees herself in her mind's eye: she is the embodiment of "self-seeing as conscience."[122] As Aristotle remarked, "Shame is a mental picture of disgrace," which, as Robert Kaster notes, also entails "some expressive use of the body, a posture or movement that signals a breaking-off of contact with others: silence, downcast eyes, an averted glance, a turning away, or an actual withdrawal."[123]

Caught thus in the grieving misery of pudor, her "sad head" bent down with hooded eyes, this she-wolf is the very image of what the eminent zoologist Konrad Lorenz called "the animal with a conscience," referring specifically, but not only, to one of his dogs. This dog, having accidentally bitten his owner Lorenz, was so upset at his mistake that he was virtually paralyzed and lay on the rug breathing shallowly for days, "an occasional deep sigh coming from his tormented soul," as Lorenz put it.[124] Earlier I mentioned that many contemporary animal behaviorists agree that animals have complex emotions like chagrin, grief, and shame. Indeed, the Dutch primatologist Frans de Waal includes such ethical sensibility as one of the main features of the continuity between human and animal behavior; he has been quoted as saying, "Sometimes I read about someone saying with great authority that animals have no intentions and no feelings, and I wonder, 'Doesn't this guy have a dog?'"—or a wolf, we might add.[125] The monk's lupa has feelings aplenty; indeed, she is like the shamed Roman as evoked by Carlin Barton, one whose "inability to sustain the regard of others' eyes felt like quivering in darkness."[126]

Like modern animal studies, ancient Christian storytelling knowledge found the animal body to be a compelling ground for meditating on morality. In the course of imagining ethical sensibilities in terms of structures of affect shared by animals and humans, ancient Christian narratives focused again and again on one particularly strong emotion: shame.[127] Sulpicius's story about the she-wolf and the monk not only articulates the experience of deep intimacy in the language of animality, it also uses the language of animality in the form of an abject wolf to picture shame. As a shamed being, the wolf is actually a mirror image of the ascetic himself, since shame, humiliation, and humility were cardinal emotions in the literature of the desert. One desert ascetic, for example, said that the heart of his ascetic practice was "to blame and reproach myself without ceasing," while another declared, "Humility and the fear of God are above all virtues."[128] And even though the monk in Sulpicius's story is not himself shamed, his refusal to judge the she-wolf, extending to her a caress rather than a reprimand, enacts a major feature of the compassionate ethics of desert Christianity, the bearing of the other's burdens. As Douglas Burton-Christie observes, "The willingness to 'be with' another in an experience of suffering and to redeem that person through this action is one of the most striking aspects of the practice of compassion found in the desert."[129] As he goes on to conclude, in the literature of desert asceticism, love is inflected with tenderness.[130] The caressing hand on the shamed head restores the broken relationship.

As Ellen Finkelpearl has noted, in antiquity shame was considered to be a complex cognitive emotion and was connected with worth and social status.[131] Further, the ability to feel shame entails self-consciousness and identity formation.[132] Thus the monk's caressing hand restores the she-wolf's sense of worth and, at the same time, her sense of shame establishes her as one endowed with an ethical subjectivity. Both monk and she-wolf have an embodied sensibility, and it shows itself through the medium of shame and the bodily affects that it calls forth. As one contemporary theorist has noted, "Shame is truly the most interpersonal of affects."[133] Its very interrelationality establishes the human and the animal in Sulpicius's tale in a relationship of reciprocity that—ironically, given the painfulness of shame—has the positive effect of valuing animal-human belonging in a shared ethical world.

In her study of shame in ancient Christianity, Burrus suggests another positive role for shame. She notes that, especially for ascetic practitioners, "a plunge into the abyss of abjection was necessarily undertaken by those who aspired to transcendence."[134] She observes further that shame need not be "a sheerly destructive or paralyzingly inhibiting force"; "there is no escape from shame, but there may be many possibilities for a productive transformation of shame and through shame."[135] These observations are pertinent to the story of the she-wolf, whose shame is inextricable from repentance and leads to restoration of relationship. And her shamed presence has a salutary effect on the hermit; it elicits empathy, "the ability to be vicariously affected by someone else's feelings and situation."[136] To be empathic is to care, and "the capacity to care for others is," as de Waal remarked, "the bedrock of our moral systems."[137] It should be clear by now that these stories from the Christian desert, far from reinforcing alienation between humans and animals, instead find a shared fundament of bodily, emotional, and ethical life. The recent comic strip shown in Figure 9 aptly sums up the tale of the monk and the she-wolf: unconditional love binds human and animal together.

I shall close with a second modern story about a real wolf that demonstrates in a compelling way the power of reading texts for their animal-human relationships. In *A Sand County Almanac*, a set of essays on nature, the eminent twentieth-century environmental conservationist Aldo Leopold recalled an incident from his early days in the U.S. Forest Service. As summarized by Gavin Van Horn, "[Leopold] describes how he and a group of his colleagues were eating lunch above a river in eastern Arizona when, below them, they saw a mother wolf and her pups greeting one another, oblivious to the government workers above them."[138]

FIGURE 9. Cartoon, *Syracuse Post-Standard*. Mutts: © 2016 Patrick McDonnell, distributed by King Features Syndicate.

In those days [Leopold explained], we had never heard of passing up the chance to kill a wolf. In a second we were pumping lead into the pack, but with more excitement than accuracy. When our rifles were empty the old wolf was down and a pup was dragging a leg into impassable slide rocks. We reached the old wolf in time to watch a fierce green fire dying in her eyes. I realized then, and have known ever since, that there was something new to me in those eyes—something known only to her and to the mountain. I was young then, and full of trigger-itch; I thought that because fewer wolves meant more deer, that no wolves would mean hunters' paradise. But after seeing the green fire die, I sensed that neither the wolf nor the mountain agreed with such a view.[139]

The death of the fierce green fire was Leopold's moment of conversion in this very religious story of an idea of paradise turned upside down by a wolf's dying light. Leopold went on to become the father of wildlife and wilderness conservation in the United States. The clash of perspectives in this story could not be clearer, and it is very like the situation we encountered in Sulpicius's story of a she-wolf: the long life of the biblical image of the wolf as rapacious predator is subverted by a seeing with the eye of the wolf, a seeing that suggests that "to meditate on the wolf is to meditate on ourselves."[140] Here is another form of intimacy, and another form of shame. Sulpicius's monk grieved when the she-wolf stayed away; perhaps he then became conscious for the first time of his love for her comforting presence. Similarly, Aldo Leopold recognized his own rapacity when he saw the fading of the green life force in the mother wolf's eyes. He lost the dominical point of view just as surely as did Sulpicius (at least when he was in the midst of storytelling). In its place he was left with an experience of suffering, care, and connection.

Finally, I would be remiss if I did not address the erotic flow that electrifies Sulpicius's story of the monk and the she-wolf. I suggest, following affect theory, that the love between the two is a circuit of intensity rather than a characteristic only of the wolf, whose erotic allure as lupa I discussed earlier in this chapter. As we have seen, the two protagonists in this tale speak, affectively, with their bodies: the she-wolf licks, the monk caresses. Here is what Merleau-Ponty, an affect theorist *avant la lettre*, called an erotic chiasm, "a relation of embrace in which surfaces or boundaries are not frontiers but rather contact surfaces" of kinship.[141] The being of other animals is a meditative sounding board for powerful human emotions. As this story, and others like it in this chapter, testifies, at least one dimension of ancient Christian self-conception seems to have depended on how one imagines other animals, especially in terms of intense and intimate experiences and emotions. Not only are there animal-human relationships, there is a continuum and a reciprocity that recognizes shared cognitive sensibility. With regard to Sulpicius's monk and she-wolf, I shall end with a question. Despite the story's characterization of the lupa's rash act of theft, the monk's awareness of it, and the she-wolf's extreme self-abasement, there is not a hint of castigation, reprisal, or disapproval on the part of the monk. He prays and caresses. His delight at the return of his companion is so great that he gives her two loaves of bread instead of the usual crumbs. Might we say, quoting Wallace Stevens, that "His anima liked its animal / And liked it unsubjugated"?[142]

Coda

Many of the stories from the literature of the Christian desert analyzed in this chapter feature touch as an important medium of communication and relationship between humans and other—especially wild—animals. The body is the medium of reciprocity, and it seems crucial that touch is paramount in the intensity of the resonances circulating between animals and their monastic companions. As Donna Haraway has argued, "Touch ramifies and shapes accountability. Accountability, caring for, being affected, and entering into responsibility are not ethical abstractions; these mundane, prosaic things are the result of [animals and humans] having truck with each other." As she goes on to say, touch "peppers its partners with attachment sites for world making. Touch, regard, looking back, becoming with—all these make us responsible in unpredictable ways for

which worlds take shape." And she concludes: "Touch and regard have consequences."[143] In the case of these stories from the desert, one of the consequences
of touch and regard is to sidestep the usual rhetoric of human superiority and
domination of animals. The stories disclose another, more intimate and profound, relationship between human beings and animals. Why this should be so
is difficult to say with any certainty, except that ethical subjectivity was such an
important concern among the ascetic inhabitants of the desert. The monks'
cultivation of compassion and love extends in these stories beyond intraspecies
relationships to include the animals as well. Animal lore is ethically therapeutic.

Why *wild* animals? One answer has already been explored, namely, the
placing of desert ascetics by their interpreters in settings that idealize their practices as indicative of paradise regained, in which all enmity is erased, including
that between the wild and the tame. From this perspective, Christianity, in the
persons of the desert saints, is positioned as a religion exercising miraculous
power over the natural world. In addition, perhaps the wild animals teach the
monks something about their own "wildness," whether that wildness concerns
ethics, as in those stories that expose monks' transgressive behavior vis-à-vis
animals, or whether it concerns society, monastic cultivation of relationships
with lions, hyenas, antelopes, and wolves being at least implicitly an embrace of
an ethos that is critical of the values of civilization. But there is also wildness
that is psychological, as when animal sufferings of various kinds elicit deep and
unselfish kindliness from the old men of the desert. As Carl Sandburg wrote in
a poem entitled "Wilderness," "I got a menagerie, inside my ribs, under my bony
head, under my red-valve heart. . . . For I am the keeper of the zoo . . . I came from
the wilderness."[144] The pedagogy of wild animals embeds ascetic Christianity in
a corporeal matrix that is also deeply spiritual.

Psychologically speaking, however, animal depths could also be negative, as
in this final story, which was written by Cyril of Scythopolis in the mid-sixth
century. The story concerns the Palestinian monk Sabas who, like Gerasimos,
had extracted a thorn from the paw of a lion. This lion, like Jordanes, then
became the monk's companion. Sabas, as the story continues, had a disciple
named Flavius, who owned a beast of burden, an ass; whenever Sabas sent him
away on a commission, Flavius would get the lion to watch over the ass. Here is
the rest of the story.

> So in the morning the lion would go off with the halter of the ass in
> its mouth, let it graze the whole day, and in the evening take it to
> water and then bring it back. Some time later, while the lion was

performing this office, Flavius, who had been sent on a commission, apparently neglected his salvation and was carried away by presumption; in his consequent state of abandonment, he fell into fornication. On the very same day the lion struck down the ass and made it his food. On discovering this, Flavius realized that his own sin was the cause of the ass's being eaten and, no longer daring to appear before the elder, gave himself up for lost, acting wrongly. Going away, he settled on his own property, lamenting his sin. The godly old man, however, in imitation of the Master's mercy did not despise him but carried out a lengthy search for him. When by the grace of Christ he found him, he admonished and exhorted him, raised him from his fall and restored him. Flavius went into reclusion, repented from the bottom of his soul, and became extremely well-pleasing to God.[145]

In this tale, the focus is not on animal-human relationships, since the lion drops out of the story fairly early on. Instead, the spotlight is on the spiritual arrogance and concomitant fall of the sinful monk. There is no tender or healing touching here; instead, touch runs amok, and a different world takes shape, a world of fornication and the deadly tearing of flesh.

A compelling psychological reading of Cyril's story is offered by Blake Leyerle, who sees it as a picture of what happens when the monastic ideal of self-restraint is punctured. The critical moment in the story, on her reading, is when Flavius links his sin to the lion's rapacity as cause to effect. She remarks: "Here the lion—and for that matter the ass as well—image, quite transparently, aspects of the monk's soul. When the monk loses control of his passions, all restraint is lifted from the lion."[146] The resulting carnage, then, is psychological. I find this reading compelling, even though it shows that Cyril's story confines the animals, and especially the lion, to the register of the symbolic.[147] Still, as a cautionary tale about ethical formation, it makes interesting contact with other stories from the literature of desert asceticism explored in this chapter, and its conclusion, with its touching picture of the merciful old monk Sabas, circles back to the motif of compassion that is so much on view in these tales of animal-human relationships.

CHAPTER 5

Small Things

The Vibrant Materiality of Tiny Creatures

In Arundhati Roy's novel *The God of Small Things*, the God in question is a God of loss and sorrow, a God who presides over the seemingly incidental, "small" events that actually (and especially in hindsight) mark momentous changes in the human lives affected by them. This contemporary God of small things is also a "Small God" who laughs "a hollow laugh"; "the source of his brittle elation was the relative smallness of his misfortune. He climbed into people's eyes and became an exasperating expression."[1] Similarly, what I shall call the "small things" of ancient Christian zoological imaginings are also momentous in terms of the meaningful supercharge that their tiny bodies carry. By contrast with contemporary small things, however, these ancient diminutive beings embody not loss but rather an exuberance of theological wonder, and also of disgust. It seems that it is not an accident that ancient Christian small things—worms, flies, mosquitoes, frogs—teem, swarm, and croak in abundance. And the God whose presence is intimated by these small but mighty creatures may well, we might imagine, laugh, but it is a complicated "laugh" that acknowledges intricate design, cosmic mystery, and soteriological hope. In terms that I think such authors as Augustine of Hippo and Basil of Caesarea would not only understand but also approve, these ancient Christian "small things" are indicative of a vibrancy and a vibration of matter, or what the "new materialist" author Jane Bennett calls "vibrant matter."[2]

The new materialism in which Bennett is a participant derives its interpretive energy from a readjustment of focus on "matter," both animate and inanimate, such that matter is no longer viewed simply as passive and lacking in agency. Bennett's interest, like that of others in this movement, is in "returning to the most fundamental questions about the nature of matter and the place of embodied humans within a material world."[3] For new materialists like Bennett, matter is lively: "Materiality is always something more than 'mere' matter: an excess, force, vitality, relationality, or difference that renders matter active, self-creative, productive, unpredictable."[4] Bennett asks, "Why advocate the vitality of matter?" And she answers: "Because my hunch is that the image of dead or thoroughly instrumentalized matter feeds human hubris and our earth-destroying fantasies of conquest and consumption. It does so by preventing us from detecting (seeing, hearing, smelling, tasting, feeling) a fuller range of the nonhuman powers circulating around and within human bodies."[5] In other words, an instrumental view of matter goes hand in hand with a rhetoric of human dominion over the earth, including earth's animals. Thus imagining matter as animate or vibrant, rather than as dead or inert, allows other views of animals to emerge. In the context of this chapter's interest in ancient Christian attention to small zoological phenomena, then, two of Bennett's aims are pertinent: "to paint a positive ontology of vibrant matter" and to attenuate such "onto-theological binaries" as life/matter and human/animal.[6]

Meaningful Worms: Augustine

Laudable as they are from a new materialist perspective, such efforts to value the material world, including animals, positively and to de-center the human (or to bring the human down from an imagined apex of a vertically organized structure of being) might seem to be odd or even inappropriate contexts in which to consider the views of Augustine, who will be the focus of the first part of this discussion. As Gillian Clark has pointed out, Augustine did not formulate a "sustained theological argument about the nature of animals and their relationship to God and to humans."[7] It is true that Augustine did not write a *sustained* treatise devoted to the inferiority of animals. Yet, as we saw in earlier chapters, when he spoke about animals as a classification of beings, it is clear that he accepted the *idea* of a human-centered order in which human beings are superior to animals by virtue of their possession of reason, which animals are said to lack. Animals were the intellectual and spiritual inferiors of humans, sentient but irrational.[8] As Clark has observed, when Augustine referred to animals in the "lump sum," as a generality, "he rarely uses the neutral term *animalia*, a Latin equivalent of the Greek *zôa*, 'living creatures,' which could in principle include humans. Instead, he uses words for animals as seen by humans: either tame flocks and herds for human use, or wild beasts which war against humans and (it was believed) each other. His most common word is *pecus*, 'cattle' in the general sense, but he also uses *belua*, which connotes monstrosity, and *bestia*, which connotes ferocity."[9] There would seem to be no doubt that, when he adopts this kind of generalized or generic view of animals, Augustine is participant in the sort of Western thought that confines animals "in vast concept spaces from which they are not supposed to be able to exit," as Jean-Christophe Bailly has written in his meditation on animals.[10] The anthropological corollary to this confinement of animals, as Bailly continues, is that "human beings are to be defined precisely—if only it were that simple—by the fact that they have managed to get themselves out of these enclosures, leaving behind *bestiality*—condemned as disgraceful— and *animality*, deeply feared, as if these were stages in a journey and bad (though haunting) memories."[11] As Augustine puts it, "The human soul is made in the image of God, but God does not grant that image of himself to a dog or a pig."[12]

However, and by contrast, when Augustine discussed, not "the animal" or animality as a conceptual category, but rather animals in their "plural singularity," a more positive zoontology of vibrant matter emerges.[13] Let us join Augustine as, to borrow a phrase from Wallace Stevens, he follows "the course of a particular," in this instance, worms.[14] Writing about the ordering function of soul, Augustine remarks:

> We must admit that a weeping man is better than a happy worm.
> And yet I could speak at great length without any falsehood in praise
> of the worm. I could point out the brightness of its coloring, the slen-
> der rounded shape of its body, the fitness of its parts from front to
> rear, and their effort to preserve unity as far as is possible in so lowly a
> creature. There is nothing anywhere about it that does not corre-
> spond to something else that matches it. What am I to say about its
> soul animating its tiny body? Even a worm's soul causes it to move
> with precision, to seek things suitable for it, to avoid or overcome dif-
> ficulties as far as possible. Having regard always to the sense of safety,
> its soul hints much more clearly than its body at the unity which cre-
> ates all natures. I am speaking of any kind of living worm.[15]

Here we encounter yet another of those curious passages among patristic texts on animals in which the dominical perspective that elevates human beings above all other life-forms is at marked odds with the zoological imagination. A weeping man may be "better" than the happy but "lowly" worm, and yet it is the worm, not the man, that functions as the vehicle for a brief but lively meditation on creation's design and order. Vibrant in color and the symmetry of its parts, the worm is a striking instance of animated matter whose soul conforms it perfectly to its environment, even endowing it with a sort of agency as it successfully negotiates its habitat. Such is Augustine's "search for the universal within the infinitesimally small," to borrow a phrase from the zoologist David George Haskell.[16] The worm's "tiny body" with its animating soul encapsulates the creative, unifying energy of "all natures." On the basis of a passage like this, one might think that Augustine, like his fellow worm enthusiast Charles Darwin, "was a tinkerer, interested as much in nature's minutiae as in its grandeur."[17]

Indeed, like Augustine, Darwin spoke unabashedly "in praise of the worm," though at greater length. Both at the beginning of his career, in a paper delivered to the Geographical Society of London in 1837, and at the end, in a book entitled *Formation of Vegetable Mould Through the Action of Worms* published in 1881, Darwin touted the worm's ability to create, through digestion and excretion, the rich topsoil (then called vegetable mold) that accounts for the fecundity of the earth.[18] As for Augustine, so for Darwin, the small was mighty in terms of design and order, indeed, order on quite a grand scale. As Bennett remarks, "Darwin describes the activities of worms as one of many 'small agencies' whose 'accumulated effects' turn out to be quite big": by making topsoil, worms enable agriculture, which "makes possible the cultural artifacts, rituals, plans, and endeavors of human history."[19] In regard to these kinds of claims, the psychologist Adam Phillips observes (no doubt with a smile) that Darwin wanted "to justify the ways of worms to Man."[20]

In his own way Augustine also engaged in such a justification. In *On Genesis: A Refutation of the Manichees*, he was at one point responding to a Manichaean question about God's motive in making so many animals that were hostile to and induced fear in humans. He replies—ultimately—with a vision of God's intricate cosmic design:

> I must confess that I have not the slightest idea why mice and frogs were created, and flies and worms; yet I can still see that they are all beautiful in their own specific kind, although because of our sins so many of them seem to be against our interests. There is not a single living creature, after all, in whose body I will not find, when I reflect upon it, that its measures and numbers and order are geared to a harmonious unity. Where these should all come from I cannot conceive, unless it be from the supreme measure and number and

order which are identical with the unchanging and eternal sublimity of God himself.[21]

As Augustine goes on to say, "all such beauties" ought to elicit praise for "God the craftsman."[22] In a statement such as this one, he of course parts company with the perspective of the contemporary new materialism, which, to use Bennett's perspective on it once more, "aims to theorize a vitality intrinsic to materiality as such, and to detach materiality from the figures of . . . divinely infused substance. This vibrant matter is not the raw material for the creative activity of humans or God."[23] For Augustine, creatures such as worms testify precisely to the sublimity of a creator God. And yet, insofar as he embraces both high and "lowly" creatures as testaments to cosmic harmony—"From the highest to the lowest," he argues, "none of these things is offensive to reason"[24]—one can see what Bennett calls "a positive ontology of vibrant matter" taking shape. In the worm, one sees "metaphysics scrawled into flesh."[25] To paraphrase Phillips's statement, Augustine justifies the ways of worms not only to man but also to God.

At the very least, then, it would seem that, as for Darwin, for Augustine the earthworm was not "a mere blind, dumb, senseless, and unpleasantly slimy annelid" as it was to others.[26] In a remarkable reminiscence of an experience he had with two of his students, Augustine shows just how far the connections among worms, material vibrancy, and soulful animation could go. In a dialogue with his friend Evodius, in which the topic of discussion was the magnitude or greatness (*quantitas*) of the soul, he recalls the following:

> Not long ago when we were in the Ligurian countryside, our young men, who were then pursuing their studies with me, noticed, while lying on the ground in a shady spot, a many-footed little animal [*bestiolam multipedem*] crawling along; I call it a long slender worm [*longum dico quondam vermiculum*]. It is quite common. Yet what I am going to say about it I had never observed before. One of the students cut the animal in half with the edge of the stylus that he was holding, and both parts of the body then moved in opposite directions away from the cut with as much speed and energy as if they had been two living animals. Astonished at this phenomenon, and curious to know the cause, they brought the living parts to where Alypius and I were seated. We too were astonished to see those two living pieces running on a tablet in all directions. One of the pieces, touched by the stylus, writhed at the point of contact; the other, feeling nothing,

continued to move elsewhere. In short, in order to test how far this would continue, we cut the worm—or rather worms—into many parts. All these parts moved about in such a way that if we had not done the cutting, and if the flesh wounds were not visible to us, we should have thought that each of these parts had been created as a separate worm, and that each had lived its life distinct from the others.[27]

Augustine does not go on to inform his readers about the fate of these vermicular bits, although, biologically speaking, none of the "wormlets" would have survived this surgery by stylus; the various parts would have wriggled only so long as the nerve cells stayed alive.

And yet, biology aside, Augustine's story presents as vibrant a picture of matter as any new materialist might wish for—"active, productive, unpredictable," as Bennett says.[28] Augustine treats his reader to an astonishing multiplication of being. Indeed, it is tempting to imagine that Augustine might have agreed with Bailly's view of animals as "*thoughts* through which the verb 'to be' is conjugated, played out, produced."[29] In his "thought" of the worm, however, Augustine does not "conjugate" ontology in quite the way that his memory of the worm experiment might lead one to believe. In the section of *De quantitate animae* in which the memory occurs, he has been trying to show his partner in dialogue, Evodius, that the soul does not have spatial extension, and cannot be confined to place or body. He lets Evodius in on a secret regarding the meaning of the experiment with the worm: "If I had not been well versed in questions about the nature of a body, the form that is in the body, about place, time, and motion . . . I should be inclined to bestow the palm of victory on the proponents of the doctrine that the soul is a body."[30] And that seems to be precisely what the account *does* prove, although Augustine does not want it to. As he says to Evodius: "Since, therefore, from the many arguments set forth earlier, which you accepted as most certain, it was made clear to you that the soul is not contained in place and for that reason lacks the quantity that we notice in bodies, why do you not take it for granted that there is some cause why a certain animal, when cut up, continues to live in each segment and that the cause is not that the soul can be divided with the body? If it is beyond our power to discover that cause, is it not better to continue our search for the true cause, rather than accept one that is false?"[31] In succeeding passages in the dialogue, Augustine shows that the soul is not divisible by using as analogy the relation of sound and meaning in a word. The crux of his argument is that "since a word is made up of sound and meaning, and the sound refers to the hearing, but the meaning to the under-standing, does it not seem to you that, just as in some living body, the sound of the word is the body and the meaning is, as it were, the soul?"[32] Still with those wormlets on his mind, Augustine concludes that his analogy "makes it clear enough" how "the segments of a body can live, although the soul does not suffer any division. . . . The meaning—which is like the soul of the sound that is made in uttering a word—cannot possibly be divided, while the sound itself—which is like the body, can be divided."[33]

The gist of Augustine's argument is that the soul has intangible power, not literal magnitude. That is not an especially surprising conclusion. What *is* surprising is that so much of the argument should hang on a zoological fantasy, and furthermore that the relation between the worm's body and soul is explained by way of an analogy drawn from language—a word's sound, which is divisible, and its meaning, which is not. The "wildness of the disparity" between a worm and a word ought to give us pause except that, as Michael Cameron explains in another context, "the enveloping unlikeness makes the threads of likeness all the more instructive."[34] Many centuries later, the wildly disparate connection between worms and words was not lost on Wallace Stevens, either. In his poem "The Man with the Blue Guitar," he compares the activity of the blue guitar—a figure for both the poet and the poetic imagination—to "a worm composing on a straw."[35] And there is also Bailly, whose meditations on animals entertain the possibility that "the whole animal realm is . . . like a grammar," "a nonfinite possibility of phrasings."[36] In Augustine, the worm, like grammar, structures his thought, enabling an articulation—a meaningful phrasing—of a philoso-phy of soul.

There are still more "phrasings" of worms in Augustine's works. One is Christological. Like a long Christian exegetical tradition before him, Augustine was drawn to Psalm 22 because, according to two gospels in the New Testa-ment, Jesus had cried out the psalm's first verse ("My God, my God, why hast thou forsaken me?") in his anguish on the cross.[37] Among the Christological hermeneutics that developed as a way of interpreting the psalms, one, the proso-pological method, posited that Christ was the speaking voice of many of the psalms, and much of what he spoke revealed his humanity.[38] What this meant for Psalm 22, a psalm typically approached by means of prosopological interpre-tation, was that interpreters could not limit the Christic voice to the psalm's first verse. They had to imagine that the entire Psalm was spoken by Christ. This included Psalm 22:6, "But I am a worm, and no man." What could it pos-sibly mean? Here is Augustine's explanation: "I am a worm, and no man. In what sense 'no man'? Because he is God. Why then did he so demean himself as to say 'worm'? Perhaps because a worm is born from flesh without intercourse, as Christ was born from the Virgin Mary? A worm, and yet no man. Why a worm? Because he was mortal, because he was born from flesh, because he was born without intercourse. Why 'no man'? Because in the beginning was the Word, and the Word was with God, and he was God (Jn. 1:1)."[39] This is all that Augustine has to say about worms in his exposition of Psalm 22, yet despite its brevity it is rhetorically brilliant. The same question, "Why 'no man'?" opens and closes the passage; it establishes the divine nature of Christ. With Christ's divinity established as the frame of his remarks, Augustine can then deal with the troubling aspect of the verse, again with a dramatic repetition of a question, "Why worm?" The worm's relationship to Christ's humanity takes center stage in Augustine's exegesis.

The fact that the Word of God might make the demeaning declaration "I am a worm," and mean it, engaged the exegetical energy of many patristic authors prior to Augustine.[40] Origen's interpretation, which emphasizes the degradation of Christ's mortality, can stand as typical of Augustine's predecessors:

> The Savior himself says, "But I am a worm and not a man." . . . In his
> mother's womb he saw the uncleanness of bodies. He was walled in
> on both sides by her innards; he bore the straits of earthly dregs. So he
> compares himself with a worm and says, "I am a worm and not a
> man." A man is normally born from a male and a female; but I was
> not born from a male and a female, according to nature and the ways
> of men. I was born like a worm. A worm does not get seed from out-
> side itself. It reproduces in itself and from itself, and it produces off-
> spring from its own body.[41]

As Martine Dulaey has pointed out, it is probable that, lying in the background of the connection that Origen makes between the worm and Christ's human body, is a passage from Job that questions whether human beings can be righteous before God, since man is a "maggot" and "the son of man" is a "worm."[42] In any case, while Origen's description of gestation and bodies carries intense disgust, he sidesteps the outright identification of the "I am" passage by converting the worm into a simile ("I was born *like* a worm")—a comparison that weakens the force of the verse. Even though Augustine's references to Christ as "mortal" and as "flesh" carry a sense of human deficiency, there is no weakening of the

Christ/worm identification in his interpretation. Augustine takes the metaphor seriously: as worm, Christ is human.

Unlike Origen, however, Augustine takes into account both aspects of the statement "I am a worm and no man."[43] Christ is both animal and God. From the perspective of the zoological imagination, it is significant that Augustine never points out the literal absurdity of the Christ/worm metaphor. Here is one moment when one of the goals of the new materialism, the attenuation of onto-theological binaries like life/matter and human/animal, makes an appearance. Actually, with the Christian paradox of the God-Man on his side, Augustine goes further than the new materialists: *he* attenuates the divisions among human, animal, *and* divine.

Otherwise, Augustine is in accord with Origen: the other significant feature of the worm passage in Psalm 22 from a Christological perspective is an ancient conviction about the spontaneous generation of worms, which links the birth of worms to the virginal birth of Christ. The view that worms were born "without intercourse," as Augustine wrote, being generated instead from decaying matter and animal corpses, carried the authority of no less an "observer" than Aristotle.[44] Here is Augustine the "zoologist" at work in his *Literal Commentary on Genesis*, where the question of the origin of "certain very small forms of animal life"—presumably including worms—is at issue: "There is a question as to whether they were produced in the first creatures or were a later product of the corruption of perishable beings. For most of them come forth from the diseased parts or the excrement or vapors of living bodies or from the corruption of corpses; some also from decomposed trees and plants, others from rotting fruit."[45] Augustine concludes that the tiny creatures that stem from water and earth belong to the six days of creation, whereas those that originate from decomposing bodies came later.[46]

The real import of this material is not Augustine's obvious knowledge of a naturalist tradition stemming from Aristotle. Rather, it is that Augustine (and many Christian authors before him) used part of the life cycle of the worm as an appropriate image of an exalted theological doctrine, the virginal birth of Christ. From a philosophy of soul to the God-bearer: worms led Augustine to unusual flights of zoological imagination. And the theological uses to which he put worms did not stop there. For Augustine, worms could be truly cosmic in their excessive vibrancy, functioning in visions both of hell and of heaven. Thus the final "phrasing" of worms in Augustine's thought that this chapter will address concerns theological doctrines of punishment and salvation.

First, hell. Late in the *City of God*, Augustine was searching for evidence to convince scoffers that eternal torment in the fires of hell was possible. At issue was whether the human body could remain intact in order to suffer being burned forever. Responding to pressure from such unbelievers to come up with a convincing example of a body that remains alive and whole in intense heat, Augustine offers the following: "We may reply that there are examples of animals which are undoubtedly subject to decay, because they are mortal, which nevertheless can live in the middle of a fire; and that there is also a species of worm to be found in the gushing springs of hot baths. These are too hot for anyone to put a hand in with impunity, whereas the worms not only live in it without damage but are unable to exist elsewhere." In response to his critics' rejection of this explanation, their critique being that the hot springs are the natural habitat for such worms and not a place of torment, Augustine huffs, "We are asked to suppose that it is not more incredible that creatures should thrive in such an environment than that they should be tortured in it! For it is amazing that any creature should be in pain in the fire and yet should continue to live; but it is more astonishing that it should live in the fire without feeling pain. But if the latter is believed to be a fact, why should the former be incredible?"[47] Whatever one might think of Augustine's logic in this passage, there is no doubt about the exuberance, now on a cosmic theological scale, that is fostered by the tiny worm. This constitutes finding the universal in the infinitesimally small with a vengeance. And it will be no less the case as Augustine follows "the worms at heaven's gate," to borrow the title of another poem by Stevens.[48]

"Your creation has its being from the fullness of your goodness."[49] This statement of the positive ontology of the created world in the *Confessions* is echoed in the *Tractates on the Gospel of John*, where Augustine is concerned to emphasize as strongly as possible that the "Creator Word" (*Verbo creatore*) of the Gospel of John 1:1–5 was responsible for the creation of all the world's creatures, including their form, structure, agreement of parts, and their weight, number, and measure.[50] Insisting that the Word made "every creature whatsoever," both "spiritual and corporeal," Augustine says (just in case anyone could possibly have missed his meaning):

> I will speak more plainly, brethren, that you may understand me. I
> will say, from an angel even to a worm (*ab angelo usque ad vermicu-
> lum*). What is more splendid among created things than an angel?
> What is lower than a worm? He who made the angel made the worm
> also; but the angel is fit for heaven, the worm for earth. He who created

also arranged. If He had placed the worm in heaven, you might have found fault; if He had willed that angels should spring from decaying flesh, you might have found fault: and yet God nearly does this (*et tamen prope hoc facit Deus*), and He is not to be faulted. For all men born of flesh, what are they but worms? And of these worms God makes angels (*de vermibus angelos facit*).[51]

Having imagined the created order as a "vast, sprawling mesh of interconnection"[52] based on the Word's ordering of all the things He made, Augustine drives home his point by conjuring that order's extremes, from the most spiritual beings, the angels, to the most terrestrial, the worms. And then—revealing his very high hopes for worms—he triumphantly notes how God makes the one kind into the other. Worms are indeed at heaven's gate, having been turned into angels.

As Augustine suggests in the passage just quoted, this strange kinship between the worm and the angel is based on an anthropology that envisions human transformation; the worms are human beings who will find themselves transported from earthly decaying flesh to heaven. As he continues in this part of his lecture, it becomes clear that the soteriology of the passage is based on the sort of vermicular Christology that we have already encountered in this chapter. "And of these worms God makes angels. For if the Lord Himself says, 'But I am a worm and no man' (Ps. 22:6), who will hesitate to say what is written also in Job (25:6), 'How much more is man rottenness, and the son of man a worm?' . . . Behold what for your sake He was willing to become, who in the beginning was the Word, and the Word was with God, and the Word was God!"[53] Augustine's basic argument here is that the Word of God became a "worm" so that human beings might become angels. At its heart, it is a message about divine love and human salvation.[54] Here we have, not metaphysics, but theology "scrawled into flesh," and once again the incongruous worm provides the body for thought.

Worms and Metamorphosis: Basil of Caesarea and the *Physiologus*

Augustine's willingness to see theological truth in such a body may be regarded as an instance of Karmen MacKendrick's view of the ancient tradition of "understanding the world as divine text": this tradition entails "reading the divine name in [the world], as traced, as belonging somehow to the bodies in which it is always improper, a bit of a scandal."[55] One can imagine Augustine's parishioners shaking their heads at the somewhat scandalous thought of a worm's metamorphosis into an angel as figure for the resurrection. And yet perhaps it was that very impropriety that made worms "good to think," as Claude Lévi-Strauss remarked about totemic animals.[56] In any case, Augustine was not alone in his view of the theological import of worms, and a similar "bit of scandal" wafts about the worm of Basil of Caesarea's zoological imagination. Like Augustine's worm become angel that functions as a figure for resurrection, the worm in Basil's *Hexaemeron* also pictures metamorphosis. He introduces the worm as the first of the land creatures to be treated following his exposition of the other living species:

> The land, ready in turn to exhibit creatures rivaling the plants, the swimming species, and the winged creatures, calls us to present wild beasts and reptiles and herds. "Let the earth bring forth living creatures, cattle and wild animals and crawling creatures of different kinds" (Gen. 1:24). What do you say, you who mistrust Paul concerning the transformation made at the resurrection [τῆς κατὰ ἀνάστασιν ἀλλοιώσεως] when you see many creatures of the air changing their forms [τὰς μορφὰς μεταβάλλοντα]? What stories are told about the Indian silkworm, the horned one! First, it changes into a caterpillar, then goes on to become a buzzing insect; however, it does not remain in this shape, but clothes itself with light, wide metallic wings. Whenever, therefore, you women sit unwinding the product of these, the threads, I mean, which the Chinese send to you for the preparation of soft garments, recall the metamorphoses [μεταβολῆς] in this creature, conceive a clear idea of the resurrection, and do not refuse to believe the change which Paul announces for all men.[57]

The matter of this animal is so vibrant that it changes *itself* from worm to winged creature. And its material changes carry such visual force, at least to Basil's mind, that those changes are appropriate for imaging "a clear idea of the resurrection" (ἐναργῆ . . . τῆς ἀναστάσεως ἔννοιαν). This tiny body is quite a heady beast!

The introduction of this first land animal into his text is the occasion for one of the highly rhetorical second-person interruptions by Basil of his third-person narration of the days of creation, and the transition from narration to expostulation is very abrupt. It seems clear that the earthy being of this silkworm (and its transformations that he will later depict) fires up Basil's anger at those who reject Christian belief in the resurrection. Yet in what sense do the transformations in the life cycle of a silkworm provide a "clear idea" of the doctrine of the resurrection? When juxtaposed, as in the present chapter, with Augustine's statement about the worm-to-angel change, it might seem that this is what Basil has in mind: the silkworm's final shape, in his telling, is characterized by wide and soft (χαύνοις) wings—like an angel's, perhaps? Yet the thoroughgoing materiality of the silkworm's metamorphosis introduces a jarring note into his use of it as an image of human resurrection. After all, according to Paul, who is being petitioned here, the resurrected body will *not* be like the earthly body: as Paul writes in 1 Corinthians 15:44, "It is sown a physical body, it is raised a spiritual body." From "perishable" to "imperishable," "we shall be changed" (I Corinthians 15:52). The ethereal materiality that Paul seems to have in mind in this passage is rather oddly visualized by the silkworm become moth.

And yet, perhaps ethereal materiality vis-à-vis the silkworm is precisely the point. In the Greco-Roman philosophical culture in which Basil participated, "matter" and "spirit" were not as radically distinct as many modern interpreters, following in the footsteps of Descartes, have imagined. Reading ancient philosophical and theological ideas through the lens of Cartesian ontological dualism has led to "misguided discussions of ancient notions of body and soul," as Dale Martin has argued.[58] There were certainly dualisms—Basil himself used dualisms such as transient/eternal, rational/irrational, visible and invisible nature, and so on[59]—but as Martin has pointed out, for the ancient mind-set, "instead of an ontological dualism, we should think of a hierarchy of essences," which he also describes as "the spectrum of stuff," ranging "from fine, thin, rarified stuff down to gross, thick, heavy stuff."[60] Thus, Martin concludes, the cosmic organizing principle "is not an ontological dichotomy between physical and spiritual reality but a gradual hierarchical scale ranging from heaviness to lightness, from inert and lifeless mass to living, eternal divinity."[61] Basil himself had described the mighty metamorphosis that awaited human beings as a "coming back to natural beauty" through the restoration of the image of God in which they had been made.[62] For Basil, this was a slow but sure transition from the "humiliation" of humans' earthy animal selves to the realization of their godlike, rational selves—a movement along a spectrum from the heavy to the fine.[63] Thus perhaps the endpoint of Basil's image of the earthbound silkworm, the aerial moth with its soft wings, provided an image of that final attainment of beauty that really did, as Basil said, give a clear idea of resurrection.

Of course, it is the process of change per se, rather than materiality in and of itself, that is the salvific theme that the silkworm suggests to Basil's mind in the passage from the *Hexaemeron* quoted above.[64] And the seeming incongruity of using a material metamorphosis to recall a spiritual one might be just to the point of aiding the limited imagination of those who were inclined to scoff at the momentous but mysterious change that resurrection entailed. As Basil wrote in a sermon, "If you open your eyes to the beauties of the earth, they in their turn will augment your belief in God."[65] In the final analysis, Basil agreed with Augustine about the signifying power of tiny bodies: "The Lord has placed within the smallest living creature the visible traces of his own great wisdom."[66] Visible and invisible beauties come together in the envisaging by Basil of the transformative process central to his view of Christian belief and practice.

Basil's use of the metamorphosing body of a worm that ultimately becomes a winged creature as an image that gives clarity to belief in resurrection had a curious counterpart in the lore collected by the *Physiologus*, which was, as we have seen in earlier chapters, a bestiary written in the late third century.[67]

On the Phoenix

Our Lord Jesus Christ says in the holy gospel: "I have the power to lay down my life and I have the power to take it [again]" (John 10:18). The Jews were vexed at this saying. Now there is a bird in India called the phoenix. After five hundred years it comes to the trees of Lebanon and fills its wings full of spices. And it gives a sign to the priest of Heliopolis on the first day of the month (Nisan or Adar), that is to say, Phamenothi or Pharmouthi. The priest, receiving the sign, goes and fills the altar full of vine wood. The bird comes into Heliopolis, laden with spices, and goes up into the altar, kindles its fire, and sets itself on fire. On the next day, the priest, searching the altar, finds a worm in the ashes. On the second day, the worm grows feathers [or: sprouts wings], and is found to have become a young bird. On the third day, it is found to be as it was before (and it salutes the priest and flies away), and it goes away to its former place. If then this bird has the power to kill itself and to regenerate itself, how do mindless men feel angry when our Lord Jesus Christ says, "I have the power to lay down my life, and I have the power to take it again"? For the phoenix represents the person of our Savior since, coming out of the heavens, he carried two wings full of fragrance, that is, virtuous, heavenly words, so that we might stretch out our hands in holy vows, and send up spiritual fragrance through good lives. Thus fittingly has the Physiologus spoken about the phoenix.[68]

Here is yet another way in which one could picture resurrection, this time specifically Christ's resurrection, by petitioning a worm.

In this fabulous tale, the author of the *Physiologus* departs from the usual structure of its individual narratives. Rather than opening with a quotation from the Hebrew Bible and closing with a quotation from the New Testament, as per usual, the story of the phoenix omits mention of the Hebrew Bible and twice quotes the same verse, "'I have the power to lay down my life, and I have the power to take it again,'" from the New Testament. This deviation from its usual structure allows the *Physiologus* to highlight the phenomenon of resurrection as the context for understanding the death and regeneration of the bird. Furthermore, and again unlike this text's usual procedure, the biblical quotations do not contain mention of the animal in question.[69] Instead, the quotation of Christ's statements about his death-and-life power point immediately to the theological exuberance of the wondrous phoenix and the self-regenerating vibrancy that it shares with the Savior.

Although most of the accounts that make up the two major versions of the myth of the phoenix in classical and Greco-Roman antiquity mention the worm as part of the rebirthing process, not all did.[70] One example is the early third-century naturalist Aelian, who thought that the phoenix was a "divine bird," but not because it signified rebirth. Instead, he admired the phoenix's mathematical prowess: it "knows how to reckon five hundred years without the aid of arithmetic, for it is a pupil of all-wise nature, so that it has no need of fingers or anything else to aid it in the understanding of numbers."[71] While the priests squabble about their differing calculations of the phoenix's five-hundred-year cycle, the phoenix reads the signs correctly and makes its appearance at the altar, ready for self-immolation.[72]

By contrast, a different kind of "arithmetic" struck the author of the *Physiologus* as important. As R. Van Den Broek points out, "Only the *Physiologus* and the texts related to it say that the worm developed into a phoenix in three days."[73] Of course the three days are related, like the saying of Jesus about laying down and taking up his life, to the passion and resurrection, but they also allow readers to linger on the worm and its unusual successor, a worm with feathers! This is not quite the worm-to-angel transformation of Augustine's zoological fantasy or the worm-to-moth of Basil's, although it is related to their brand of theology on the wing, as it were. The author of the *Physiologus* adds his own vermicular intimation of divinity by articulating the truth of the resurrection on the basis of the life cycle, not of a real worm, but of a mythical bird and its wormy stages of development. Nonetheless, evoking one of the aphorisms of

Wallace Stevens, one might say of all of these worm-to-winged-creature images
of resurrection that "there is no wing like meaning."[74] Or perhaps, given the
soteriological thrust of all of this material, one might best petition these lines of
a poem by Emily Dickinson:

> "Hope" is the thing with feathers—
> That perches in the soul—
> And sings the tune without the words—
> And never stops at all.[75]

Saintly Worms: Simeon the Stylite

This chapter's penultimate picturing of worms in the ancient Christian imagination petitions, not feathery wonder, but disgust, at least at first sight. The text in
question is a hagiography, the *Life and Daily Mode of Living of the Blessed Simeon
the Stylite*, written by one Antonius, who positions himself as one of the saint's
ardent disciples.[76] As Antonius presents him, Simeon was an ascetic whose practice was not only unflinchingly corporeal but also grotesquely self-lacerating.
The text explains the holy man's mortifications as responses to his crushing sense
of his own sinfulness, and perhaps also that of humankind as a whole, since the
young Simeon, replying to an abbot who questioned the gravity of the sinfulness of one so young, quoted Psalm 50:7: "Behold, I was brought forth in iniquities, and in sins did my mother conceive me."[77] Referring to his body, Simeon
then states: "I was clothed the same as everyone else."[78] Simeon thus used practices of the body—material performances such as throwing himself into a rep-
tile and insect-ridden well and taking up residence there, and of course the most
famous of his actions, inhabiting pillars of ever-increasing height—to give
graphic expression to *the*, and not simply *his*, ascetic self.[79] Simeon's body is
everyman's body.

Worms first appear in conjunction with an act that Simeon tries to keep
secret. Subsequent to his entry into a monastery, Simeon bound his body with a
rope and covered it with a hair shirt so that no one could see what he had done.
A year or so later, the rope had eaten into his flesh "so that the rope was covered
by the rotted flesh of the righteous man. Because of his stench no one could
stand near him [and] his bed was covered with worms, but no one knew what
had taken place."[80] Eventually the other monks complain to their abbot about
Simeon's harsh regimen, not to mention the stench and the worms. The abbot

goes to see the worms for himself and orders Simeon to be stripped in order to discover the source of his body's odor. The monks have to soak Simeon in a tub of water in order to loosen his garment, which was "stuck fast because of the putrefied flesh"; when they finally manage to undress him, only the ends of the rope can be seen, so deeply had the rope lacerated his flesh. "There was no guessing how many worms were on him. Then all the monks were astonished when they saw that terrible wound." Simeon responds by asking to be left alone to die, "'For I am an ocean of sins.'"[81] Here is a theology of the human being "scrawled into flesh" in no uncertain terms.

This episode of Simeon and his worms is clearly playing upon the ancient conviction, which we have already seen at work in Augustine's thought, that worms were spontaneously generated from decaying matter. But in this hagiography, the decaying fundament is a live human body, not dead leaves or animal corpses. What is alive is "dead," and what is dead is alive—with worms. Simeon with his putrefying, worm-producing flesh presents an image of what Virginia Burrus, in another context, has called "carnal excess"—a vision of "flesh exceeding its own bounds."[82] Surely it is the intensity of Simeon's treatment of his own material being, as well as his use of it as a signifying ground, that would catch the attention of a new materialist like Bennett. But my guess is that she would not find this material particularly vibrant, even though it does diminish an ontotheological binary, namely, the divide between the spiritual anguish of the saint and his physical being. It is rather difficult to read Simeon's story thus far as an instance of the new materialism's "positive ontology." Indeed, as Susan Ashbrook Harvey has observed, Antonius's *Life of Simeon* "is an anguished text." It "presents the ugliness of the saint's practice as exactly that. It is not the angelic life, nor is it transcendent."[83]

There are yet more worms in Simeon's story. Following his move to the final pillar, one that was forty cubits high, Simeon, now famous, was, at the behest of the devil, afflicted with a tumor in his thigh. "His thigh grew putrid and . . . such huge numbers of worms fell from his thigh to the earth that those near him had no other job but to collect them and take them back from where they had fallen, while the saint kept saying, 'Eat from what the Lord has given to you.'"[84] Here the worms are connected not only with the saint's putrefying body but also with his ability to withstand an attack by the devil. Further, he complicates the devilish origin of his wound by his statement, presumably to the replaced worms, "Eat from what the Lord has given you." God is somehow involved in both the wound and the nourishment of the worms, making Simeon into a Job-like figure, as indeed the text itself notes.[85] While still provocative of disgust rather than theological wonder, the zoological imagination that is constructing the hagiographical Simeon has taken a decidedly more positive turn, especially by suggesting God's care for the worms that feed off Simeon's body.

The grotesque exuberance of Simeon's excessive flesh takes one more turn in this curious text. This is an incident that deserves quotation in full.

> By God's will the king of the Arabs came to [Simeon] to have the saint pray for him. As soon as he came near the pillar to be blessed by holy Simeon, the saint of God, when he saw him, began to admonish him. While they were talking together, a worm fell from [Simeon's] thigh; it caught the king's attention and, since he did not yet know what it was, he ran and picked it up. He placed it on his eyes and onto his heart and went outside holding it in his hand. The saint sent a message to him, saying, "Come inside and put away what you have taken up, for you are bringing misery upon me, a sinner. It is a stinking worm from stinking flesh. Why soil your hand, you, a man held in honor?" When the righteous man had said this, the Arab came inside and said to him, "This will bring blessing and forgiveness of sins to me." When he opened his hand, a precious pearl was in his hand. When he saw it, he began to glorify God and said to the righteous man, "Look! What you said was a worm is a pearl—in fact, a priceless one—by means of which the Lord has enlightened me." On hearing this, the saint said to him, "As you have believed, so may it be to you all the days of your life—not only to you, but to your children also." So blessed, the king of the Arabs returned home safe and sound, rejoicing.[86]

The shock in this text is that Simeon as sinful everyman—"stinking flesh"—is also a saintly body able to transform a "stinking worm" into a "precious pearl."

Worms seem ineluctably associated with transformation in the ancient Christian zoological imagination. Augustine's worms-to-angels are surely rivaled by this worm-to-pearl, which is a conveyer of forgiveness, enlightenment, and blessing. How many more of Simeon's worms might be pearls, if one only had the eyes to see them properly? The worm as pearl is soteriological, having had a role in the conversion of the pagan king to Christianity; perhaps there is a touch of transcendence in this story after all, and not only anguish, as Harvey argued. In fact, if the transformation of worm to pearl can be said to be part of the perceptual ability induced by witnessing Simeon's ascetic practice, then that practice is not only ugly but also beautiful: the pearl, after all, is "priceless." Pinning a saint's significance on the turn of a worm might seem rather too exuberant even for the zoological imagination at work in Simeon's hagiography, yet, as Burrus astutely observes, "Hagiographical writing demands belief, and it does so precisely when its claims are the most fantastic: the life of a saint is typically extreme, stretching the limits of both imagination and credulity—and thereby also (in theory at least) transforming the reader's sense of possibility."[87] From this perspective, the thought that a small thing like a worm might embody high theology of various kinds is not so surprising, or even so grotesque, as one might at first have imagined.

Vermicular Exegesis: Pseudo-Dionysius the Areopagite

Or perhaps the grotesquerie is just the point. At least, this is the perspective of Pseudo-Dionysius the Areopagite, the final "vermicular exegete" whom we will encounter.[88] As is well known, Dionysius viewed the language of scripture as paradoxical, arguing that its images of such invisible beings as angels and of course God were both like and unlike their referents.[89] As he explained in *Celestial Hierarchy*, "Sacred revelation works in a double way. It does so, first, by proceeding naturally through sacred images in which like represents like, while also using formations which are dissimilar and even entirely inadequate and ridiculous."[90] With regard to intelligible beings such as angels, for example, Dionysius argued that they were most appropriately represented by biblical images that are dissimilar, incongruous, even deformed or misshapen, since these images are least likely to be taken as literal representations of their referents.[91] Biblical authors were wise to use "incongruous dissimilarities," for by doing this they took account of our inherent tendency toward the material, especially our tendency to literalize images of beauty.[92] Lowly images uplift: "The sheer crassness [δυσμορφία: misshapenness] of the signs is a goad so that even the materially inclined cannot accept that it could be permitted or true that the celestial and divine sights could be conveyed by such shameful things."[93] However, even images "drawn from the lowliest matter can be used, not unfittingly, with regard to heavenly beings" because matter owes its existence to God and "keeps, throughout its earthly ranks, some echo of intelligible beauty."[94] The point is that one must keep dissimilarity in mind, lest anyone think that the heavens are filled with "the great moos" of angels represented as oxen![95]

By contrast, images that are "similar" by virtue of their beauty or elevated quality—angels as golden and radiant humans, for example—are dangerous because they might lead one to think that such images actually disclose the reality of the beings they purport to represent.[96] "Positive affirmations," Dionysius argues, "are always unfitting to the hiddenness of the inexpressible," so "one must be careful to use the similarities as dissimilarities to avoid one-to-one correspondences."[97] Yet, as he also argued, the similar and the dissimilar are not mutually exclusive categories of images, since every image, whether lofty or lowly, has a double character: "The very same things are both similar and dissimilar."[98] That is, every image is characterized by a simultaneity of lack and plenitude; all images are incongruous, but all are nonetheless epiphanic.

What is true of scriptural images of angels is also true of the Bible's images of God. That is, the foregoing discussion provides the conceptual framework for Dionysius's understanding of the worm in Psalm 22:6, "I am a worm and no man." Dionysius notes in *Celestial Hierarchy* that scriptural imagery of God is not only exalted but also extremely lowly: "Sometimes the imagery is even derived from animals so that God is described as a lion or a panther, a leopard or a charging bear. Add to this what seems the lowliest and most incongruous of all, for the experts in things divine gave him the form of a worm."[99] The incongruous image of the worm both protects the "inaccessibility" of the divine and conveys a theophanic glimmer. As Enrica Ruaro has observed, "The vile comparison does, in a certain odd way, make sense, because there is no creature so low as to lack a sparkle of the divine light of its cause, so that no creature is completely devoid of beauty.[100] Like Augustine before him, Dionysius thought that matter was vital.

Nonetheless, the main function of the "deformed" image of the worm is to deliver a shock to the interpretive endeavor, ruling out complacency in seekers after theological truth.[101] We have moved from Augustine's celebration of the "happy worm" as image of cosmic design and harmony to Dionysius's use of the worm as a capstone example of a full-blown theory of the incongruity of biblical imagery of divinity. With the dissonant vibrancy of Dionysius's incongruous worm, Wallace Stevens's "worm composing on a straw" may here make another appearance, this time as a figure for the complex vitality of language itself.

Mosquitoes and Flies

Worms were not the only "small things" that could be "a help to contemplation," as Dionysius remarked about dissimilar similarities.[102] Let us return to Augustine. Just as he spoke "in praise of the worm" in *De vera religione*, so he also spoke in praise of the mosquito. In a passage from *De Genesi ad litteram* referred to earlier in which he ponders the origin of "certain very small forms of animal life," he goes on to expostulate about the "special beauty" proper to the nature of all small creatures.[103] He concludes the passage as follows: "He creates them tiny in body, keen in sense, and full of life, so that we may feel a deeper wonder at the agility of the mosquito on the wing than at the size of a beast of burden on the hoof, and may admire more intensely the works of the smallest ants than the burdens of the camels."[104] With this privileging of the small over against the large, Augustine placed himself in a Greco-Roman naturalist tradition as typified by Pliny the Elder, who remarks in his *Natural History*, "In the contemplation of nature nothing can appear superfluous."[105] Thus, Pliny continues, "we marvel at elephants' shoulders, carrying towers of war, the necks of bulls and the fierce tossings [of their heads] high in the air, the predation of tigers and the manes of lions, although nature is nowhere more wholly herself than in her smallest creatures." Augustine shared with Pliny a fascination with the perfection of the tiny.[106] What for Pliny is nature "wholly herself" is for Augustine an exuberance of theological wonder.

Commenting on this and similar passages in Augustine's works, Richard Sorabji has argued that Augustine's sense of nature's beauties was qualified by the context in which he placed them: "Animals are to be admired not for their own sake, but as pointers to God. We must not let the creature take hold of us, so that we forget the Creator."[107] Sorabji means this comment about not taking animals seriously in their own right as a critique, and there is something to be said for it, especially if one reads the comment by Augustine about the mosquito side by side with his lament in the *Confessions* over what he calls daily life's "buzz of distractions."[108] Augustine notes as one of his own distractions watching a dog chase a rabbit in the countryside, which "distracts me . . . from thinking out some weighty matter."[109] He then offers a second example:

> When I am sitting at home, a lizard catching flies or a spider entrapping them as they rush into its web often fascinates me. The problem is not made any different by the fact that the animals are small. The sight leads me to praise you, the marvelous Creator and orderer of all things; but that was not how my attention first began. . . . My life is full of such lapses, and my one hope is in your great mercy. When my heart becomes the receptacle of distractions of this nature and the container for a mass of empty thoughts, then too my prayers are often

interrupted and distracted; and in your sight, while I am directing
the voice of my heart to your ears, frivolous thoughts somehow rush
in and cut short an aspiration of the deepest importance.[110]

Once again Augustine has linked small animals and their activities with God's
orderly creative achievement. As he notes, however, watching spiders and lizards
catch flies was not in its inception undertaken for the purpose of praising God's
creation. Instead, it was an example of curiosity understood negatively as a hunger of the eye for frivolous things.[111] What might seem like the simple act of
watching spiders and lizards catch flies becomes instead a state of distracted
attention that leads Augustine away from his heart's desire.

In this self-punishing reflection from the *Confessions*, then, "ocular curios-
ity distracts [Augustine] from the path of self-discipline."[112] If one were to read
Augustine's passage on the mosquito in the light of the passage in the *Confessions*, the mosquito might well beckon as a fateful temptation from which
Augustine is saved only by contextualizing his wonder in God's creative activity.
There is no doubt that the tiny but agile "mosquito on the wing" does indeed
call up in Augustine's mind an "intense admiration" of its "all-powerful Maker."
And yet, *pace* Sorabji's perspective, I would suggest that Augustine's wonder at
the mosquito—and fascination with worms—conveys a positive form of attention to the animal in itself and an admiration of it for its own sake. This is due
to Augustine's obvious fascination not only with how creatures that are so tiny
can nonetheless be "keen in sense and full of life" but also with how impressive
they are, so much so that they provoke deep wonder. The verb used in this passage to describe the wonder-provoking mosquito is *stupeo*, a strong verb that
means "to stun, astonish, amaze." The wondrous mosquito does not lead
Augustine into a "state of fragmented desire"; on the contrary, here is an example
of transient beauty that is affirmed.[113] Indeed, this mosquito can be seen as one
of what Bennett as a new materialist calls a "site of enchantment," where
enchantment means "to be struck and shaken by the extraordinary that lives
amid the familiar and the everyday."[114] Enchantment is found in moments of
"pure presence" and "acute sensory activity"—how like Augustine's mosquito,
"keen of sense and full of life."[115]

If Augustine were to be consistent, the enchantment that inflects the mosquito ought also to inflect the being of all animals. This is because, in the passage of *De Genesi ad litteram* in which Augustine presents a mosquito in flight
as an object of wonder, all animals are kin as products of divine wisdom: "For
He has wrought them all [all creatures] in His wisdom [Ps. 104:24] which,

reaching from end to end, governs all graciously [see Wis. 8:1]."[116] This is a rather formal kind of kinship, however, based as it is on each creature's testimony to God's governing and ordering activities. We are kin by virtue of the patterning of Wisdom. Thus Augustine ultimately parts company with Bennett, however much he is (somewhat strangely) enchanted by a mosquito and positions it positively in the ontological order of creatures. He differs from Bennett because her sense of enchantment is founded on a thoroughgoing materialism, "an onto-picture of a vibrant, quirky, and overflowing material world" whose interconnections are more radically intimate than are those that Augustine envisions in this passage.[117] Augustine's mosquito doesn't bite. That is, its being is not entangled in the flesh of human beings, and its flesh is not implicated in processes of human transformation as was the worm of Augustine's zoological imagination.

Modern mosquitoes do bite, and so, in fact, do some ancient ones. In other words, there are mosquitoes other than Augustine's that can be understood as providing "sensory access" to a cosmos considered as "energetic and rumbling."[118] One instance of a modern mosquito can serve to set the context—actually, the counterpoint—for pondering those other ancient mosquitoes and their energetic rumbling. Here is zoologist David George Haskell in his book *The Forest Unseen*, narrating his encounter with a swarm of mosquitoes, one of which lands on his hand.

> Hungry ladies dance in the air, swoop at my arms and face, then land and probe. They have flown upwind, excited by my smelly mammalian promise. . . . What an easy meal! One of the mosquitoes lands on the back of my hand, and I let her probe my skin. . . . A needle juts from under her head. She slowly moves this lance across my skin, seeming to test for a suitable spot. She stops, holds steady, then I feel a burn as her head drops between her forelegs and the needle slides in. The sting continues as she penetrates deeper, sliding in several millimeters. The mosquito on my hand has evidently pierced a productive vessel. In just a few seconds her light brown underbelly balloons into a shining ruby. When her belly is stretched into a half globe, she abruptly lifts her head and, in a blink, flies off. I am left with a slight burn on my hand and two milligrams less blood. The first thing she'll do after finishing her meal is rest on a tree trunk and offload by urination some of the water she has swallowed. Human blood is much saltier than a mosquito body, so she'll also pump salts into the urine,

preventing my blood from disrupting her physiological equilibrium. Within an hour she will have dumped about half the water and salt from her meal. What remains, the blood cells, will be digested, and my proteins will find themselves turned into yolk in a batch of mosquito eggs. The mosquito will also take some of my nutrients for herself, but the vast majority will be used for egg production. The millions of mosquito bites inflicted on us every year are therefore preliminaries to mosquito motherhood. Our blood is their ticket to fecundity.[119]

Here is a description of a mosquito bite, willingly suffered for the sake of biological observation, that is both aesthetic and scientific at once. The female mosquito's "shining ruby" of an underbelly becomes a vessel of transformation, as protein from human blood becomes yolk in the insect's eggs. Here too is wonder, but of a very material and intimate sort. If Haskell and his "small thing" form a mini-cosmos, the mosquito definitely provides sensory access to a world of energetic interconnection.[120]

In his poem "Mosquito" John Updike too relates enduring this kind of interconnection, but not with interest either scientific or aesthetic. While in bed one evening, he is stung by a mosquito. He slaps at the stinger:

A cunning, strong Gargantua, I struck
When he was pinned in the feast of my flesh,
Lulled by my blood, relaxed, half-sated, stuck,
Engrossed in the gross rivers of myself.

Success! Without a cry the creature died,
Became a fleck of fluff upon the sheet.
The small welt of remorse subsides as side
By side we, murderer and murdered, sleep.[121]

Unlike the appreciative biologist, the poet adopts a parodic heroic stance, Gargantua to the tiny mosquito. He "slays" his enemy, unscientifically marked as male.[122] The poetic form is aesthetic, but the sentiment is not: no "shining rubies" here but rather "gross rivers" and violent death.

The mood of an ancient story about mosquitoes that bite is more in tune with Updike's poem than it is with Haskell's appreciative meditation that, as we shall see, shows in effect how an ascetic *ought* to react to a mosquito's sting.

Here is Palladius's account of an event and its aftermath in the life of Macarius of Alexandria, a monk who lived in the late fourth century in a region of the Egyptian desert south of Alexandria called Kellia, or the Cells.

> Early one morning when he [Macarius] was sitting in his cell a mosquito stung him on the foot. Feeling the pain, he killed it with his hands, and it was gorged with his blood. He accused himself of acting out of revenge and he condemned himself to sit naked in the marsh of Scete out in the great desert for a period of six months. Here the mosquitoes lacerate even the hides of the wild swine just as wasps do. Soon he was bitten all over his body, and he became so swollen that some thought he had elephantiasis. When he returned to his cell after six months he was recognized as Macarius only by his voice.[123]

If only Macarius had seen a ruby underbelly rather than a bug gorged with his own blood! As an ascetic, he should have controlled his passions and let his fellow creature live.

Unlike the modern biologist, however, the ancient ascetic suffered his bite by surprise and reacted in angry revenge. For an ascetic devoted to cultivating a state of virtue in himself, the act of revenge was an especially self-defeating one: as one of Macarius's monastic contemporaries, Abba Isaiah, is quoted as saying, "When someone wishes to render evil for evil, he can injure his brother's soul even by a single nod of the head."[124] It is difficult to cultivate the single eye and the heart at rest while swatting at a mosquito, and so it was precisely that vengeful act of swatting that Macarius set out to purge himself of by sitting in a swamp and becoming, in effect, mosquito bait.[125]

Mosquito killing and remorse are common to the dark moods both of Palladius's story and Updike's poem. Both tellings are inflated—Updike's by his positioning of the poem's protagonist lying beside a dead "speck of fluff" and preposterously naming himself and the mosquito "murderer and murdered," and Palladius's by indulging his "sometimes gothic taste in spirituality" that tends to favor portrayals of unduly harsh ascetical regimens.[126] While the inflation in the poem is the engine of its satirical vision, the inflation in Palladius's text is indeed spiritual, however gothic it may be. And whether or not one agrees with William Harmless's characterization of the swollen because much-bitten Macarius in his post-swamp condition as "cartoonish" and comically entertaining, he is surely right that Macarius's mosquito is moral in its ultimate effect.[127] It leads the monk to detect disorder in his psyche, and to act to purge and purify an untamed dimension of himself. Indeed, as Burrus has observed, in the case of Macarius "the grotesque swelling of the flesh, manifesting a self-chastisement itself grossly in excess of the sin committed, is clearly productive of virtue."[128] And finally, as Harmless notes, the moral of the mosquito story is, as are so many of Palladius's anecdotes, ascetically therapeutic: Macarius's stint in the swamp was a discipline of the body as a means for disciplining the soul.[129]

Elsewhere in the zoological imagination of ancient Christian authors, mosquitoes and their aerial cousins, flies, were not especially wondrous, nor were they intimately entangled with an ascetic's self-discipline. For Origen, for example, they were "vibrant" not as "matter" but rather as jibes at his philosophical and theological enemies and as negative snapshots of their behavior. In the course of his *Homilies on Exodus*, Origen set about to try to make contemporary sense of the plagues that God inflicted on the Egyptians. After interpreting the Nile once it was turned to blood as "the erring and slippery teachings of the philosophers," he observed that mosquitoes, the third plague on Egypt, are "so fine and small" that one can't see them unless one looks closely; but when a mosquito sits on one's body, "it bores with the sharpest sting so that what one cannot see flying he feels stinging."[130] With this stealthy aspect of the mosquito's being established, Origen then compares the mosquito to "the art of dialectic, which bores souls with minute and subtle stinging words and circumvents so shrewdly that the one who has been deceived neither sees nor understands the deception."[131] As for flies, he has less to say: he compares them "to the sect of Cynics who, in addition to other depravities of their deception, proclaim pleasure and lust as the highest good."[132] Why flies should be emblems of pleasure and lust is not explained, unless Origen knew the lore stemming from Aristotle, who wrote that flies' copulation lasted a long time.[133] In any case, flies and mosquitoes, with their stinging and deceptive ways, become in Origen's hands an occasion to expose and critique harmful viewpoints and activities of rival sects.

Origen also compared "the stings of the fly" with "the bites of the passions."[134] Addressing the moral application of the plagues in Exodus by way of allegory, he argues that when the "Law of God" (the scriptures) rescues the soul lost in the "ignorance" that is Egypt, "it purifies its evil thoughts and scatters the stinging mosquitoes which are like the power of craftiness to sting. It also removes the bites of the passions which are like the stings of the fly and destroys the foolishness and brutish understanding in the soul."[135] Here, what might be rather abstract, that is, the psychological or spiritual wounds caused by a disordered soul, takes on physical affect as the sharp pain of the bites of flies and mosquitoes. At the behest of these stings, bodily affect, even when imagined metaphorically, assumes an ethical role. As with Macarius, mosquitoes (and flies) seem to entail an embodied sensibility.[136]

For Gregory of Nyssa too flies signified a negative entanglement in material life. He mentions flies in the course of his interpretation of the psalms, which in his view instruct the reader about the five stages of the spiritual life imagined as an ascent, during which the soul recovers its likeness to God.[137] For Gregory the text of the Psalter is an ethical primer: "The whole book of Psalms is full of the praises of virtue and the condemnation of those who live in evil."[138] Gregory imagines the one who attains the fifth and final stage, when one recovers one's original angel-like nature, with a metaphor of an eagle.[139] It will become evident that the positive image of the strong wings of an eagle in flight must have suggested to Gregory the puny wings of a fly as an appropriate (negative) counterpoint. In any case, here is Gregory's zoological fantasia on the final stage of spiritual ascent:

> In the sequence, by means of the fifth part of the Psalter, he [David] brings the one who is able to follow him to the height to the most sublime step of contemplation, as though it were a peak, once he has flown with firm wing through the entanglements of the webs of material life. For those who are soft and without vigour, and are greedy, like flies, for the sticky things of life, are entangled in their weak and feeble flight, and bound up in the mantle of such threads as if they were nets. I am referring to those who are entangled in luxuries, honours, popular repute, and various desires, as if they were spider-webs, and who become the prey and food of that beast which hunts by such means. But if someone who has the nature of an eagle, and looks more sharply with the unchanging eye of his soul to the ray of light as he strains onward to the height, should happen to approach such spider-webs, he utterly destroys every such thing, whatever it might be that he approaches, by the wind alone that accompanies the swift beating of the long feathers of his wings in his rushing flight.[140]

In this passage the image of the fly signifies the dreadful condition of those whose values are earthbound. In the positive form of this sensibility, as signified by the up-rushing eagle, there is nothing vibrant about materiality. When one inhabits a "fly self," everything material is sticky, and that stickiness is not only enfeebling but in fact imprisoning, like a fly caught in a spider's web. There was no falling into reverie at the sight of a fly in a spider's web for Gregory, as there was for Augustine (however much he regretted it). From the vantage point of "eagles," "flies" are doomed to a life bereft of virtue.

In a less metaphorical mode, Augustine too could use the fly to make an ethical point, in his case a point about the absurdity of human pride. In one passage, he asks his reader, "'Do you presume on your strength? You are surpassed by wild beasts. Do you presume on your swiftness? You are surpassed by a fly [*a muscis vinceris*].'"[141] In this case the fly is an agent of humiliation. Augustine shames human presumption by using the comical image of a tiny fly besting a much larger human being.[142] In another passage, Augustine changes gears, moving from pride based on bodily prowess to pride stemming from the passions, that is, psychological or emotional pride. Again he addresses his reader directly from the text: "'Why is it that you are puffed up with human pride? A man has insulted you, and you become swollen with anger. Drive away the fleas that you may sleep; know who you are. For that you my know, brethren, those things which annoy us were created to subdue our pride; God could have subdued the proud people of Pharaoh by bears, lions, and serpents; but He sent flies and frogs against them that their pride might be subdued by the vilest things.'"[143] Interestingly, in a passage quoted earlier in this chapter, Augustine had exclaimed that he had no idea why such creatures as flies (and frogs and mice and worms) were created, though he is sure that they all have their own special beauty.[144] Now, however, in the context of deflating human *superbia*, Augustine assures his flock that he in fact does know the purpose of these "tiniest and most abject creatures": it is to torment us on account of our pride.[145] Again he appeals to the grotesquerie of flagrant disproportion: the tiniest creature torments a much larger one, all in the cause of ethical improvement.

Augustine's flies have moral cachet! It is not an exaggeration to emphasize the significance that their association with human pride accords to the flies. As mentioned in Chapter 2, superbia was always for Augustine the primal sin.[146] As he wrote in the *City of God*, pride had been "the start of the evil will. . . . And what is pride except a longing for a perverse kind of exaltation?"[147] Pride, he goes on to say, stems from finding satisfaction in oneself rather than in God. Whether pride was understood, as in Augustine's early work, as "a violation of the divine order of the cosmos, a deliberate turning away from higher to lower goods," or whether it entailed "a perverse self-love that seeks its private good over the common good" as in the passage above, it is clear that pride was a crucial element in Augustine's anthropology.[148] Thus when flies literally sting us, the punishing physical bite also has the spiritual effect of psychic improvement by subduing the arrogance of the retreat into the closed-off self.[149]

Frogs

If flies, then, are implicated in this most basic aspect of the self, so too, it would seem, are frogs, which will lead this discussion to its final "small things" in the ancient Christian zoological imagination. In the passage above from Augustine, frogs and flies are associated together as two of the plagues of "the vilest things" (*rebus villissimis*) that God sent as punishments against Pharaoh and his proud people (Ex. 8:2–14, frogs; 8:21–24, flies). It was indeed the biblical idea of the frog as plague that persisted in most ancient Christian engagements with this small animal. Augustine did not specify what he found to be so vile about frogs. Origen, however, was very specific: the problem with frogs is their noisy croaking. Extending the significance of the story of the plagues in Exodus so that he might "take some digs" at those he opposed, he wrote: "I think the songs of the poets are indicated figuratively by the second plague in which frogs are produced. The poets with a certain empty and puffed up melody introduced deceptive stories to this world as if by the sounds and songs of frogs. For that animal is useless except that it produces an inferior harsh sound."[150] Here Origen follows Plato in viewing poets as purveyors of morally questionable stories, mere "phantoms" and not real knowledge.[151] The deceptive stories of poets are puffed-up opinion, a false song. Yet castigating poets for their imitative mischief, as Plato did, is one thing; imagining poets as harsh croakers is quite another. When Exodus and Plato come together in Origen's imagination, the frog is matter alive with a cacophonous agency.

For his view of frogs and their relation to mere opinion, Origen may well have been inspired, as he so often was, by Philo of Alexandria.[152] In one of his comments on the plagues in Exodus, Philo wrote,

> But Pharaoh, the squanderer of all things, not being able himself to receive the conception of virtues unconnected with time, inasmuch as he was mutilated as to the eyes of his soul, by which alone incorporeal natures are comprehended, would not endure to be benefited by virtues unconnected with time; but being weighed down by soulless opinions, I mean here by the frogs, animals which utter a sound and noise wholly void and destitute of reality, when Moses says, "Appoint a time to me when I may pray for you and for your servants that God will make the frogs to disappear" [Ex. 8:9], though he ought, as he was in very imminent necessity, to have said, Pray this moment, nevertheless postponed it, saying, "Pray tomorrow," in order that he might in every case preserve the folly of his impiety.[153]

What Origen apparently drew from Philo was the association of frogs' noise with valueless opinions that for Philo are an affliction—a mutilation, even—of the soul. Origen too moved from gibes against poets to a moral concern for the soul's well-being in his engagement with frogs. In a later passage in his *Homilies on Exodus*, he imagines the import of the plague of frogs for every human soul: "But now if we are also to discuss the moral nature, we will say that any soul in this world, while it lives in errors and ignorance of the truth is in Egypt. If the Law of God begins to approach this soul it turns the waters into blood for it, that is, it changes the fluid and slippery life of youth to the blood of the Old or New Testament. Then it draws out of the soul the vain and empty talkativeness and complaining against the providence of God which is like the noise of frogs."[154] In Origen's view, every soul that lives apart from scriptural guidance is Pharaoh, and the blindness of such a soul to timeless truth and divine providence binds it in misery to the earthbound "frogs" of baseless words. The frog was for Origen what the fly was for Augustine, an anthropological image, a means for imagining the soul's unattractive proclivities. As the poet Theodore Roethke once remarked, "I'm sure I've been a toad, one time or other," and Origen would no doubt have agreed with this unflattering but all-too-true assessment of human nature.[155]

In the ancient Christian zoological imagination, frogs were handy as mirrors of distorted human behavior in contexts other than exegeses of the plagues of Egypt. Various authors found in these small creatures not an excess of theological wonder but rather an excess of moral disgust. In his *Lausiac History*, for example, Palladius attributed the following observation to two of the pious old men of the desert whose lives he recorded, Chronius and Paphnutius: "The souls of the sinful resemble different fountains. The gluttons and lovers of wine resemble springs that have been fouled; the greedy and fraudulent are like fountains with frogs."[156] Here once more the frog bears the onus of human defects. Although Palladius does not specify what the presence of frogs actually does to a fountain, the visual image that the text conjures is surely grotesque, especially in a culture that valued gardens with their sparkling fountains as paradisal oases.[157]

In its presentation of frogs, the *Physiologus* was a bit more differentiated, imagining two kinds of frog and the two kinds of people that they are like. The text reads:

> There is a land frog and a marine frog. The Physiologus said of the
> land frog that it bears the heat of the sun and the flaming fire, but

when harsh winter takes it, it dies. If the marine frog comes out of the water and the sun touches it, it dives back into the water at once. The most noble Christians are like the land frog, for they bear the heat of temptations. If then winter violently comes upon them, that is, persecution because of virtue, they will die. But those of the world are marine, for when a light heat of temptation or lust touches them they cannot endure it but dive again on to the same longing for sexual intercourse. The Physiologus spoke well about the frog.[158]

In this text, the frogs are hardly frogs at all; they don't even croak! They are simply ciphers for virtue and vice. In this ascetically oriented text, virtue means resistance to temptation, while vice is associated with sexual desire. This association of the marine frog with desire and lust is interesting in light of Greco-Roman zoological lore about frogs as reported by the naturalist Aelian who—somewhat surprisingly, in light of reactions to frogs' croaks discussed earlier—reports that croaks are love spells (ἴυγγας ἐρωτικάς). He continues: "The frog, as a signal for sexual intercourse, emits a certain cry to the female, like a lover singing a serenade, and this cry is called its croak, so they say. And when it attracts the female to itself they wait for the night. They cannot copulate under water, and they shun mutual embraces on land in the daytime. But when night descends they emerge with complete fearlessness and take their pleasure of one another."[159] In this text, desire is a song, and the sexuality of frogs is naturalized as sensual pleasure.

Such a positive view of the vital materiality of the being of frogs did not, to my knowledge, find expression in ancient Christian texts. A return to a final meditation on the frogs in Exodus will show just how supercharged—in an extremely negative sense—these small bodies could be. Gregory of Nyssa did not like frogs. In the interpretive section of his *Life of Moses*, Gregory presents them as "ugly and noisy amphibians, leaping about, not only unpleasant to the sight, but also having a foul-smelling skin; they entered the houses, beds, and storerooms of the Egyptians, but they did not affect the life of the Hebrews."[160] In his *Homilies on the Song of Songs*, he asks rhetorically (in a brief aside about the plagues in Egypt), "What deeds it is that one does to produce a stink of frogs in his own house?"[161] He gives no answer to this question in the homily, but he does give an answer in no uncertain terms in the *Life of Moses*: frogs are the evils that spring from the "sordid heart of men as though from some slimy mire."[162] Since for the sternly ascetic Gregory mud is often associated with the passions, and especially sexual passions, the frogs associated with sordid slime are very far from intimating creation's intricate design and soteriological hope.[163] How different are Gregory's frogs from Augustine's worms.

Not content with simply mentioning frogs in conjunction with sensuality, Gregory expands upon just what this sordid frog self is: "One sees in the sordid and licentious life that which is indeed born out of clay and mire and that which, through imitation of the irrational, remains in a form of life neither altogether human nor frog. Being a man by nature and becoming a beast by passion, this kind of person exhibits an amphibious form of life ambiguous in nature."[164] With this reference to an ambiguous, amphibious form of life, one might almost think that Gregory knew something about the sexual development of frogs. In *The Biology of Frogs*, Samuel Holmes reports that it is difficult to distinguish between male and female frogs when they are young because the males have gonads, sometimes containing egg follicles, that look like ovaries. Thus in Holmes's terms young frogs are "juvenile hermaphrodites," a phrase humorously glossed by David Miller as "a sort of frog version of polymorphous perversity."[165]

Gregory couldn't agree more, although his sense of polymorphous perversity is unrelievedly negative rather than playful. The ambiguous frog-man, "neither altogether human nor frog," is "profligate in everything."[166] As Gregory's rather feverish denunciation of the froggish life continues, the muddy passions in the heart spread out, displaying their contaminating influence even in the frog-man's domicile: "In the house of the one there are frescoes on the wall which by their artful pictures inflame the sensual passions. These things bring out the nature of the illness, and through the eye passion pours in upon the soul from the dishonorable things which are seen."[167] And these visible "sensual spectacles" in the house are as nothing when compared with what lurks in the "storeroom," "that is to say, the secret and unmentionable things of his life, [where] you will discern in his licentiousness a much greater pile of frogs."[168] Thus does the full weight of sexual licentiousness fall on the small body of the frog. In this particular case, the zoological imagination is as excessive as the negative vibrancy attributed to the animal. Gregory has used the image of the frog to theorize an intensity of material being quite as forcefully as might any contemporary new materialist.

Given the negative view of frogs that emerges from ancient Christian texts, it is stunning to find that artifacts from material culture tell quite a different story. Archaeologists have unearthed a large group of small oil lamps, indigenous to Egypt, that they call "frog lamps" (Figure 10). Incised with naturalistic-looking frogs, the lamps were produced beginning in the second century CE and continued through the Christian period in Egypt. Beginning in the late third century and extending throughout the fourth, lamps incised with a frog and a cross monogram were produced; sometimes frog and cross were so closely identified that the frog's body formed the Chi of the Chi Rho monogram and its head formed the top of the Rho (Figure 11).[169] A frog with the Christian symbol of the Chi Rho figured either alongside or as its body is surely a surprising counterpoint to the frog as plague. In fact, literal frogs, as contrasted with textual ones, held a special place in Egyptian life and lore. As the authors of *Art and Holy Powers in the Early Christian House* explain about the frog,

> This animal held a special meaning for the inhabitants of Egypt. . . . Frogs were significant for the Egyptians because the amphibians appeared after the annual summer rising of the Nile, an event upon which all life in Egypt depended. The sources of the Nile were unknown to the people who lived along its banks, and so it is small wonder that the rising of the river was regarded as a miracle, the gift, first of the pagan gods, then of Christ. The frogs, which seemed to spring spontaneously from the wet mud when it was warmed by the sun, became a symbol of that miracle, and thus of creation and life.[170]

In material culture and imagination, then, frogs were guarantees of the continuing abundance of the natural world created by God. They were also theological signs of the highest degree: many frog lamps were marked with the inscription "I am the Resurrection."[171] Here is an unexpected vibrancy of matter, as the despised frog of the ancient Christian textual imagination becomes a light-giving Christological image, a bringer of life rather than a carrier of moral pollution. Liberating frogs from the conceptual space in which their association with plague had imprisoned them, these frog lamps, like Augustine's Christological worms, command attention as what I called earlier a positive ontology of vibrant matter. Conceptually, small is large.

Indeed, the idea that small is large, that small things loomed large in the ancient Christian zoological imagination, has been the guiding theme of this chapter. The various small things considered here—worms, flies, mosquitoes, frogs—may be tiny in size, but they are immense as loci of surplus value. One might even describe them as triggers for ethical and theological thought. Or perhaps the musings of the French philosopher Gaston Bachelard on miniatures puts the point more elegantly. In *The Poetics of Space*, Bachelard wrote that the miniature "is one of the refuges of greatness," by which he meant that "immen-

FIGURE 10. Lamp with frog motif. Egypt, late third–early fourth century CE, earthenware. Courtesy of Spurlock Museum, University of Illinois at Urbana-Champaign.

FIGURE 11. Lamp with frog-cross monogram. Egypt, third–fourth century CE. Kelsey Museum of Archaeology, #22432, University of Michigan.

sity in the intimate domain is intensity, an intensity of being."[172] It is precisely the intensity that accompanied the ancient Christian gaze at small things that has sparked this chapter's explorations of one form of zoological imagination in Christian antiquity.

Coda

It may seem odd that a discussion of small things has not included such tiny creatures as bees, ants, and spiders in its purview. As one scholar of ancient animals has pointed out, "The spider is one of the most common stock illustrations of intelligent behavior among animals in antiquity," and the same is true of bees and ants.[173] Ancient Christians, no less than their cultural fellows of other religious persuasions, often petitioned the practical wisdom of such insects, while at the same time, however, demeaning them for their lack of rationality. This rather uncomfortable jostling of admiration and debasement is the topic of discussion in Chapter 2, where I consider exactly what ancient Christians meant by the irrationality of animals, especially in the light of positive estimations of their behavior and character. Thus bees, ants, and spiders make their appearance in that chapter rather than here.

With that said, however, I shall offer here one more anecdote about bees. It will be an appropriate way to end this chapter because it is a concrete image of the concept of theological wonder petitioned at the chapter's beginning. Not surprisingly, bees and flowers form a pair in the modern as well as the ancient zoological imagination. Here is a line from a poem by Anne Carson: "Flowers sigh and two noon bees float backwards"—backward perhaps in time, to the fourth century when Ambrose of Milan was composing his treatise *On Virginity*.[174] Ambrose, among others, read the biblical Song of Songs as an ascetic text in which the bride was understood as a virgin, the highest calling for a young Christian woman.[175] At one point in his treatise on virgins, Ambrose had in mind Song of Songs 4:11 (Vulgate), in which the bridegroom says, "Your lips are like a dripping honeycomb, my bride; honey and milk are under your tongue."[176] With honeycomb, honey, and bees thus in mind, Ambrose wrote the following: "The labor of bees as well as their continence affords a comparison with virginity: the bee feeds on dew, knows no marriage, makes honey—How I wish you, daughter, to be an imitator of this bee, whose food is flowers, whose produce is collected by the mouth, stored up by the mouth."[177] In the zoological imagination of Ambrose, the tiny, continent bee that makes honey—or honeyed words—is a fitting carrier of one of Ambrose's highest theological construals of the human body. Bee and virgin together do indeed convey a sense of theological wonder concerning the soteriological potential embedded in the bodies of women.

And as if the nectar-gathering bee weren't exuberant enough, Ambrose adds the charming image of the bee whose food is flowers. His vibrant, flower-eating bee is of course a bearer of serious ascetic advice. Happily, however, it also passes naturalist inspection. In *The Forest Unseen*, the zoologist David George Haskell, to whom the discussions in this chapter have already appealed, devoted some of his observatory powers to bees. Sounding somewhat like a latter-day Ambrose, he wrote: "The larval bee that hatches from the egg will munch its way through the pollen paste and emerge several weeks later, its body built wholly out of flowers. This dependence on pollen and nectar will continue for the rest of the bee's life. Bees eat nothing else; they are the original 'flower power' creatures."[178] And with this image of the flower power of (virginal) bees, I close this discussion of the role of small things in the ancient Christian zoological imagination.

Afterword

In Plato's dialogue the *Statesman*, an Eleatic Stranger who is the main interlocutor tells a myth of a golden age, the Age of Cronos, when the earth was bounteous, the seasons were gentle, and human beings, at leisure, went naked and slept outside on the beds of grass that the earth provided.[1] As in the biblical book of Genesis, animals were a part of this paradise:

> Stranger: Well then, if the foster-children of Cronos, with that much leisure attending them and the possibility of being able to engage in conversations not only with humans but also with beasts, made full use of all these advantages for the purpose of philosophy, by associating both with beasts and with one another, and by learning from every nature whether one of them that has some special power has perceived something distinctive that set it apart from the others and contributed to the gathering of intelligence, then it's easy to judge that the people back then excelled a thousand-fold those of the present in point of happiness.[2]

In Plato's imagination of a blissful and happy existence, humans could talk to animals, and animals could talk to us. As David Farrell Krell comments on this passage, "Our conversations all went in the direction of philosophy. . . . Humans and other animals told one another their stories, their μύθοι, and all were alike in their enthusiasm for insight and for the riches of language, ἐπιθυμίας . . . περί τε ἐπιστημῶν καί τῶν λόγων χρείας [272d]."[3]

Centuries later, these philosophizing animals were followed by ancient Christianity's theologizing animals, alike in their possession of insight and logos. Krell thinks of the phenomenon of the talking animal as a kind of dream that bespeaks "the necessity of learning a new way to speak and think" about animals and their relationships to metaphysics, ethics, and philosophical anthropology. Plato, for him one of the best at this kind of learning, "dreamed that once upon a time humans and other animals spoke together, which is to say that they listened to one another. Is there room for such a dream today?"[4] This is, I surmise, a rhetorical question, since Krell himself is fully aware of the out-pouring of publications in the field of animal studies in the past fifteen years, an outpouring by now so vast that a single person would have trouble reading it all. Yet this is, from my perspective, an apposite rhetorical question because it keeps the "turn to the animal" in the foreground as a pressing area of inquiry.

My work in this book has been to explore whether there was room for "such a dream" in ancient Christianity. I hope I have shown that the answer is yes. This is not, however, a book that attempts to "save" Christianity for the animal rights movement. Christianity's anthropocentric rhetoric is a major impedi-ment, since "human exceptionalism is what sanctions human violence against other life-forms."[5] What this book *does* show, however, is that there are resources in ancient Christian texts for imagining otherwise the basis of human-animal relations, even when those relations are paradoxically presented as both positive and negative in the same text. In many ways, one can see in many ancient Chris-tian texts an opening out of the human self to an engagement with other ani-mals in matters of vulnerability and finitude, emotional expressions and psychological needs, in short a shared fundament of bodily life that had striking theological and ethical dimensions. We have seen animals positioned as friends, role models, pedagogues, occasions for theological reflection, metaphors, and allegories.

And, as Chapter 5 on tiny animal beings attests, there was wonder. In a succinct gloss on Derrida's musings on paradise in Genesis as read through the lens of the prologue of the Gospel of John, philosopher Krell writes: "In the . . . biblical Paradise, animals precede the human animal, since the Word that was in the beginning spoke up for the animals first of all. In the incipient Logos was Life, ζωή, and such Life was the light, φῶς, of human beings. Human beings did not get a biography; they got a luminous zoology."[6] Derrida argues that human beings follow the animals, not only in terms of following them in thought but also sequentially, since in Genesis the animals were created first, before the human beings. The word that was life and light is shared by humans and ani-mals. Hence the luminous zoology. Such a luminous view of animals—indeed, of the entire creation—was powerfully expressed in the hexaemeral tradition in ancient Christianity. I have saved a discussion of these expressions of a vibrant, spirit-infused material world until now because these expressions present such a significant departure from ancient Christian exceptionalism.

The idea that God can be known through the created order was expressed in the Christian tradition already in the apostle Paul's letter to the Romans: "Ever since the creation of the world his [God's] eternal power and divine nature, invisible though they are, have been understood and seen through the things he has made [1:20]." Forty-some years later, the author of 1 Clement wrote a virtual hymn to the universe, emphasizing the creator's presence in terms of the cosmos's order, harmony, and peace. Even "the tiniest creatures come together in harmony and peace," he remarks.[7] This theme of cosmic wonder, which eventually spawned the view of the cosmos as a "book" whose components can be "read," did not reach its fullest expression until the fourth century. As Paul Blowers has observed,

> Though pre-Nicene Christian theologians certainly recognized the value of Christians perusing the book of creation as a basis for extolling the virtues of the Creator, the formal discipline of natural contemplation (θεωρία φυσική) did not truly come into its own in ecclesial and monastic contexts until the fourth century. The Peace of Constantine brought with it an increasing sense—undoubtedly still tentative for many ascetics—that the church was now more at home in the world and that its vocation was not just to transcend the cosmos but to participate in its transformation. Both in churchly devotion and in the evolving traditions of monastic piety, there was markedly greater focus on the contemplation of nature as a formative discipline for all Christians.[8]

Augustine, though not writing in the hexaemeral tradition, indicated how "zoology" might be "luminous" when he wrote the following: "I will not be idle in seeking out the substance of God [*substantiam dei*], either through his scriptures or his creatures. For both these are offered us for our observation and scrutiny in order that in them he may be sought, he may be loved, who inspired the one and created the other."[9]

This is the ancient Christian version of vibrant materiality, when the very substance of God can be sought through the earth's creatures. In the hexaemeral tradition, Basil of Caesarea, for example, called the created world (τῆς κτίσεως) a "wonder" (θαῦμα).[10] God, says Basil, is an artist who has given everything in the creation the beauty of harmonious proportion.[11] Indeed, Basil insists on the beauty of the whole created order and, even though, when compared with the grandeur of divine beauty, neither cosmic bodies like the sun and the moon nor

earthly creatures like ants and gnats can give an adequate sense of that beauty—
still they *all* reflect God, however faintly.[12] Suffice it to say that the "majestic
and blessed [τοῦ σεμνοῦ τούτου καὶ μακαρίου]" cosmos of Basil's exclamations is
echoed in the hexaemeral commentaries of both John Chrysostom and
Ambrose.[13] Chrysostom, for example, commands his audience to "notice how
the divine nature shines out of the very manner of creation," while Ambrose
exclaims over the "true beauty" of God's work as cosmic artist.[14]

All of these writers are in accord with the late ancient assumption of "a
general principle of sympathy between all the parts of this visible and invisible
world that, in their order, are the cosmos."[15] As Basil put it, the creator "bound
together the whole world, consisting of dissimilar parts, by an unbroken bond
of affection [φιλίας θεσμῷ] into a single communion [κοινωνίαν] and harmony
[ἁρμονίαν], so that things positioned at the greatest distance from each other
appear to be united through affinity [διὰ τῆς συμπαθείας]."[16] In a study of cosmos, Catherine Chin remarks that "the late ancient cosmos, as cosmos, insists
on a multiplicity of connected parts."[17] And just as Basil insists on the harmony
and affinity of the dissimilar parts, Chin continues: "In a real, physical sense,
then, the late ancient cosmos was made out of resemblances and connections:
the microcosms and macrocosms that made up the cosmos were intricate sets
of materially enchained reflections, constantly in the process of coming into
accord."[18]

Earlier in this book I wrote about the "strange kinship" of humans and
animals and about "the flesh of the world" in which there is a "shared creatureliness," and also about the "mutual entanglement" of humans and other animals.
Now, from the broader perspective of the late ancient view of the cosmos, which
includes Christian views, these phrases, as well as the material in this book,
assume their full significance. Alongside the rhetoric of human exceptionalism—to which all of the authors in the hexaemeral tradition subscribed—there
was *another* rhetoric, a rhetoric of cosmic resemblance, connection, harmony,
and affinity that does not debase animals but includes them along with everything else in the material and spiritual enchainments that are the created order.
This is a perspective that supports, even celebrates, difference without recourse
to hierarchical valuations. I think it is a perspective that continuously announces
itself in the forms of ancient Christian literature that this book presents. Perhaps, "in the eye of the animal," this perspective hints at what Derrida imagined
as "the regeneration of paradise." As Krell explains, "The key to such a regeneration of paradise, of the Golden Age to come, in Derrida's view, is to recognize

the Earth's surface as a garden of infinite differences and differentiations, a garden not spoiled by any single sovereign division, which always amounts to an 'us' versus 'them.' Especially where other animals are concerned."[19] So we end where we began, with Adam and the other animals, existing together in a paradisal fundament, a luminous zoology indeed.

Ancient Christian and Other Authors

For readers who are not specialists in the study of Christianity in late antiquity, the following brief descriptions will aid in providing historical contexts for the book's discussions of, or references to, these authors and their works.

Aelian (ca. 170–235). This Roman author and teacher of rhetoric is best known for his *De natura Animalium* (*On the Nature of Animals*). This work is a collection in seventeen books of anecdotes and tales from the natural world that showcase animal behavior and include comparisons with human behavior. Aelian often brought out the moral implications of the (sometimes fantastical) animal lore he presented.

Ambrose (ca. 339–397). Ambrose was bishop of Milan from 374 to 397 and is remembered as one of the four leading ecclesiastics of the Western Church (along with Augustine, Jerome, and Gregory the Great). Among his many literary works were treatises on virginity, in which he positioned the Virgin Mary as the patroness of Christian women embracing celibacy as a religious calling. Among his biblical exegetical works was a commentary on the six days of creation in the book of Genesis, his *Hexaemeron,* which is indebted to the *Hexaemeron* of Basil of Caesarea.

Antonius. A hagiography of the Stylite saint Simeon (ca. 390–459), who spent almost forty years standing atop a pillar in the Syrian desert, was attributed to this author. He is otherwise unknown. Since Antonius claims to be Simeon's contemporary, the hagiography may have been written sometime during the second half of the fifth century.

Athanasius (ca. 300–373). Athanasius was bishop of Alexandria from 328 to 373 and was a leading theologian and ecclesiastic in Egyptian Christianity in the fourth century. Among his major literary works were apologetic treatises refuting the theological positions of the Arians as well as a hagiography, the *Life of Saint Antony*, which became the model for subsequent lives of the saints.

Augustine (354–430). Augustine was bishop of Hippo, a town in the Roman province of Numidia in North Africa, from 395 to 430. A prolific author, Augustine is best known for three works, the *Confessions*, *On the Trinity*, and the *City of God*. His sweeping vision of the creation, fall, and redemption of humankind, as well as his articulation of views of human sinfulness in relation to the biblical Adam, the individual's dependence on divine grace, and the role of the body and sexuality in human self-definition have had profound influence on the development of Western Christianity. This book draws on many of his writings; of special importance are his many sermons in which exegesis of animal imagery in the Bible—particularly the psalms—is prominent.

Basil of Caesarea (ca. 330–379). Basil was bishop of Caesarea in Cappadocia, a region of ancient Asia Minor, from 370 until his death. He is remembered both for his fervent support of an ascetic lifestyle for all Christians as well as for his social concern, especially for the poor and the sick. Of lasting value among his writings was an *Asceticon*, a "rule" that was foundational for the establishment of monasteries in the eastern part of the Roman Empire. Also important was his *Hexaemeron*, a commentary on the six days of creation in Genesis that combines biblical exegesis with contemporary philosophy and science, including detailed discussions of animals and fish. This Christian cosmology was imitated (and large portions copied) by Ambrose in the composition of his own *Hexaemeron*.

Clement of Alexandria (ca. 160–215). Clement was a Christian teacher who appears to have led a "school" or independent study circle. He was deeply conversant with Greek philosophy and culture and is notable for his attempts to show that Christianity represented the pinnacle of philosophy. He wrote numerous works that addressed both beginners and advanced students of Christian doctrine and practice.

Cyprian (ca. 200–258). An influential bishop of Carthage in North Africa from ca. 248 until his death, Cyprian is perhaps best remembered for his entanglements in ecclesiastical and political conflicts during the rule of the emperor Decius (249–251) and its aftermath. Decius's imperial edict of 250, requiring all citizens of the empire to demonstrate their loyalty to the gods by offering sacrifice, caused a serious rift between those Christians who com-

plied and those who did not. Cyprian wrote treatises that opposed faction-
alism and attempted to promote unity in the church.

Cyril of Scythopolis (ca. 525–ca. 558). Cyril's *Lives of the Monks of Palestine* is the
major historical source for knowledge of Palestinian monasticism in the
fifth and sixth centuries. Cyril presents the monks whose lives he represents
as holy men who functioned as conduits of spiritual power, especially in the
form of miracles. Several of his stories feature encounters between monks
and wild animals.

Didymus of Alexandria (313–398). Also known as Didymus the blind, this
author wrote extensively on theological and biblical topics. He followed
Origen of Alexandria in his use of the allegorical method for interpreting
scripture. His *Commentary on Genesis* provides examples of this method of
biblical interpretation.

Dionysius the Areopagite (ca. 500). A pseudonymous author who adopted his
name from Acts 17:34, which mentions a member of the Athenian court of
Areopagus named Dionysius who was converted to Christianity by the
apostle Paul, Dionysius was a theologian who famously used Neoplatonic
philosophy to interpret Christian theology. He adhered to an apophatic
approach to the divine and was a major influence on the development of
Christian mysticism.

Gregory of Nyssa (ca. 331–ca. 394). One of the major theologians writing in
Greek in the fourth century, Gregory was also active in ecclesiastical politics
and was ordained bishop of Nyssa in Asia Minor in 372. In addition to writing a biography of his sister Macrina, which extolled virginity as the most
virtuous Christian lifestyle for women, and a *Life* of Moses in which Gregory's philosophical approach to theology is on display, he wrote commentaries on Psalms and on the Song of Songs that showcase his allegorical
interpretation of scripture, including scripture's animal images, in the Origenist tradition.

Hippolytus of Rome (ca. 170–ca. 236). Presbyter in the church in Rome, and
ultimately bishop of a schismatic faction there, Hippolytus was a learned
writer whose work reflects the traditions of the Greek-speaking eastern part
of the Roman Empire. Today he is most well known for the *Refutation of All
Heresies* ascribed to him, although he also wrote an exegetical treatise on the
biblical book of Daniel as well as liturgical and theological texts.

Irenaeus (ca. 115–ca. 202). Born in Smyrna in Asia Minor, Irenaeus traveled to
Rome for study and was later made bishop of Lyons. He was a defender of

apostolic authority as vested in the church's bishops. His most important work was the *Adversus haereses* (*Against Heresies*). He directed his heresiological polemic against a number of comtemporary Christian groups such as the Valentinians, the Marcosians, and others that are loosely associated together as "Gnostic."

Isaac the Syrian (d. ca. 700). Sometimes referred to as Isaac of Nineveh, this writer's works participate in the Syriac spiritual tradition. Isaac wrote homilies espousing an ascetic lifestyle as well as prayers and aphorisms expressing a mystical theological perspective.

Jerome (ca. 347–419 or 420). Jerome was a major figure in fourth-and early fifth-century Latin Christianity. He was for a time influential in the circle of Pope Damasus in Rome in the 380s, but ecclesiastical politics forced him out, and he moved to Bethlehem, where he founded a monastery and spent the rest of his life, engaging in such major projects as the translation of the Hebrew Bible into Latin and the learned exegesis of scriptural texts. He was active as a theological polemicist but also as a biographer of ascetic heroes and as a translator, and so disseminator, of the works of Origen of Alexandria from Greek into Latin.

John Chrysostom (ca. 347–407). One of the most eloquent orators in Christian antiquity, John became a priest in 386 and served the churches in the city of Antioch. His sermons were notable for their crafting of an ideal Christian ethos based especially on the Gospels and Pauline epistles. John was appointed bishop of Constantinople in 398, but ecclesiastical politics forced him out in 404. His extensive homiletic corpus covers exegesis of biblical texts as well as social reform and celebration of martyrs. Like many leading churchmen of his day, he spent time as a monk and adhered to the tenets of asceticism.

John Moschos (ca. 550–619). John was a Palestinian monk who lived for most of his life in monasteries in the Judean and Egyptian deserts. Known for his *Pratum spirituale* (*The Spiritual Meadow*), an assemblage of anecdotes and stories about Palestinian and Egyptian monks, John celebrated the ascetic spirituality and lifestyle of these holy men. His collection, probably compiled around 600, is akin to such earlier compilations of monastic tales as Palladius's *Lausiac History* and the anonymous *Historia monachorum in Aegypto* (*History of the Monks in Egypt*).

Martial (ca. 40–ca. 104). A prominent literary figure, Martial was a Roman poet and writer of epigrams that depicted the mores of his fellow Romans from all social ranks.

Origen of Alexandria (ca. 185–ca. 251). Origen was a learned philosophical theologian and prolific biblical exegete as well as an apologist for Christianity against pagan critique. One of his major theological treatises, *De principiis* (*On First Principles*), constructed a Christian cosmology. The vast corpus of Origen's commentaries and homilies on various biblical books is notable for his insistence on teasing out the spiritual import of scriptural words and passages. Origen's development of allegorical interpretation of the Bible was influential on such later exegetes as Gregory of Nyssa.

Ovid (43 BCE–CE 17). A Roman poet devoted to the topics of erotic love and seduction as well as to myths of metamorphosis, Ovid also wrote *Fasti*, a calendar of the Roman year in verse; it is a valuable chronicle of the festivals and other customs associated with Roman religion.

Palladius (ca. 365–425). Eventually chosen as bishop of Helenopolis in Bithynia, Palladius was a monk who lived for a time with the austerely ascetic monks of the Egyptian desert communities of Cellia and Nitria. Toward the end of his life he wrote his *Historia Lausiaca* (*Lausiac History*), which contains anecdotes and brief biographical snapshots of the lives of the Christian ascetics of those desert areas.

Philo of Alexandria (ca. 20 BCE–ca. CE 50). Scion of an important Jewish family in Alexandria, Egypt, and a leader of the Jewish community there, Philo is best known as a philosophical thinker who used contemporary Platonic concepts to interpret Judaism, especially Jewish scripture. His use of the allegorical method to interpret biblical texts, as well as his philosophical approach to the Bible, were deeply influential on the exegetical theories and interpretations of such Christian authors as Origen of Alexandria.

Pliny (the Elder) (23/24–79). Pliny was a Roman polymath who wrote military history and a rhetorical training manual as well as his famous *Naturalis historia* (*History of Nature*). A monumental work in thirty-seven books, Pliny's *Naturalis historia* contained "facts" (some false) and observations about human beings and other animals, the uses of plants and animals in medicine, and a variety of other topics, such as metals and architecture.

Plutarch (ca. 50–ca. 120). A learned polymath like Pliny the Elder, Plutarch was a rhetorician, biographer, philosopher in the Platonic tradition, and antiquarian. In addition, he was one of only two prominent thinkers in pagan antiquity (Porphyry was the other) who held that animals are reasoning beings. His treatise *De sollertia animalium* (*On the Cleverness of Animals*) refuted Stoic philosophy's view of animals as irrational and argued that animals are rational.

Porphyry (ca. 232–ca. 305). A student of the noted Neoplatonic philosopher Plotinus, Porphyry became a Neoplatonic philosopher in his own right. He was a defender of pagan religion and wrote about oracles as well as about Homer, part of whose work he allegorized. In addition, he wrote the now-lost treatise *Against the Christians*, whose historical-critical attack on scriptures venerated by Christians was considered important enough that several Christian apologists wrote refutations of it. Along with Plutarch, Porphyry was one of the two prominent philosophers in antiquity who defended the intelligence of animals, a position to which he devoted an entire treatise, *De abstinentia* (*On Abstinence from Killing Animals*), which is in part an argument in favor of vegetarianism.

Quintillian (ca. 35–ca. 100). Orator, literary critic, and teacher, Quintillian wrote a twelve- volume work on Latin rhetoric.

Sappho (fl. seventh century BCE). Arguably the most famous woman poet in Greek antiquity, Sappho wrote love poems, wedding songs, and hymns to the goddess Aphrodite.

Sophronius (fl. seventh century). A monk who lived in both Palestinian and Egyptian monasteries, Sophronius was bishop of Jerusalem from 634 to 639. In addition to hagiographical writings, he wrote theological defenses of the doctrines promulgated at the Council of Chalcedon as well as odes devoted to festivals of the church.

Stobaeus (fl. fifth century). Stobaeus compiled an anthology of excerpts of the poetry and prose of pagan authors from Homer through the philosopher Themistius in the fourth century.

Sulpicius Severus (ca. 360–ca. 420). Sulpicius converted to the ascetic life as an adult and founded a monastery in southern France (ancient Gaul). He was an enthusiastic supporter of Martin, bishop of Tours, and wrote an influential hagiography in which he emphasized Martin's miracles of healing. He also wrote a text entitled *Dialogi* (*Dialogues*), in which the ascetic feats of Martin are shown to be comparable to those of the heroes of monastic practice in the Egyptian desert.

Tertullian (ca. 160–ca. 225). Centered in Carthage in North Africa, Tertullian was a prolific author who was both an apologist for Christianity and a heresiologist, taking aim at so-called Gnostic groups and especially at the theologian Marcion. In his later years he embraced Montanism, a rigorist prophetic movement within Christianity.

Theodoret (393–ca. 460). Historian, theologian, and exegete, Theodoret, following a monastic education, was appointed bishop of Cyrrhus in Syria in

423. For much of his career he was embroiled in politico-theological controversies that centered on Christological doctrine. Aside from his role in ecclesiastical controversy, he is best known for his hagiographical collection, *A History of the Monks of Syria.*

Theon (fl. second century). Theon, an Alexandrian, was a rhetorician who wrote a teacher's manual, the *Progymnasmata* (*Preliminary Exercises*) for use in schools of rhetoric. The manual introduced students to basic rhetorical forms such as fables, anecdotes, and maxims.

Theophilus of Antioch (fl. second century). An apologist who ultimately became bishop of Antioch, Theophilus wrote his only surviving work, *Ad Autolycum* (*To Autolycus*), to instruct an otherwise unknown individual about the immorality of paganism when compared with Christianity. The treatise contains attacks on idolatry, mythology, and emperor worship as well as exegeses of the opening chapters of the book of Genesis.

NOTES

INTRODUCTION

1. For the dating of the diptych, see Maguire, "Adam and the Animals," 365, n. 15. The provenance of the diptych has been variously suggested to be Constantinople or Italy. A few of my comments at the outset of this Introduction are taken from my "Adam, Eve, and the Elephants."

2. As noted by Konowitz, "The Program of the Carrand Diptych," 484, the left leaf of the Carrand diptych presents the earliest known artistic representation of Adam with the animals in Eden. The right leaf of the diptych represents scenes from the life of the apostle Paul, including the incident on Malta when Paul was unharmed by the bite of a viper (see Acts 28:3–6).

3. Peers, "Adam's Anthropocene," 164.

4. Ibid., 162.

5. See, for example, Konowitz, "The Program of the Carrand Diptych," 485; Toynbee, *Animals in Roman Life and Art*, 294; Kessler, "Diptych with Old and New Testament Scenes," 505.

6. Morris, "Animals into Art in the Ancient World," 198.

7. Peers, "Adam's Anthropocene," 164.

8. See, for example, Konowitz, "The Program of the Carrand Diptych," 488; Maguire, "Adam and the Animals," 364–66; Toynbee, *Animals in Roman Life and Art*, 294, allows for some mutuality in the image by noting that several of the animals "are open-mouthed, as though they were answering to the name assigned to them."

9. Peers, "Adam's Anthropocene," 164.

10. Historical snapshots of ancient Christian authors such as Basil, Ambrose, and John Chrysostom are provided in the Appendix as an aid to readers who are not specialists in the history of Christianity in late antiquity. For passages linking human beings, reason, and dominion, see Basil of Caesarea, *Hex.* 10.6–7; 19; Ambrose, *Hex.* 6.43; John Chrysostom, *Hom. in Gen.* 9.8. See also the discussion of various passages in Augustine's works that follow this line of thought regarding Adam in Clark, "The Fathers and the Animals."

11. Basil of Caesarea, *Hex.* 9.3. I have followed the numbering of this text in the Sources Chrétiennes series.

12. John Chrysostom, *Hom. in Gen.* 14.19.

13. Ibid., 14.20.

14. I should hasten to say at this point that this book's treatment of animals in early Christian texts is by no means exhaustive. Indeed, my hope is that the book will provoke further investigation into this fascinating area.

15. I have appropriated this phrase from Mitchell, *What Do Pictures Want?* 59. Speaking of paintings as things that are drawn toward objects, he writes: "Desire just *is*, quite literally, drawing, or *a* drawing—a pulling or attractive force, and the trace of this force in a picture" (59).

16. Bataille, *Theory of Religion*, 19, 24.

17. Ibid., 22 (italics in original).

18. Bailly, *Animal Side*, 10.

19. See Wolfe, "Human, All Too Human," 565.

20. Moore, "Introduction: From Animal Theory to Creaturely Theology," 1. See also Weil, *Thinking Animals*, 3–24.

21. Wolfe, "Human, All Too Human," 568.

22. See, for example, Baker, *Picturing the Beast* and *Postmodern Animal*.

23. See, for example, Kuzniar, *Melancholia's Dog*; Payne, *Animal Part*.

24. Good overviews are Calarco, *Zoographies*; Cavell et al., *Philosophy and Animal Life*; and Oliver, *Animal Lessons*.

25. See Gross, *Question of the Animal and Religion*; Moore, *Divinanimality*.

26. Fudge, "History of Animals," quoted by Wolfe, "Human, All Too Human," 566 (italics in original).

27. Wolfe, "Human, All Too Human," 566–67, quoting Derrida, *Animal*, 31.

28. Lundblad, "From Animal to Animality Studies," 500.

29. Wolfe, "Human, All Too Human," 570.

30. Weil, *Thinking Animals*, 20. On the problems with the singular "the animal," see Derrida, *Animal*, 23, 32, 47–48. I discuss Derrida's critique of "the animal" in Ch. 3, pp. 81–82.

31. Payne, *Animal Side*, 8.

32. Derrida, *Animal*, 3–4.

33. Ibid., 6.

34. Ibid., 48.

35. Ibid., 29. For discussion, see Calarco, *Zoographies*, 106, 110; Oliver, *Animal Lessons*, 132.

36. On animal suffering, see Derrida, *Animal*, 25–29.

37. Calarco, *Zoographies*, 118.

38. Derrida, *Animal*, 28.

39. Ibid., 51.

40. Rilke, "The Black Cat," in Mitchell, trans., *Selected Poetry*, 65, quoted in Weil, *Thinking Animals*, 40.

41. Weil, *Thinking Animals*, 40.

42. Derrida, *Animal*, 34 (emphasis in original).

43. Calarco, *Zoographies*, 125.

44. Derrida, *Animal*, 10 (emphasis in original).

45. Calarco, *Zoographies*, 125.

46. Bailly, *Animal Side*, 39.

47. Ibid., 59 (italics and ellipses in original).

48. Rilke, *Duino Elegies*, trans. Cohn, 67.

49. Bailly, *Animal Side*, 14.

50. Ibid., 15.

51. Ibid.

CHAPTER 1

1. Hughes, *Poetry in the Making*, 15.

2. Ibid., *Collected Poems*, 21.

3. Proulx, *Fine Just the Way It Is*, 48.

4. Collins, ed., "Introduction," 2.

5. Clare, "Autumn Birds," in Morton, *Ecological Thought*, loc. 671–72; Carlile, "The Cardinal," in Collins, ed., *Bright Wings*, 203.

6. Thoreau, in *Writings of Thoreau*, 339, quoted in Bennett, *Enchantment of Modern Life*, 95.

7. Ambrose, *Hex.* 5.12.36. For descriptions of ancient Christian and other ancient authors, see the Appendix.

8. Stevens, "Thirteen Ways of Looking at a Blackbird," in *Collected Poems*, 93.

9. Lingis, *Dangerous Emotions*, 56.

10. Ibid., 58.

11. Origen, *Hom. Lev.* 5.2.3.

12. Ibid.

13. Stevens, "Thirteen Ways of Looking at a Blackbird," in *Collected Poems*, 94; Sandburg, "Wilderness," in *Complete Poems*, 100.

14. Rilke, *Notebooks of Malta Laurids Brigge*, 26.

15. *Hom. opif.* 8.5, trans. Ladner, "Philosophical Anthropology of Gregory of Nyssa," 70 (translation slightly emended).

16. See *Hom. opif.* 18. For discussion, see Behr, "Rational Animal," 226–31.

17. Ambrose, *Hex.* 6.2.3: *Simul quia non possumus plenius nos cognoscere, nisi prius quae sit omnium natura animantium cognouerimus.*

18. Ambrose, *Hex.* 6.2.3.

19. On the use of animals "to shape the landscape of our humanity," see Foer, "Foreword," loc. 111. As Foer remarks further, "Our self-conception has always depended on how we imagine animal others" (loc. 142). As for interior birds, one wonders whether Origen is at this point relying on Plato to help him interpret Genesis. In his *Theaetetus* 197e, Plato has Socrates muse, "Let us suppose that every mind contains a kind of aviary stocked with birds of every sort, some in flocks apart from the rest, some in small groups, and some solitary, flying in any direction among them all." As Socrates goes on to explain, "The birds stand for pieces of knowledge" that are enclosed in the mind (*Collected Dialogues of Plato*, 904). Origen definitely knew the *Theaetetus*, since he quotes from it in his *C. Cels.* 4.62.

20. Origen, *Hom. in Gen.* 1.8.

21. Ibid.

22. Ibid. See also *Hom. in Gen.* 1.11: "Those things which are brought forth from the waters ought to be understood as the impulses and thoughts of our mind which are brought forth from the depth of the heart."

23. Ibid.

24. Bachelard, *Air and Dreams*, 66.

25. On the "spiritual metanarrative" as "the deepest meaning of the biblical text," see Dawson, *Christian Figural Reading*, 59. See also Irvine, *Making of Textual Culture*, 252–57, for a discussion of Origen's allegorical interpretation in connection with his "notion of an Eternal Gospel—a master discourse forming a kind of hypertext for any act of interpretation" (252). On the bestial inhabitants of the human soul in Origen's work at large, see Cox, "Origen and the Bestial Soul."

26. Origen, *Hom. in Gen.* 1.11.

27. See Origen, *De prin.* 4.3.4.

28. Dawson, *Christian Figural Reading*, 54.

29. Ingold, "Hunting and Gathering," 44.

30. Gross, "Introduction,"15.

31. Boyarin, *A Radical Jew*, 105.

32. Dawson, *Christian Figural Reading*, 48.

33. Ibid., 49, characterizing the position of Boyarin, whose perspectives he engages for much of the book.

34. Dawson, *Christian Figural Reading*, 59.

35. Ibid., 59.

36. Bailly, "Animals Are Masters of Silence," 89.

37. Sappho, Fragment 31.

38. Basil of Caesarea, *Hex.* 8.8; Ambrose, *Hex.* 5.12.38.

39. Bailly, "Animals Are Masters of Silence," 88.

40. Laux, "The Ravens of Denali," in Collins, ed., *Bright Wings*, 146.

41. Augustine, *Ex. 3 Ps.* 103.5 (RSV 104), *WSA*, p. 143. As Michael Cameron has pointed out, "references to Augustine's Psalms expositions can be confusing" (*Christ Meets Me Everywhere*, 326, n. 8). I have followed the numbering in the *Works of Saint Augustine* (*WSA*) translation by Maria Boulding. As Cameron explains, Boulding's translation "groups all the expositions of an individual psalm together [rather than separating the expositions into two series, one preached by Augustine as priest, the second as bishop] and counts them in a sequence" (*Christ Meets Me Everywhere*, 327, n. 8). The citation in this footnote thus refers to the third exposition of Ps. 103, section 5. I have given the page numbers in *WSA*, which is easily available online, for convenience.

42. Bachelard, *Air and Dreams*, 8.

43. Theophilus of Antioch, *Ad Autolycum* 2.17.

44. Ibid.

45. Clement of Alexandria, *Strom.* 5.83, 1–2 (trans. Murphy, 72).

46. Clement of Alexandria, *Protr.* 106.2–3 (trans. Murphy, 22).

47. Gregory of Nazianzus, *Or.* 28.26.

48. Ibid., 28.28.

49. Didymus of Alexandria, *Comm. in Gen.* 46.

50. Wallace Stevens's aphorism "There is no wing like meaning" is also quoted in Chapter 5. See Stevens, *Opus Posthumous*, 162.

51. For discussion of the notion of a cultural encyclopedia, see Irvine, *Making of Textual Culture*, 246.

52. Plato, *Phaedrus* 248c.

53. Plato, *Phaedrus* 249d–252e.

54. Gregory of Nazianzus, *Or.* 28.24. For discussion, see Maguire, *Earth and Ocean*, 39.

55. Maguire, *Earth and Ocean*, 39.

56. The annual cycle of shedding and regrowth of peacock feathers was noted by Pliny, *NH* 10.22.

57. Maguire, *Earth and Ocean*, 39.

58. Augustine, *Civ. Dei* 21.4 (trans. Bettenson).

59. Apicius, *Romanae artis coquinariae liber* 2.6. Jennison offers further culinary tidbits: "Peacocks' brains were among the more fantastic dishes served to the Emperor Vitellius, who enjoyed dining extravagantly as well as heavily. Juvenal refers to peacock as the rich glutton's food, and Martial to the waste of beauty in giving this bird to the cook" (*Animals for Show*, 108–9).

60. *Infancy Gospel of Thomas* 2.1–4.

61. Davis, *Christ Child*, 50, following the interpretation of Aasgaard, *Childhood of Jesus*.

62. Augustine, *Conf.* 1.19.30.

63. Davis, *Christ Child*, 51.

64. Nemerov, "On Metaphor," 223.

65. Ibid.

66. *Life and Miracles of St. Thecla*, Mir. 24.

67. Proulx, *Fine Just the Way It Is*, 103.

68. Ibid.

69. Aristotle, *HA* 9.10.614b; Pliny, *NH* 10.28.59–60; Aelian, *NA* 3.13.

70. Basil of Caesarea, *Hex.* 8.5.

71. Ambrose, *Hex.* 5.15.50.

72. Ibid.

73. Ibid.

74. Ibid., 5.15.52.

75. Ibid.

76. Ambrose, *On Paradise* 3.15–18.

77. See Chapter 3, where Basil's use of shame is analyzed.

78. I have (mis)appropriated this line of verse from Stein's poem "Arts of Joy," in Collins, ed., *Bright Wings*, 125.

79. See Ambrose's descriptions of birdsong as well as birds' migratory and other habitual behaviors in *Hex.* 5.12.39; 5.14.45.

80. Basil of Caesarea, *Hex.* 8.2.

81. Basil of Caesarea, *Hex.* 1.11. Other remarks about the physiology of birds include very brief remarks about bats' eyes and wings, owls' eyes, and swans' necks; see *Hex.* 8.7.

82. Basil of Caesarea, *Hex.* 8.5.

83. For discussion, see Arterbury, *Entertaining Angels*. See also Brown, *Through the Eye of a Needle*, 53–90.

84. For references, see Thompson, *A Glossary of Greek Birds*, 231.

85. Ibid.

86. The lines of poetry are from Creeley, "The Birds," in Collins, ed., *Bright Wings*, 21.

87. *Physiologus* 6 (trans. Curley, 9–10). For a discussion of the *Physiologus*'s treatment of the pelican as compared with other ancient texts, see Nicklas and Spittler, "Christ and the Pelican." I thank Georgia Frank for referring me to this article.

88. Augustine, *Ex. 1 Ps.* 101.7 (RSV 102), *WSA*, p. 52; for the solitary place as the Virgin's womb, see *Ex. 1 Ps.* 101.8 (RSV 102), *WSA*, p. 54.

89. Augustine, *Ex. 1 Ps.* 101.8 (RSV 102), *WSA*, p. 53.

90. Later in his exegesis, Augustine remarks, "However, it is for those who have written about pelicans to settle the question (about the mother pelican killing her chicks); we must not base our interpretation on a doubtful report." And yet he has just engaged in a rather lengthy exegesis based precisely on the lore surrounding the pelican, a fact that unsettles, at the very least, the seriousness of his doubt. He then goes on to speculate about the virgin birth and the pelican. See Augustine, *Ex. 1 Ps.* 101.8 (RSV 102), *WSA*, p. 54.

91. Ibid., pp. 53–54.

92. Ibid., p. 53.

93. Augustine, *Ex. 1 Ps.* 58.2 (RSV 59), *WSA*, p. 149.

94. Augustine, *Ex 1 Ps.* 58.10 (RSV 59), *WSA*, p. 156.

95. Augustine, *Ex. 1 Ps.* 90.4 (RSV 91), *WSA*, pp. 319–20. Note that the Holy Spirit was also imagined as a brooding bird: see Basil of Caesarea, *Hex.* 2.6, and Augustine, *Gen. litt.* 1.18.36, both of whom imagine the scene of the Holy Spirit hovering over the waters in Gen. 1:2 under the figure of a bird sitting on its eggs.

96. The passage about the hen's body being a fluffy muddle reads as follows: *quomodo fit hispidum totum corpus*. Presumably Augustine is referring to broody hens' propensity to leave their eggs or chicks briefly to take dirt baths.

97. Mk. 1:10; Mt. 3:16; Lk. 3:22; Jn. 1:32.

98. For a representative discussion of the Holy Spirit as dove that brings out the themes of salvation, peace, and innocence, see Tertullian, *De bap.* 8.

99. Ambrose, *Hex.* 6.9.68.

100. Cornell Lab of Ornithology, www.allaboutbirds.org/guide/Mourning_Dove/life-history, accessed 19 November 2014.

101. Cyprian, *De ecclesiae catholicae unitate* 9 (trans. Penn, *Kissing Christians*, 48).

102. Penn, *Kissing Christians*, 12.

103. Ibid., 49.

104. Ibid., 49. For Martial's remark, see Mart. 12.65.7

105. Augustine, *Io. Ev. Tr.* 6.4.

106. Augustine, *Serm.* 64.4 (CCL 38.426), quoted in Penn, *Kissing Christians*, 48.

107. Isidore of Seville, *Etymologiae* 12.61, quoted in Penn, *Kissing Christians*, 148, n. 100.

108. Augustine, *Ex. Ps.* 54.8 (RSV 55), *WSA*, p. 61.

109. Basil of Caesarea, *Hex.* 8.3, which translates λάνιοι as "amorous."

110. Lewis and Short, *A Latin Dictionary*, s.v. "gemitus."

111. Augustine, *Ex. Ps.* 54.8, *WSA*, p. 61.

112. Pastan, "After Reading Peterson's Guide," in Collins, ed., *Bright Wings*, 87.

113. Augustine, *Io. Ev. tr.* 6.1 (translation slightly emended).

114. Ibid., 6.2.

115. Augustine, *Io. Ev. tr.* 6.2.

116. Rilke, Untitled Poem, in *Ahead of All Parting*, 191. "Ah, Not to Be Cut Off," translation copyright © 1995 by Stephen Mitchell; from *Selected Poetry of Rainer Maria Rilke*, translated by Stephen Mitchell. Used by permission of Random House, an imprint and division of Penguin Random House LLC. All rights reserved. I thank Professor Karmen MacKendrick for bringing this poem to my attention.

117. Gregory of Nyssa, *Hom. in Cant.* 4. It should be noted that Gregory is not only relying on the notion of "beholding" in Plato's *Phaedrus*; he is also appealing to his era's theory of vision: "We see faces in the clear pupils of eyes that are focused on someone (for people who can give the scientific explanations of such things say that the eye activates its vision by receiving the impressions of the images given off by visible bodies), and for this reason it becomes a commendation of the eyes' form that the shape of a dove shows in their pupils. For people receive in themselves the likeness of whatever they gaze upon intently" (*Hom. in Cant.* 4).

118. Origen, *Comm. in Cant.* 3.3.

119. Ibid., 3.1.

120. Origen, *Comm. in Cant.* 3.1.

121. The phrase in quotation is from Billy Collins, "Christmas Sparrow," in Collins, ed., *Bright Wings*, 213.

122. The phrases in quotation marks are from Amy Clampitt, "The Kingfisher," in Collins, ed., *Bright Wings*, 118.

123. Origen, *Hom. in Lc.* 27.6.

124. Origen, *Hom. Lk.* 27.6.

125. See Maguire, Maguire, and Duncan-Flowers, *Art and Holy Powers*, 66.

126. I have borrowed and slightly altered the phrase "one impossible bright bird" from Ciardi, "Bird Watching," in Collins, ed., *Bright Wings*, 201.

127. Stevens, "Of Mere Being," in *Opus Posthumous*, 117–18.

128. Celsus, it should be noted, was one of only a handful of philosophers in Greco-Roman antiquity who held this position. For discussion, see Spittler, *Animals in the Apocryphal Acts of the Apostles*, 15–26. For ancient sources on the topic of animal rationality and irrationality, see Newmyer, *Animals in Greek and Roman Thought*, 3–26.

129. Origen, *C. Cels.* 4.81. Spittler's comment is succinct: "The Stoic sources give the impression that the issue of animal rationality was a philosophical line in the sand: to grant reason to animals was to fundamentally misunderstand the nature of human beings and their *summum bonum*" (*Animals in the Apocryphal Acts of the Apostles*, 15).

130. Origen, *C. Cels.* 4.88.

131. Ibid., 4.96.

132. Ibid., 4.96–97. On demonic inspiration of so-called prophetic animals, see *C. Cels.* 4.92–93. Long after Origen's era, early Christians were still commenting on divination and demons. As Morwenna Ludlow explains, "The Cappadocians were concerned with the place of augury in Roman religion. Gregory of Nyssa is typical in explicitly claiming that all the means by which certain persons claim to predict the future—'through divination by the examination of livers, or by watching the flight of birds, through omens, through the summoning of ghosts, through astrology'—all these are deception controlled by demons" (quoting Gregory of Nyssa, *Contra Fatum* [*Against Fate*], in "Demons, Evil, and Liminality in Cappadocian Theology," 206.

133. Beard, "Cicero and Divination," 41.

134. Origen, *C. Cels.* 4.95. Origen quotes Lev. 19:26 ("You shall not employ augury nor study the omens of birds"); Deut. 18:14, 12, 15 ("For the nations, which the Lord thy God shall utterly destroy before thy face, will listen to omens and divination; but as for thee, the Lord thy God has not allowed this. . . . The Lord thy God shall raise up a prophet for thee from thy brethren"); Num. 23:23 ("For there is no augury in Jacob nor divination in Israel; in due time it shall be told to Jacob and Israel what God will do").

135. Green, "Malevolent Gods and Promethean Birds," 147. Green argues that the positive understanding of augury was contested in first-century Rome, long before the Christian critique.

136. Bailly, *Animal Side*, 20.

137. Hicok, "Keeping track," in Collins, ed., *Bright Wings*, 235.

138. Bailly, *Animal Side*, 43–44. For Rilke on "the open," see his *Duino Elegies* 8.

139. Bailly, *Animal Side*, 44.

CHAPTER 2

1. For dating, see the chronological charts in Brown, *Augustine of Hippo*.

2. *C. Acad.* 1.20: *Non enim, si miramur apiculam melle posito nescio qua sagacitate, qua hominem vincit, undeunde advolare, ideo eam nobis praeponere aut saltem comparare debemus.* (Trans. slightly altered.)

3. *Ord.* 2.49 (trans. Holman, 7).

4. I was going to entitle this chapter with the phrase "anthropocentrism and its discontents" until I discovered a book by that title by Steiner, *Anthropocentrism and Its Discontents*.

5. Steiner, *Anthropocentrism and Its Discontents*, 1.

6. Gross, "Introduction," 2.

7. Philo, *De animalibus* 20. As Terian notes, in his *De providentia* 1.25 Philo brings bees even closer to human intelligence by calling them φρόνιμο, endowed with understanding (p. 135, n. 20). In *De animalibus* 92, however, Philo takes a Stoic position against his nephew's high estimation of bees' intelligence. Noting the bee's dutiful gathering of pollen and its creation of "a beautiful honeycomb which it fills with honey in a most amazing manner," Philo nonetheless insists that "these are not accomplished through the animals' foresight, but are to be ascribed to nature. . . . They do nothing by thought." See, for discussion, Peder Borgen, "Man's Sovereignty over Animals and Nature According to Philo of Alexandria."

8. Pliny, *NH* 11.12 (trans. slightly altered).

9. Aelian, *NA* 1.59 (trans. slightly altered).

10. Morton, *Ecological Thought*, loc. 941.

11. Ibid., loc. 914.

12. Ibid., loc. 921. The quotation is from Darwin, *Descent of Man*, 375.

13. Morton, *Ecological Thought*, loc. 926.

14. Bailly, *Animal Side*, 15. See my Introduction for a full statement of the meaning of the phrase "pensivity of animals."

15. See Bailly, *Animal Side*, 61, for the phrase in quotation marks; for discussion of animals as products of the contemplation of nature (where Bailly is following the thought of Plotinus), see pp. 56–57.

16. Chadwick, *Origen: Contra Celsum*, xxvi, calls Celsus an "eclectic Platonist." For discussion, see Wilken, *Christians as the Romans Saw Them*, 94–125; see also Hoffman, trans., *Celsus, On the True Doctrine*, 31–32.

17. Origen, *C. Cels.* 4.74–77.

18. Ibid. 4.77; Hume, "Of Suicide," 410.

19. Origen, *C. Cels.* 4.78.

20. See Dickerman, "Some Stock Illustrations of Animal Intelligence." Along with earlier classical authors, early Christians also celebrated the ant and the bee together. See, for example, John Chrysostom, *De statuis hom*.12.5 "On the Statues": "The ant is industrious and performs a laborious task. . . . Consider then how prudent the ant is, and consider how God has implanted in so small a body, such an unceasing desire of working! But while from this animal you learn industry, take from the bee at once a lesson of neatness, industry, and social concord."

21. Origen, *C. Cels.* 4.81.

22. Ibid.

23. Ibid.

24. Ibid.

25. Ibid.

26. Ibid., 4.84, for the quotation about ants and language.

27. Ibid., 4.89–96, on the issue of animals' knowledge of and closeness to God. See my discussion of Origen's view of birds and divination in Ch. 1 for details. For discussion of ancient defenses of animal reason, see Sorabji, *Animal Minds and Human Morals*, 78–93. See also Newmyer, "Animals in Ancient Philosophy"; Spittler, *Animals in the Apocryphal Acts of the Apostles*, 39–42, has nicely summarized the stakes in the debate between Origen and Celsus.

28. Steiner, *Anthropocentrism and Its Discontents*, 245.

29. Ibid., 247.

30. Griffin, *Animal Minds*, 190. For a detailed discussion of dance communication in honeybees, see Hölldobler and Wilson, *Superorganism*, 169–78.

31. Ibid., 169; Griffin, *Animal Minds*, 191–92.

32. Hölldobler and Wilson, *Superorganism*, 169–70.

33. Griffin, *Animal Minds*, 190, 202; Wilson, *Insect Societies*, 94.

34. Ingold, "The Animal in the Study of Humanity," 93.

35. See Gould and Gould, "Invertebrate Intelligence," 24.

36. Steiner, *Anthropocentrism and Its Discontents*, 245–46. See also Griffin, *Animal Minds*, 202–3, for a survey of positions skeptical of dance communication as akin to language use.

37. The question of whether ancient observers had or had not identified the waggle dance of bees is discussed by Davies and Kathirithamby, *Greek Insects*, 55–56.

38. Balcombe, *Exultant Ark*, loc. 186–88.

39. De Waal, *The Ape and the Sushi Master*, 69.

40. De Waal, *Good Natured*, loc. 249–53.

41. Gould, *Ever Since Darwin*, 261.

42. Payne, *The Animal Part*, 15.

43. De Waal, *Good Natured*, loc. 883; the second quotation is from Bekoff, *Emotional Lives of Animals*, 30.

44. Bekoff, *Emotional Lives of Animals*, 123.

45. Balcombe, *Exultant Ark*, loc. 171–72.

46. Rigby, "Animal Calls," 124. I want to highlight the difference between this understanding of anthropomorphism and its negative use "to censure the attribution of humanlike traits and experiences to other species," as articulated and discussed by de Waal, "What I Learned Tickling Apes," 4.

47. Wendy Doniger, "Epilogue," 350–51.

48. White, "Historical Roots of our Ecologic Crisis." For discussion, see Bauckham, *Living with Other Creatures*, 15–19 and passim.

49. See Chapter 5 for a discussion of Augustine's view of pride.

50. *Ex. 2 Ps.* 31.22 (32 RSV), *WSA*, p. 383.

51. I have taken this term from Moore, "Introduction," 11.

52. *Ex. 2 Ps.* 31.23 (32 RSV), *WSA*, p. 383. Note that the translator has blunted the force of Augustine's metaphor by making the first sentence of this passage into a simile ("The sinner wanted to be *like* an unbroken animal."). But the Latin does not contain "likeness" language (*Indomitum enim animal esse cupiebat*).

53. Psalm 32.9 (RSV), "Do not be like a horse or mule, without understanding, whose temper must be curbed with bit and bridle," provoked considerable commentary among patristic authors, especially regarding the importance of reason and the danger of bestial ignorance. See Blaising and Hardin, eds., *Ancient Christian Commentary*, 241–43, for English translations of many of these passages.

54. *Ex. 2 Ps.* 31.23 (32 RSV), *WSA*, p. 384.

55. *Ex. 2 Ps.* 31.23 (32 RSV), *WSA*, p. 384 (translation slightly altered). Note once again that the translator has blunted the force of Augustine's metaphor, rendering *populus mitis et mansuetus portans bene dominum, asellus est* as "This donkey *stands for* the humble and docile people." The words "stands for" are not in the Latin.

56. Derrida, *The Beast and the Sovereign*, 1:13.

57. Mathews, *Clash of Gods*, 45.

58. *Exp. 2 of Ps.* 33.5 (34 RSV), *WSA*, p. 26.

59. *Ex. 2 Ps.* 33.5 (34 RSV), *WSA*, p. 26.

60. *Ex. Ps.* 123.3 (124 RSV), *WSA*, p. 45.

61. *Ex. 1 Ps.* 103.4 (104 RSV), *WSA*, p. 110. See also *Ex. 4 Ps. 30.1* (31 RSV), *WSA*, p. 347: "Everything written here [the psalms] is like a mirror held up to us."

62. Cameron, "Augustine and Scripture," 213.

63. Bruns, "The Problem of Figuration in Antiquity," 148.

64. See, for example, *Ex. 1 Ps.* 103.1 (104 RSV), *WSA*, p. 107, where Augustine says, "The psalm which has been read to us is almost entirely composed of figurative statements and mysterious expressions, which demand close attention not on our part only but also on yours."

65. Augustine, *Doc. chr.* 3.5.9; 3.10.14.

66. *Ex. 2 Ps.* 33.5 (34 RSV), *WSA*, p. 27 (translation slightly emended).

67. The quotation is from Knickerbocker, *Ecopoetics*, 24.

68. The phrase is from Bailly, *Animal Side*, 15.

69. I know of only two instances. First, see *Ex. 4 Ps.* 103.2 (104 RSV), *WSA*, p. 168: "There are other creatures, such as all wild beasts, domestic animals, and trees, which lack intelligence and are unable to participate in wisdom. But does this inability mean that they were not made in wisdom and by wisdom? Far from it. God does not demand understanding from a horse or a mule; but to human beings he says, 'Do not be like a horse or a mule, devoid of understanding [Ps. 31(32):9].' What is natural in a horse is a matter for reproach in a man or woman. God says to us, 'I do not expect creatures that I not have made in my own image to participate in my wisdom. But from you, who are made in my image, I do demand it. I require you to use the gift I have given you.'" Second, see *Ex. Ps.* 146.18 (147 RSV), *WSA*, pp. 438–39, where Augustine is commenting on v. 9 ("He provides the cattle with their food and feeds the ravens' squabs that call upon him"): "Are we meant to think that raven squabs really do cry out to God to feed them? No, you should not assume that irrational beings invoke God; no soul knows how to invoke God except a rational soul. You must take the psalm's statement in a figurative sense or you may fall into the error of some unbelievers who say that human souls are reincarnated in cattle, dogs, pigs, or ravens. Banish such a notion from your hearts and from your faith. The human soul is made in the image of God, but God does not grant that image of himself to a dog or a pig."

70. Formisano, "Towards an Aesthetic Paradigm of Late Antiquity," 283.

71. See, for example, Augustine, *Ex. Ps.* 77.26 (78 RSV), *WSA*, p. 112. See also Augustine's discussion of the various literary tropes in *Doc. Chr.* 3.29.40.

72. Augustine, *Ex. Ps.* 41.1 (42 RSV), *WSA*, p. 239.

73. Ibid.

74. Ibid.

75. Ibid.

76. Burnaby, *Amor Dei*, 96.

77. Augustine, *Serm.* 53.11 (trans. Burnaby, *Amor Dei*, 97).

78. Augustine, *Io. Ev. Tr.* 40.10 (trans. Burnaby, *Amor Dei*, 97). As Asiedu points out, "It is the language of being inflamed that sets Augustine's sensibilities in its characteristic hue." Further, "Singing the songs of ascent allows Augustine to capture his longing in the language of desire found in the Psalms: desire (*desiderium*) without eros, love (*caritas, amor, dilectio*) without self-possessiveness (*cupiditas*)." See "The Song of Songs and the Ascent of the Soul," 315–16. On desire in Augustine, especially in his *Confessions*, see Burrus, Jordan, and MacKendrick, *Seducing Augustine*, esp. Ch. 4.

79. Bekoff, *Emotional Lives of Animals*, 19.

80. Augustine, *Ex. Ps.* 41.2 (42 RSV), *WSA*, pp. 240–41.

81. Ibid., p. 241.

82. Ibid. (translation slightly altered). The *WSA* translator renders the final line of this passage (*inuenimus enim insigne velocitatis in ceruo*) as "I say this because the deer *stands for* fleetness of foot." The passage does not contain any such language of representation, and this translation blunts the force of Augustine's use of the deer as a powerful metaphor.

83. Augustine, *Ex. Ps.* 41.3 (42 RSV), *WSA*, p. 241.

84. Ibid. (translation slightly emended). *WSA* translates *serpentes vitia tua sunt* as "These snakes represent your vices." Augustine's sentence does not have any "representational" language in it. The idea that deer kill snakes was part of ancient naturalists' lore; see Pliny, *NH* 8.118, and Aelian, *NA* 2.9; 8.6.

85. Augustine, *Ex. Ps.* 41.3 (42 RSV), *WSA*, p. 242.

86. The phrase in quotation comes from Kuzniar, *Melancholia's Dog*, 70.

87. Augustine, *Ex. Ps.* 41.4 (42 RSV), *WSA*, p. 242.

88. Ibid. This behavior of deer is noted in the naturalists' lore. See Pliny, *NH* 8.50.114; Aelian, *NA* 5.56.

89. Pliny, *NH* 8.50.114.

90. Augustine, *Ex. Ps.* 41.5 (42 RSV), *WSA*, pp. 242–43.

91. On the turn to the animal, see Moore, "Introduction," 1, and the discussion in my Introduction to this book.

92. Augustine, *Ex. Ps.* 41.5 (42 RSV), *WSA*, p. 242.

93. Gregory of Nyssa, *Hom. op.* 8.4.

94. Behr, "Rational Animal," 225. See Gregory of Nyssa, *Hom. op.* 2.1, for Gregory's use of kingly language to describe the human being.

95. Gregory of Nyssa, *Hom. op.* 8.4–5.

96. See Moore, "Introduction," 6, for discussion.

97. Gregory of Nyssa, *In inscrip.* I.5.40. I have followed Heine's numbering of this text.

98. Gregory of Nyssa, *In inscrip.* I.5.41 (emphasis added). As Heine points out, lying in the background of Gregory's image of the snake-eating deer is Origen's *Hom. in Cant.* 2.11 and other similar passages in Origen's writings. See Heine, *Gregory of Nyssa's Treatise on the Inscriptions*, 97, n. 49.

99. On this aspect of Gregory's anthropology, see, for example, *Hom. in Cant.* 1.25: "Let not any passionate and fleshly person, who still gives off the deathly smell of the old humanity, drag the meaning of the divinely inspired ideas and words down to the level of brutish irrationality. No, let each depart from himself and get beyond the material cosmos and ascend somehow, by way of impassibility, into paradise, and having by purity been made like to God, let him in this fashion journey to the inner shrine of the mysteries manifested to us in this book [the Song of Songs]." Gregory's thirsting deer with teeth of self-control is one of the images for the journey described in this passage. There are several good discussions of various aspects of Gregory's spiritual anthropology in Coakley, ed., *Re-Thinking Gregory of Nyssa*.

100. Mosshammer, "Disclosing but Not Disclosed," 119.

101. For other patristic comments on the thirsty deer of Psalm 42 (RSV), see Blaising and Hardin, eds., *Ancient Christian Commentary*, 328–29.

102. In the prologue to his *Homilies on the Song of Songs*, Gregory discusses the role of tropology and allegory, including enigmas and other figures, as incitements to interpretation. See *Hom. in Cant.*, prologue, 4–9.

103. Gregory of Nyssa, *Hom. in Cant.* 5.144.

104. Ibid., 5.142: "Since, therefore, it is proper to the nature of the fawn to destroy wild things and, by its breath and the special character of its color, to put the serpent-kind to flight . . . for this reason because he treads down and destroys the opposing Energy—which in figurative language is called 'mountains and hills'—he is likened to a young hart."

105. For discussion, see Cox, "*Physiologus*," reprinted in Miller, *Poetry of Thought in Late Antiquity*.

106. Gregory of Nyssa, *Hom. in Cant.* 5.143–44.

107. See *Physiol.* 1 (lion) and 16 (panther) and my n. 105, above, for reference.

108. Gregory of Nyssa, *Hom. in Cant.* 7.240.

109. On the role of fragrance in Gregory's *Homilies on the Song of Songs*, see Harvey, *Scenting Salvation*, 178–79.

110. Gregory of Nyssa, *Hom. in Cant.* 7.241.

111. Harvey, *Scenting Salvation*, 178.

112. Gregory of Nyssa, *Hom. in Cant.* 7.241–42.

113. For the etymology, see Norris, trans., *Gregory of Nyssa*, 253, n. 34.

114. The phrase in quotation is taken from Moore, "Introduction," 19, who is describing Jacques Derrida's critique of the Western philosophical tradition's "de-vitalizing" of animals.

115. Some of the material in the discussion of the *Physiologus* that follows has been drawn from Miller, "*Physiologus*," in Miller, *Poetry of Thought in Late Antiquity*, 61–73, original published as Cox, "*Physiologus*: A Poiesis of Nature," *Church History* 52 (1983): 433–43.

116. Stevens, *Letters of Wallace Stevens*, 364.

117. For dating, see Scott, "Date of the *Physiologus*."

118. Scott, "Zoological Marvel," 81. On p. 87, n. 5, Scott offers as a notable parallel Origen's and the *Physiologus*'s bringing together of various scriptural passages that mention foxes (Song of Songs 2:15, Lk. 13:32, and Mt. 8:20).

119. Scott, "Zoological Marvel," 85.

120. *Physiol.* 1. All translations of the *Physiologus* are my own.

121. Scott, "Zoological Marvel," 86.

122. Curley, trans., *Physiologus*, xiii.

123. Origen of Alexandria, *Comm. in Cant.* 3.12, quoted and discussed by Curley, trans., *Physiologus*, xiii. I am following the numbering of Origen's treatise in the translation in the Ancient Christian Writers series.

124. Origen of Alexandria, *Comm. in Cant.* 3.12.

125. This view of Christ's descent through heavenly spheres, during which he takes on the form of the spiritual denizens in each sphere, is of course heterodox, although the cosmology it presupposes was widespread in Greco-Roman antiquity. Some texts from the Nag Hammadi Library, such as the *Apocryphon of John* and *Hypostasis of the Archons*, for example, feature heavenly spheres occupied by inimical spirits, as do such "magical" texts as the *Mithras Liturgy*. The closest parallel to the *Physiologus*'s representation of the descent through cosmic realms is in the pseudepigraphical *Ascension of Isaiah* 10.

126. *Physiol.* 16.

127. 2 Cor. 2:14–16; Origen, *Hom. in Cant.* 1.3.

128. Note that the Septuagint substitutes "panther" for "lion" in the Hebrew text of Hosea.

129. On reversal in the *Physiologus*'s presentation of the nature of the panther, see Curley, trans., *Physiologus*, xxv–xxvi.

130. See, for discussion, Otto, *Dionysus, Myth and Cult*, 110–12, and Detienne, *Dionysus Slain*, 93–94.

131. Pliny, *NH* 8.23.62; Oppian, *Cynegetica* 3.63–80; Aesop, *Fables* 37 and 119, cited and discussed by Detienne and Vernant, *Cunning Intelligence*,19, 35–36.

132. Detienne and Vernant, *Cunning Intelligence*, 18–21.

133. Pliny, *NH* 8.23.62.

134. Aelian, *NA* 5.40. Note that Aelian refers to the leopard in this passage, but his reference to its seductive fragrance suggests that this is the same animal as the panther.

135. Hamilton, "Selection of Selfish and Altruistic Behavior," 83.

136. For an in-depth exploration of the role of bestial imagery in Origen's thought, see Cox, "Origen on the Bestial Soul," reprinted in Miller, *The Poetry of Thought in Late Antiquity*.

137. Origen of Alexandria, *Hom. in Lev.* 7.4.1.

138. Ibid., 7.4.3.

139. Ibid., 7.4.2.

140. Ibid., 7.4.4–7.

141. Ibid., 5.2.3 (translation emended).

142. Ibid., 16.6.2 (translation emended).

143. See Origen of Alexandria, *Comm. in Cant.* 3.12, for a lengthy discussion of the spiritual or heavenly import of scriptural animals.

144. For the birds, see Origen of Alexandria, *Hom. in Gen.* 1.11, discussed in my Ch. 1; for the hart, see *Comm. Cant.* 3.12.

145. Origen of Alexandria, *Hom. in Jer.* 10.8.

146. Ibid..

147. Origen of Alexandria, *Hom. in Lc.* 8.3.

148. Origen of Alexandria, *Hom. in Lev.* 16.6.2, commenting on Lev. 26:6, "I shall drive out the evil beasts from your land." Origen remarks, "These physical beasts are neither evil nor good, but something in between; for they are mute animals. But those other evil beasts are spiritual which the Apostle calls 'wicked spirits in the heavens' [see Eph. 6:12]."

149. See Sorabji, *Animal Minds and Human Moral*, esp. Ch. 1: "The Crisis: The Denial of Reason to Animals," 7–16.

150. Passages in Origen's work in which the process of making the soul conscious of its depths through bestial imagery is discussed at length in Cox, "Origen on the Bestial Soul," passim.

151. Origen of Alexandria, *Dial.* 12.30–13.10.

152. Bachelard, *Lautréamont*, 16, quoting the *Maldoror* of Isidore Ducasse.

153. Origen of Alexandria, *Dial.* 13.28–14.16.

154. Further references to human transformation in relation to beasts are in Cox, "Origen on the Bestial Soul," 128.

CHAPTER 3

1. For discussions of the text's date, see Junod, "Vie et conduit des saintes femmes," 91; Szepessy, "Narrative Model of the *Acta Xanthippae et Polyxae*," 318; Pervo, "Dare and Back," 162–66. I am using the conventional title of the text, *Acts of Xanthippe and Rebecca*, but as Pervo notes, the manuscript title of the text is *The Life and Conduct of the Women Saints Xanthippe, Polyxena, and Rebecca* (161, n. 2). Junod adds that the text's original editor, M. R. James, may have chosen *Acta* as the title because of the text's numerous allusions to and outright borrowings from several of the Apocryphal Acts (83).

2. *Acts of Xanthippe and Polyxena* 27.

3. Ibid., 30 (translation slightly emended). I thank Virginia Burrus for calling my attention to this passage. The motif of the talking lion(ess) is one of this text's borrowings from the *Acts of Paul*; see Pervo, "Dare and Back," 171.

4. *Acts of Xanthippe and Polyxena* 30 (slightly emended).

5. For a discussion of the phrase "pensivity of animals," see my Introduction.

6. Kuzniar, *Melancholia's Dog*, 29.

7. Ibid., 3, 6.

8. Ibid., 108.

9. Ibid., 6.

10. Pervo, "Dare and Back," 161.

11. Kuzniar, *Melancholia's Dog*, 33.

12. Derrida, *Animal*, 23.

13. Ibid., 32.

14. Ibid., 34, 32. Here I would like to remind the reader of a point made in my Introduction. Although I occasionally use the singular "animal," I intend it to be read and heard as *animot*, Derrida's neologism, which is an aural pun on the plural of the word "animal" in French ("animaux") as well as an extension of words to animals ("mot" = "word" in French). As Derrida explains, "I would like to have the plural *animals* heard in the singular" (*Animal*, 47; see also pp. 37, 41).

15. Derrida, *Animal*, 32. It should be noted that Derrida's question is a pun on the title of his book in French, *L'animal que donc je suis*, in which "je suis" can mean both "I am" and "I am following."

16. Clark, "The Fathers and the Animals," 68.

17. This phrase comes from Williams, "When a Dolphin Loves a Boy," 201. My thanks go to Virginia Burrus for alerting me to this article.

18. I have taken the phrase "to unseat human exceptionalism" from Williams's brief discussion of recent efforts in philosophy, literature, and politics to do just that ("When a Dolphin Loves a Boy," 201).

19. *Acts of Xanthippe and Polyxena* 6.

20. Pervo, "Dare and Back," 180.

21. François Bovon, "Canonical and Apocryphal Acts of the Apostles," 215.

22. Merleau-Ponty, *Nature*, 271.

23. Kuzniar, *Melancholia's Dog*, 6.

24. Foer, "Foreword," loc. 111.

25. De Waal, *Primates and Philosophers*, 65.

26. Ancient Christians used the term "anthropomorphism" to refer, negatively, to pagan representations of the gods and goddesses in human form and with human emotions; see, for example, Clement of Alexandria, *Strom.* 7.4. Origen used the term to describe, again negatively, the position of those who understood God's use of the dust of the earth to create human beings "in his image" to mean that human bodies are the image of God; see *Dial.* 12. Two centuries later, the so-called Anthropomorphites, who held that God had human form, played a role in the Origenist controversy; see Clark, *Origenist Controversy*, esp. 44–47, 50–52, 57–60.

27. Heidegger, *Fundamental Concepts of Metaphysics*, 210–11.

28. Ibid., 264. For discussion of Heidegger's position on animals, see (among many) Steiner, *Anthropocentrism and Its Discontents*, 204–14; Oliver, *Animal Lessons*, 193–207; Calarco, *Zoographies*, 15–53.

29. I owe the phrase "metaphysical anthropocentrism" to Calarco, *Zoographies*, 15.

30. Merleau-Ponty, *Nature*, 268. See Oliver, "Stopping the Anthropological Machine," 17–19.

31. Merleau-Ponty, *Nature*, 271.

32. Oliver, *Animal Lessons*, 222.

33. See, e.g., Merleau-Ponty, *Le visible et l'invisible*, 301, 180–82.

34. Ibid., 154.

35. Ibid., 181–82.

36. Westling, *Logos of the Living World*, 26–27.

37. Toadvine, "How Not to Be a Jellyfish," 51, quoted in Oliver, *Animal Lessons*, 224.

38. Merleau-Ponty, *Phenomenology of Perception*, 217, quoted and discussed by Oliver, *Animal Lessons*, 218. See also Toadvine, "'Strange Kinship,'" 30–31: "But perhaps an ontology of life cannot avoid listening more carefully to the upheavals and turbulence of Being, to the contrapuntal refrains that constitute each organism's characteristic style of 'singing the world'" (quoted in Oliver, *Animal Lessons*, 330, n. 12).

39. Sorabji, *Animal Minds and Human Morals*, 80.

40. The views of these two authors have been thoroughly discussed by others, and I shall not elaborate upon them in great detail here. See, inter alia, Newmyer, "Animals in Ancient Philosophy"; Spittler, *Animals in the Apocryphal Acts of the Apostles*, 15–26; Steiner, *Anthropocentrism and Its Discontents*, 93–111. On the difficulty of dating Porphyry's *De abstinentia* with certainty, see Clark, trans., *Porphyry: On Abstinence from Killing Animals*, 5–8.

41. Newmyer, "Animals in Ancient Philosophy," 163. For a discussion of Aristotle's views on animals, see ibid., 160–63; Sorabji, *Animal Minds and Human Morals*, 12–16.

42. Plutarch, *Soll. an.* 962C.

43. Newmyer, "Animals in Ancient Philosophy," 170–71.

44. Plutarch, *Soll. an.* 973A.

45. Ibid.

46. Porphyry, *De abs.* 3.3.1–3.

47. Ibid., 3.4.4.

48. Ibid., 3.7.2.

49. Ibid., 3.19.2.

50. See Clark, *Porphyry: On Abstinence from Killing Animals*, p. 124, n. 17, who notes that *oikeios* and related words carry the sense of family, one's own, or part of the household. "Belonging" is the main thrust of this cluster of words, which, as Clark observes, are central to Porphyry's argument in *De abstinentia*.

51. *Acta Pauli*, P. Bodmer LXI, 4.12–5.24. For the dating of the text, see Schneemelcher and Kasser, "The Acts of Paul," 234–35; for a summary of the complex reconstruction of the text, see Matthews, "Articulate Animals, 206–8.

52. Aune, *The New Testament in its Literary Environment*, 186.

53. On the speaking animal as a teratological motif, see Söder, *Die Apokryphen Apostelgeschichten*, 110–12. For the text's revision of the story of Androcles and the lion, see Metzger, "St. Paul and the Baptized Lion"; Spittler, *Animals in the Apocryphal Acts of the Apostles*, 184–85; and Adamik, "The Baptized Lion in the Acts of Paul," 68–73. For the argument about the baptized lion as a sign of divine οἰκονομία, see Schneemelcher, "Der getaufte Löwe in den Acta Pauli," especially p. 325: "Auch die Kreatur nicht ausserhalb dieses Heilsplanes steht."

54. Of course the term "ΟΙΚΟΝΟΜΙΑ" is in the Coptic text as indicated in the long quotation from the *Acts of Paul* above. There, however, the "plan" appointed by God has a vague, unspecified referent.

55. Drijvers, "Der getaufte Löwe," esp. 186–88. Spittler, *Animals in the Apocryphal Acts of the Apostles*, 186–87, thinks that "a stronger case can be made for the connection of lions and death" than for the connection of lions and sexuality: "The lion is a frequent subject in sepulchral art, in depictions either of lion hunts or of lions devouring their prey. Toynbee has argued that the latter is 'a symbol of the ravening power of death,' while the former 'can be interpreted as victories of the soul over death'" (*Animals in Roman Life and Thought*, 65–68).

56. Rordorf, "Quelques jalons pour une interprétation symbolique des *Actes de Paul*," esp. 260–63. For a critique of Rordorf's argument, see Snyder, *Acts of Paul*, 228–29.

57. Jerome, *Vir. ill.* 7. For the dating of *Vir. ill.*, see Kelly, *Jerome*, 174.

58. Tertullian, *De bap.* 17.5. For the translations of "fabula," see Lewis and Short, *A Latin Dictionary*, s.v. "fabula."

59. Quintillian, *Institutio Oratoria* 1.9.1: "Let them learn first to tell the fables orally in clear, unpretentious language, then to write them out with the same simplicity of style; first putting the verses into prose and translating the substance in different words, then paraphrasing it more freely, in the course of which they may abbreviate some things and elaborate others, so long as they preserve the poet's meaning." As Perry explains, since Quintillian thought that the early education of Roman boys should begin with "practice in the speaking and writing of Greek, it is very probable, if not quite certain, that what he has in mind in this passage is Aesopic fables written in Greek verse, rather than in Latin" ("Introduction," l–li).

60. Perry, "Introduction," xix–xx, quoting Theon, *Progymnasmata* 3.

61. Bland, "Cain, Abel, and Brutism," 167.

62. The first quotation is from Bland, "Construction of Animals in Medieval Jewish Philosophy," 181; the second quotation is from Bland, "Cain, Abel, and Brutism," 167.

63. Bland, "Construction of Animals in Medieval Jewish Philosophy," 181. Bland is quoting from Hadot, *Philosophy as a Way of Life*, 212.

64. Amsler, *Acta Philippi: Commentarius*, 285. The text's encratic views—notably sexual continence and a particular dietary regimen (abstinence from wine, vegetarianism)—are discussed by Amlser on pp. 36, 429–31, 469–520. See also Bovon, "Facing the Scriptures," 275, 285.

65. Gilhus, *Animals, Gods and Humans*, 251.

66. *Acta Philippi* VIII.16 (hereafter *APhil*).

67. Ibid., VIII.16–17.

68. Ibid., VIII.17.

69. Amsler, *Acta Philippi: Commentarius*, 267, n. 41.

70. *APhil*. VIII.17.

71. Ibid.

72. Amsler, *Acta Philippi: Commentarius*, 267, n. 43; Bovon, "Introduction," 23.

73. Bovon, "The Child and the Beast," 229. See also Amsler, *Acta Philippi: Commentarius*, 322, for a similar argument concerning the text's hope for "a universal reconciliation of the millenarian kind." Note that Amsler also argues that the text is a covert attack on the Phrygian cult of Cybele. The leopard was one of her animal symbols, and the goat kid was the symbol of Cybele's companion Attis. By claiming these two animals for Christianity, the text thus mounts a polemic against a rival religion (pp. 305–12).

74. Bovon, "The Child and the Beast," 228.

75. Gilhus, *Animals, Gods and Humans*, 254, and I agree on this point. As she notes, in the *Acts of Philip* "animals as such were not necessarily regarded as positive, only animals that had become human." See also Matthews, "Articulate Animals," 225, on "the humanization of animals and their incorporation into an all-encompassing salvation."

76. *APhil*. VIII.19.

77. Ibid., VIII.20.

78. Ibid., VIII.21.

79. Ibid., XII.1.

80. Ibid., XII.4.

81. Ibid., XII.5.

82. Ibid., XII.6.

83. Modern interpreters have suggested that this is a purificatory ritual that prepares the animals for receiving the Eucharist. See Spittler, *Animals in the Apocryphal Acts of the Apostles*, 230; Bovon, Bouvier, and Amsler, eds., *Acta Philippi*, pp. 278–79, n. 8; and Matthews, "Articulate Animals," 230, who wonders whether the text's failure to narrate the administering of the Eucharist to the animals is the result of censorship. This point is noted also by Amsler, *Acta Philippi: Commentarius*, 366.

84. *APhil.* XII.7–8.

85. Matthews, "Articulate Animals," 231.

86. Amsler, *Acta Philippi: Commentarius*, 365.

87. *APhil.* XIII.5.

88. Ibid., XIV.9. These two final appearances of the animals *as animals* is noted by Amsler, *Acta Philippi: Commentarius*, 306–7, n. 10: "Il faut noter cependant que l'assimilation à la forme humaine reste incomplète." The ambiguity attendant upon the animals' metamorphosis has also been noted by Perkins, "Animal Voices," 391–92.

89. Bailly, "Animals Are Masters of Silence," 87.

90. *APhil.* VIII.18.

91. See Philip's plea to Christ in *Martyrdom of the Holy and Glorious Apostle Philip* 38: "Transform the form of my body in angelic glory" (μεταμόρφοσον τὴν μορφὴν τοῦ σώματός μου ἐν ἀγγελικῇ δόξῃ). This human plea is echoed by the bestial transformation noted in *APhil.* XII.7: Philip says to Christ, "Just as you changed the form of the soul of these animals" (ὥσπερ ἤλλαξας τὴν μορφὴν τῆς ψυχῆς τῶν ζῴων τούτων).

92. While I have not attempted to be all-inclusive, it should be noted that there are other talking animals in ancient Christian literature. Most notable among these are the talking asses in the *Acts of Thomas*, who are every bit as theologically sophisticated as the leopard in the *Acts of Philip*. See Spittler, *Animals in the Apocryphal Acts of the Apostles*, 199–23, and Czachesz, *The Grotesque Body*, 130–40, for discussion.

93. *Historia monachorum in Aegypto* 21.16 (hereafter *HM*).

94. On Derrida's following the animal, see my n. 14 above.

95. Bailly, *Animal Side*, 6.

96. I use this title in accord with Lipsius and Bonnet, eds., *Acta Apostolorum Apocrypha*, Part 1, 235.

97. *Acts of Paul and Thecla* 26–27.

98. Ibid., 28.

99. Ibid. Spittler, *Animals in the Apocrypal Acts of the Apostles*, 170, suggests that this scene may be a "fatal charade" in which Thecla, as the condemned prisoner, is made to play the role of a divinity, Cybele being the likeliest candidate.

100. Other commentators are agreed that this is the same lioness; see Spittler, *Animals in the Apocryphal Acts of the Apostles*, 172, and Davis, *Cult of St. Thecla*, 10.

101. *Acts of Paul and Thecla* 42.

102. "Helper" was a term used frequently in early Christian literature from the second century onwards to designate both God and Christ. See Lampe, ed., *Patristic Greek Lexicon*, s.v. "βοηθός."

103. Davis, *Cult of St. Thecla*, 10.

104. I owe the first phrase in quotation to Burrus, *The Sex Lives of Saints*, 32.

105. Jerome, *Vita Pauli* 16.

106. Ibid., 16.

107. See Lewis and Short, eds., *A Latin Dictionary*, s.v. "*mutus.*"

108. On behalf of the text's anthropomorphic presentation of the lions, it should be noted that the male lions echo the male monks; as Burrus has noted, the lions compete with each other to dig the grave just as, in an earlier episode of the *Vita Pauli* (11), Paul and Antony are pictured "arguing and tugging at the bread" given them by a raven (*Sex Lives of the Saints*, 32). On the topic of helpful lions, mention needs also to be made of Sophronius's *Life of St. Mary of Egypt*, in which a helpful lion comes to the rescue of the old monk Zossima, who is too feeble to dig Mary's grave. This lion too recognizes holiness by licking the saint's feet, and he understands the little speech that Zossima delivers to him asking that the lion dig the grave—a task that the lion anticipated and in fact completed before Zossima finished his speech.

109. Athanasius, *De vita Antonii* 50.

110. Ibid.

111. In regard to this passage, Spittler, *Animals in the Apocryphal Acts of the Apostles*, 46–47, agrees with Gilhus's observation in *Animals, Gods and Humans*, 222: "Antony makes the animals leave by talking in a friendly way to them. But Antony is not really friendly towards these creatures. When ordering the animals away, he also prevents them from drinking water in the only place in the desert where water could be found. So even if it is said of Antony that 'the wild animals made their peace with him' (51.5; cf. Job 5:23), although he does not kill them, his relationship with animals does not imply a peaceful cohabitation. He has made his Garden of Eden in the desert . . . and made animals obey him as they did Adam, but he does not want them. The message that comes through is that there was no place for animals in the new paradise that Antony had made in the desert." I think this is an overinterpretation. In the first place, its implication that Antony was cruel in depriving the animals of water is not supported by the text. In the second place, I think Antony's gentleness with the animals, plus the application to him of the passage from Job, need to be taken more seriously as positive indications of human-animal relationships. Finally, nowhere in Genesis does it say that the animals "obeyed" Adam, and although it is true that Antony commands the animals to leave, the command is preceded by an ethical argument that he no doubt presumes the animals will understand.

112. *Historia monachorum in Aegypto* XII.6.

113. Ibid., XII.7–9.

114. *Acta Iohannis* 60–61.

115. Ibid., 60. On the disputed meaning of this term in the text, see the discussion by Spittler, *Animals in the Apocryphal Acts of the Apostles*, 106–7, and 105 on the companions' laughter.

116. For the phrase in quotation, see my n. 60 above.

117. Kuzniar, *Melancholia's Dog*, 33.

118. Basil of Caesarea, *Hex.* 9.4.

119. The instinctual behavior of animals as a natural pedagogue for love, care, and self-protection, among other virtues, is the gist of *Hex.* 9.3–4.

120. I thank David Miller for giving me a framed poster of this *New Yorker* cartoon to hang on my wall while writing this book. As Tapper has pointed out, "Animals are good to teach and learn with, particularly in those central areas of life clouded by taboos and inhibitions. It is not so long ago that the realities of sex and procreation were so unmentionable in the English family that children were gently initiated into the harsh truth through stories of birds and bees and the

stork." He goes on to quote several educators: "Children can readily relate to real or imagined feelings in animals, when they often have great difficulty in relating to or comprehending the feelings of other people. This fact is clearly recognized by the authors and publishers of children's literature who frequently use anthropomorphic animal characters, rather than more realistic images, as a medium for conveying social values and rules" ("Animality, Humanity, Morality, Society," 51). Basil was astute enough to realize that adults also respond to animals as pedagogues.

121. Bailly, "Animals Are Masters of Silence," 87.

122. For discussion of ascetics and angel images, see Miller, "Desert Asceticism and 'The Body from Nowhere,'" reprinted in Miller, *The Poetry of Thought in Late Antiquity*, 159–74.

123. See the discussion of Merleau-Ponty's concept of "the flesh of the world" earlier in this chapter.

124. On the ascetic cast of the *Physiologus*, see Scott, "Zoological Marvel," 85. Some of the material on the elephant is based on Miller, "Adam, Eve, and the Elephants."

125. *Physiologus* 20 "On the Elephant," trans. Curley, text in *Physiologus Latinus Versio Y*. As noted by Curley, trans., *Physiologus*, 79, in antiquity the mandrake was thought to promote conception and to function as an aphrodisiac.

126. This use of animals to tell (or retell) the story of Christian salvation history is typical of many of the chapters of the *Physiologus*.

127. Bekoff, *Emotional Lives of Animals*, 47.

128. Pliny the Elder, *NH* 8.1.1.

129. Aelian, *NA* 7.2; 4.10; 7.44, respectively. See also Pliny the Elder, *NH* 8.1.1 and Plutarch, *Moralia* 17.972.

130. Aelian, *NA* 7.44. The humans that Aelian appears to be disparaging vis-à-vis religious devotion may have been Epicureans; see Hammond and Scullard, eds., *Oxford Classical Dictionary*, s.v. "Aelianus (1)."

131. Bekoff, *Emotional Lives of Animals*, 7, 13, 37, 66; see also Sheldrick, *Love, Life, and Elephants*, loc. 2082 and passim.

132. Pliny the Elder, *NH* 8.5.13; Aelian, *NA* 8.17. For discussion and multiple citations, see Scullard, *The Elephant in the Greek and Roman World*, 208–31, and Newmyer, "Paws to Reflect," 121–24.

133. For discussion and examples, see Dickerman, "Some Stock Illustrations of Animal Intelligence." Animals whose instinctual behavior was especially admired were ants, bees, spiders, and birds. Indeed, as Clark, "The Fathers and the Animals," 70–71, points out, Theodoret admonished his flock not to envy spiders for their skill in weaving. See Theodoret, *De prov.* 5.553c–554a.

134. Renehan, "The Greek Anthropocentric View of Man," 242.

135. Augustine, *Quant.* 28.54.

136. Leyerle, "Monks and Other Animals," 163.

137. Basil of Caesarea, *Hex.* 9.4: "We also possess natural virtues toward which there is an attraction of soul not from the teaching of men, but from nature itself"; Rousseau, *Basil of Caesarea*, 337.

138. Rousseau, *Basil of Caesarea*, 339.

139. Basil of Caesarea, *Hex.* 8.2 (translations slightly modified).

140. Basil of Caesarea, *Hex.* 1.11; see also *Hex.* 9.5, where Basil remarks that "everything in existence is the work of Providence."

141. Basil of Caesarea, *Hex.* 9.1. On Basil's skittishness about allegory in the *Hexaemeron*, see Lim, "The Politics of Interpretation in Basil of Caesarea's 'Hexaemeron.'"

142. Basil of Caesarea, *Hex.* 7.6.

143. In the *Hexaemeron* as in other works, one of Basil's chief concerns was "the moral discipline of good works," in Rousseau's words (*Basil of Caesarea*, 181). For an overall view of Basil's extension of ascetic ideals to all Christians, see Gribomont, *Histoire du texte des ascétiques de S. Basile*, passim.

144. Basil of Caesarea, *Hex.* 8.6.

145. Rousseau, *Basil of Caesarea*, 55; 55, n. 24

146. Ibid., 181–82.

147. Basil of Caesarea, *Hex.* 7.3. Some of the material on Basil's crab is based on Miller, "'Intricate Evasions of As,'" 183–87.

148. Miller, "Tradition and Difference," 10.

149. The first quotation in this sentence is from Bachelard, *L'air et les songes*, 7; the second quotation is from Miller, *The New Polytheism*, 20.

150. For Pound's definition of images, see Sullivan, ed., *Ezra Pound: A Critical Anthology*, 41, 57; for a discussion of Pound's notion of the luminous detail, see Gallagher and Greenblatt, *Practicing New Historicism*, 19.

151. Burrus, *Sex Lives of Saints*, 3.

152. The phrase "force field of desire" is from Mitchell, *What Do Pictures Want?* 59, where it refers to "the pulling or attracting force" of desire and "the trace of this force in a picture"—and, I would add, a textual image.

153. Newmyer, "Paws to Reflect," 169, n. 38.

154. Basil of Caesarea, *Hex.* 7.5.

155. Bailly, "Animals Are Masters of Silence," 87.

156. Basil of Caesarea, *Hex.* 8.5.

157. Derrida, *Animal*, 3–6, on the cat; 51, on destitution in the gaze of the animal.

158. Derrida, *Animal*, 51.

159. Basil of Caesarea, *Hex.* 9.3.

160. Rousseau, *Basil of Caesarea*, 191.

161. Mitchell, *What Do Pictures Want?* 92.

162. Burrus, *Saving Shame*, xi.

163. Ibid., xii.

164. Ibid., 2.

165. Ibid., 3.

166. *Historia monachorum in Aegypto* 6, "On Theon."

167. The phrase in quotation is from Bataille, *Theory of Religion*, 24, describing animals' envelopment in the world along the lines of Bailly's description in this chapter.

168. Jerome, *Vita Sancti Pauli Primi Eremitae* 7. Much of the material in this "Coda" is a condensation and adaptation of Miller, "Jerome's Centaur: A Hyper-icon of the Desert."

169. The phrase in quotation comes from Jane Bennett, *Enchantment of Modern Life*, 29.

170. See *Vita Sancti Pauli Primi Eremitae* 10, where Paul is described as having a body "covered with unkempt hair." On the tradition of the wild and hairy anchorites whose traditions were to proliferate in the medieval period, see Williams, "Oriental Affinities of the Legend of the Hairy Anchorite," *Illinois Studies in Language and Literature* 10, no. 2 (1925); 11, no. 4 (1926). More recently, see Bartra, *Wild Men in the Looking Glass*.

171. Jerome, *Vita Pauli Primi Eremitae* 7.

172. See duBois, *Centaurs and Amazons*, 27–48.

173. Ibid., 31.

174. Bartra, *Wild Men in the Looking Glass*, 16.

175. Ibid.

176. duBois, *Centaurs and Amazons*, 30.

177. White, "The Forms of Wildness," 22, 28.

178. On the complex dynamics of ascetics' relation to temptation, see Harpham, *The Ascetic Imperative*, 45–66. Jerome himself was witness to this phenomenon by his own admission. Escaping to the desert which he once thought of as paradise, he engaged in ascetic practices designed to elicit the inner turmoil of passions, confront them, and conquer their stranglehold; but the passions—especially sexual passions in his case (the famous troops of dancing girls)— were not so easily quelled once summoned. See Miller, "Jerome's Centaur," 210–14, for discussion especially of Jerome's ambivalent view of desert life. See also Miller, "The Blazing Body," passim.

179. The phrase in quotation marks comes from Bennett, *Enchantment of Modern Life*, 104.

CHAPTER 4

1. *Historia monachorum in Aegypto* 21.5–12.

2. Jannes and Jambres were among the magicians whom Pharaoh sent to compete against Moses in Ex. 7:11ff. See 2 Tim. 3:8.

3. For a discussion of the development of the myth of the desert as a heaven on earth, see Goehring, "The Dark Side of Landscape: Ideology and Power in the Christian Myth of the Desert."

4. Brown, *The Body and Society*, 221.

5. Vivian, "Peaceable Kingdom," 490–91. The quotation is from Isaac the Syrian, *Ascetical Homilies*, p. 383, as quoted by Vivian, 491.

6. Osborne, *Dumb Beasts and Dead Philosophers*, 160. On the rapport with animals as a sign of the peaceable kingdom and a recovery of the lost paradise, see Elliott, *Roads to Paradise*, 133–67. On monasticism "instantiating the peaceable kingdom," see Leyerle, "Monks and Other Animals," 161.

7. *Historia monachorum in Aegypto*, prologue 9.

8. *Life of Macarius of Alexandria* 3.

9. Vivian, "Peaceable Kingdom," 478. Macarius of Alexandria seems to have had a problem with anger, as the anecdote of the gnat, recounted in my Chapter 5, suggests. On killing, see the story of Abba Helle and the crocodile in my Chapter 3. For an in-depth analysis of one patristic author's take on the serpent of Genesis 3, including its connection with the devil's evil schemes, see Dunning, "Chrysostom's Serpent."

10. John Moschos, *Prat. Spir.* 163.

11. On vegetarianism among the desert monks, see Leyerle, "Monks and Other Animals," 152–56.

12. See Harmless, *Desert Christians*, 245, who lists "the core themes" of desert spirituality as "repentance, renunciation, vigilance, the combat with evil, humility, forgiveness of enemy, and love of God and neighbor." For discussion of desert monks' hospitality, charity, and refusal to judge others, see Ward, "Foreword," xxiv–xxv. For in-depth discussion of the themes of forgiveness, withholding judgment, and compassion, see Burton-Christie, *Word in the Desert*, 275–87.

13. In "Monks and Other Animals," Leyerle remarks about this story that "the lion's daily visits to Abba Paul . . . must surely impress the spectator with the colonizing prowess of the

monks: their ability to tame the savage desert" (161). I think that the story can just as easily be read as a failure to tame the desert, as well as a picture of the savagery in the self.

14. Vivian, "Peaceable Kingdom," 479.

15. Marsden, "Bataille and the Poetic Fallacy of Animality," 40. Commenting on Georges Bataille's approach to animality, Marsden remarks: "Poetic language 'intimates' that which resists conceptuality—the 'draw of intimacy' that subtends the snare of calculative thought" (40).

16. See Gaita, *Philosopher's Dog*, 111.

17. Seigworth and Gregg, "An Inventory of Shimmers," 1. It should be noted that affect theory is not a singular phenomenon but rather is composed of a variety of definitions and approaches, as indeed *The Affect Theory Reader* itself attests. I find Gregg and Seigworth's perspective most helpful for the purposes of this chapter.

18. Seigworth and Gregg, "An Inventory of Shimmers," 1.

19. Ibid., 2.

20. Bailly, *Animal Side*, 4.

21. Bettini, *Women and Weasels*, 138–39. For the quotation, see Wittgenstein, *Philosophical Investigations*, 223.

22. Westling, *Logos of the Living World*, 13.

23. Seigworth and Gregg, "An Inventory of Shimmers," 2: "In practice, then, affect and cognition are never fully separable—if for no other reason than that thought is itself a body, embodied."

24. Rowlands, *The Philosopher and the Wolf*, 57–58.

25. Bataille, *Theory of Religion*, 22. See my Introduction for discussion of Bataille.

26. Other anecdotes from Haskell's book are presented in Chapter 5.

27. Haskell, *Forest Unseen*, 193–94.

28. The phrase in quotation is from de Waal, *Good Natured*, loc. 883.

29. See Bataille, *Theory of Religion*, 39: "The animal has lost its status as man's fellow creature, and man, perceiving the animality in himself, regards it as a defect."

30. The phrase in quotation is from Bennett, *Enchantment of Modern Life*, 104, who uses it to describe the mood that she calls "enchantment," also described by her as "affective fascination" (12).

31. Sulpicius Severus, *Dialogi* 1.13.

32. Ibid., 1.15.

33. *The Virtues of Saint Macarius of Egypt* 14. I have altered the translation slightly by changing the neuter pronouns ("it" and "its") to feminine pronouns ("she" and "her"), since the subject of the story, the mother antelope, is obviously feminine. It should be noted that this kind of story, which emphasizes human compassion and animal suffering and gratitude, had precedents in the naturalist literature. Pliny, for example, tells the story of a female panther grief-stricken at the loss of her cubs, which had fallen into a pit, and of her use of touch to ask for human help (*NH* 8.59–60). For discussion of this and other passages, see Finkelpearl, "Elephant Tears," 177–78. See also Tilley, "Martyrs, Monks, Insects, and Animals," 96.

34. Payne, *Animal Part*, 8.

35. Burrus, "Introduction" to "Troubled Boundaries," a workshop that was part of "Senses, Affect, and the Imagination in Late Antiquity: A Symposium," April 10–11, 2015, sponsored by Colgate University, Late Antique Religion in Central New York (LARCeNY), and the Central New York Humanities Corridor. Quoted from notes by permission of the author.

36. Vivian, "Peaceable Kingdom," 486.

37. For a discussion of bodily suffering as a language shared by all animals, including human ones, a language that recognizes shared creatureliness and compassionate contact, see Rigby, "Animal Calls," 123–24.

38. For the story of the sinful woman, see Luke 7:36–50.

39. The gazing eye has been the topic of much analysis in recent scholarship. For a brief discussion, see Miller, *Corporeal Imagination*, 86–89. Recent notable discussions of ancient looking can be found in Frank, *Memory of the Eyes*; Bartsch, *Mirror of the Self*; Fredrick, ed., *Roman Gaze*; and Elsner, *Roman Eyes*.

40. On the sometime confusion between the two monks named Macarius, see Guillaumont, "Le problème des deux Macaires."

41. *Life of Macarius of Alexandria* 1.

42. Rigby, "Animal Calls," 124.

43. Bennett, *Enchantment of Modern Life*, 158; see also her discussion on 131–32.

44. John Moschus, *Prat. Spir.* 107.

45. Quoting Payne, *Animal Part*, 8, once again.

46. Grant, *Early Christians and Animals*, 18.

47. Pliny, *NH* 8.21.56.

48. Aelian, *NA* 7.48; Osborne, *Dumb Beasts and Dead Philosophers*, 137. See her comparison of Aelian's tale with that of John Moschus on pp. 150–53.

49. Aelian, *NA* 5.39. On lions as pets in the early Roman Empire, see Toynbee, *Animals in Roman Life and Art*, 64.

50. Gilhus, *Animals, Gods and Humans*, 28–31, cautions against calling animals in antiquity pets; she prefers "personal animals" in order to avoid misleading comparisons with modern pet culture.

51. Hippolytus of Rome, *Comm. in Dan.* 3.29.4.

52. John Moschus, *Prat. Spir.* 2.

53. *Acts of Paul and Thecla* 33; Sophronius, *Vitae Mariae Aegyptae* 26–27; Jerome, *Vita Sancti Pauli* 16. It should be noted that not all ancient Christian texts viewed lions positively. In the *Apocryphon of John* 10.11, for example, the flawed creator-god, Yaldabaoth, is said to be lion-faced. As Karen King remarks, "He [Yaldabaoth] is not even human in appearance, but bestial, having at once 'the face of a serpent and the face of a lion.' He is, in form and in fact, a monster. This bestiality is the outward representation of his inward nature—violent, uncontrolled, and irrational" (*Secret Revelation of John*, 92). For a detailed discussion of leontomorphic figures in antiquity, see Jackson, *The Lion Becomes Man*; see also Gilhus, *Animals, Gods and Humans*, 236–38.

54. See Leyerle, "Monks and Other Animals," 158–59, for other examples.

55. Ibid., 161.

56. Ibid.

57. See Barthes, "The Reality Effect." For my discussion of fabulae, see Chapter 3.

58. See humanesociety.org/issues/exotic_pets/facts/dangerous-exotic-pets-big-cats.html, accessed 28 January 2016.

59. Leyerle, "Monks and Other Animals," 161.

60. Ibid.

61. Ibid.

62. Ibid., 162.

63. Ibid., 162–63. I have revised one typo in this quotation ("faction" for "fraction").

64. See Elliott, *Roads to Paradise*, 165, who argues as follows: "At first glance, the lions [in monastic tales from the desert] might seem to have reversed the spatial movement of the hermits, moving from nature to culture, serving man in the capacity of domesticated animals.... But it is more correct to see in this animal's behavior a movement paralleling the saints', for they have abandoned their post-lapsarian nature and returned to their original [paradisal] state," which, she argues, is most obvious in their adoption of a vegetarian dietary regimen.

65. Osborne, *Dumb Beasts and Dead Philosophers*, 156.

66. Ibid., 152.

67. Ibid., 157.

68. Ibid., 153.

69. Bauckham, *Living with Other Creatures*, 124.

70. Some representative examples of the scriptural figure of the ravening lion are: Deuteronomy 33:20, Judges 14:5, 1 Kings 20:36, Job 4:10, Psalms 17:12 and 22:13, Jeremiah 2:30, and Ezekiel 22:25 in the Hebrew Bible; 1 Peter 5:8 in the New Testament. For commentary on the long historical tradition of the lion as "a potent, bi-valent symbol, evoking both good and evil," see Elliott, *Roads to Paradise*, 166–67.

71. I am indebted for this sentence to Burton-Christie, *Word in the Desert*, 231, who observes the following about stories pertaining to desert ascetics and animals: "While there is no direct mention of Adam in these stories, the echoes of paradise reverberate through them."

72. Bekoff, *Emotional Lives of Animals*, 12.

73. Ibid., 6, discussing Darwin, and 10–11, on secondary emotions such as empathy and compassion.

74. Ibid., 22.

75. Ibid., 15. For depth of animal feeling and cognition, see Finkelpearl, "Elephant Tears," 179.

76. Pliny, *NH* 9.25–26, trans. Williams, 206. Williams discusses such love stories in detail, focusing on narratives of Pliny, Aelian, and Aulus Gellius.

77. Vivian, "Peaceable Kingdom," 479.

78. Williams, "When a Dolphin Loves a Boy," 204. It should be noted that Williams also suspends questions of ethology, phrased by him in the context of the material he treats as "Can animals *really* fall in love with human beings?" while I do not. I think that the findings of contemporary ethology, especially on the topic of animal minds and emotions, are immensely helpful as an aid in reading early Christian zoological lore with an animal eye, as it were.

79. Williams, "When a Dolphin Loves a Boy," 204.

80. Sulpicius Severus, *Dialogi* 1.14 (trans. Waddell, *Beasts and Saints*, 6–7, translation revised).

81. Bekoff, *Emotional Lives of Animals*, 15.

82. Mech, *The Wolf*, 4. For a description of wolf personalities, see Mowat, *Never Cry Wolf*, 86–98, esp. 90–92.

83. See Lewis and Short, *A Latin Dictonary*, s.v. "sensus."

84. Mech, *The Wolf*, 9, 295–98.

85. Basil of Caesarea, *Hex.* 9.3.

86. Augustine, *Civ. Dei* 12.22.

87. Mech, *The Wolf*, 181.

88. Barthes, "The Reality Effect," 141–42.

89. Clark, "Holy Women, Holy Words," 420, discussing Barthes's reality effect.

90. All biblical quotations are from the Revised Standard Version.

91. Clement of Alexandria, *Protrepticus* I.3, 2–4, 3.

92. Irenaeus, *Adversus haereses* 1, pref. 2.

93. Athanasius, *De vita Antonii* 9.

94. John Moschus, *Prat. Spir.* 165.

95. Origen of Alexandria, *C. Cels.* 4.93. It might be noted at this point that this fear and loathing of wolves has continued into the present. As naturalist Farley Mowat has noted, European and Asiatic hunting cultures lived in a symbiotic relationship with the wolf, but when "they divest[ed] themselves of their hunting heritage in order to become farmers or herdmen, they lost this ancient empathy with the wolf and became its inveterate enemy. So-called civilized man eventually succeeded in totally extirpating the *real* wolf from his collective mind and substituting for it a contrived image, replete with evil aspects that generated almost pathological fear and hatred. European man brought this mind-set to the Americas where, spurred on by bounties and rewards and armed with poison, trap, snare, and gun (together with new weapons provided by an enlightened technology, including helicopters and fragmentation grenades), we moderns have since waged war to the death against the wolf"—and largely succeeded, as he goes on to point out (*Never Cry Wolf*, vi–vii). On current "wolf-animus" in the United States, see Downes, "Wolf Haters."

96. Kelly, "Patronage." It might also be noted here that *familiaris* also means belonging to a household or family, thus enfolding the wolf into the intimate domestic world of the monk. The *lupa*, in other words, is family. I thank Virginia Burrus for this suggestion.

97. On Sulpicius's use of scripture, see Stancliffe, *St. Martin and His Hagiographer*, 38–44. On reading practices and biblical literacy among ascetic writers such as Sulpicius, see Clark, *Reading Renunciation*, 45–69, and Burton-Christie, *Word in the Desert*, passim.

98. Burrus, "Speaking in Other Tongues"; phrase used by permission.

99. Derrida, *Of Grammatology*, 144–45, quoted and discussed in Clark, *Reading Renunciation*, 6–7.

100. Agamben, *The Open*, 21.

101. See Derrida, *Animal*, 32, as discussed in my Chapter 3.

102. See Brown, *Body and Society*, 236: "Life in the desert revealed, if anything, the inextricable interdependence of body and soul."

103. Gross, "Introduction," 1.

104. Sellbach, "Lives of Animals," 314.

105. Foer, "Foreword," loc. 126–38.

106. See Chapter 3.

107. Buchanan, "Being with Animals," 266, quoting Steeves, "Introduction," 8.

108. Bailly, "Animals Are Masters of Silence," 86.

109. The phrase in quotation is from Erdrich, *The Antelope Wife*, 56. It is from a story about love between an antelope and a woman.

110. Kinnell, "Saint Francis and the Sow," 81. From *Mortal Acts, Mortal Words*, by Galway Kinnell. Copyright © 1980, and renewed 2008 by Galway Kinnell. Reprinted by permission of Houghton Mifflin Harcourt Publishing Company. All rights reserved.

111. Osborne, *Dumb Beasts and Dead Philosophers*, 153. On monastic resistance to temptation, see Burton-Christie, *Word in the Desert*, 198–203, and Harpham, *The Ascetic Imperative*, 45–66.

112. Osborne, *Dumb Beasts and Dead Philosophers*, 154.

113. Mazzoni, *She-Wolf*, 186.

114. Ovid, *Fasti* 2.39, quoted in Mazzoni, *She-Wolf*, 109.

115. Augustine, *Civ. Dei* 18.21 (trans. Dyson).

116. Mazzoni, *She-Wolf*, 114. See also Flemming, *"Quae Corpore Quaestum Facit,"* 47–48.

117. Mazzoni, *She-Wolf*, 114.

118. Ibid., 118. See also Goldberg, "Jerome's She-Wolf," for a discussion of the sexualized she-wolf of Jerome's imagination in *Life of Paul*.

119. Burrus, *Sex Lives of the Saints*, 3, 10.

120. Goldberg, "Jerome's She-Wolf," 628.

121. See Carson, *Eros the Bittersweet*, 20, on Stobaeus, *Flor.* 4.230M: *"Aidōs* dwells upon the eyelids of sensitive people as does *hybris* upon the insensitive." See also Clark, "Sex, Shame, and Rhetoric," 229, discussing the ancient association of shame with sight.

122. The phrases in quotation are from Kaster, *Emotion, Restraint, and Community*, 56, 60.

123. Aristotle, *Rhet.* 1384a.

124. This anecdote is told by de Waal, *Good Natured*, loc. 1515–22.

125. On ethical sensibility as a feature of animal-human continuity, see de Waal, *Good Natured*, loc. 26–27, 76–77, and passim. The quotation of de Waal is in Bekoff, *Emotional Lives of Animals*, 111.

126. Barton, *Roman Honor*, 254. Barton observes about *pudor* that it "comprised the fear that inhibited one from transgressing one's bonds and the remorse that one felt as a result of transgressing" (200).

127. For Basil of Caesarea's and Ambrose's use of animal behavior to shame human misconduct, see my Chapters 1 and 3. As Clark has observed, "In the third century and beyond, examples of the rhetoric of shame were constructed via unflattering comparisons between alleged Christians and 'others' whom Christians might consider religiously or socially inferior. To throw in the face of confessing Christians that their behavior was no better than that of Jews, pagans, barbarians, slaves, or even dumb animals . . . became a standard rhetorical device productive of ethical norms" ("Sex, Shame, and Rhetoric," 224).

128. The first quotation is from *Vitae Patrum* 5.15.22; this text has a lengthy section of sayings regarding humility. The second quotation is from *Apophthegmata Patrum*, "Iota: John the Dwarf," 22.

129. Burton-Christie, *Word in the Desert*, 287; on refraining from judgment among the desert fathers, see 273–82, and 282–83 on bearing the other's burdens.

130. Ibid., 287–91.

131. Finkelpearl, "Elephant Tears," 180–81.

132. Kaster, *Emotion, Restraint, and Community*, 29, who writes about *pudor* that "seeing oneself as discredited depends on having a sense of personal worthiness and value." Modern theories of shame are also centered around the notion of self-consciousness: "Shame is such an important affect for it is constitutive of the subjective experience of selfhood" (Kuzniar, *Melancholia's Dog*, 71).

133. Kuzniar, *Melancholia's Dog*, 71.

134. Burrus, *Saving Shame*, 81.

135. Ibid., xi, xii. Burrus's study of shame is also discussed earlier in this book, in Chapter 3.

136. De Waal, *Good Natured*, loc. 573–76.

137. Ibid., loc. 1234–36.

138. Adapted from Van Horn, "The Making of a Wilderness Icon," 212.

139. Leopold, *A Sand County Almanac*, 129–30.

140. Van Horn, "The Making of a Wilderness Icon," 223.

141. Westling, *Logos of the Living World*, 40–41, discussing Merleau-Ponty, *The Visible and the Invisible*, 271.

142. Stevens, "Esthétique du Mal," in *Collected Poems*, 321.

143. Haraway, *When Species Meet*, loc. 699–706.

144. Sandburg, "Wilderness," in *Complete Poems*, 100.

145. Cyril of Scythopolis, *Lives of the Monks of Palestine*, 139,5–139,15.

146. Leyerle, "Monks and Other Animals," 162.

147. A point also noted by Leyerle, ibid., 164.

CHAPTER 5

1. Roy, *The God of Small Things*, 316–18.

2. Bennett, *Vibrant Matter*.

3. The phrase is from Coole and Frost, "Introducing the New Materialisms," 138–39.

4. Ibid., 246–48.

5. Bennett, *Vibrant Matter*, 89–90.

6. Ibid., 100–101.

7. Clark, "The Fathers and the Animals," 67.

8. Among the many passages in which Augustine expresses such convictions, see *Div. qu.* 13 and *Lib. Arb.* 1.53; these and others are cited by Clark, "The Fathers and Animals," passim.

9. Clark, "The Fathers and the Animals," 68.

10. Bailly, *Animal Side*, 4.

11. Ibid., 5.

12. *Ex. Ps.* 146.18 (147 RSV), *WSA*, p. 439.

13. For the contrast between "the animal" and animals in their heterogeneous multiplicity, see Derrida, *Animal*, 47–48. See the discussion of Derrida in my Introduction, above.

14. This phrase is the title of one of Stevens's poems in *Opus Posthumous*, 46–47.

15. *Vera rel.* 77.9–22.

16. Haskell, *Forest Unseen*, xii.

17. Stewart, "Darwin's Worms," p. 7 of the electronic version, accessed 29 April 2014.

18. On Darwin's publications regarding the worm, see Bennett, *Vibrant Matter*, 95–121; Phillips, *Darwin's Worms*, 38–58; Sacks, "Mental Life of Plants and Worms"; Stewart, "Darwin's Worms," 48–58.

19. Bennett, *Vibrant Matter*, 95–96.

20. Phillips, *Darwin's Worms*, 47.

21. Augustine, *Gen. adv. Man.* 1.26.1–3. For discussion of this passage, see MacCormack, "Augustine Reads Genesis," 13–14, 28.

22. Augustine, *Gen. adv. Man.* 1.26.39–40, 59 (*deum artificem*). As Karmen MacKendrick notes in her theological meditation on Augustine, "It is beauty that draws attention, and beauty that answers the very question it draws—but the answer is not at all pregiven. In that beauty, Augustine is not turned away from the world (which would in any case risk a return to his rejected Manicheanism), but is drawn more deeply into it, as a way toward the infinite and elusive 'source'—or better, perhaps, the ultimately elusive *sense*—of that beauty" (*Divine Enticement*, 7; italics in original).

23. Bennett, *Vibrant Matter*, loc. 152–53.

24. Augustine, *Gen. adv. Man.* 1.26.39–41.

25. Haskell, *Forest Unseen*, 47. Haskell uses the sentence "Metaphysics was scrawled into flesh" to characterize Jakob Böhme's view that "God's purpose for his creation was signed into the forms of worldly things" (47). This close connection between metaphysics and flesh seems appropriate for Augustine's position as well, given the very close connection he draws between "the measure and number and order" of animal bodies and God.

26. Stewart, "Darwin's Worms," 3, quoting an unnamed critic of Darwin's work on worms: "Another critic dryly observed, 'In the eyes of most men . . . the earthworm is a mere blind, dumb, senseless, and unpleasantly slimy annelid. Mr. Darwin undertakes to rehabilitate his character, and the earthworm steps forth at once as an intelligent and beneficent personage, a worker of vast geological changes, a planer down of mountainsides . . . a friend of man.'"

27. Augustine, *Quant.* 31.62.6–24 (trans. Holman, emended). For a brief discussion of this dialogue in the context of the dialogue format as used by Augustine, see Fuhrer, "Conversationalist and Consultant."

28. Bennett, *Vibrant Matter*, 246–48.

29. Bailly, *Animal*, 57 (italics in original); see also p. 46.

30. Augustine, *Quant.* 31.63.17–21 (trans. McMahon).

31. Ibid., 31.64.5–13.

32. Ibid., 32.66.20–24.

33. Ibid., 32.67.16–23.

34. Cameron, *Christ Meets Me Everywhere*, 270.

35. Stevens, "The Man with the Blue Guitar," XVII, in *Collected Poems*, 174.

36. Bailly, *Animal Side*, 49. See also MacKendrick's view of the relationships that Augustine sees among God, the world, and language: "The whole world *reads* for Augustine as a sign of God; it *says* God to him" (*Divine Enticement*, 8).

37. Mt. 27:46; Mk. 15:34. Note that, in Augustine's numbering, this is Psalm 21.

38. Cameron, *Christ Meets Me Everywhere*, 165–212, on Augustine's Christological interpretation of the Psalms. See his comment on p. 168: "Augustine took up the Psalms in order to think deeply and intentionally about the human Christ." Ultimately, as Cameron notes, Augustine thought that the Psalms were soteriological: his interest was in "Christ's redeeming humanity" (199). On the prosopological method of interpretation, see the discussion by Fiedrowicz, "General Introduction," 50–52.

39. *Ex. 2 Ps.* 21.7, *WSA*, p. 231.

40. See Bertrand, "Le Christ comme ver."

41. Origen, *Hom. in Luc.* 14.8.

42. Job 25:4–6. See Dulaey, "L'interprétation du Psaume 21," 326.

43. Dulaey, "L'interprétation du Psaume 21," 326–27, suggests that an insistence on "no man" as indicative of Christ's status as Son or Word of God was unique to Augustine.

44. Aristotle, *Hist. an.* 539a–b, 550b–557b, 569a; *De gen. an.* 733a, 758a–b, 762a–763a. For patristic sources and discussion, see Ruaro, "God and the Worm," 588.

45. Augustine, *Gen. litt.* 3.14.22.

46. Ibid.

47. Augustine, *Civ. Dei* 21.2 (trans. Bettenson).

48. Stevens, "The Worms at Heaven's Gate," *Collected Poems*, 49.

49. Augustine, *Conf.* 13.ii (2).

50. Augustine, *Io. Ev. tr.* 1.13.

51. Ibid. (translation slightly emended).

52. Morton, *Ecological Thought*, 119.

53. Augustine, *Io. Ev. tr.* 1.13.

54. For an important exploration of Augustine's view of redemption as "Christ's incorporation of us into himself," see Ayres, "Augustine on Redemption," 427. See also Cameron, *Christ Meets Me Everywhere*, 208: "When Christ transposes all humanity into himself on the cross he trades humanity's death for divine life." For an exposition of a range of Augustine's views on salvation, see Burns, "How Christ Saves," especially p. 207: "The manifestation of divine love in bearing the self-inflicted sufferings of humanity elicited and encouraged a response of love: not simply of gratitude but a recognition and appreciation of the divine goodness. That love, in its beginnings, its growth and its fullness, constituted human salvation."

55. MacKendrick, *Divine Enticement*, 27. For a discussion of patristic authors (including Augustine) who viewed the creation as a book that reveals God, see Blowers, *Drama of the Divine Economy*, 318–22.

56. Lévi-Strauss, *Totemism*, 89: "Natural species are chosen not because they are 'good to eat' but because they are 'good to think.'" For discussion of this remark about animals used as totemic signifiers, see Patton, "'Caught with Ourselves in the Net of Life and Time,'" 30.

57. Basil of Caesarea, *Hex.* 8.8. Basil follows Aristotle, *Hist. an.* 5.19.551b9, on the silkworm.

58. Martin, *Corinthian Body*, 11.

59. See, for example, *Hex.* 6.1, 8.2, 1.5.

60. Martin, *Corinthian Body*, 15, 116. See pp. 3–15 for his argument that Cartesian oppositions "are misleading when retrojected into ancient language" (15).

61. Ibid., 116.

62. Basil of Caesarea, *Spir.* 9.23. On the theme of metamorphosis and natural beauty in Basil's thought, see Pelikan, *Christianity and Classical Culture*, 285–87.

63. On the "humiliation" that earthly human beings share with animals, see Basil of Caesarea, *Hex.* 8.2.

64. As Philip Rousseau has noted, the *Hexaemeron* was, among other things, "a study of salvation" (*Basil of Caesarea*, 321).

65. Basil of Caesarea, *Hom.* 350.3 (trans. Rousseau, *Basil of Caesarea*, 324).

66. Basil of Caesarea, *Hex.* 7.5 (trans. Rousseau, *Basil of Caesarea*, 324).

67. Alan Scott, "Date of the *Physiologus*."

68. *Physiologus* 7 (my translation).

69. On the structure of the individual chapters of the *Physiologus*, see Cox, "*Physiologus*" 434.

70. Van Den Broek, *Myth of the Phoenix*, 146–62, on the two versions.

71. Aelian, *NA* 6.58.

72. Ibid.

73. Van Den Broek, *Myth of the Phoenix*, 214.

74. Stevens, *Opus Posthumous*, 162.

75. Dickinson, "'Hope' Is the Thing with Feathers," in *Complete Poems*, no. 254.

76. Hereafter *Life of Simeon*. See Doran, "Introduction," 41–42, for a discussion of authorship.

77. Antonius, *Life of Simeon* 8.

78. Ibid.

79. Ibid., 9–10, the well; Simeon ascends the first of his three pillars in *Life of Simeon* 12. On desert ascetics' behaviors as performances, see Miller, "Desert Asceticism and 'The Body from Nowhere.'"

80. Antonius, *Life of Simeon*, 5.

81. Ibid., 8.

82. Burrus, "Carnal Excess," 250.

83. Harvey, "Sense of a Stylite," 387. In Harvey's view, Antonius's text is moralistic rather than celebratory.

84. Antonius, *Life of Simeon*, 17.

85. Ibid.

86. Ibid., 18.

87. Burrus, "Introduction," 46.

88. Hereafter "Dionysius," as per Charles Stang: "He does not merely sign the name of Dionysius the Areopagite to his writings. He goes much further and literally assumes the identity of this first-century figure" (*Apophasis and Pseudonymity*, 3).

89. For a concise discussion, see Louth, "'Truly Visible Things.'" See also Stang, *Apophasis and Pseudonymity*, 128–35.

90. *Celestial Hierarchy* 2.2–3 (hereafter *CH*).

91. For discussion, see Rorem, *Pseudo-Dionysius*, 53–57; Louth, "'Truly Visible Things,'" 21–22.

92. Dionysius, *CH* 2.3.

93. Ibid.

94. Ibid., *CH* 2.4.

95. Ibid., *CH* 2.2.

96. Ibid., *CH* 2.3.

97. Ibid., *CH* 2.3; 2.4.

98. Dionysius, *Divine Names* 9.7.

99. Dionysius, *CH* 3.5.

100. Ruaro, "God and the Worm," 584. See also Louth, "'Truly Visible Things,'" 19: "Though [Dionysius] does not use the word, he sees the whole cosmos, both visible and invisible, as a theophany: a manifestation of God, in which God is calling the whole order of things 'after him' back into union with him."

101. Dionysius, *CH* 3.5, on deformed imagery.

102. Ibid., *CH* 3.4.

103. Augustine, *Gen. litt.* 3.14.22.

104. Ibid. Augustine makes the same point in *Gen. adv. Man.* 1.16 26: quoting Wisdom 11:20 (God has "arranged all things in measure and number and weight"), he remarks: "You will perhaps find more genuine satisfaction when you praise God in the tiny little ant down on the ground, than when you are crossing a river high up, let us say, on an elephant."

105. Pliny the Elder, *NH* 11.4 (trans. Kaster, *Emotion, Restraint, and Community*, 115).

106. For an example of this perspective on small things in the Latin Christian tradition prior to Augustine, see the following passage from Tertullian, who is arguing against the Marcionite view that God is an inferior creator: "Since you put to scorn those tiny animals which the great artificer has designedly made great in competence and ability, so teaching us that greatness approves itself in littleness, even as the apostle says, strength does in weakness: imitate, if you can, the bee's house-building, the ant's stablings, the spider's net-work, the silkworm's spinning: tolerate, if you can, even those creatures in your bed and on your bed-cover, the poison of the cantharis, the midge's sting, *the mosquito's trumpet and spear*. How great must the greater things be, when by things so little you are so gratified or distressed that not even in those little things can you dispute their creator" (*Adv. Mar.* 1.14.1, emphasis added).

107. Sorabji, *Animal Minds and Human Morals*, 204.

108. Augustine, *Conf.* 10.55.56.

109. Ibid., 10.55.57.

110. Ibid.

111. On curiosity as a form of fascination in ancient Roman culture, see Barton, *Sorrows of the Ancient Romans*, 85–95.

112. Stock, *Augustine the Reader*, 231.

113. See Burrus, Jordan, and MacKendrick, *Seducing Augustine*, 93, where their discussion of *distentio*, while it does not refer to animals, nonetheless is relevant here: "*Distentio* suggests "a state of fragmented desire that results from the frantic pursuit of elusively transient beauties."

114. Bennett, *Enchantment of Modern Life*, 4.

115. Ibid., 5.

116. Augustine, *Gen. litt.* 3.14.22.

117. Bennett, *Enchantment of Modern Life*, 162. On the "radical intimacy" of the new materialism, see Morton, *Ecological Thought*, 119.

118. The phrases in quotation are borrowed from Bennett, *Enchantment of Modern Life*, 166.

119. Haskell, *Forest Unseen*, 107–9.

120. As Haskell notes about the mosquito bite: "This physical connection to the rest of nature is often unseen. The mosquito bite, the breath, the mouthful are acts that create a community, that keep us welded into existence, but that mostly pass unacknowledged. A few people say grace at a meal, but no one does so with every inhalation or insect bite. This unconsciousness is partly self-defense. The connections through the millions of molecules we eat or breathe or lose to mosquitoes are too many, too multifariously complex for us to attempt comprehension" (*Unseen Forest*, 112).

121. Updike, "Mosquito."

122. As Haskell, *Unseen Forest*, 108, notes, "Male mosquitoes . . . feed like bees or butterflies, sipping nectar from flowers or drinking sugars from rotting fruit." Only breeding females seek out human and other animals' blood.

123. Palladius, *Historia Lausiaca* 18.4. I have changed Meyer's translation of κώνωψ as "gnat" to "mosquito" in order to make this part of the story cohere with the scene of the mosquitoes in the swamp. According to Liddell, Scott, and Jones, *Greek-English Dictionary*, the word can mean either "gnat" or "mosquito," and it seems clear that it designates mosquitoes in Palladius's telling of this story. On the ancient lack of clear distinction between gnats and mosquitoes, see Davies and Kathirithamby, *Greek Insects*, 164–65, and 165–67 on ancient testimonies to mosquitoes as nuisances.

124. *Apophthegmata Patrum*, Isaiah 8.

125. On cultivating the single eye as a monastic goal, see Ward, "Introduction," 29–38. On the monastic cultivation of serenity and its connection with the "heart," see Brown, *The Body and Society*, 224–29.

126. See Harmless, *Desert Christians*, 285, for the quotation; 285–87 for a discussion of Palladius's representations of the ascetic life.

127. Harmless, *Desert Christians*, 286–87.

128. Burrus, *Saving Shame*, 86.

129. Harmless, *Desert Christians*, 287.

130. Origen, *Hom. in Ex.* 4.6, in Heine, trans., *Origen: Homilies on Genesis and Exodus*, 208–9.

131. Origen, *Hom. in Ex.* 4.6.

132. Ibid..

133. Aristotle, *HA* 542a12, in Davies and Kathirithamby, *Greek Insects*, 151.

134. Origen, *Hom. in Ex.* 4.8.

135. Ibid.

136. See Bennett, *Enchantment of Modern Life*, 131, on the connection between ethics and embodied sensibility.

137. See Heine, "Introduction," 50–71, for a full discussion of Gregory's vision of the five stages.

138. Gregory of Nyssa, *In inscriptiones Psalmorum* 1.4.35.

139. On the fifth stage of ascent, see the discussion of Heine, "Introduction," 67–71.

140. Gregory of Nyssa, *In inscriptions Psalmorum* 1.8.76.

141. Augustine, *Io. Ev. tr.* 3.4 (trans. Holman, 61).

142. On the positive effects of humiliation in early Christian thinking, see Burrus, *Saving Shame*, 81–109.

143. Augustine, *Io. Ev. tr.* 1.15 (trans. Holman, 61).

144. See n. 21 above.

145. Augustine, *Io. Ev. tr.* 1.15, lines 7–8: *Nam propter superbiam instuit deus istam creaturam minimam et abiectissimam, ut ipsa nos torqueret.*

146. See, for example, *Civ. Dei* 14.13, where Augustine quotes a version of Ecclesiasticus 10:13, "The beginning of all sin is pride." For a brief discussion, see Sorabji, *Emotion and Peace of Mind*, 336.

147. Augustine, *Civ. Dei* 14.13 (trans. Bettenson, 571).

148. The phrases in quotation are from Hunter, "Augustine on the Body," 357.

149. Markus, *Conversion and Disenchantment*, 32.

150. Origen, *Hom. in Ex.* 4.6. The idea that patristic authors could be a little "lighthearted" in some of their interpretations of the Pentateuch, using, for example, "[a] passage like the ten plagues of Egypt" to "take some digs at their enemies," comes from Lienhard, "Christian Reception of the Pentateuch," 381.

151. Plato, *Republic* III.398a–b; X.595a–605e, on the dangers of imitative poetry. This was not, of course, Plato's only view of poetry.

152. For Philo's influence on Origen's thought, see Van Den Hoek, "The Catechetical School of Early Christian Alexandria;" Van den Hoek, "Philo and Origen"; Runia, *Philo in Early Christian Literature: A Survey*, 157–83. For an overall view, see Runia, "Philo of Alexandria."

153. Philo of Alexandria, *De sacrificiis* 69. I owe this reference to Robin Darling Young.

154. Origen of Alexandria, *Hom. in Ex.* 4.8.

155. Theodore Roethke, "Slug," in *Collected Poems of Theodore Roethke*, 145. I owe this reference to David L. Miller.

156. Palladius, *Historia Lausiaca* 47.10.

157. Even a Christian ascetic like Paulinus of Nola, for example, delighted in the lovely array of fountains that he supplied for the inner courtyard of the complex in Cimitile devoted to St. Felix. See Kiely, "Interior Courtyard," 455. In the region of Campania, Italy, for example, water was readily available due to the construction of an aqueduct just prior to the imperial period. Thus "water features became integral to the décor of gardens around the Bay of Naples. Fountains, grottoes, canals shaded by trellises, waterfalls, pools, and fishponds were as popular as garden sculptures in creating the setting and atmosphere for *otium* (Mattusch et al., *Pompeii and the Roman Villa*, 169. For wall paintings of gardens with fountains, see Mazzoleni, *Domus*, esp.

pp. 6, 33. For more on gardens and their fountains, see Farrar, *Ancient Roman Gardens*; MacDougall and Jashemski, *Ancient Roman Gardens*.

158. *Physiologus* 29 (trans. Grant, 64).

159. Aelian, *NA* 9.13.

160. Gregory of Nyssa, *De vita Moysis* 2.68 (trans. Malherbe and Ferguson, 69).

161. Gregory of Nyssa, *Homilies on the Song of Songs* (ed. and trans. Norris, 87).

162. Gregory of Nyssa, *De vita Moysis* 2.69.

163. For a discussion, with references, of Gregory's use of the metaphors of mud and mire, see Malherbe and Ferguson, trans., *Gregory of Nyssa: The Life of Moses*, 167, n. 91.

164. Gregory of Nyssa, *De vita Moysis* 2.70.

165. Holmes, *Biology of the Frog*, 55–56; I owe this reference, plus the remark about polymorphous perversity, to an unpublished paper by David L. Miller.

166. Gregory of Nyssa, *De vita Moysis* 2.71.

167. Ibid.

168. Ibid., 2.71–72.

169. Maguire, Maguire, and Duncan-Flowers, *Art and Holy Powers*, 76.

170. Ibid., 10.

171. Ibid.

172. Bachelard, *Poetics of Space*, 155, 193.

173. Spittler, *Animals in the Apocryphal Acts of the Apostles*, 165.

174. The quotation is a line from a poem by Carson, "Guillermo's Sigh Symphony," in her *Decreation*, 77.

175. On consecrated women as brides of Christ, see (among many) Clark, "Devil's Gateway and Bride of Christ"; Cooper, *The Virgin and the Bride*; Brown, *The Body and Society*, 259–60, 274–76; 345–57 on Ambrose. On the "desexualization" of the Song of Songs, see Clark, *Reading Renunciation*, 87–88.

176. *Favus distillans labia tua, sponsa; mel et lac sub lingua tua.*

177. Ambrose, *De virginitate* 1.8.40–41.

178. Haskell, *Forest Unseen*, 57.

AFTERWORD

1. Plato, *Politicus* 272a–b.

2. Ibid., 272b–c.

3. Krell, "'Talk to the Animals,'" 29.

4. Krell, *Derrida and Our Animal Others*, 5.

5. With this sentence, Krell, *Derrida and Our Animal Others*, 84, succinctly summarizes a major focal point of many recent works in animal studies. See, for example, Weil, *Thinking Animals*, 3–24; Oliver, *Animal Lessons*, 303–6; Steiner, *Anthropocentrism and Its Discontents*, 4–38 and passim

6. Krell, *Derrida and Our Animal Others*, 31. See Derrida, *The Beast and the Sovereign*, 1: 313–14; *Animal*, 16–17.

7. 1 Clement 20.1–12.

8. Blowers, *Drama of the Divine Economy*, 322.

9. Augustine, *Trin.* 2, prol. 1.1 (trans. Blowers, *Drama of the Divine Economy*, 325).

10. Basil of Caesarea, *Hex.* 5.2.

11. Ibid., 3.10.

12. On beauty, see ibid., 1.11; 8.7. On all created things as faint reflections of the creator, see ibid., 6.11.

13. Ibid., 6.1.

14. John Chrysostom, *Hom. in Gen.* 2.11; Ambrose, *Hex.* 2.21.

15. Chin, "Cosmos," 99.

16. Basil of Caesarea, *Hex.* 2.2 (trans. Blowers, *Drama of the Divine Economy*, 220).

17. Chin, "Cosmos," 99.

18. Ibid., 100.

19. Krell, *Derrida and Our Animal Others*, 101.

BIBLIOGRAPHY

ANCIENT WORKS

Acta Iohannis. In *Corpus Christianorum, Series Apocryphorum* 1. Ed. Eric Junod and Jean Daniel Kaestli. Turnhout: Brepols, 1983. Trans. Knut Schäferdiek. *New Testament Apocrypha*, vol. 2: *Writings Relating to the Apostles, Apocalypses, and Related Subjects*. Ed. Wilhelm Schneemelcher and Edgar Hennecke, 172–209. Trans. R. McL. Wilson. Louisville: Westminster/John Knox Press, 1992, rev. ed.

Acta Pauli. P. Bodmer LXI. In *New Testament Apocrypha*, rev. ed., vol. 2: *Writings Relating to the Apostles, Apocalypses, and Related Subjects*. Ed. Edgar Hennecke and Wilhelm Schneemelcher, 263–65. Trans. R. McL. Wilson. Louisville: Westminster/John Knox, 1992.

Acta Philippi. *Corpus Christianorum, Series Apocryphorum* 11. Ed. François Bovon, Bertrand Bouvier, and Frédéric Amsler. Turnhout: Brepols, 1999. Trans. François Bovon and Christopher R. Matthews. *The Acts of Philip: A New Translation*. Waco: Baylor University Press, 2012.

Acts of Paul and Thecla. Ed. Richard Adelbert Lipsius and Maximilian Bonnet. *Acta Apostolorum Apocrypha*, Part 1. Leipzig: H. Mendelssohn, 1891. Trans. Wilhelm Schneemelcher and Rodolphe Kasser. *New Testament Apocrypha*, vol. 2: *Writings Relating to the Apostles, Apocalypses, and Related Subjects*. Ed. Wilhelm Schneemelcher and Edgar Hennecke, 239–46. Trans. R. McL. Wilson. Louisville: Westminster/John Knox Press, 1992, rev. ed.

Acts of Xanthippe and Polyxena. Ed. Montague Rhodes James, *Apocrypha Anecdota: A Collection of Thirteen Apocryphal Books and Fragments*. Texts and Studies 2. Cambridge: Cambridge University Press, 1893. Trans. David L. Eastman. *The Life and Conduct of the Holy Women Xanthippe, Polyxena, and Rebecca*. In *New Testament Apocrypha: More Noncanonical Scriptures*, 416–52. Ed. Tony Burke and Brent Landau. Grand Rapids, MI: Wm. B. Eerdmans, 2016. I thank Professor Eastman for sharing the manuscript of his translation with me.

Aelian. *De natura animalium*. 3 vols. Ed. and trans. A. F. Scholfield. Loeb Classical Library. Cambridge, MA: Harvard University Press, 1958.

Ambrose. *De paradiso*. *Patrologia Latina* 14.275–314. Trans. John J. Savage. *Saint Ambrose: Hexaemeron, Paradise, and Cain and Abel*. Fathers of the Church 42. New York: Fathers of the Church, 1961.

———. *De virginitate*. *Patrologia Latina* 16.197–243. Trans. Sister M. Theresa of the Cross Springer. *Nature-Imagery in the Works of Saint Ambrose*. Washington, DC: Catholic University of America Press, 1931.

———. *Hexaemeron*. *Patrologia Latina* 14.123–274. Trans. John J. Savage. *Saint Ambrose: Hexaemeron, Paradise, and Cain and Abel*. Fathers of the Church 42. New York: Fathers of the Church, 1961.

Antonius. *Life and Daily Mode of Living of the Blessed Simeon the Stylite.* Trans. Robert Doran. *The Lives of Simeon Stylites.* Cistercian Studies 112. Kalamazoo: Cistercian Publications, 1992.

Apicius. *Romanae Artis Coquinariae Liber.* Trans. Barbara Flower and Elisabeth Rosenbaum. *The Roman Cookery Book.* London: Peter Nevill, 1958.

Apocryphon of John. Trans. Karen L. King. *The Secret Revelation of John.* Cambridge, MA: Harvard University Press, 2006.

Apophthegmata patrum. Patrologia Graeca 65.71–440. Trans. Benedicta Ward, S.L.G. *The Sayings of the Desert Fathers: The Alphabetical Collection.* Kalamazoo: Cistercian Press, 1975.

Aristotle. *De generatione animalium.* Trans. A. L. Peck. *Aristotle,* vol. 13: *On the Generation of Animals.* Loeb Classical Library. Cambridge: Harvard University Press, 1942.

———. *Historia Animalium.* Ed. and trans. D. M. Balme. Loeb Classical Library. Cambridge: Harvard University Press, 1991.

———. *Rhetoric.* Trans. W. Rhys Roberts. In *The Basic Works of Aristotle.* Ed. Richard McKeon. New York: Random House, 1968.

Ascension of Isaiah. In *New Testament Apocrypha,* vol. 2: *Writings Relating to the Apostles; Apocalypses and Related Subjects,* 644–63. Ed. Edgar Hennecke and Wilhelm Schneemelcher. Trans. R. McL. Wilson. Philadelphia: Westminster Press, 1965.

Athanasius. *De vita Antonii.* Ed. and trans. G. J. M. Bartelink. *Athanase: Vie d'Antoine.* Sources Chrétiennes 400. Paris: Les Éditions du Cerf, 1994. Trans. Robert C. Gregg. *Athanasius: The Life of Antony and the Letter to Marcellinus.* The Classics of Western Spirituality. Mahwah: Paulist Press, 1980.

Augustine. *Confessiones. Corpus Christianorum Series Latina* 27. Ed. L. Verheijen. Turnhout: Brepols, 1981. Trans. Henry Chadwick. *Saint Augustine: Confessions.* Oxford: Oxford University Press, 1991.

———. *Contra Academicos. Corpus Christianorum Series Latina* 29. Ed. W. M. Green and K. D. Daur. Turnhout: Brepols, 1970. Trans. Sister Mary Patricia Garvey, R.S.M. *Saint Augustine: Against the Academicians.* Milwaukee: Marquette University Press, 1957.

———. *De civitate dei. Corpus Christianorum Series Latina* 47–48. Ed. B. Dombart and A. Kalb. Turnhout: Brepols, 1955. Trans. Henry Bettenson. Ed. David Knowles. *Augustine: City of God.* Harmondsworth: Penguin Books, 1972. Also consulted: R. W. Dyson, ed. and trans. *Augustine: The City of God Against the Pagans.* Cambridge: Cambridge University Press, 1998.

———. *De diversis quaestionibus octoginta tribus. Corpus Christianorum Series Latina* 44A. Ed. Almut Mutzenbecher. Turnhout: Brepols, 1975. Trans. Boniface Ramsay. Ed. Raymond Canning. *Works of Saint Augustine: A Translation for the Twenty-First Century,* I.12. Hyde Park, NY: New City Press.

———. *De doctrina christiana. Corpus Christianorum Series Latina* 32. Ed. K. D. Daur and J. Martin. Turnhout: Brepols, 1962. Trans. D. W. Robertson, Jr. *Saint Augustine: On Christian Doctrine.* Upper Saddle River, NJ: Prentice-Hall, 1958.

———. *De Genesi ad litteram. Corpus Scriptorum Ecclesiasticorm Latinorum* 28/1. Ed. Joseph Zycha, 1894. Trans. John Hammond Taylor, S.J. *St. Augustine: The Literal Meaning of Genesis.* 2 vols. Ancient Christian Writers 41, 42. New York: Newman Press, 1982.

———. *De Genesi adversus Manichaeos. Corpus Augustinianum Gissense* and CSEL 91. Trans. Edmund Hill, O.P. *Works of Saint Augustine,* electronic edition: *On Genesis: A Refutation of the Manichees,* p. 55. Charlottesville, VA: Intelex Corporation, 2001.

———. *De libero arbitrio. Corpus Christianorum Series Latina* 29. Ed. W. M. Green and K. D. Daur. Turnhout: Brepols, 1970. Trans. Robert P. Russell. *Saint Augustine (The Teacher, The Free Choice of the Will, Grace and Free Will)*. Fathers of the Church 59. Washington, DC: Catholic University Press of America, 1968.

———. *De ordine. Corpus Christianorum Series Latina* 29. Ed. W. M. Green and K. D. Daur. Turnhout: Brepols, 1970. Trans. Sister Mary John Holman, *Nature-Imagery in the Works of St. Augustine*. Washington, DC: Catholic University Press of America, 1931.

———. *De quantitate animae. Corpus Scriptorum Ecclesiasticorum Latinorum* 89. Trans. John J. McMahon, S.J. *Writings of Saint Augustine*, vol. 2. The Fathers of the Church 4. New York: CIMA, 1947. Also consulted: Sister Mary John Holman, trans. *Nature-Imagery in the Works of St. Augustine*. Washington, DC: Catholic University of America, 1931.

———. *De trinitate. Corpus Christianorum Series Latina* 50A, 50. Ed. W. J. Mountain and F. Glorie. Turnhout: Brepols, 1968, 2001.

———. *De vera religione. Corpus Christianorum Series Latina* 32. Ed. K. D. Daur and J. Martin. Turnhout: Brepols, 1962. Trans. John H. Burleigh. *Augustine: Earlier Writings*. The Library of Christian Classics 6. Philadelphia: Westminster Press, 1953.

———. *Enarrationes in Psalmos. Corpus Augustinianum Gissense, Opera Omnia*: Part 9. Online edition. Trans. Maria Boulding, O.S.B. *The Works of Saint Augustine: A Translation for the 21st Century* (Hyde Park, NY: New City Press), III.15–20: *Expositions on the Psalms*. Electronic edition (*WSA*).

———. *In Iohannis Evangelium tractatus CXXIV. Corpus Scriptorum Series Latina* 36. Ed. D. Radbotus Willems, O.S.B. Turnhout: Brepols, 1953. Trans. John Gibb and James Innes. *Tractates on the Gospel of John. Nicene and Post-Nicene Fathers*, 1st Series, vol. 7. Grand Rapids, MI: Wm. B. Eerdmans, repr. ed., 1991. Also consulted: Sister Mary John Holman, trans. *Nature-Imagery in the Works of St. Augustine*. Washington, DC: Catholic University Press of America, 1931.

Basil of Caesarea. *Homiliae. Patrologia Graeca* 29.209–494.

———. *Homiliae in Hexaemeron*. Ed. and trans. Stanislas Giet. *Basile de Césarée: Homélies sur L'Hexaéméron*. Sources Chrétiennes 26 bis. Paris: Les Éditions du Cerf, 1968. Trans. Sister Agnes Clare Way, C.D.P. *Saint Basil: Exegetic Homilies*. Fathers of the Church 46. Washington, DC: Catholic University Press of America, 1963.

———. *Homiliae in Hexaemeron* 10. Ed. and trans. Alexis Smets and Michel Van Esbroeck. *Basile de Césarée: Sur l'Origine de l'Homme (Hom. X et XI de l'Hexaéméron)*. Sources Chrétiennes 160. Paris: Les Éditions du Cerf, 1970.

———. *De spiritu sancto*. Ed. and trans. Benoît Pruche. *Basile de Césarée, Sur le Saint-Esprit*. Sources Chrétiennes 17 bis. Paris: Les Éditions du Cerf, 1968.

Clement of Alexandria. *Protrepticus*. Ed. and trans. Claude Mondésert, S.J. *Clément d'Alexandrie: Le Protreptique*. Sources Chrétiennes 2 bis. Paris: Les Éditions du Cerf, 1949.

———. *Stromata*. Ed and trans. Claude Mondésert. *Clément d'Alexandrie: Les Stromates*, 7 vols. Sources Chrétiennes 30, 38, 278, 279, 428, 446, 463. Paris: Les Éditions du Cerf, 1981–2001.

———. *Stromata* 7. Trans. J. B. Mayor. In *Alexandrian Christianity*, ed. John Ernest Leonard Oulton and Henry Chadwick, 93–165. Library of Christian Classics 2. Philadelphia: Westminster Press, 1954.

1 Clement. Trans. Cyril C. Richardson. *Early Christian Fathers* 1. Philadelphia: Westminster Press, 1953.

Cyprian. *De ecclesiae catholicae unitate*. Ed. M. Bévenot. *Corpus Scriptorum Ecclesiasticorum Latinorum* 3. Turnhout: Brepols, repr. ed., 1972.

Cyril of Scythopolis. *Lives of the Monks of Palestine*. Ed. Eduard Schwartz. *Kyrillos von Skythopolis*. Texte und Untersuchungen 49:2. Leipzig, 1939. Trans. R. M. Price. *Lives of the Monks of Palestine by Cyril of Scythopolis*. Kalamazoo: Cistercian Publications, 1991.

Didymus of Alexandria. *Commentarium in Genesim*. Ed. and trans. Pierre Nautin. Sources Chrétiennes 233. Paris: Les Éditions du Cerf, 1976.

Dionysius the Areopagite. *Celestial Hierarchy. Patrologia Graeca* 3. Trans. Colm Luibheid. *Pseudo-Dionysius: The Complete Works*. New York: Paulist Press, 1987.

———. *Divine Names. Patrologia Graeca* 3. Trans. Colm Luibheid. *Pseudo-Dionysius: The Complete Works*. New York: Paulist Press, 1987.

Gregory of Nazianzus. *Oratio* 28 (*Second Theological Oration*). Ed. and trans. Paul Gallay with Maurice Jourjon. *Grégoire de Nazianze: Discours 27–31*. Sources Chrétiennes 250. Paris: Les Éditions du Cerf, 1978. Trans. E. H. Gifford. *Nicene and Post-Nicene Fathers* 7: *Cyril of Jerusalem and Gregory Nazianzen*, 288–301. Grand Rapids, MI: Wm. B. Eerdmans, repr. ed., 1989.

Gregory of Nyssa. *De hominis opificio. Patrologia Graeca* 44.123–256. Trans. *Nicene and Post-Nicene Fathers* 5: *On the Making of Man*, 387–427. Ed. Philip Schaff and Henry Wace. Grand Rapids, MI: Wm. B. Eerdmans, repr. ed., 1994.

———. *De vita Moysis*. Ed. and trans. Jean Daniélou. *Grégoire de Nysse: La Vie de Moïse*. Sources Chrétiennes 1 bis. Paris: Les Éditions du Cerf, 1955. Trans. Abraham J. Malherbe and Everett Ferguson. *Gregory of Nyssa: The Life of Moses*. The Classics of Western Spirituality. New York: Paulist Press, 1978.

———. *Homiliae in Canticum Canticorum*. Greek text and trans. in Richard A. Norris Jr., *Gregory of Nyssa: Homilies on the Song of Songs*. Writings from the Greco-Roman World 13. Atlanta: Society of Biblical Literature, 2012.

———. *In inscriptiones Psalmorum*. Ed. and trans. Jean Reynard. *Grégoire de Nysse: Sur les Titres des Paumes*. Sources Chrétiennes 466. Paris: Les Éditions du Cerf, 2002. Trans. Ronald E. Heine. *Gregory of Nyssa's Treatise on the Inscriptions of the Psalms: Introduction, Translation, and Notes*. Oxford: Clarendon Press, 1995.

Hippolytus of Rome. *Commentarium in Danielem*. Ed. and trans. Maurice LeFèvre. *Hippolyte: Commentaire sur Daniel*. Sources Chrétiennes 14. Paris: Les Éditions du Cerf, 1947. Trans. Robert M. Grant, *Early Christians and Animals*. London, 1999 (selected passages).

Historia monachorum in Aegypto. Ed. A.-J. Festugière. Subsidia Hagiographica 34. Brussels: Société des Bollandistes, 1961. Trans. Normal Russell, *The Lives of the Desert Fathers*. Kalamazoo: Cistercian Publications, 1981.

Infancy Gospel of Thomas. Trans. David R. Cartlidge and David L. Dungan. *Documents for the Study of the Gospels*. Minneapolis: Augsburg Press, 1980; repr. in Bart Ehrman, *After the New Testament: A Reader in Early Christianity*, 255–59. New York: Oxford University Press, 1999.

Irenaeus. *Adversus haereses*. Ed. and trans. A. Rousseau, L. Doutreleau, and C. Mercier. *Irénée de Lyon: Contre les hérésies*. Sources Chrétiennes 100, 152, 153, 210, 211, 263, 264, 293, 294. Paris: Les Éditions du Cerf, 1965–1982. Trans. Alexander Roberts and James Donaldson. Ante-Nicene Fathers 1: *The Apostolic Fathers with Justin Martyr and Irenaeus*. Grand Rapids, MI: Wm. B. Eerdmans, repr. ed., 1979.

Isaac the Syrian. *The Ascetical Homilies*. Trans. Father Panteleimon et al. Boston: Holy Transfiguration Monastery, 1984.

Jerome. *De viris illustribus*. Ed. Aldo Ceresa-Gastaldo. *Gerolamo: Gli uomini illustri. De viris illustribus*. Biblioteca Patristica 12. Florence: Nardini, 1988.

———. *Vita Sancti Pauli Primi Eremitae*. Ed. William Abbott Oldfather. *Studies in the Text Tradition of Jerome's Vitae Patrum*. Urbana: University of Illinois Press, 1943. Trans. Paul B. Harvey, Jr., *Jerome: Life of Paul, the First Hermit*. In *Ascetic Behavior in Greco-Roman Antiquity: A Sourcebook*, ed. Vincent L. Wimbush, 357–69. Minneapolis: Fortress Press, 1990.

John Chrysostom. *Homiliae in Genesim. Patrologia Graeca* 53. Trans. Robert C. Hill, *Saint John Chrysostom: Homilies on Genesis 1–17*. Fathers of the Church 74. Washington, DC: Catholic University of America Press, 1986.

———. *De statuis homilia 12. Patrologia Graeca* 49.127–36. Trans. W. R. W. Stephens, *Saint Chrysostom: Homilies on the Statues*. In *Nicene and Post-Nicene Fathers* 9, ed. Philip Schaff, 418–25 (= *Homily* 12). Grand Rapids, MI: Wm. B. Eerdmans, repr. ed., 1989.

John Moschos. *Pratum Spirituale. Patrologia Graeca* 87.3: 2852A–3112B. Trans. John Wortley. *John Moschos: The Spiritual Meadow*. Cistercian Studies Series 139. Collegeville: Cistercian Publications, 2008.

Life and Miracles of St. Thecla. Ed. and trans Gilbert Dagron. *Vie et miracles de Sainte Thècle: Texte Grec, traduction, et commentaire*. Brussels: Société des Bollandistes, 1978.

Life of Macarius of Alexandria. Trans. Tim Vivian. *Four Desert Fathers: Pambo, Evagrius, Macarius of Egypt and Macarius of Alexandria*. Crestwood: St. Vladimir's Seminary Press, 2004.

Martial. *Epigrammata*. Ed. and trans. H. J. Izaac. *Martial: Épigrammes*. 3 vols. 2nd ed. Paris: Société "Les Belles Lettres," 1961.

Martyrdom of the Holy and Glorious Apostle Philip. Corpus Christianorum, Series Apocryphorum 11. Ed. François Bovon, Bertrand Bouvier, and Frédéric Amsler. Turnhout: Brepols, 1999. Trans. François Bovon and Christopher Mathews. *The Acts of Philip: A New Translation*. Waco: Baylor University Press, 2012.

Origen. *Commentarium in Canticum Canticorum*. Ed. and trans. Luc Brésard, O.C.S.O., Henri Crouzel, S.J., and Marcel Borret, S.J. *Origène: Commentaire sur le Cantique des Cantiques*. 2 vols. Sources Chrétiennes 375, 376. Paris: Les Éditions du Cerf, 1991, 1992. Trans. R. P. Lawson. *Origen: The Song of Songs, Commentary and Homilies*. Ancient Christian Writers 26. New York: Newman Press, 1956.

———. *Contra Celsum*. Ed. and trans. M. Borret. *Origène: Contre Celse*, vol. 2. Sources Chrétiennes 136. Paris: Les Éditions du Cerf, 1968. Trans. Henry Chadwick. *Origen: Contra Celsum*. Cambridge: Cambridge University Press, 1965.

———. *De principiis*. Ed. and trans. Henri Crouzel, S.J., and Manlio Simonetti. *Origène: Traité des Principes*, 4 vols. Sources Chrétiennes 252, 253, 268, 269. Paris: Les Éditions du Cerf, 1978–1980. Trans. G. W. Butterworth. *Origen: On First Principles*. New York: Harper and Row, 1966.

———. *Dialogue with Heraclides*. Ed. and trans. Jean Scherer. *Entretiene d'Origène avec Héraclide*. Sources Chrétiennes 67. Paris: Les Éditions du Cerf, 1960. Trans. Robert J. Daly, S.J. *Origen: Treatise on the Passover and Dialogue of Origen with Heraclides and His Fellow Bishops on the Father, the Son, and the Soul*. Ancient Christian Writers 54. New York: Paulist Press, 1992.

———. *Homiliae in Canticum Canticorum*. Ed. and trans. Olivier Rousseau. O.S.B. *Origène: Homélies sur Le Cantique des Cantiques*. Sources Chrétiennes 37 bis. Paris: Les Éditions du Cerf, 2007. Trans. R. P. Lawson. *Origen: The Song of Songs, Commentary and Homilies*. Ancient Christian Writers 26. New York: Newman Press, 1956.

———. *Homiliae in Exodum*. Ed. and trans. P. Fortier. *Origène: Homélies sur l'Exode*. Sources Chrétiennes 16. Paris: Les Éditions du Cerf, 1947. Trans. Ronald E. Heine. *Origen: Homilies on Genesis and Exodus.* The Fathers of the Church 71. Washington, DC: Catholic University of America Press, 1982.

———. *Homiliae in Genesim.* Ed. and trans. Louis Doutreleau. *Origène: Homélies sur la Genèse.* Sources Chrétiennes 7 bis. Paris: Les Éditions du Cerf, 1976. Trans. Ronald E. Heine. *Origen: Homilies on Genesis and Exodus.* The Fathers of the Church 71. Washington, DC: Catholic University of America Press, 1982.

———. *Homiliae in Jeremiam.* Ed. and trans. Pierre Nautin and Pierre Husson. *Origène: Homélies sur Jérémie,* 2 vols. Sources Chrétiennes 232, 238. Paris: Les Éditions du Cerf, 1976, 1977.

———. *Homiliae in Leviticum.* Ed. and trans. Marcel Borret, S.J. *Origène: Homélies sur le Lévitique.* Sources Chrétiennes 286. Paris: Les Éditions du Cerf, 1981. Trans. Gary Wayne Barkley. *Origen: Homilies on Leviticus 1–16.* The Fathers of the Church 83. Washington, DC: Catholic University of America Press, 1990.

———. *Homiliae in Lucam.* Ed. and trans. Henri Crouzel, François Fournier, and Pierre Périchon. *Origène: Homélies sur S. Luc.* Sources Chrétiennes 87. Paris: Les Éditions du Cerf, 1962. Trans. Joseph T. Lienhard, S.J. *Origen: Homilies on Luke, Fragments on Luke.* The Fathers of the Church 94. Washington, DC: Catholic University Press of America, 1996.

Ovid. *Fasti.* Trans. Sir James George Frazier. Loeb Classical Library. Cambridge, MA: Harvard University Press, 2nd ed., 1996.

Palladius. *Historia Lausiaca.* Ed. Cuthbert Butler. *The Lausiac History of Palladius,* vol. 2: *The Greek Text Edited with Introduction and Notes.* Cambridge: Cambridge University Press, 1904. Trans. Robert T. Meyer. *Palladius: The Lausiac History.* Ancient Christian Writers 34. New York: Paulist Press, 1964.

Philo. *De animalibus.* Trans. Abraham Terian. *Philonis Alexandrini De Animalibus: The Armenian Text with an Introduction, Translation, and Commentary.* Studies in Hellenistic Judaism 1. Chico, CA: Scholars Press, 1981.

———. *De Sacrificiis.* Trans. Charles Duke Yonge. *The Works of Philo, Complete and Unabridged.* New updated ed. Ed. David M. Scholer. Peabody, MA: Hendrickson, 1993.

Physiologus. Ed. Friedrich Lauchert. *Geschichte des Physiologus.* Strasbourg: K. J. Trübner, 1889. Also consulted: *Physiologus Latinus Versio* Y. Ed. Francis J. Carmody. *University of California Publications in Classical Philology* 12, no. 7. Berkeley: University of California Press, 1941. Trans. Michael J. Curley. *Physiologus.* Austin: University of Texas Press, 1979. Also consulted: Robert M. Grant, trans. *Early Christians and Animals.* London: Routledge, 1999.

Plato. *The Collected Dialogues of Plato Including the Letters.* Ed. Edith Hamilton and Huntington Cairns. Bollingen Series 71. Princeton: Princeton University Press, 1961.

———. *Phaedrus.* Trans. William S. Cobb. *The Symposium and The Phaedrus: Plato's Erotic Dialogues.* Albany: State University of New York Press, 1993.

———. *Politicus [Statesman].* Trans. Eva Brann, Peter Kalkavage, and Eric Salem. *Plato: Statesman: Translation, Glossary, and Essay.* Indianapolis: Focus /Hackett, 2012.

Pliny. *Naturalis Historia,* 10 vols. Ed. and trans. H. Rackham. Loeb Classical Library. London: William Heinemann, 1967.

Plutarch. *De sollertia animalium.* In *Plutarch: Moralia,* vol. 12. Trans. Harold Cherniss and William C. Helmbold. *Plutarch: On the Cleverness of Animals.* Loeb Classical Library. Cambridge, MA: Harvard University Press, 1957.

———. *Moralia. Plutarch's Moralia,* 15 vols. Ed. and trans. Harold Cherniss and William C. Helmbold. Loeb Classical Library. Cambridge, MA: Harvard University Press, 1957.

Porphyry. *De abstinentia*. In *Porphyre: De l'abstinence*, vol. 2. Ed. Jean Bouffartique and Michel Patillon. Paris: Société d'Édition "Les Belles Lettres," 1979. Trans. Gillian Clark. *Porphyry: On Abstinence from Killing Animals*. Ithaca, NY: Cornell University Press, 2000.

Quintillian, *Institutio Oratoria*. In "Introduction," *Babrius and Phaedrus*. Ed. and trans. Ben Edwin Perry. Loeb Classical Library. Cambridge, MA: Harvard University Press, 1965.

Sappho. Fragment 31. Trans. Anne Carson. *If Not, Winter: Fragments of Sappho*. New York: Vintage Books, 2003.

Sophronius. *Vita Mariae Aegyptae*. *Patrologia Graeca* 87.3697–3726. Trans. Benedicta Ward, S.L.G. *Harlots of the Desert: A Study of Repentance in Early Monastic Sources*. Kalamazoo: Cistercian Publications, 1987.

Stobaeus. *Anthologium [Florilegium]*. 5 vols. Ed. Curtius Wachsmuth and Otto Hense. Berlin: Weidmans, repr. ed., 1958.

Sulpicius Severus. *Dialogi*. *Corpus Scriptorum Ecclesiasticorum Latinorum* 1. Trans. Alexander Roberts. *The Dialogues of Sulpicius Severus*. In *Nicene and Post-Nicene Fathers* 11, 24– 54. Grand Rapids, MI: Wm. B. Eerdmans, 1991. Also consulted: Helen Waddell, trans. *Beasts and Saints*. Grand Rapids, MI: William B. Eerdmans, 1996.

Tertullian. *Adversus Marcionem*. Ed. and trans. Ernest Evans. *Tertullian: Adversus Marcionem*. Oxford: Oxford University Press, 1972.

———. *De baptismo*. In *De baptismo liber, Homily on Baptism*. Ed. and trans Ernest Evans. London: SPCK, 1964.

Theodoret. *De providentia*. *Patrologia Graeca* 83.556–773.

Theon. *Progymnasmata*, In "Introduction," *Babrius and Phaedrus*. Ed. and trans. Ben Edwin Perry. Loeb Classical Library. Cambridge, MA: Harvard University Press, 1965.

Theophilus of Antioch. *Ad Autolycum*. Ed. and trans. Robert M. Grant. Oxford Early Christian Texts. Oxford: Clarendon Press, 1970.

The Virtues of Saint Macarius of Egypt. Trans. Tim Vivian. In *St. Macarius the Spiritbearer: Coptic Texts Relating to Saint Macarius the Great*. Crestwood: St. Vladimir's Seminary Press, 2004.

Vitae Patrum. *Patrologia Latina* 73.855–1022. Trans. Benedicta Ward. *The Desert Fathers: Sayings of the Early Christian Monks*. London: Penguin Books, 2003.

MODERN WORKS

Aasgaard, Reidar. *The Childhood of Jesus: Decoding the Apocryphal Infancy Gospel of Thomas*. Eugene, OR: Cascade Books, 2009.

Adamik, Tamás. "The Baptized Lion in the Acts of Paul." In *The Apocryphal Acts of Paul and Thecla*, ed. Jan. N. Bremmer, 60–74. Kampen: Kok Pharos, 1996.

Agamben, Giorgio. *The Open: Man and Animal*. Trans. Kevin Attell. Meridian: Crossing Aesthetics. Stanford: Stanford University Press, 2004.

Amsler, Frédéric. *Acta Philippi: Commentarius*. Corpus Christianorum, Series Apocryphorum 12. Turnhout: Brepols, 1999.

Arterbury, Andrew. *Entertaining Angels: Early Christian Hospitality in Its Mediterranean Setting*. Sheffield: Sheffield Phoenix Press, 2005.

Asiedu, F. B. A. "The Song of Songs and the Ascent of the Soul: Ambrose, Augustine, and the Language of Mysticism." *Vigiliae Christianae* 55 (2001): 299–317.

Aune, David Edward. *The New Testament in Its Literary Environment*. Philadelphia: Westminster Press, 1987.

Ayres, Lewis. "Augustine on Redemption." In *A Companion to Augustine*, ed. Mark Vessey, 416–27. Oxford: Wiley-Blackwell, 2011.

Bachelard, Gaston. *L'air et les songes: Essai sur l'imagination du movement*. Paris: Librairie José Corti, 1943. Trans. Edith R. Farrell and C. Frederick Farrell. *Air and Dreams*. Dallas: Dallas Institute Publications, 1988.

———. *Lautréamont*. Paris: Librairie José Corti, 1939.

———. *The Poetics of Space*. Trans. Maria Jolas. Boston: Beacon Press, 1969.

Bailly, Jean-Christophe. *The Animal Side*. Trans. Catherine Porter. New York: Fordham University Press, 2011.

———. "Animals Are Masters of Silence." *Yale French Studies* 127 (2015): 84–94. Ed. Matthew Senior, David L. Clark, and Carla Freccero. *Animots: Postanimality in French Thought*. New Haven: Yale University Press, 2015.

Baker, Steve. *Picturing the Beast: Animals, Identity, and Representation*. Urbana: University of Illinois Press, 2001.

———. *The Postmodern Animal*. London: Reaktion Books, 2000.

Balcombe, Jonathan. *The Exultant Ark: A Pictorial Tour of Animal Pleasure*. Berkeley: University of California Press, 2011. Kindle edition.

Barthes, Roland. "The Reality Effect." In *The Rustle of Language*, trans. Richard Howard, 141–48. New York: Hill and Wang, 1986.

Barton, Carlin A. *Roman Honor: The Fire in the Bones*. Berkeley: University of California Press, 2001.

———. *The Sorrows of the Ancient Romans: The Gladiator and the Monster*. Princeton: Princeton University Press, 1993.

Bartra, Roger. *Wild Men in the Looking Glass: The Mythic Origins of European Otherness*. Ttrans. Carl T. Berrisford. Ann Arbor: University of Michigan Press, 1994.

Bartsch, Shadi. *The Mirror of the Self: Sexuality, Self-Knowledge, and the Gaze in the Early Roman Empire*. Chicago: University of Chicago Press, 2006.

Bataille, Georges. *Theory of Religion*. Trans. Robert Hurley. New York: Zone Books, 1989.

Bauckham, Richard. *Living with Other Creatures: Green Exegesis and Theology*. Waco: Baylor University Press, 2011.

Beard, Mary. "Cicero and Divination: The Formation of a Latin Discourse." *Journal of Roman Studies* 76 (1986): 33–46.

Behr, John. "The Rational Animal: A Rereading of Gregory of Nyssa's *De hominis opificio*." *Journal of Early Christian Studies* 7 (1999): 219–47.

Bekoff, Marc. *The Emotional Lives of Animals: A Leading Scientist Explores Animal Joy, Sorrow, and Empathy—and Why They Matter*. Novato, CA: New World Library, 2007. Kindle edition.

Bennett, Jane. *The Enchantment of Modern Life: Attachments, Crossings, and Ethics*. Princeton: Princeton University Press, 2001.

———. *Vibrant Matter: A Political Ecology of Things*. Durham: Duke University Press, 2010. Kindle edition.

Bertrand, D. A. "Le Christ comme ver. A propos du Ps 22 (21), 7." In *Le Psautier chez les Pères*. Cahiers de Biblia Patristica 4, 221–34. Turnhout: Brepols, 1993.

Bettini, Maurizio. *Women and Weasels: Mythologies of Birth in Ancient Greece and Rome*. Trans. Emlyn Eisenach. Chicago: University of Chicago Press, 2013.

Blaising, Craig A., and Carmen S. Hardin, eds. *Ancient Christian Commentary on Scripture, Old Testament 7: Psalms 1–50*. Downers Grove, IL: InterVarsity Press, 2008.

Bland, Kalman P. "Cain, Abel, and Brutism." In *Scriptural Exegesis: The Shapes of Culture and the Religious Imagination: Essays in Honour of Michael Fishbane*, ed. Deborah A. Green and Laura S. Lieber, 165–85. Oxford: Oxford University Press, 2009.

———. "Construction of Animals in Medieval Jewish Philosophy." In *New Directions in Jewish Philosophy*, ed. Aaron W. Hughes and Elliot R. Wolfson, 175–204. Indianapolis: Indiana University Press, 2009.

Blowers, Paul M. *Drama of the Divine Economy: Creator and Creation in Early Christian Theology and Piety*. Oxford: Oxford University Press, 2012.

Borgen, Peder. "Man's Sovereignty over Animals and Nature According to Philo of Alexandria." In *Texts and Contexts: Biblical Texts in Their Textual and Situational Contexts: Essays in Honor of Lars Hartman*, trans. Tord Fornberg and David Hellholm, 369–89. Oslo: Scandinavian University Press, 1995.

Bovon, François. "Canonical and Apocryphal Acts of the Apostles." In his *New Testament and Christian Apocrypha: Collected Studies II*, ed. Glenn E. Snyder, 197–222. Tübingen: Mohr Siebeck, 2009. Originally published in *Journal of Early Christian Studies* 11 (2003): 165–94.

———. "The Child and the Beast: Fighting Violence in Ancient Christianity." In his *New Testament and Christian Apocrypha: Collected Studies II*, ed. Glenn E. Snyder, 223–45. Tübingen: Mohr Siebeck, 2009.

———. "Facing the Scriptures: Mimesis and Intertextuality in the *Acts of Philip*." In his *New Testament and Christian Apocrypha, Collected Studies II*, ed. Glenn E. Snyder, 273–85. Wissenschaftliche Untersuchungen zum Neuen Testament 237. Tübingen: Mohr Siebeck, 2009.

———. "Introduction." *The Acts of Philip: A New Translation*. Trans. François Bovon and Christopher R. Matthews, 1–30. Waco: Baylor University Press, 2012.

Boyarin, Daniel. *A Radical Jew: Paul and the Politics of Identity*. Berkeley: University of California Press, 1994.

Brown, Peter. *Augustine of Hippo: A Biography*. Berkeley: University of California Press, 1969, 2000.

———. *The Body and Society: Men, Women, and Sexual Renunciation in Early Christianity*. New York: Columbia University Press, 1988.

———. *Through the Eye of a Needle: Wealth, the Fall of Rome, and the Making of Christianity in the West 350–550 AD*. Princeton: Princeton University Press, 2012.

Bruns, Gerald L. "The Problem of Figuration in Antiquity." In *Hermeneutics: Questions and Prospects*, ed. G. Shapiro and A. Sica, 147–64. Amherst: University of Massachusetts Press, 1984.

Buchanan, Brett. "Being with Animals: Reconsidering Heidegger's Animal Ontology." In *Animals and the Human Imagination: A Companion to Animal Studies*, ed. Aaron Gross and Anne Vallely, 265–88. New York: Columbia University Press, 2012. Kindle edition.

Burnaby, John. *Amor Dei: A Study of the Religion of St. Augustine*. London: Hodder and Stoughton, 1938.

Burns, J. P. "How Christ Saves: Augustine's Multiple Explanations." In Ronnie J. Rombs and Alexander Y. Hwang, eds., *Tradition and the Rule of Faith in the Early Church: Essays in Honor of Joseph T. Lienhard, S.J.*, 193–210. Washington, DC: Catholic University of America Press, 2010.

Burrus, Virginia. "Carnal Excess: Flesh at the Limits of Imagination." *Journal of Early Christian Studies* 17 (2009): 247–65.

———. "Introduction." In Virginia Burrus and Marco Conti, eds. and trans., *The Life of Saint Helia: Critical Edition, Translation, Introduction, and Commentary*, 1–59. Oxford Early Christian Texts. Oxford: Oxford University Press, 2013.

———. *Saving Shame: Martyrs, Saints, and Other Abject Subjects.* Divinations: Rereading Late Ancient Religion. Philadelphia: University of Pennsylvania Press, 2008.

———. *The Sex Lives of Saints: An Erotics of Ancient Hagiography.* Divinations: Rereading Late Ancient Religion. Philadelphia: University of Pennsylvania Press, 2004.

———. "Speaking in Other Tongues: Ancient Christianity and the Dialogical Imagination." Lecture delivered at Syracuse University, 20 February 2013.

Burrus, Virginia, Mark D. Jordan, and Karmen MacKendrick. *Seducing Augustine: Bodies, Desires, Confessions.* New York: Fordham University Press, 2010.

Burton-Christie, Douglas. *The Word in the Desert: Scripture and the Quest for Holiness in Early Christian Monasticism.* New York: Oxford University Press, 1993.

Calarco, Matthew. *Zoographies: The Question of the Animal from Heidegger to Derrida.* New York: Columbia University Press, 2008.

Cameron, Michael. "Augustine and Scripture." In *A Companion to Augustine*, ed. Mark Vessey, 200–214. Oxford: Blackwell, 2012.

———. *Christ Meets Me Everywhere: Augustine's Early Figurative Exegesis.* Oxford Studies in Historical Theology. Oxford: Oxford University Press, 2012.

Carlile, Henry. "The Cardinal." In Billy Collins, ed., *Bright Wings: An Illustrated Anthology of Poems About Birds.* New York: Columbia University Press, 2010.

Carson, Anne. *Decreation: Poetry, Essays, Opera.* New York: Vintage Books, 2005.

———. *Eros the Bittersweet: An Essay.* Princeton: Princeton University Press, 1986.

Cavell, Stanley, Cora Diamond, John McDowell, Ian Hacking, and Cary Wolfe. *Philosophy and Animal Life.* New York: Columbia University Press, 2008.

Chadwick, Henry, trans. *Origen: Contra Celsum.* Cambridge: Cambridge University Press, 1965.

Chin, Catherine M. "Cosmos." In *Late Ancient Knowing: Explorations in Intellectual History*, ed. Catherine M. Chin and Moulie Vidas, 99–116. Berkeley: University of California Press, 2015.

Ciardi, John. "Bird Watching." In *Bright Wings: An Illustrated Anthology of Poems About Birds*, ed. Billy Collins. New York: Columbia University Press, 2010.

Clampitt, Amy. "The Kingfisher." In *Bright Wings: An Illustrated Anthology of Poems About Birds*, ed. Billy Collins. New York: Columbia University Press, 2010.

Clare, John. "Autumn Birds." In Timothy Morton, *The Ecological Thought*, loc. 671–72. Cambridge, MA: Harvard University Press, 2010. Kindle edition.

Clark, Elizabeth A. "Devil's Gateway and Bride of Christ." In her *Ascetic Piety and Women's Faith: Essays on Late Ancient Christianity*, 23–60. Lewiston: Edwin Mellen Press, 1986.

———. "Holy Women, Holy Words: Early Christian Women, Social History, and the 'Linguistic Turn.'" *Journal of Early Christian Studies* 6 (1998): 413–30.

———. *The Origenist Controversy: The Cultural Construction of an Early Christian Debate.* Princeton: Princeton University Press, 1992.

———. *Reading Renunciation: Asceticism and Scripture in Early Christianity.* Princeton: Princeton University Press, 1999.

———. "Sex, Shame, and Rhetoric: Engendering Early Christian Ethics." *Journal of the American Academy of Religion* 59 (1991): 221–45.

Clark, Gillian. "The Fathers and the Animals: The Rule of Reason?" In *Animals on the Agenda: Questions About Animals for Theology and Ethics*, ed. Andrew Linzey and Dorothy Yamamoto, 67–79. Urbana: University of Illinois Press, 1998.

———. trans. *Porphyry: On Abstinence from Killing Animals*. Ithaca, NY: Cornell University Press, 2000.

Coakley, Sarah, ed. *Re-Thinking Gregory of Nyssa*. Oxford: Blackwell, 2003.

Collins, Billy. "Christmas Sparrow." In *Bright Wings: An Illustrated Anthology of Poems About Birds*, ed. Billy Collins. New York: Columbia University Press, 2010.

———, ed. "Introduction." *Bright Wings: An Illustrated Anthology of Poems About Birds*, 1–6. New York: Columbia University Press, 2010.

Coole, Diana, and Samantha Frost. "Introducing the New Materialisms." In *New Materialisms: Ontology, Agency, and Politics*, ed. Diana Coole and Samantha Frost, 1–44. Durham: Duke University Press, 2010. Kindle edition.

Cooper, Kate. *The Virgin and the Bride: Idealized Womanhood in Late Antiquity*. Cambridge, MA: Harvard University Press, 1996.

Cox, Patricia. "Origen on the Bestial Soul: A Poetics of Nature." *Vigiliae Christianae* 36 (1982): 115–40, repr. in Patricia Cox Miller, *The Poetry of Thought in Late Antiquity: Essays in Imagination and Religion.*, 35–59. Aldershot: Ashgate, 2001.

———. "The *Physiologus*: A Poiesis of Nature." *Church History* 52 (1983): 433–43; repr. in Patricia Cox Miller, *The Poetry of Thought in Late Antiquity: Essays in Imagination and Religion.*, 61–73. Aldershot: Ashgate, 2001.

Creeley, Robert. "The Birds." In *Bright Wings: An Illustrated Anthology of Poems About Birds*, ed. Billy Collins. New York: Columbia University Press, 2010.

Curley, Michael J. "Introduction" to his translation of *Physiologus*. Austin: University of Texas Press, 1979, ix–xliii.

Czachesz, István. *The Grotesque Body in Early Christian Discourse*. Sheffield: Equinox, 2012.

Darwin, Charles. *The Descent of Man, and Selection in Relation to Sex*. Harmondsworth: Penguin, 2004.

Davies, Malcolm, and Jeyaraney Kathirithamby. *Greek Insects*. New York: Oxford University Press, 1986.

Davis, Stephen J. *Christ Child: Cultural Memories of a Young Jesus*. New Haven: Yale University Press, 2014.

———. *The Cult of St. Thecla: A Tradition of Women's Piety in Late Antiquity*. Oxford Early Christian Studies. Oxford: Oxford University Press, 2001.

Dawson, John David. *Christian Figural Reading and the Fashioning of Identity*. Berkeley: University of California Press, 2002.

Derrida, Jacques. *The Animal That Therefore I Am*. Ed. Marie-Louise Mallet. Trans. David Wills. New York: Fordham University Press, 2008.

———. *The Beast and the Sovereign*, 2 vols. Trans. Geoffrey Bennington. Chicago: University of Chicago Press, 2009.

———. *Of Grammatology*. Trans. Gayatri Chakravorty Spivak. Baltimore: Johns Hopkins University Press, 1976.

Detienne, Marcel. *Dionysus Slain*. Trans. Mireille Muellner and Leonard Muellner. Baltimore: Johns Hopkins University Press, 1979.

Detienne, Marcel, and Jean-Pierre Vernant. *Cunning Intelligence in Greek Culture and Society.* Trans. Janet Lloyd. Sussex: Harvester Press, 1978.

Dickerman, Sherwood Owen. "Some Stock Illustrations of Animal Intelligence in Greek Psychology." *Transactions of the American Philological Association* 42 (1911): 123–30.

Dickinson, Emily. *The Complete Poems of Emily Dickinson.* Ed. Thomas H. Johnson. Cambridge, MA: Harvard University Press, 1983.

Doniger, Wendy. "Epilogue: Making Animals Vanish." In *Animals and the Human Imagination: A Companion to Animal Studies*, ed. Aaron Gross and Anne Vallely, 348–53. Kindle edition. New York: Columbia University Press, 2012.

Doran, Robert. "Introduction." In *The Lives of Simeon Stylites*, 15–66. Trans. Robert Doran. Cistercian Studies 112. Kalamazoo: Cistercian Publications, 1992.

Downes, Lawrence. "Wolf Haters." Editorial, *New York Times*, 28 December, 2013.

Drijvers, Han J. W. "Der getaufte Löwe und die Theologie der Acta Pauli." In *Carl-Schmidt-Kolloquium an der Martin-Luther Universität 1988*, ed. Peter Nagel, 181–89. Halle-Wittenberg: Martin-Luther-Universität, 1990.

duBois, Page. *Centaurs and Amazons: Women and the Pre-History of the Great Chain of Being.* Ann Arbor: University of Michigan Press, 1982.

Dulaey, Martine. "L'interpretation du Psaume 21 (22 TM) chez saint Augustin." In *David, Jésus et la reine Esther: Recherches sur le Psaume 21 (22 TM)*, ed. Gilles Dorival, 315–40. Louvain: Peeters, 2002.

Dunning, Benjamin H. "Chrysostom's Serpent: Animality and Gender in the *Homilies on Genesis.*" *Journal of Early Christian Studies* 23 (2015): 71–95.

Elliott, Alison Goddard. *Roads to Paradise: Reading the Lives of the Early Saints.* Hanover, NH: University Press of New England/Brown University Press, 1987.

Elsner, Jaś. *Roman Eyes: Visuality and Subjectivity in Art and Text.* Princeton: Princeton University Press, 2007.

Erdrich, Louise. *The Antelope Wife.* New York: HarperCollins, 2009.

Farrar, Linda. *Ancient Roman Gardens.* Stroud: Sutton, 2000.

Fiedrowicz, Michael. "General Introduction. " In *Expositions of the Psalms 1–32. Works of Saint Augustine*, III/15, trans. Maria Boulding, 13–66. Charlottesville, VA: InteLex, 2001.

Finkelpearl, Ellen. "Elephant Tears: Animal Emotion in Pliny and Aelian." In *Kinesis: The Ancient Depiction of Gesture, Motion, and Emotion: Essays for Donald Lateiner*, ed. Christina A. Clark, Edith Foster, and Judith P. Hallett, 173–87. Ann Arbor: University of Michigan Press, 2015.

Flemming, Rebecca. "*Quae Corpore Quaestum Facit*: The Sexual Economy of Female Prostitution in the Roman Empire." *Journal of Roman Studies* 89 (1999): 38–61.

Foer, Jonathan Safran. "Foreword." In *Animals and the Human Imagination: A Companion to Animal Studies*, ed. Aaron Gross and Anne Vallely, loc. 108–47. New York: Columbia University Press, 2012. Kindle edition.

Formisano, Marco. "Towards an Aesthetic Paradigm of Late Antiquity." *Antiquité Tardive* 15 (2007): 277–84.

Frank, Georgia. *The Memory of the Eyes: Pilgrims to Living Saints in Late Antiquity.* The Transformation of the Classical Heritage 30. Berkeley: University of California Press, 2000.

Fredrick, David, ed. *The Roman Gaze: Vision, Power, and the Body.* Baltimore: Johns Hopkins University Press, 2002.

Fudge, Erica. "The History of Animals." *H-Animal.* H-Net, 25 May 2006.

Fuhrer, Therese. "Conversationalist and Consultant: Augustine in Dialogue." In *A Companion to Augustine*, ed. Mark Vessey, 270–83. Oxford: Wiley-Blackwell, 2012.

Gaita, Raimond. *The Philosopher's Dog: Friendships with Animals*. New York: Random House, 2009. Kindle edition.

Gallagher, Catherine and Stephen Greenblatt. *Practicing New Historicism*. Chicago: University of Chicago Press, 2001.

Gilhus, Ingvild Sælid. *Animals, Gods and Humans: Changing Attitudes to Animals in Greek, Roman and Early Christian Ideas*. London: Routledge, 2006.

Goehring, James E. "The Dark Side of Landscape: Ideology and Power in the Christian Myth of the Desert." In *The Cultural Turn in Late Ancient Studies: Gender, Asceticism, and Historiography*, ed. Dale B. Martin and Patricia Cox Miller, 136–49. Durham, NC: Duke University Press, 2005.

Goldberg, Charles. "Jerome's She-Wolf." *Journal of Early Christian Studies* 21 (2013): 625–28.

Gould, James L., and Carol Grant Gould. "Invertebrate Intelligence." In *Animal Intelligence: Insights into the Animal Mind*, ed. R. J. Hoage and Larry Goldman, 21–36. Washington, D. C.: Smithsonian Institute, 1986.

Gould, Stephen Jay. *Ever Since Darwin*. Harmondsworth: Penguin, 1980.

Grant, Robert M. *Early Christians and Animals*. London: Routledge, 1999.

Green, Steven. "Malevolent Gods and Promethean Birds: Contesting Augury in Augustus's Rome." *Transactions of the American Philological Association* 139 (2009): 147–67.

Gribomont, Jean. *Histoire du Texte des Ascétiques de S. Basile*. Bibliothèque du *Muséon* 32. Louvain: Publications Universitaires/Institut Orientaliste, 1953.

Griffin, Donald R. *Animal Minds: Beyond Cognition to Consciousness*. Chicago: University of Chicago Press, 1992.

Gross, Aaron. "Introduction and Overview: Animal Others and Animal Studies." In *Animals and the Human Imagination: A Companion to Animal Studies*, ed. Aaron Gross and Anne Vallely, 1–22. New York: Columbia University Press, 2012. Kindle edition.

———. *The Question of the Animal and Religion: Theoretical Stakes, Practical Implications*. New York: Columbia University Press, 2014.

Gross, Aaron, and Anne Vallely, eds. *Animals and the Human Imagination: A Companion to Animal Studies*. New York: Columbia University Press, 2012. Kindle edition.

Guillaumont, Antoine. "Le problème des deux Macaires dans les *Apophthegmata Patrum*." *Irénikon* 48 (1975): 41–59.

Hadot, Pierre. *Philosophy as a Way of Life: Spiritual Exercises from Socrates to Foucault*. Ed. Arnold I. Davidson. Oxford: Blackwell, 1995.

Hamilton, W. D. "Selection of Selfish and Altruistic Behavior." In *Man and Beast: Comparative Social Behavior*, ed. J. F. Eisenberg and W. S. Dillon, 59–91. Washington, DC: Smithsonian Institution Press, 1971.

Hammond, N. G. L., and H. H. Scullard, eds. *The Oxford Classical Dictionary*. Oxford: Clarendon Press, 2nd ed., 1970.

Haraway, Donna J. *When Species Meet*. Posthumanities, vol. 3. Minneapolis: University of Minnesota Press, 2008. Kindle edition.

Harmless, William, S.J. *Desert Christians: An Introduction to the Literature of Early Monasticism*. Oxford: Oxford University Press, 2004.

Harpham, Geoffrey Galt. *The Ascetic Imperative in Culture and Criticism*. Chicago: University of Chicago Press, 1987.

Harvey, Susan Ashbrook. *Scenting Salvation: Ancient Christianity and the Olfactory Imagination*. The Transformation of the Classical Heritage 42. Berkeley: University of California Press, 2006.

———. "The Sense of a Stylite: Perspectives on Simeon the Elder." *Vigiliae Christianae* 42 (1988): 376–94.

Haskell, David George. *The Forest Unseen: A Year's Watch in Nature*. New York: Viking, 2012. Kindle edition.

Heidegger, Martin. *The Fundamental Concepts of Metaphysics*. Trans. William MacNeill and Nicholas Walker. Bloomington: Indiana University Press, 1995.

Heine, Ronald E. "Introduction." In his *Gregory of Nyssa's Treatise on the Inscriptions of the Psalms: Introduction, Translation, and Notes*, 1–80. Oxford Early Christian Studies. Oxford: Clarendon Press, 1995.

Hicok, Bob. "Keeping Track." In *Bright Wings: An Illustrated Anthology of Poems About Birds*, ed. Billy Collins. New York: Columbia University Press, 2010.

Hoffman, R. Joseph, trans. *Celsus, On the True Doctrine; A Discourse against Christians*. Oxford: Oxford University Press, 1987.

Hölldobler, Bert, and Edward O. Wilson. *The Superorganism: The Beauty, Elegance, and Strangeness of Insect Societies*. New York: W. W. Norton, 2009.

Holmes, Samuel J. *The Biology of the Frog*. New York: Macmillan, 1928.

Hughes, Ted. *Collected Poems*. Ed. Paul Keegan. New York: Farrar, Straus and Giroux, 2003.

———. *Poetry in the Making: An Anthology of Poems and Programmes from Listening and Writing*. London: Faber and Faber, 1967.

Hume, David. "Of Suicide." In *Essays Moral, Political, and Literary*, 2:406–14. Ed. T. H. Green and T. H. Grose. London: Longmans, Green, 1882, new ed.

Hunter, David G. "Augustine on the Body." In *A Companion to Augustine*, ed. Mark Vessey, 353–64. Oxford: Wiley-Blackwell, 2012.

Ingold, Tim. "The Animal in the Study of Humanity." In *What Is An Animal?* ed. Tim Ingold, 84–99. London: Unwin Hyman, 1988.

———. "Hunting and Gathering as Ways of Perceiving the Environment." In Aaron Gross and Anne Vallely, eds., *Animals and the Human Imagination: A Companion to Animal Studies*, 31–54. New York: Columbia University Press, 2012.

Irvine, Martin. *The Making of Textual Culture: "Grammatica" and Literary Theory, 350–1100*. Cambridge: Cambridge University Press, 1994.

Jackson, Howard. *The Lion Becomes Man: The Gnostic Leontomorphic Creator and the Platonic Tradition*. SBL Dissertation Series 81. Atlanta: Society of Biblical Literature, 1985.

Jennison, George. *Animals for Show and Pleasure in Ancient Rome*. Manchester: Manchester University Press, 1935; repr. Philadelphia: University of Pennsylvania Press, 2005.

Junod, Eric. "Vie et conduit des saintes femmes Xanthippe, Polyxène, et Rébecca (BHG 1877)." In *Oecumenica et patristica: Festschrift für Wilhelm Schneemelcher zum 75. Geburtstag*, ed. Damaskinos Papandreou, Wolfgang A. Bienert, and Knut Schäferdiek, 83–106. Stuttgart: Kohlammer, 1989.

Kaster, Robert A. *Emotion, Restraint, and Community in Ancient Rome*. Classical Culture and Society. Oxford: Oxford University Press, 2005.

Kelly, Christopher. "Patronage." In *Late Antiquity: A Guide to the Postclassical World*, ed. G. W. Bowersock, Peter Brown, and Oleg Grabar, 637–38. Cambridge, MA: Harvard University Press, 1999.

Kelly, J. N. D. *Jerome: His Life, Writings, and Controversies*. New York: Harper and Row, 1975.

Kessler, Herbert L. "Diptych with Old and New Testament Scenes." In *Age of Spirituality: Late Antique and Early Christian Art, Third to Seventh Century*, ed. Kurt Weitzmann, 505– 7. New York: Metropolitan Museum of Art and Princeton University Press, 1979.

Kiely, Sr. Maria M., O.S.B. "The Interior Courtyard: The Heart of Cimitile/Nola." *Journal of Early Christian Studies* 12 (2004): 443–79.

Kinnell, Galway. "Saint Francis and the Sow." In *Three Books*. New York: Mariner Books, 2002.

Knickerbocker, Scott. *Ecopoetics: The Language of Nature, the Nature of Language*. Amherst: University of Massachusetts Press, 2012.

Konowitz, Ellen. "The Program of the Carrand Diptych." *Art Bulletin* 66 (1984): 484–88.

Krell, David Farrell. *Derrida and Our Animal Others: Derrida's Final Seminar, "The Beast and the Sovereign."* Studies in Continental Thought. Bloomington: Indiana University Press, 2013.

———. "'Talk to the Animals': On the Myth of Cronos in the *Statesman*." In *Plato's Animals: Gadflies, Horses, Swans, and Other Philosophical Beasts*, ed. Jeremy Bell and Michael Naas, 27–39. Studies in Continental Thought. Bloomington: Indiana University Press, 2015.

Kuzniar, Alice. *Melancholia's Dog: Reflections on Our Animal Kinship*. Chicago: University of Chicago Press, 2006.

Ladner, Gerhart B. "The Philosophical Anthropology of Gregory of Nyssa." *Dumbarton Oaks Papers* 12 (1958): 61–94.

Lampe, G. W. H., ed. *A Patristic Greek Lexicon*. Oxford: Clarendon Press, 1962.

Laux, Dorianne. "The Ravens of Denali." In Billy Collins, ed., *Bright Wings: An Illustrated Anthology of Poems About Birds*. New York: Columbia University Press, 2010.

Leopold, Aldo. *A Sand County Almanac and Sketches Here and There*. New York: Oxford University Press, 1949.

Lévi-Strauss, Claude. *Totemism*. Trans. Rodney Needham. Boston: Beacon Press, 1963.

Lewis, Charlton T., and Charles Short, eds. *A Latin Dictionary*. Oxford: Clarendon Press, 1969.

Leyerle, Blake. "The Consolation of Nature: Fields and Gardens in the Preaching of John Chrysostom." In *Ascetic Culture: Essays in Honor of Philip Rousseau*, ed. Blake Leyerle and Robin Darling Young, 269–92. Notre Dame: University of Notre Dame Press, 2013.

———. "Monks and Other Animals." In *The Cultural Turn in Late Ancient Studies: Gender, Asceticism, and Historiography*, ed. Dale B. Martin and Patricia Cox Miller, 150–71. Durham, NC: Duke University Press, 2005.

Leyerle, Blake, and Robin Darling Young, eds. *Ascetic Culture: Essays in Honor of Philip Rousseau*. Notre Dame, IN: University of Notre Dame Press, 2013.

Liddell, Henry George, Robert Scott, and Henry Stuart Jones, eds. *A Greek-English Lexicon*. Oxford: Clarendon Press, rev. ed., 1968.

Lienhard, Joseph T., S.J. "The Christian Reception of the Pentateuch: Patristic Commentaries on the Books of Moses." *Journal of Early Christian Studies* 10 (2002): 373–88.

Lim, Richard. "The Politics of Interpretation in Basil of Caesarea's 'Hexaemeron.'" *Vigiliae Christianae* 44 (1990): 351–70.

Lingis, Alphonso. *Dangerous Emotions*. Berkeley: University of California Press, 2000.

Louth, Andrew. "'Truly Visible Things Are Manifest Images of Invisible Things': Dionysios the Areopagite on Knowing the Invisible." In *Seeing the Invisible in Late Antiquity and the Early Middle Ages*, ed. Giselle de Nie, Karl F. Morrison, and Marco Mostert, 15–24. Utrecht Studies in Medieval Literacy. Turnhout: Brepols, 2005.

Ludlow, Morwenna. "Demons, Evil, and Liminality in Cappadocian Theology." *Journal of Early Christian Studies* 20 (2012): 179–211.

Lundblad, Michael. "From Animal to Animality Studies." *Proceedings of the Modern Language Association* 124 (2009): 496–502.

MacCormack, Sabine. "Augustine Reads Genesis." *Augustinian Studies* 38, no. 2 (2008): 5–47.

MacDougall, Elizabeth B., and Wilhelmina F. Jashemski. *Ancient Roman Gardens*. Washington, DC: Dumbarton Oaks Trustees for Harvard University, 1981.

MacKendrick, Karmen. *Divine Enticement: Theological Seductions*. New York: Fordham University Press, 2013.

Maguire, Eunice Dauterman, Henry P. Maguire, and Maggie J. Duncan-Flowers. *Art and Holy Powers in the Early Christian House*. Illinois Byzantine Studies 2. Urbana: University of Illinois Press, 1989.

Maguire, Henry. "Adam and the Animals: Allegory and the Literal Sense in Early Christian Art." *Dumbarton Oaks Papers* 41 (1987): 363–73.

———. *Earth and Ocean: The Terrestrial World in Early Byzantine Art*. University Park: Pennsylvania State University Press, 1987.

Markus, R. A. *Conversion and Disenchantment in Augustine's Spiritual Career*. Villanova: Villanova University Press, 1989.

Marsden, Jill. "Bataille and the Poetic Fallacy of Animality." In *Animal Philosophy: Ethics and Identity*, ed. Peter Atterton and Matthew Calarco, 37–44. London: Continuum, 2004.

Martin, Dale B. *The Corinthian Body*. New Haven: Yale University Press, 1995.

Mathews, Thomas F. *The Clash of Gods: A Reinterpretation of Early Christian Art,* rev. ed. Princeton: Princeton University Press, 1999.

Matthews, Christopher R. "Articulate Animals: A Multivalent Motif in the Apocryphal Acts of the Apostles." In *The Apocryphal Acts of the Apostles*, ed. François Bovon, Ann Graham Brock, and Christopher R. Matthews, 205–32. Harvard Divinity School Studies. Cambridge, MA: Harvard University Press, 1999.

Mattusch, Carol C., et al. *Pompeii and the Roman Villa*. New York: Thames and Hudson, 2008.

Mazzoleni, Donatella. *Domus: Wall Painting in the Roman House*. Los Angeles: Getty Trust, 2004.

Mazzoni, Cristina. *She-Wolf: The Story of a Roman Icon*. Cambridge: Cambridge University Press, 2010.

Mech, L. David. *The Wolf: The Ecology and Behavior of an Endangered Species*. Minneapolis: University of Minnesota Press, 1970.

Merleau-Ponty, Maurice. *Le visible et l'invisible*. Paris: Éditions Gallimard, 1964. Trans. Alphonso Lingis. *The Visible and the Invisible*. Evanston: Northwestern University Press, 1968.

———. *Nature: Course Notes from the Collège de France*. Trans. Robert Vallier. Evanston: Northwestern University Press, 2003.

———. *Phenomenology of Perception*. Trans. Colin Smith. New York: Routledge, 2002.

Metzger, Bruce. "St. Paul and the Baptized Lion: Apocryphal vs. Canonical Books of the New Testament." *Princeton Seminary Bulletin* 39 (1945): 11–21.

Miller, David L. *The New Polytheism*. Dallas: Spring Publications, 2nd ed., 1981.

Miller, J. Hillis. "Tradition and Difference." *Diacritics* 2 (1972): 6–13.

Miller, Patricia Cox. "Adam, Eve, and the Elephants: Asceticism and Animality." In *Ascetic Culture: Essays in Honor of Philip Rousseau*, ed. Blake Leyerle and Robin Darling Young, 253–68. Notre Dame: University of Notre Dame Press, 2013.

———. "The Blazing Body: Ascetic Desire in Jerome's *Letter to Eustochium*." *Journal of Early Christian Studies* 1 (1993): 21–45; repr. in Miller, *The Poetry of Thought in Late Antiquity: Essays in Imagination and Religion*, 135–58. Aldershot: Ashgate, 2001.

———. *The Corporeal Imagination: Signifying the Holy in Late Ancient Christianity.* Divinations: Rereading Late Ancient Religion. Philadelphia: University of Pennsylvania Press, 2009.

———. "Desert Asceticism and 'The Body From Nowhere.'" *Journal of Early Christian Studies* 2 (1994): 137–53; repr. in Miller, *The Poetry of Thought in Late Antiquity: Essays in Imagination and Religion*, 159–74. Aldershot: Ashgate, 2001.

———. "'Intricate Evasions of As': History, Imagination, and Saint Basil's Crab." In *Disturbances in the Field: Essays in Honor of David L. Miller*, ed. Christine Downing, 179–91. New Orleans: Spring Journal Books, 2006.

———. "Jerome's Centaur: A Hyper-icon of the Desert." *Journal of Early Christian Studies* 4 (1996): 209–33; repr. in Miller, *The Poetry of Thought in Late Antiquity: Essays in Imagination and Religion*, 75–99. Aldershot: Ashgate, 2001.

———. *The Poetry of Thought in Late Antiquity: Essays in Imagination and Religion.* Aldershot: Ashgate, 2001.

Mitchell, W. J. T. *What Do Pictures Want? The Lives and Loves of Images.* Chicago: University of Chicago Press, 2005.

Moore, Stephen D. "Introduction: From Animal Theory to Creaturely Theology." In *Divinanimality: Animal Theory, Creaturely Theology*, ed. Stephen D. Moore, 1–16. New York: Fordham University Press, 2014.

Morris, Christine. "Animals into Art in the Ancient World." In *A Cultural History of Animals*, vol. 1: *A Cultural History of Animals in Antiquity*, ed. Linda Kalof, 175–98. Oxford: Berg, 2007.

Morton, Timothy. *The Ecological Thought.* Cambridge, MA: Harvard University Press, 2010. Kindle edition.

Mosshammer, Alden A. "Disclosing but Not Disclosed: Gregory of Nyssa as Deconstructionist." In *Studien zu Gregor von Nyssa und der christlichen Spätantike*, ed. Hubertus Drobner and Christoph Klock, 99–123. Leiden: E. J. Brill, 1990.

Mowat, Farley. *Never Cry Wolf: The Amazing True Story of Life Among Arctic Wolves.* New York: Back Bay Books/Little, Brown, 1963.

Murphy, Mable Gant, trans. *Nature Allusions in the Works of Clement of Alexandria.* The Catholic University of America Patristic Studies 65. Washington, DC: Catholic University of America Press, 1941.

Nemerov, Howard. "On Metaphor." In *A Howard Nemerov Reader*, 223–36. Columbia: University of Missouri Press, 1991.

Newmyer, Stephen T. "Animals in Ancient Philosophy." In *A Cultural History of Animals in Antiquity*, ed. Linda Kalef, 151–222. Oxford: Berg, 2007.

———. *Animals in Greek and Roman Thought: A Sourcebook.* London: Routledge, 2011.

———. "Paws to Reflect: Ancients and Moderns on the Religious Sensibilities of Animals." *Quaderni urbinati di cultura classica*, n.s., 75 (2003): 111–29.

Nicklas, Tobias, and Janet E. Spittler. "Christ and the Pelican: Function, Background and Impact of an Image." *Ephemerides Theologicae Lovanienses* 92 (2016): 323–37.

Oliver, Kelly. *Animal Lessons: How They Teach Us to Be Humans.* New York: Columbia University Press, 2009.

———. "Stopping the Anthropological Machine: Agamben with Heidegger and Merleau-Ponty." *PhaenEx* 2 (2007): 1–23.

Osborne, Catherine. *Dumb Beasts and Dead Philosophers: Humanity and the Humane in Ancient Philosophy and Literature.* Oxford: Clarendon Press, 2007.

Otto, Walter F. *Dionysus, Myth and Cult*. Trans. Robert B. Palmer. Bloomington: Indiana University Press, 1965.

Pastan, Linda. "After Reading Peterson's Guide." In *Bright Wings: An Illustrated Anthology of Poems About Birds*, ed. Billy Collins. New York: Columbia University Press, 2010.

Patton, Kimberley. "'Caught with Ourselves in the Net of Life and Time': Views of Animals and Religion." In *A Communion of Subjects: Animals in Religion, Science, and Ethics*, ed. Paul Waldau and Kimberley Patton, 27–39. New York: Columbia University Press, 2006.

Payne, Mark. *The Animal Part: Human and Other Animals in the Poetic Imagination*. Chicago: University of Chicago Press, 2010.

Peers, Glenn. "Adam's Anthropocene." *Postmedieval: A Journal of Medieval Cultural Studies* 7 (2016): 161–71.

Pelikan, Jaroslav. *Christianity and Classical Culture: The Metamorphosis of Natural Theology in the Christian Encounter with Hellenism*. New Haven: Yale University Press, 1993.

Penn, Michael Philip. *Kissing Christians: Ritual and Community in the Late Ancient Church*. Divinations: Rereading Late Ancient Religion. Philadelphia: University of Pennsylvania Press, 2005.

Perkins, Judith. "Animal Voices." *Religion and Theology* 12 (2005): 385–96.

Perry, Ben Edwin. "Introduction." In *Babrius and Phaedrus*, ed. and trans. Ben Edwin Perry, xi– cii. Loeb Classical Library. Cambridge, MA: Harvard University Press, 1965.

Pervo, Richard I. "Dare and Back: The Stories of Xanthippe and Polyxena." In *Early Christian and Jewish Narrative: The Role of Religion in Shaping Narrative Forms*, ed. Ilaria Ramelli and Judith Perkins, 161–204. Tübingen: Mohr Siebeck, 2015.

Phillips, Adam. *Darwin's Worms: On Life Stories and Death Stories*. New York: Basic Books, 2000.

Proulx, Annie. *Fine Just the Way It Is*. Wyoming Stories 3. New York: Scribner, 2008.

Renehan, Robert. "The Greek Anthropocentric View of Man." *Harvard Studies in Classical Philology* 85 (1981): 239–59.

Rigby, Kate. "Animal Calls." In *Divinanimality: Animal Theory, Creaturely Theology*, ed. Stephen D. Moore, 116–33. New York: Fordham University Press, 2014.

Rilke, Rainer Maria. *Ahead of All Parting: The Selected Poetry and Prose of Rainer Maria Rilke*. Ed. and trans. Stephen Mitchell. New York: Modern Library, 1995.

———. *Duino Elegies*. Trans. J. B. Leishman and Stephen Spender. The Norton Library. New York: W. W. Norton, 1939.

———. *Duino Elegies: A Bilingual Edition*. Trans. Stephen Cohn. Evanston, IL: Northwestern University Press, 1998.

———. *Notebooks of Malta Laurids Brigge*. Trans. M. D. Herter. New York: W. W. Norton, 1949.

———. *Selected Poetry of Rainer Maria Rilke*. Trans. Stephen Mitchell. New York: Vintage, 1982.

Roethke, Theodore. *The Collected Poems of Theodore Roethke*. Garden City, NY: Anchor Books, 1975.

Rordorf, Willy. "Quelques jalons pour une interprétation symbolique des *Actes de Paul*." In *Early Christian Voices in Texts, Traditions, and Symbols: Essays in Honor of François Bovon*, ed. David H. Warren, Ann Graham Brock, and David H. Pao, 251–65. Biblical Interpretation Series 66. Leiden: Brill, 2003.

Rorem, Paul. *Pseudo-Dionysius: A Commentary on the Texts and an Introduction to Their Influence*. New York: Oxford University Press, 1993.

Rousseau, Philip. *Basil of Caesarea*. The Transformation of the Classical Heritage 20. Berkeley: University of California Press, 1994.

Rowlands, Mark. *The Philosopher and the Wolf: Lessons from the Wild on Love, Death, and Happiness*. New York: Pegasus Books, 2010. Kindle edition.

Roy, Arundhati. *The God of Small Things: A Novel*. New York: Random House, 2008. Kindle edition.

Ruaro, Enrica. "God and the Worm: The Twofold Otherness in Pseudo-Dionysius's Theory of Dissimilar Images." *American Catholic Philosophical Quarterly* 82, no. 4 (2008): 581–92.

Runia, David T. *Philo in Early Christian Literature: A Survey*. Compendium Rerum Iudaicarum ad Novum Testamentum 3, 3. Minneapolis: Fortress Press, 1993.

———. "Philo of Alexandria." In John Anthony McGuckin, ed., *The Westminster Handbook to Origen*, 169–71. The Westminster Handbooks to Christian Theology. Louisville: Westminster John Knox Press, 2004.

Sacks, Oliver. "The Mental Life of Plants and Worms, Among Others." *New York Review of Books* 61, no. 7 (24 April 2014): 4–8.

Sandburg, Carl. *The Complete Poems of Carl Sandburg*. New York: Harcourt, Brace, Jovanovich, 1970.

Schneemelcher, Wilhelm. "Der getaufte Löwe in den Acta Pauli." In *Mullus: Festschrift Theodor Klauser*, ed. Alfred Stuidber and Alfred Hermann, 315–26. Münster: Aschendorffsche, 1964.

Schneemelcher, Wilhelm, and Rodolphe Kasser. "The Acts of Paul." In *New Testament Apocrypha*, rev. ed., vol. 2: *Writings Relating to the Apostles, Apocalypses, and Related Subjects*, ed. Edgar Hennecke and Wilhelm Schneemelcher, 213–70. Trans. R. McL. Wilson. Louisville: Westminster/John Knox Press, 1992.

Scott, Alan. "The Date of the *Physiologus*." *Vigiliae Christianae* 52 (1998): 430–41.

———. "Zoological Marvel and Exegetical Method in Origen and the *Physiologus*." In *Reading in Christian Communities: Essays on Interpretation in the Early Church*, ed. Charles A. Bobertz and David Brakke, 80–89. Christianity and Judaism in Antiquity Series 14. Notre Dame, IN: University of Notre Dame Press, 2002.

Scullard, H. H. *The Elephant in the Greek and Roman World*. Ithaca, NY: Cornell University Press, 1974.

Seigworth, Gregory J. and Melissa Gregg. "An Inventory of Shimmers." In *The Affect Theory Reader*, ed. Melissa Gregg and Gregory J. Seigworth, 1–25. Durham: Duke University Press, 2010.

Sellbach, Undine. "The Lives of Animals: Wittgenstein, Coetzee, and the Extent of the Sympathetic Imagination." In *Animals and the Human Imagination: A Companion to Animal Studies*, ed. Aaron Gross and Anne Vallely, 306–30. New York: Columbia University Press, 2012.

Sheldrick, Daphne. *Love, Life, and Elephants: An African Love Story*. New York: Farrar, Straus and Giroux, 2012. Kindle edition. (First published Notre Dame, IN: University of Notre Dame Press, 2002.)

Snyder, Glenn E. *Acts of Paul: The Formation of a Pauline Corpus*. Wissenschaftliche Untersuchungen zum Neuen Testament 2. Reihe 352. Tübingen: Mohr Siebeck, 2013.

Söder, Rosa. *Die apokryphen Apostelgeschichten und die romanhafte Literatur der Antike*. Würzburger Studien zur Altertumswissenschaft 3. Stuttgart: Kohlhammer, 1932.

Sorabji, Richard. *Animal Minds and Human Morals: The Origins of the Western Debate*. Ithaca, NY: Cornell University Press, 1993.

———. *Emotion and Peace of Mind: From Stoic Agitation to Christian Temptation*. The Gifford Lectures. Oxford: Oxford University Press, 2000.

Spittler, Janet E. *Animals in the Apocryphal Acts of the Apostles: The Wild Kingdom of Early Christian Literature*. Wissenschaftliche Untersuchungen zum Neuen Testament. Second Series, vol. 247. Tübingen: Mohr Siebeck, 2008.

Stancliffe, Clare. *St. Martin and His Hagiographer: History and Miracle in Sulpicius Severus*. Oxford: Clarendon Press, 1983.

Stang, Charles M. *Apophasis and Pseudonymity in Dionysius the Areopagite: "No Longer I."* Oxford Early Christian Studies. Oxford: Oxford University Press, 2012.

Steeves, H. Peter. "Introduction." In *Animal Others: On Ethics, Ontology, and Animal Life*, ed. H. Peter Steeves, 1–14. Albany: SUNY Press, 1999.

Stein, Kevin. "Arts of Joy." In *Bright Wings: An Illustrated Anthology of Poems About Birds*, ed. Billy Collins. New York: Columbia University Press, 2010.

Steiner, Gary. *Anthropocentrism and Its Discontents: The Moral Status of Animals in the History of Western Philosophy*. Pittsburgh: University of Pittsburgh Press, 2005.

Stevens, Wallace. *The Collected Poems of Wallace Stevens*. New York: Alfred A. Knopf, 1977.

———. *Letters of Wallace Stevens*. Ed. Holly Stevens. New York: Alfred A. Knopf, 1977.

———. *Opus Posthumous*. Ed. Samuel French Morse. New York: Alfred A. Knopf, 1977.

Stewart, Amy. "Darwin's Worms." *Wilson Quarterly* 28, no. 1 (2004): 48–58.

Stock, Brian. *Augustine the Reader: Meditation, Self-Knowledge, and the Ethics of Interpretation*. Cambridge, MA: Harvard University Press, 1996.

Sullivan, J. P., ed. *Ezra Pound: A Critical Anthology*. Baltimore: Harmondsworth, 1970.

Szepessy, Tibor. "Narrative Model of the *Acta Xanthippae et Polyxae*." *Acta Antiqua Academiae Scientiarum Hungaricae* 44 (2004): 317–40.

Tapper, Richard. "Animality, Humanity, Morality, Society." In *What Is an Animal?* ed. Tim Ingold, 47–62. London: Unwin Hyman, 1988.

Thompson, D'Arcy Wentworth. *A Glossary of Greek Birds*. London: Oxford University Press, 1936.

Thoreau, Henry David. *The Writings of Thoreau: A Week on Concord and Merrimack Rivers*. Ed. Carol Hovde. Princeton: Princeton University Press, 1980.

Tilley, Maureen A. "Martyrs, Monks, Insects, and Animals." In *The Medieval World of Nature: A Book of Essays*, ed. Joyce E. Salisbury, 93–107. New York: Garland, 1993.

Toadvine, Ted. "How Not to Be a Jellyfish: Human Exceptionalism and the Ontology of Reflection." In *Phenomenology and the Non-Human Animal*, ed. Corinne Painter and Christian Lotz, 39–56. Dordrecht: Springer, 2007.

———. "'Strange Kinship': Merleau-Ponty on the Human-Animal Relation." *Analecta Husserliana* 93 (2007): 17–32.

Toynbee, J. M. C. *Animals in Roman Life and Art*. Ithaca, NY: Cornell University Press, 1973.

Updike, John. "Mosquito." *New Yorker*, 11 June 1960, 32.

Van Den Broek, Roelof. *The Myth of the Phoenix According to Classical and Early Christian Traditions*. Leiden: E. J. Brill, 1972.

Van Den Hoek, Annewies. "The Catechetical School of Early Christian Alexandria and Its Philonic Heritage." *Harvard Theological Review* 90 (1997): 59–87.

———. "Philo and Origen: A Descriptive Catalogue of their Relationship." *Studia Philonica Annual* 12 (2000): 44–121.

Van Horn, Gavin. "The Making of a Wilderness Icon: Green Fire, Charismatic Species, and the Changing Status of Wolves in the United States." In Aaron Gross and Anne Vallely, *Animals and the Human Imagination*, 203–36. New York: Columbia University Press, 2012. Kindle edition.

Vessey, Mark, ed. *A Companion to Augustine*. Oxford: Wiley-Blackwell, 2012.

Vivian, Tim. "The Peaceable Kingdom: Animals as Parables in the *Virtues of Saint Macarius*." *Anglican Theological Review* 85 (2003): 477–91.

de Waal, Frans. *The Ape and the Sushi Master*. New York: Basic Books, 2001.

———. *Good Natured: On the Origins of Right and Wrong in Humans and Other Animals*. Cambridge, MA: Harvard University Press, 1996. Kindle edition.

———. *Primates and Philosophers: How Morality Evolved*. Princeton: Princeton University Press, 2006.

———. "What I Learned Tickling Apes." *New York Times*. "Sunday Review" section, Sunday, 10 April 2016, 1, 4.

Ward, Benedicta, S.L.G. "Foreword." *The Sayings of the Desert Fathers: The Alphabetical Collection*, trans. Benedicta Ward, S.L.G., xvii–xxvii. Kalamazoo: Cistercian Publications, 1975.

———. "Introduction." In *The Lives of the Desert Fathers*, trans. Norman Russell, 3–46. Kalamazoo: Cistercian Publications, 1980.

Weil, Kari. *Thinking Animals: Why Animal Studies Now?* New York: Columbia University Press, 2012.

Westling, Louise. *The Logos of the Living World: Merleau-Ponty, Animals, and Language*. New York: Fordham University Press, 2014.

White, Hayden. "The Forms of Wildness: Archaeology of an Idea." In *The Wild Man Within: An Image in Western Thought from the Renaissance to Romanticism*, ed. Edward Dudley and Maximillian E. Novak, 3–38. Pittsburgh: University of Pittsburgh Press, 1972.

White, Lynn, Jr. "The Historical Roots of our Ecologic Crisis." *Science* 155 (1967): 1203–7.

Wilken, Robert L. *The Christians as the Romans Saw Them*. New Haven: Yale University Press, 1984.

Williams, Charles Allyn. "Oriental Affinities of the Legend of the Hairy Anchorite." *Illinois Studies in Language and Literature* 10, no. 2 (1925): 9–56; 11, no. 4 (1926): 57–139.

Williams, Craig. "When a Dolphin Loves a Boy: Some Greco-Roman and Native American Love Stories." *Classical Antiquity* 32 (2013): 200–242.

Wilson, Edward O. *The Insect Societies*. Cambridge, MA: Belknap Press of Harvard University Press, 1971.

Wittgenstein, Ludwig. *Philosophical Investigations*. Trans. G. E. M. Anscombe. New York: Macmillan, 1968.

Wolfe, Cary. "Human, All Too Human: 'Animal Studies' and the Humanities." *Proceedings of the Modern Language Association* 124 (2009): 564–75.

ACKNOWLEDGMENTS

Like the narrator of Carl Sandburg's poem "Wilderness" quoted in Chapter 4, I too "got a zoo, I got a menagerie, inside my ribs, under my bony head"—and have had, almost since the beginning of my academic career when I wrote on such topics as Adam eating from an animal tree and Origen's musings on the bestial human soul. Somewhat later the animal allegories of the *Physiologus* and the unsettling centaur of Jerome's imagination took center stage. The most recent "turn to the animal" in my work grew out of my studies of ancient Christian asceticism, the body, and corporeality: a consideration of animality seemed like a natural next step as well as an intriguing return to the question of the animal with a somewhat different set of perspectives.

I would like to thank those who entertained my first latter-day foray into the topic of ancient Christian animals. My colleagues in the North American Patristics Society provided a welcoming forum for my presentation, "Adam, Eve, and the Elephants: Asceticism and Animality," at the society's annual meeting in May 2009. Subsequently, I gave two revised versions of this presentation: in February 2010 at the University of Texas, Austin, where my sponsors were the Departments of Religious Studies, Classics, and Art History as well as the Middle Eastern Studies Program; and in April 2012, at the University of Mary Washington, where the primary sponsor was the Department of Classics, Philosophy, and Religion. Special thanks for genial hosting go to Professor Glenn Peers at UT, Austin, and to Professor James Goehring and Linda LaFave for a charming evening of good food and conversation at UMW.

Several other invited lectures provided occasions for further explorations of ancient Christian animal imagery. "Sensing Religion: A View from Late Antiquity" was the title of my keynote address delivered during the "Sensual Faiths: Religion and the Senses" conference at Stanford University in May 2011, which was sponsored by graduate students in the Department of Religious Studies and by the Stanford Humanities Center. I thank all of the graduate students for making this a delightful occasion. It was a special honor to present another keynote address during "Late Antiquity Made New: A Conference in Celebration of the Work of Elizabeth Clark," which was held at Duke University in April 2013. My address, "Caressing the She-Wolf's Head: Reading Animals in Early Christianity," provided the occasion to branch out into new texts both ancient and modern, and I am grateful for the opportunity to do new research and also to honor Liz, a friend and colleague of long standing. The planning committee for this conference deserves special mention: Professors Laura Lieber, Jeremy Schott, Caroline Schroeder, Annabel Wharton, and above all Maria Doerfler, for her untiring efforts to make sure everything ran smoothly.

A return trip to the University of Texas, Austin, this time sponsored by the Late Antiquity Workshop there, afforded me the chance to experiment with contemporary theories as lenses through which to view ancient texts. "Of Wolves and Worms: Affect Theory, The New Materialism, and Early Christianity" was delivered in October 2014, and I thank Professor Na'ama Pat-El for being a cordial host. The Department of Religious Studies at the University of North Carolina, Chapel Hill, gave me a very special invitation, in March 2016, to share two of the drafts that eventually became chapters in this book. One of those drafts, "Of Bees and Anxiety," was a public address that, with a good deal of reworking, became Chapter 2. The other draft, "Signifying Animals: Anthropomorphism," was the focus of a reading group of professors and graduate students; it became Chapter 3, and I greatly benefited from the observations and questions of the members of the reading group. I thank my affable host, Professor Bart Ehrman, for two fabulous dinner parties and stimulating conversation. I also thank the two graduate students who shepherded me about and in general contributed to a pleasant visit: Candace Buckner and Travis Proctor. "Of Bees and Anxiety" was also delivered in April 2016 at the Five Colleges in Amherst, Massachusetts. I thank Mark Roblee, at that time an advanced graduate student, for being an engaging host.

Finally, there is the always-supportive regional scholarly group, Late Ancient Religion in Central New York (locally known and pronounced as LARCeNY). This group, with the help of funds from the Central New York Humanities Corridor and an award by the Andrew W. Mellon Foundation, held a symposium in April 2015 entitled "Liturgy and Aesthetics in Late Antiquity." My contribution, "Augustine's Liturgical *Asini*," allowed me to discuss, for the first time in public, my newfound interest in Augustine's sermons. I continue to value highly the collegial spirit and good cheer of the members of LARCeNY.

I have been the recipient of much collegial generosity over the many years of work on this book. I am especially grateful to Professors Georgia Frank, Elizabeth Clark, Robin Darling Young, Jennifer Glancy, Virginia Burrus, and David Miller for supplying references to animals in ancient and modern texts. Professor Karmen MacKendrick gave early chapters an appreciative reading, as did Professor Virginia Burrus, and I am very grateful for their support. Virginia, as one of the members of the Divinations series editorial board, ultimately read the entire manuscript; her insightful comments were immensely helpful. I also thank the anonymous reader.

Two other kinds of generosity deserve mention here. First, the staff at the University of Pennsylvania Press have been unfailingly helpful and even cheerful: thanks go to Hannah Blake and Noreen O'Connor-Abel, and special thanks go to my senior editor, Jerome Singerman, who believed in this project from the start and was encouraging and patient until the last moment when I hit the "send" key. Second, I owe many thanks to Professor Philip Arnold, chair of the Department of Religion at Syracuse University, for providing subvention funds for the cost of permissions for the art and some of the poetry in this book and for the indexing. I am greatly appreciative of such generous support.

Finally, I owe more gratitude than I can express to my husband, David L. Miller, who once again read my work as it emerged from the printer, page by (sometimes painful) page, and offered his imaginatively critical and supportive comments. This book is dedicated, appropriately, I think, to the four Old English Sheepdogs who have kept such good company with David and me over many, many years: Wissenschaft, Jessie, Sophie, and Ben, avatars of animal grace.

9 780812 250350